W9-AVH-458

Writing with Confidence
Writing Effective Sentences and Paragraphs

Alan Meyers
Harry S Truman College

Longman

New York   San Francisco   Boston
London   Toronto   Sydney   Tokyo   Singapore   Madrid
Mexico City   Munich   Paris   Cape Town   Hong Kong   Montreal

To my two Anns

Vice President and Editor-in-Chief: Joseph Terry
Senior Acquisitions Editor: Steven Rigolosi
Development Editor: Ann Hofstra Grogg
Senior Marketing Manager: Melanie Craig
Supplements Editor: Donna Campion
Media Supplements Editor: Nancy Garcia
Senior Production Manager: Valerie Zaborski
Project Coordination, Text Design, and Electronic Page Makeup: Elm Street Publishing Services, Inc.
Cover Design Manager: Wendy Ann Fredericks
Cover Designer: Joseph DePinho
Cover and Interior Opening Photos: ©PhotoDisc Imaging/PhotoDisc/PictureQuest
Photo Researcher: Photosearch, Inc.
Manufacturing Buyer: Lucy Hebard
Printer and Binder: Von Hoffmann Press, Inc./Owensville
Cover Printer: The Lehigh Press, Inc.

For permission to use copyrighted material, grateful acknowledgment is made to the copyright holders on p. 446, which is hereby made part of this copyright page.

Library of Congress Cataloging-in-Publication Data

Meyers, Alan, 1945–
    Writing with confidence writing effective sentences and paragraphs / Alan Meyers. — 7th ed.
        p. cm.
    Includes index.
    ISBN 0-321-08915-4
        1. English language—Rhetoric. 2. English language—Sentences. 3. English language—paragraphs. 4. English language—Grammar. 5. Report writing. I. Title.

PE1408.M52 2003
808'.042-dc21

                                                                    2001050776

Please visit our website at http://www.ablongman.com/meyers.

ISBN 0-321-08915-4

1 2 3 4 5 6 7 8 9 10—VHO—05 04 03 02

Brief Contents

Detailed Contents

Rhetorical Contents

The following list classifies the reading selections and student essays according to the rhetorical modes they employ or include. Many of the additional readings are mixed modes.

EXEMPLIFICATION

The Writing Process

Hints and Help for Writers

IF YOUR FIRST LANGUAGE IS NOT ENGLISH

COMBINING AND REFINING SENTENCES

WORKING WITH VERBS

Preface

Building on a foundation established in 1979, this seventh edition of *Writing with Confidence* offers more—and less. There are more readings (including sixteen in a special section at the back of the book). There are more writing assignments—especially those based on the readings. And there's much more emphasis on editing and proofreading where they belong: in the final stage of the writing process. There are more visual aids: in-chapter blueprints outlining the stages of the writing process; and "Blueprints for Success," summarizing essential points of each unit of the book. There are more tips in the margins of each chapter—and more advice in the margins for those whose first language is not English. There is more guidance through the writing, revising, and editing process: each exercise throughout the text is keyed to one of the "Six Steps to Successful Writing and Revising" introduced in Chapter 2. And there's more opportunity for students to work independently, with answer keys to all odd numbered items of exercises and the first "Editing for Mastery Exercise" in an appendix.

But there's less, too. The explanations have been shortened, providing only what students need to know as they plan, write, revise, and edit. As always, these explanations and exercise content are student-friendly, engaging, often humorous—and practical. While, indeed, *Writing with Confidence* includes a multitude of exercises, they emphasize the activity of writing, revising, and editing—not filling in blanks. This new edition builds both writing skills and confidence in those skills.

CONTENT OVERVIEW

- **Unit I: Building Your Writing Skills.** These four chapters motivate students to write, while showing them how it is done. Separate chapters focus on the reasons for writing; a six-step writing process that begins with discovery and ends with proofreading; the shape and form of the paragraph; the connection between paragraph and essay; and ways to write concretely and concisely.

- **Unit II: Building and Repairing Sentences.** This five-chapter unit focuses on the essentials of writing and revising all types of sentences. Chapters include material on the structure of the sentence—subject, verb, and complement—and on eliminating fragments, comma splices, and run-ons. More than a fix-it kit, however, the unit promotes a deeper understanding of sentence structure by offering a variety of ways to identify clauses and join them through coordination and subordination.

- **Unit III: Revising with Care: Building on the Framework.** Chapters in this unit cover the most important grammatical and mechanical issues to address in the revising and editing stages of the writing process: subject-verb agreement, past-tense and past-participle verb forms, pronoun forms, use of modifiers, adjective and adverb forms, consistency, concrete language, and concise language.

- **Unit IV: Writing Types of Paragraphs: Shaping the Structure.** Paragraph writing instruction is consolidated in this unit on rhetorical modes. Each chapter includes a professional model followed by discussion questions; an explanation of paragraph order; a "blueprint" of that order as a visual aid; a step-by-step guide through a single writing assignment; revision guidelines that encourage collaborative revision; a student model (two of which are new); and additional writing assignments.

- **Unit V: Editing for Grammar and Mechanics: Finishing the Job.** This handbook-like section includes five chapters of additional lessons on and practice with punctuation, spelling, sound-alike and look-alike words, and issues aimed primarily at non-English dominant, or ESL, writers: articles, prepositions, verb constructions, and phrasal verbs.

- **Reading Selections.** These sixteen high-interest essays [seven of which are new] are arranged from most accessible to most challenging. They provide models of the rhetorical modes, practice in close reading, questions for analysis, and prompts for additional writing.

FEATURES

The following continuing features make the text a valuable and flexible tool for both instructor and student.

- **Simple and Direct Explanations.** Discussions of the writing process, grammar, and mechanics focus on what students should know to generate effective essays, paragraphs, and sentences while increasing their facility with language and eliminating errors. Key terms are highlighted and explained in the text, and, for continuing reference, they are repeated in a glossary at the back of the book.

- **Multi-faceted Presentation of Each Paragraph Mode.** Professional and student models exemplify the skills students aim for. Discussion questions focus student attention on these models, followed by a step-by-step guide through a single, well-developed piece of writing. Each mode is not only described in the text but also visually illustrated through an easy-to-grasp blueprint of the essentials.

- **Chapter on the Essay.** This chapter previews essay writing for those students ready to put paragraphs together.

- **Chapter Goals.** These chapter openers address student aims instead of merely foreshadowing chapter heads.

- **Continuous Discourse Exercises.** Streamlined and to-the-point exercises focus on essential concepts, not busy work. They are notable for their engaging subject matter, connected discourse, and continuous narratives. As students work with these materials, they gain skill in composing, revising, and editing sentences with meaningful content. Selections include biographies of Diamond Jim Brady, Alexandra David-Neel, Sequoyah, Jesse Owens, Dian Fossey, Amelia Earhart, Abraham Lincoln, and Harry Houdini, as well as accounts of the origins of designer jeans, the wedding cake, the waltz, the teddy bear, and high-tech sneakers. This entertaining subject matter serves a more serious purpose as well: exemplifying that people write to communicate ideas, and if ideas are worth saying, they are worth saying well. As students read and then rewrite or revise an exercise, they discover that interesting ideas become clearer and even more interesting.

- **Collaborative Activities.** These suggestions for out-of-class and in-class group work expand learning opportunities. Each paragraph writing assignment includes Revision Guidelines that encourage peer response and editing. Predicting activities throughout the text provide additional opportunities for collaboration while stressing the interrelationship between writer and reader.

- **Mastery Learning Capabilities.** The book is designed to facilitate a Mastery Learning approach, in which students complete a section on grammar and mechanics, evaluate their understanding and application of the concepts, restudy parts of the section if necessary, and then engage in further evaluation. The two Editing for Mastery exercises in each chapter (see above) and the parallel test forms in the ancillary testing package can serve as useful tools in this approach.

- **Attention to Matters of Style.** Chapter 16 explores ways to make writing more lively, vivid, and direct. It offers practice in writing strong verbs, adjectives, and expressions; eliminating unnecessary repetition of words and ideas; and avoiding clichés.

- **Comprehensive Treatment of Verbs.** Focusing on one of the most troublesome hurdles for novice writers in their first or second language—verbs—the book devotes four chapters to verb tenses, verb forms, verb phrases, and phrasal verbs.

- **Attention to the Special Needs of Students.** Unit V is a handbook-like section on punctuation, consistency, verb formation and use, quoting, spelling, apostrophe use, double negative correction, hyphenation, capitalization, articles, and prepositions. With the blueprints, glossary, and English as a Second Language boxes, the book offers aid and instruction to anyone—from native speakers to non-English dominant, or ESL, speakers—who requires additional help in specific areas. An ESL icon identifies especially pertinent instruction and exercises.

- **Tips Boxes.** Within the margins of every chapter are helpful advice and mnemonic aids.

- **English as a Second Language Boxes.** Also placed within the margins many chapters are helpful and timely suggestions for this growing segment of the student population.

- **Chapter-Ending Summary Boxes.** These highlighted summaries help students identify and review the important points to practice and serve as additional reference aids in revising and editing.

- **Glossary.** Key terms are highlighted in the text and defined in a glossary at the back of the book.

- **Quotations from Famous Authors.** Quotations in the margins of each chapter provide advice and inspiration—and often a humorous touch—while reassuring students that professional writers often encounter the same challenges as novices.

- **Full Test Bank.** The ancillary materials include two parallel forms of multiple-choice quizzes, two parallel forms of sentence writing quizzes, and two parallel forms of paragraph editing tests. Additionally, the *Test Bank* includes both a mid-term and a final examination.

NEW TO THE SEVENTH EDITION

This new edition places greater emphasis on process, accessibility to students, ease of use for instructors, and adaptability to a variety of programs and teaching approaches.

- **More Emphasis on the Writing Process.** The Six Steps to Writing with Confidence presents students with an easily mastered series of activities to perform in the writing process. Each of the chapters in Unit IV, on writing types of paragraphs, takes students through each of the six steps, which are all clearly labeled. And every exercise throughout the text is labeled to correspond to the activity it reinforces. Not only is the process thoroughly explained, but outlining, writing topic sentences, and writing conclusions are highlighted in every chapter on the paragraph modes. Conclusions also receive additional attention.

- **Answer Keys for Independent Study and Self-Correction.** Answers to the odd-numbered items in each exercise, along with the answers to the first Editing for Mastery exercise that concludes each chapter in Units II, III, and IV, are provided in an appendix on p. 426.

- **Streamlined Explanations.** Instructions have been made simpler and more direct throughout the text, focusing only on what students need to know.

- **More Emphasis on Editing.** All sentence-level instruction in Units II, III, and V is placed within the context of editing. But the emphasis on editing transcends mere instruction; it also is placed into practice. Each chapter within these units concludes with parallel **Editing for Mastery** exercises. Students are asked to find and correct a specific number and type of error in the first mastery exercise. Following this, they may consult the answer keys in the appendix, discuss and review their work, and then complete the second mastery exercise.

  Additionally, each chapter in Unit IV, in which students compose and revise paragraphs following the six steps in the writing process, includes Revision Guidelines and advice on editing.

- **More Emphasis on Reading and Writing in Response to Reading.** Recognizing the growing emphasis on the reading-writing connection, the number of additional readings has been increased from ten to sixteen, seven of which are new—and two of which are written by students. Selections stimulate student interest, exemplify rhetorical modes, guide analysis, and suggest topics for additional writing.

- **New Student Models.** Two of the sample paragraphs and essays in Unit IV— as well as two of the readings in the final unit of the book—are student written.

- **Unit-Ending Blueprints for Success.** Building on the popularity of the in-chapter blueprints for the paragraph modes in Unit IV, each unit now concludes with a two-page set of "Blueprints for Success," summarizing the key points.

- **More Writing Assignments—and Assignments Based on Readings.** Suggestions for writing follow each of the readings, both within chapters and in the Additional Readings at the end of the book. In every case, one of these assignments requires a written response to the reading.

- **New—and More Unified—Exercise Content.** This includes material on the voyage of the Kon-Tiki; fascinating information on animals such as baboons, jaguars, leopards, zebras, and insects; and mysterious and mystical information on the death of Abraham Lincoln. Most chapters throughout the book follow a thematic strand, and exercises are in continuous discourse.

THE TEACHING AND LEARNING PACKAGE

Each component of the teaching and learning package has been crafted to ensure that the course is a rewarding experience for both instructors and students.

- The *Instructor's Manual* contains teaching tips, overhead transparency masters, additional exercises and tests, and answers to all in-text questions. ISBN 0-321-08917-0

- The *Test Bank* contains a wealth of additional quizzes, tests, and exercises—keyed to each chapter in the student text. The *Test Bank* is printed on 8½ x 11 paper, perforated for easy removal and copying. ISBN 0-321-08916-2
- **Companion Web Site.** For additional activities, exercises, and resources, be sure to visit *Writing* and *Composing with Confidence* online at http://www.ablongman.com/meyers.

  In addition, a series of other skills-based supplements is available for both instructors and students. All of these supplements are available either free or at greatly reduced prices.

FOR ADDITIONAL READING AND REFERENCE

- **The Dictionary Deal.** Two dictionaries can be shrinkwrapped with *Writing with Confidence* at a nominal fee. *The New American Webster Handy College Dictionary* is a paperback reference text with more than 100,000 entries. *Merriam Webster's Collegiate Dictionary*, tenth edition, is a hardback reference with a citation file of more than 14.5 million examples of English words drawn from actual use. For more information on how to shrinkwrap a dictionary with your text, please contact your Longman sales representative.
- **Penguin Quality Paperback Titles.** A series of Penguin paperbacks is available at a significant discount when shrinkwrapped with this text. Some titles available are Toni Morrison's *Beloved,* Julia Alvarez's *How the Garcia Girls Lost Their Accents,* Mark Twain's *Huckleberry Finn, Narrative of the Life of Frederick Douglass,* Harriet Beecher Stowe's *Uncle Tom's Cabin,* Dr. Martin Luther King, Jr.'s *Why We Can't Wait,* and plays by Shakespeare, Miller, and Albee. For a complete list of titles or more information, please contact your Longman sales consultant.
- *100 Things to Write About.* This 100-page book contains 100 individual assignments for writing on a variety of topics and in a wide range of formats, from expressive to analytical. Ask your Longman sales representative for a sample copy. ISBN 0-673-98239-4
- *Newsweek* **Alliance.** Instructors may choose to shrinkwrap a 12-week subscription to *Newsweek* with any Longman text. The price of the subscription is 57 cents per issue (a total of $6.84 for the subscription). Available with the subscription is a free "Interactive Guide to *Newsweek*"—a workbook for students who are using the text. In addition, Newsweek provides a wide variety of instructor supplements free to teachers, including maps, Skills Builders, and weekly quizzes. For more information on the Newsweek program, please contact your Longman sales representative.

ELECTRONIC AND ONLINE OFFERINGS

- **[NEW] The Longman Writer's Warehouse.** The innovative and exciting online supplement is the perfect accompaniment to any developmental writing course. Developed by developmental English instructors specially for developing writers, The Writer's Warehouse covers every part of the writing process. Also included are journaling capabilities, multimedia activities, diagnostic tests, an interactive handbook, and a complete instructor's manual. The Writer's Warehouse requires no space on your school's server; rather, students complete and store their work on the Longman server, and are able to access it, revise it, and continue working at any time. For more details about how to shrinkwrap a free subscription to The Writer's Warehouse with this text, please consult your Longman sales representative. For a free guided tour of the site, visit http://longmanwriterswarehouse.com.

- **The Writer's ToolKit Plus.** This CD-ROM offers a wealth of tutorial, exercise, and reference material for writers. It is compatible with either a PC or Macintosh platform, and is flexible enough to be used either occasionally for practice or regularly in class lab sessions. For information on how to bundle this CD-ROM FREE with your text, please contact your Longman sales representative.

- **The Longman English Pages Web Site.** Both students and instructors can visit our free content-rich Web site for additional reading selections and writing exercises. From the Longman English pages, visitors can conduct a simulated Web search, learn how to write a resume and cover letter, or try their hand at poetry writing. Stop by and visit us at http://www.ablongman. com/englishpages.

- **The Longman Electronic Newsletter.** Twice a month during the spring and fall, instructors who have subscribed receive a free copy of the Longman Developmental English Newsletter in their e-mailbox. Written by experienced classroom instructors, the newsletter offers teaching tips, classroom activities, book reviews, and more. To subscribe, visit the Longman Developmental English Web site at http://www.ablongman.com/basicskills, or send an e-mail to BasicSkills@ablongman.com.

FOR INSTRUCTORS

- **[NEW] Electronic Test Bank for Writing.** This electronic test bank features more than 5,000 questions in all areas of writing, from grammar to paragraphing, through essay writing, research, and documentation. With this easy-to-use CD-ROM, instructors simply choose questions from the electronic test bank, then print out the completed test for distribution. CD-ROM: 0-321-08117-X Print version: 0-321-08486-1

- **Competency Profile Test Bank, Second Edition.** This series of 60 objective tests covers ten general areas of English competency, including fragments; comma splices and run-ons; pronouns; commas; and capitalization. Each test is available in remedial, standard, and advanced versions. Available as reproducible sheets or in computerized versions. Free to instructors. Paper version: 0-321-02224-6. Computerized IBM: 0-321-02633-0. Computerized Mac: 0-321-02632-2.

- **Diagnostic and Editing Tests and Exercises, Fourth Edition.** This collection of diagnostic tests helps instructors assess students' competence in Standard Written English for purpose of placement or to gauge progress. Available as reproducible sheets or in computerized versions, and free to instructors. Paper: 0-321-10022-0. CD-ROM: 0-321-10499-4.

- **ESL Worksheets, Third Edition.** These reproducible worksheets provide ESL students with extra practice in areas they find the most troublesome. A diagnostic test and post-test are provided, along with answer keys and suggested topics for writing. Free to adopters. 0-321-07765-2

- **Longman Editing Exercises.** Fifty-four pages of paragraph editing exercises give students extra practice using grammar skills in the context of longer passages. Free when packaged with any Longman title. 0-205-31792-8

- **80 Practices.** A collection of reproducible, ten-item exercises that provide additional practices for specific grammatical usage problems, such as comma splices, capitalization, and pronouns. Includes an answer key, and free to adopters. 0-673-53422-7

- **CLAST Test Package, Fourth Edition.** These two 40-item objective tests evaluate students' readiness for the CLAST exams. Strategies for teaching CLAST preparedness are included. Free with any Longman English title. Reproducible sheets: 0-321-01950-4 Computerized IBM version: 0-321-01982-2 Computerized Mac version: 0-321-01983-0
- **TASP Test Package, Third Edition.** These 12 practice pre-tests and post-tests assess the same reading and writing skills covered in the TASP examination. Free with any Longman English title. Reproducible sheets: 0-321-01959-8 Computerized IBM version: 0-321-01985-7 Computerized Mac version: 0-321-01984-9
- *Teaching Online: Internet Research, Conversation, and Composition,* **Second Edition.** Ideal for instructors who have never surfed the Net, this easy-to-follow guide offers basic definitions, numerous examples, and step-by-step information about finding and using Internet sources. Free to adopters. 0-321-01957-1
- *Teaching Writing to the Non-Native Speaker.* This booklet examines the issues that arise when nonnative speakers enter the developmental classroom. Free to instructors, it includes profiles of international and permanent ESL students, factors influencing second-language acquisition, and tips on managing a multicultural classroom. 0-673-97452-9

FOR STUDENTS

- **[NEW] The Longman Writer's Journal.** This journal for writers, free with *Writing with Confidence,* offers students a place to think, write, and react. For an examination copy, contact your Longman sales consultant. 0-321-08639-2
- **[NEW] The Longman Researcher's Journal.** This journal for writers and researchers, free with this text, helps students plan, schedule, write, and revise their research project. An all-in-one resource for first-time researchers, the journal guides students gently through the research process. 0-321-09530-8
- *Researching Online,* **Sixth Edition.** A perfect companion for a new age, this indispensable new supplement helps students navigate the Internet. Adapted from *Teaching Online,* the instructor's Internet guide, *Researching Online* speaks directly to students, giving them detailed, step-by-step instructions for performing electronic searches. Available free when shrinkwrapped with this text. 0-321-11733-6
- *Learning Together: An Introduction to Collaborative Theory.* This brief guide to the fundamentals of collaborative learning teaches students how to work effectively in groups, how to revise with peer response, and how to co-author a paper or report. Shrinkwrapped free with any Longman Basic Skills text. 0-673-46848-8
- *A Guide for Peer Response,* **Second Edition.** This guide offers students forms for peer critiques, including general guidelines and specific forms for different stages in the writing process. Also appropriate for freshman-level course. Free to adopters. 0-321-01948-2
- *Thinking Through the Test,* **by D. J. Henry.** This special workbook, prepared specially for students in Florida, offers ample skill and practice exercises to help students prep for the Florida State Exit Exam. To shrinkwrap this workbook free with your textbook, please contact your Longman sales representative. Available in two versions: with and without answers. Also

available: Two laminated grids (one for reading, one for writing) that can serve as handy references for students preparing for the Florida State Exit Exam.

ACKNOWLEDGMENTS

As always, I could not have achieved this result without the assistance, advice, and support of colleagues and students. I thank the administrators of Truman College and the City Colleges of Chicago, who granted me a sabbatical, part of which was devoted to revising this book. I thank my students, who continually teach me how the writing process works and should be addressed. I especially thank the students—some of them from my classes, others from other colleges—who have contributed paragraphs and essays to the text: Linder Anim, Tuyet-Ahn Van, Iman Rooker, Mirham Mahmutagic, Veronica Fleeton, Sara Sebring, Mark Schlitt, Jane Smith, Christine Mueller, and Amra Skocic. Again, Professor Patricia W. Kato of Chattanooga State Community College, Chattanooga, Tennessee, deserves my special thanks for providing several of the reading selections and student paragraphs for the book. And so does Professor Sherry F. Gott of Danville Community College, Danville, Virginia, who provided Jane Smith's student essay.

I thank the reviewers of the manuscript, whose invaluable criticisms and suggestions have helped shape this revision:

Joe Allen, Dutchess Community College
Martha Funderburk, University of Arkansas Community College of Hope
Judy G. Haberman, Phoenix College
Patsy Krech, University of Memphis
Nancy Schneider, University of Maine at Augusta
Lisa Shuchter, Naugatuck Valley Community College
James Suderman, Okaloosa-Walton Community College
Karean Williams, Miami Dade Community College

I also thank Brandi Nelson and her staff at Elm Street Publishing Services, Inc. for their outstanding work in the copyediting and production of the text. I thank my Acquisitions Editor, Steven Rigolosi, whose vision, insight, imagination, and flexibility made this whole project work. I also thank Valerie Zaborski, in-house production manager, for her many contributions; Donna Campion, for shepherding the ancillaries through their many stages, and Jennifer Krasula for helping to keep track of the assorted pieces. But most importantly, I thank my Developmental Editor, Ann Hofstra Grogg, who once again has guided me so brilliantly through a revision of this text. She is the first Ann to whom this text is dedicated and in many ways the co-author of this book.

And the second Ann to whom I dedicate not only this book is my wife and companion for almost four decades. It is she to whom I attribute whatever small successes I have achieved in my adult life, and to whom I attribute my largest successes: our children Sarah and Bradley, who continue to make us proud of their achievements.

Alan Meyers

I

Building Your Writing Skills

The word *writing* comes from a verb. That means it's an activity—a process.

Therefore, you shouldn't think of writing as merely a "paper," an "assignment," a "story"—some *thing* that magically emerges from the hands of people who have some sort of genius. Yes, some people have a natural gift for writing. But it was Thomas Alva Edison (an elementary-school dropout) who said, "Genius is 1 percent inspiration and 99 percent perspiration." All of us can write, provided we're willing to engage in the process.

Writing is a way to produce language, which you do naturally when you speak. You say something, think of more to say, perhaps correct something you've said, and then move on to the next statement. Writing isn't much different, except that you take more time to think about your subject, the person or people you'll be discussing it with, and the goal you hope to achieve in that discussion. You also take more time to form your words and then change them until they clearly express your thoughts.

The four chapters in this unit will show you how to engage in the writing process. They'll discuss why you write (and there are plenty of good reasons), how to discover and organize your thoughts, how to capture them on the page, and how to revise and rewrite them so they achieve your goals. These chapters suggest ways to make your writing interesting, direct, and clear.

Don't worry if you're new to, or unsure about, the writing process. The chapters in this unit will take you through it step by step. Follow those steps and you can indeed write well—and with confidence.■

1 Why Write?

Let's start with a basic point: writing is speaking to others on paper—or on a computer screen. If you can speak, you can write. Yes, writing is partly a talent, but it's mostly a *skill,* and like any skill, it improves with practice. Writing is also an *action*—a process of discovering and assembling your ideas, putting them on paper, and reshaping and revising them. We'll examine the writing process in Chapter 2, but here we'll look briefly at

- the relationship between speaking and writing
- the ways you can build confidence in your writing
- the ways you choose to write
- the ways you can use writing

SPEAKING AND WRITING

When you speak, you don't just make sounds. You say *words* that *mean* something. You speak because you want to share an idea, give information, express a greeting, state an opinion, or send a warning. That is, you speak because you have

1. something to say: *a subject*
2. a reason for saying it: *a purpose*
3. someone to say it to: *an audience*

When you speak, you can see and hear your listeners. They respond to you, and you respond to them. You answer their questions, restate ideas, and even change the subject if it bores them. You use your voice and body to emphasize and clarify your ideas. You raise or lower your voice, talk quickly or slowly, and pause for effect. You point with your hands, shrug your shoulders, wink your

UNIT 1	Visit the Longman Writer's Warehouse!
Chapter 1	If your text has arrived with a subscription to the Longman Writer's Warehouse, visit
Writing with Confidence	http://longmanwriterswarehouse.com
©2003	for further practice on the skills you will learn in this chapter.

eye, grin, or frown. And when you speak, you also find your thoughts coming into focus. You correct yourself, restate your ideas, illustrate your opinions, or even change your mind. In short, you are both stating and examining your ideas as you say them aloud.

Writing is much like speaking—a way to discover and communicate your ideas. Unlike speaking, however, it doesn't happen all at once. You cannot see and hear your readers, so you must predict their reactions. You must think about a subject that will interest them and try to present it in an interesting way. You must consider if an idea won't be clear to your readers and then try to make it clear. You must anticipate their questions and then try to answer them. Because you cannot emphasize your ideas through your body and speaking voice, you must pay more attention to your word choice. You must present your ideas in a logical order. You must read what you write and then rewrite it until you express your meaning strongly and clearly. In short, you must choose your language carefully, arrange it carefully, and punctuate it carefully.

You cannot do all of these things at once. Any good paragraph or essay goes through many stages before it's finished. First, you may simply explore ideas as you put them into words, lists, or charts. Afterward, you write a first draft and let it sit for a while. Then you can question and challenge it, and probably rewrite it. Perhaps you'll revise and polish your ideas and language in several drafts until you're confident that your audience will understand and care about what you have to say. You must fine-tune your message *before* you send it out.

That's what this book will help you do.

> "Writing, when properly managed . . . is but a different name for conversation."
>
> —Eighteenth-century English author Laurence Sterne

WRITING WITH CONFIDENCE

Now in its seventh edition and in print since 1979, *Writing with Confidence* has helped hundreds of thousands of people build and improve their writing skills. In fact, many of the model paragraphs and themes you'll see in the following chapters were written by students who used this book. They learned to write with confidence, and you can, too.

Perhaps you've had problems with writing in the past—getting started, organizing your thoughts, finding the right words, or mastering the rules of grammar and punctuation. Perhaps you even struggle with writing in English if it's your second (or third, or fourth) language. This book is designed to give you the best chance to improve. It divides the writing process into a series of small steps that you can master:

- ways to begin thinking about writing
- ways to explore and expand your ideas freely
- ways to shape those ideas into a plan
- ways to compose a first draft
- ways to review and revise the draft
- the way to produce final copy

Later sections of the book will give you additional help:

- suggestions for fixing problem sentences and combining sentences for variety
- strategies for organizing paragraphs and essays
- readings to serve as models of strong writing and prompts for your own essays
- advice on mastering additional grammatical and mechanical matters

As you follow the program in *Writing with Confidence,* you should discover that, although writing is rarely easy, it need not be painful and can even be fun. Flip through the pages of this book and you'll discover that many of the exercises discuss unusual people, places, animals, and events. When you revise the sentences in these exercises, you'll see how your improvements make subjects become clearer and more alive. In short, you'll learn how ideas worth reading about can get even better.

Remember that writing is a process. Remember, too, that writing is a skill that, like all skills, improves with practice. This book is filled with exercises that give you that practice. Doing them will build your confidence in your writing.

FINDING THE RIGHT WAY TO WRITE

Writing is a personal process, and no two people approach it in exactly the same way. So you should determine what works for you. Do you write best in the morning or at night? Do you write by hand or on a computer, or a combination of both? But there's one thing that you should never do: sit down to write a paper the night before it's due. You *cannot* do your best under those circumstances. Because writing is a process, you must give yourself time to work through the process.

Some writers are great planners. They see where they're going and get there with only small changes in their plans. Other writers are discoverers. They need to reach their destination by writing and then rewriting many times. But every writing task is different. Therefore, you might be a great planner in one situation, a great discoverer in another. In general, though, you should begin with a plan and then discover ideas along the way. You don't have to solve every problem before you begin. In fact, people who try that often experience *writer's block.*

The first step in planning is to prepare a schedule. Allow yourself time to list some topics, mull them over, and then choose one. Let ideas occur to you in the shower or on the way to class, and jot them down whenever you can. (You'll see specific ways to do this in Chapter 2.) Give yourself time to write a first draft, put it aside, and return to it a day or two later. You may spend three hours on an assignment, but they could be spread out in half-hour segments over five days. If you do your work in small steps, you'll accomplish something in every session. That will help you build your confidence.

WRITING FOR EVERY REASON

Now that we've looked briefly at the writing process, let's go back and answer the question in the title of this chapter: why write?

Writing to Work

We live in a technological world, where unskilled factory jobs have been sent abroad to less-developed countries and mega-malls have replaced the corner mom-and-pop stores. Today's economy requires that you write more than ever before. And with computers now a part of almost every job, word processing and e-mailing are essential skills.

Getting and keeping a job these days usually involves good writing skills. You'll get a job partly by writing a strong letter of application and résumé. You'll keep a job by writing clear memos and reports. If you're an office worker, you'll write memos and letters. If you're a health-care professional, you'll write clear records, memos, and orders. If you're a lawyer, you'll write legal briefs and documents.

Writing to Learn

Right now, of course, you're a college student, and your main job (or one of your main jobs) is to get through college. To do that, you need to take notes and write clear essays, reports, and answers to examination questions—and even an occasional letter or e-mail home.

For success in college, you should make note taking a habit. The physical act of writing will help you learn. Begin by taking notes on your readings; mark up your texts with questions, reactions, and reminders. If you have questions, write them down and bring them to class to get answers. And, of course, take good notes on your class lectures. Take notes on your assignments, too, so you know what's expected of you and when it's expected. These practices will help not only your writing but also your success as a student.

Keeping a writing log or subject journal can give your learning a big boost. You can record your progress in learning, jot down questions to ask your instructors, and explore your thoughts about new concepts and materials. Some students use a double-entry journal in which they summarize reading or lecture notes on the left-hand column or page and explore their reactions and questions to this material on the facing right-hand column or page.

Writing to Communicate

With so many computers connected to the Internet these days, people are e-mailing coworkers, friends, and relatives regularly. Why make a long-distance telephone call (and connect to an answering machine) when you can send a quick computer message, or get in a chat room to exchange messages? Students are e-mailing their professors to find out about classroom assignments—and to submit them. They're e-mailing classmates to discuss and work together on homework. They're also sharing notes about soccer practices and clubs, gossip, and philosophies of life. People are applying for jobs, conducting business, staying in touch, and even falling in love—all by writing!

In spite of computers, there will always be a place and need for the personal letter. A handwritten note from a friend, cousin, child, or parent is, and will continue to be, the best way to communicate important thoughts at important times. No matter what the content, the real message is, "I care about you and want to keep in touch." These writing practices pay off in ways that can't be measured in dollars or grades, only in the success of human relationships.

Writing for Yourself

There is another reason to write—for yourself—and this reason will last a lifetime. In this sense, all of us are writers. We write to explore our ideas, plans, sorrows, and dreams. We write to record what we've learned and done, or need to learn or do. We write to communicate with friends and relatives. We write to record family histories so our children and grandchildren can know and appreciate their heritage. We write for our own growth and pleasure. If you haven't ever written for pleasure, you may discover that, as your writing voice gains power and strength, writing can indeed be a joy.

Many writers like to keep a personal journal. It might be just a diary in which you summarize your daily activities ("Studied math for two hours, took a break to talk to Ron, and then started work on the biology project due Friday."). But the best journals serve as places to record your concerns and interests, to keep tabs on your questions and plans, to capture what surprises or puzzles you, to blow off steam, and to work through a problem and find a solution.

Take just ten minutes a day. Describe funny, dramatic, or troubling events, or examine interesting places or people. Even if you never do anything more with your journal, it will give you personal satisfaction and continual practice with writing. Often, however, college students find that their journals do become starting points for essays. They're resources for ideas that constitute the first step in the writing process. With a number of ideas already on paper, you won't have to take time searching for new material.

No matter what reason you choose to write, remember this: Good writers follow one universal practice—they write a lot.

GETTING A HEAD START

Begin the writing process now. List some topics for later writings. What has made you think, made you dream, made you mad? Jot down a few ideas. Then consider (but don't worry if you cannot yet answer) these questions on each topic: Why do I want to capture those ideas and express them? To whom do I want to tell them?

Relationship

Family

2

The Writing Process: Laying the Foundation

Writing with confidence comes from engaging in a *process* of writing. The page you're reading right now is the finished product of many hours of composing and revising. You don't see the papers that went into the wastebasket along the way: the notes, the false starts, the early drafts, and the later ones. You don't see the changes made in response to student reactions, the advice from professors who use this book in their classes, and the comments of editors. But the process does work, and it will work for you, too. In this chapter, you'll examine the steps in that process. They'll cover

■ ways to gather and shape ideas

■ ways to get your first draft on paper or in the computer

■ ways to revise and edit your work

WRITING WITH CONFIDENCE IN SIX STEPS

No two writers approach writing in exactly the same way. But they do tend to follow a series of actions that looks something like this:

1. Exploring ideas
   a. Considering subject
   b. Considering purpose
   c. Considering audience

UNIT 1	Go Electronic
Chapter 2	Use the following electronic supplements for additional practice with your writing: • For chapter-by-chapter summaries and exercises, visit the Writing with Confidence Companion Website at http://www.ablongman.com/meyers.
Writing with Confidence ©2003	• For work with the writing process, visit The Longman Writer's Warehouse at http://longmanwriterswarehouse.com (password needed). • For additional practice in grammar, use The Writer's ToolKit Plus CD-ROM.

2. Prewriting—using one or more of these methods
   a. Brainstorming
   b. Clustering
   c. Freewriting
3. Organizing
   a. Selecting
   b. Outlining
4. Writing a first draft
   a. Writing quickly to capture ideas
   b. Inserting notes and new ideas in the margins
5. Revising the draft
   a. Reviewing
   b. Reading aloud
   c. Predicting
6. Producing the final copy
   a. Editing
   b. Copying over
   c. Proofreading and copying over again

STEP 1: EXPLORING IDEAS

> "Writing is an exploration. You start from nothing and learn as you go."
>
> —Novelist E. L. Doctorow

Remember that writing is like speech, and speaking includes discovering ideas as you say them. So before you sit down to write, let your mind speak freely. Thoughts will occur to you at odd times and in odd places—while walking the dog, traveling to work, stretching out on the couch. When inspiration happens, capture it by writing on whatever you can—napkins, scraps of paper, or even the back of your hand.

Eventually, though, you should focus your exploration more systematically. As in speaking, you must have something to say, a reason for saying it, and someone to say it to. Ask yourself three questions:

- What is my subject?
- What is my purpose?
- Who is my audience?

Take notes on your answers.

Your Subject

> "There is no such thing on earth as an uninteresting subject."
>
> —English journalist G. K. Chesterton

Ask yourself, *what is my subject, and what do I know about it?* The most interesting subjects to your audience are usually those that you find most interesting. Choose a subject that you care about and know about (or can find out about). Then you'll have something interesting to say, and you'll say it more clearly and confidently.

College assignments sometimes give you freedom to choose your subject. Often, though, you must select and then narrow your subject from an assigned general topic. For example, suppose you're asked to describe a job you know well. Ask yourself:

- What jobs have I done or do now?
- What do I know about these jobs?
- Which jobs (or parts of one job) do I feel strongly about? What do I love or hate? What parts make me angry or happy?

Now choose the job, and search for more detail.

- What tools or materials do I use in my job?
- How do I perform each task?
- Which tasks are most interesting or boring?
- What examples or little stories best illustrate these points?

Make notes of your answers.

Your Purpose

Now ask yourself, *what is my purpose?* Communicating always has a purpose: to inform, to persuade, or to entertain—or maybe to do all three. You could, for example, *inform* your classmates about some procedures at your job. You could also *persuade* your classmates that they should find (or avoid) a job like yours. Or you could simply *entertain* your classmates with examples of odd incidents you've experienced at your job.

> "The first essential is to know what one wishes to say; the second is to decide to whom one wishes to say it."
>
> —Diplomat Harold Nicolson

EXERCISE 1   Defining Purpose

After each of the following opening sentences of a paragraph, label its main purpose: to inform, to entertain, or to persuade. (There may be more than one possibility.) Be prepared to explain your choices.

1. Glassmaking began almost five thousand years ago in Egypt. _to inform_____

2. Coin collecting can be an enjoyable and profitable hobby. _____

3. The United States began minting coins in 1792. _____

4. Few sights are as magnificent as the setting of the orange-red sun as it disappears beneath the roaring waves of Florida's Gulf Coast. _____

5. Smoking may be pleasurable, but can people continue to risk their lives for the sake of that pleasure? _____

6. With the score tied and just seconds left on the clock, Jordan stepped to the free-throw line. _____

EXERCISE 2   Exploring Purpose

Revise one of the sentences from Exercise 1 so that it begins three different paragraphs: one that informs, one that entertains, and one that persuades. For example:

> a. (to inform) Glassmaking began almost five thousand years ago in Egypt.
>
> b. (to entertain) Perhaps the Egyptians were really a bunch of busybodies, so they invented glass windows to look inside the houses of their neighbors.
>
> c. (to persuade) Glassmaking may seem like a small matter, but it is probably one of the most important inventions in the last five thousand years.

After writing the three sentences, list a few details that will follow each one.

Your Audience

Ask yourself, *who is my audience?* The answer to that question will determine what you say about your subject and what purpose you hope to achieve. For example, you might need to explain a great deal to a reader who's never heard of your subject, but explain a lot less to a reader who knows the subject well. Or you might need to provide a lot of evidence to persuade a reader who doesn't agree with your point of view, but provide far less for someone who tends to agree with you.

EXERCISE 3 | Adjusting for Audience

6. Edit
5. Revise
4. Write
3. Organize
2. Prewrite
1. Explore

For each of the following topics, list two or three points you would include if you were writing to the different audiences specified.

1. *Topic:* the value of popular music

   a. *Audience:* people between the ages of eighteen and thirty
   enjoyment from listening and dancing   Relaxation,

   b. *Audience:* professional musicians
   profits, enjoyment, fame

2. *Topic:* the benefits of controlled diets

   a. *Audience:* overweight adults
   Portion Control, Emotions Setting Goals

   b. *Audience:* athletes
   Strength, Drugs endurance

3. *Topic:* the benefits of attending your college

   a. *Audience:* high-school seniors with high grade-point averages

   b. *Audience:* high-school seniors with low grade-point averages

   c. *Audience:* older, returning students
   never too late, Foc04,

Collaborative Activity 1

Comparing Revisions
In a group of three to five people, discuss the sentences you wrote in Exercise 2. Does each accomplish its purpose? If not, how could it be revised? Appoint one person as the note taker, who may share your results with the whole class.

EXERCISE 4 | Recognizing Purpose and Audience

6. Edit
5. Revise
4. Write
3. Organize
2. Prewrite
1. Explore

Read this passage and then answer the questions that follow. Record your answers below or in your journal. Your instructor may also ask you to discuss them with classmates.

No Problem, But It Needs a Solution
by Bill Cosby

★ ★ ★ ★

When your fifteen-year-old son does speak, he often says one of two things: either "Okay," which, as we know, means "I haven't killed anyone," or "No problem."

"No problem" has been my son's philosophy of life. Two years ago, he was one of the top ten underachievers in our state and whenever you asked him how he was doing in school, he always said, with simple eloquence, "No problem." And, of course, his answer made sense: there *was* no problem, no confusion about how he was doing. He had failed everything; and what he hadn't failed, he hadn't taken yet. (Undoubtedly, F's had even been penciled in for next year.) He had even failed *English.*

His failing his native tongue piqued my curiosity, so I said, "How can you fail English?"

"Yeah," he replied.

Hoping to get an answer that had something to do with the question, I said again, "Please tell me: how can you fail English?"

"I don't know," he said.

"Son, you didn't really fail *English,* did you? You failed handing in the reports on time, right? Because you can understand people who speak English, can't you? And when you talk, *they* can understand *you,* can't they? So the teacher *understood* what you had written but just didn't care for the way you put it, right? You just failed *organization,* right? I mean, the teacher who failed you in English said, 'He can do the work,' right? It's just that you don't *want* to do it yet. And all it'll take is maybe leaving you out in the wilderness with no food or money in the middle of winter. Just a dime to make a collect call saying that you're ready to study."

"No problem," he said.

1. What's the writer's main purpose: to inform, persuade, or entertain? Or is it some combination of these purposes? _____

2. Who's the audience for this little article? Would you expect to find it in a college textbook, a newspaper, or in a popular magazine? What reasons can you give for your answers? _____

3. What point (or points) is the writer making? _____

4. What's the writer's attitude toward his son? Does he have more than one attitude? How do you know? _____

STEP 2: PREWRITING

The second step of the writing process involves capturing your thoughts on paper or on the computer screen. Jot down whatever comes to mind. Don't worry about spelling or punctuation or exact meanings, because you will probably change your mind and your phrasing later anyway. This step is called **prewriting**. It is a time to relax, to let the words flow, to see your ideas take shape. This process can even be fun!

Brainstorming

One way to capture your thoughts is by **brainstorming**, or listing thoughts as they come to you. Here's an example from a student who has been asked to describe a job:

> "When you come up with an idea or phrase that isn't quite right, resist the temptation to throw it out and start again. Just write it down."
>
> —Professor of English Linda Flower

Deliver pizza for Guido's Glorious Pizza

Pay: minimum wage plus tips

work nites, 6 to 10

boss is impatient

must use cell phone

hate some customers

fraternity guys who always are partying, forget to tip

fussy lady who makes me take back cold pizza

drunk guy who answers bell after six rings

You might also brainstorm a second (or even a third) time to generate more ideas.

Clustering

In **clustering**, you put your topic in a circle in the middle of the page and then add related ideas as they occur to you. These related ideas are also called *branches*.

You can then add more branches as more ideas occur to you. A completed diagram might look like this:

Freewriting

Another way to get started is through **freewriting**. You simply write about the subject without worrying about sentence structure, spelling, logic, and grammar. Write it as you would speak it. Use abbreviations and shortcuts so you can get your ideas down fast. Here's an example:

> Work part time delivering pizza for Guido's Glorious Pizzas. Nites 6 to 10 three days during week and on Saturday eve. Drive an old beater held together with duct tape and chewing gum. Have to have a cell phone because new orders come in all night, I need directions, and some customers won't open the door unless I call. Customers are a pain. One woman, I'll call her Fussy Ms. Fritzy, is very impressed with herself. Every time I deliver a pizza, she gives me a hard time. It's cold, it's not what she ordered, it smells funny. (Of course, she keeps on ordering.) All her gold bracelets and fancy hairdos. Once she looked in the box and told me she wanted triple extra cheeze, not double. And told me to give her a discount or take it back. What could I do? Either give the discount or eat the pizza myself. Another customer, Wobbly Wally, takes 4 mins to anser the door—after I ring the bell six times. Beer can in his hand and breathe to kill any infectious disease. I think I could give him cheese on cardboard and he wouldn't know the diffrence. Fumbles to find money, gives me a $20 bill and doesn't count the change. The fab fraternity four are another pleasure. Their always partying. The music is so loud my teeth rattle when one of them opens the door. They wear teeshirts with cutoff sleeves and bellys hanging out over their pants. They grab the pizza, pay me, and give me a thank you but never a tip. I guess it's not a bad job, it beats digging ditches.

Don't think of your freewriting as disorganized. It's just a way to get your creative juices flowing and put ideas into words that you can look at, expand on, change, or omit.

EXERCISE 5 | Prewriting a Paragraph

6. Edit
5. Revise
4. Write
3. Organize
2. Prewrite
1. Explore

Choose a job, hobby, or skill you know well. Consider how the topic might interest your classmates. Consider your purpose: will you inform, persuade, or entertain? Then do a brainstorming list, a clustering diagram, and a freewriting page so that you can sample each of these techniques. See which ones you find most useful.

STEP 3: ORGANIZING

With your ideas roughly captured in words, you can select from and organize them.

- Underline or highlight the most promising ideas in your brainstorming list. Then rewrite the list, putting related ideas together. Add to the list as more ideas occur to you.
- Choose the part of the clustering diagram that seems most promising. Do a second clustering diagram that explores those ideas in greater detail.
- Circle or highlight the most promising parts of your freewriting. Base a second or even a third freewriting on them. Focus more narrowly on your subject and add more details.

Selecting

Once you've narrowed your focus and generated more ideas, you can choose the ones that fit your purpose and audience. For example, the pizza delivery writer might decide that his purpose is to entertain classmates who also have part-time jobs—and to make the point that his job really isn't so bad. So he'd select only the most humorous information. That's the customers he typically serves: Fussy Ms. Fritzy, Wobbly Wally, and the fraternity boys. He'd then omit unimportant details or ones that drift off his point—perhaps the ones about his cell phone and maybe even his working hours. And he would generate more details to develop the humor.

Outlining

After deciding to focus on customers, the pizza delivery writer can make a rough outline. It might include about three examples and details in categories according to customer. The outline would look something like this:

Fussy Ms. Fritzy
  Answers door with gold bracelets dangling from her arm and $90 perm
  Complains about the pizza
    One time: too cold
    Another time: it smells funny
    Another time: wants a discount
Wobbly Wally
  Have to ring door bell six times
  Arrives after 4 minutes
  Always has beer can in hand
  Breath that could kill
  Almost unconscious
  Fumbles to find money, gives me $20 and doesn't count the change
The Fab Fraternity Four

> Always partying
> Loud music
> T-shirts with cutoff sleeves and bellies hanging out over their pants
> Never tip me

Of course, he could arrange the details in other ways: in a time sequence, perhaps with each stop on a typical delivery night, or as a comparison of the best and worst customers. There are many ways to organize paragraphs, as later chapters in this book will explain.

EXERCISE 6	Selecting and Outlining

Return to the materials you generated in Exercise 5, and consider your purpose and audience. What point do you want to make, and to whom? Select your ideas by underlining, circling, or highlighting them. Arrange the ideas in an informal outline. If you discover that some parts of the outline are thin, generate some additional details for those parts.

STEP 4: WRITING A FIRST DRAFT

You've done some prewriting, selected your best ideas, and arranged them in some reasonable order. Now you can confidently begin the first draft. Don't worry about writing something "perfect." No one gets it right on the first try. Remember that writing is a process of self-discovery. New ideas will come to you, and you may discover a different and better arrangement of ideas. So write fast, as if you were speaking your words aloud. Circle words or sentences that you want to revise later. If a new idea occurs to you that belongs earlier in the draft, make a note about it in the margin, write it on a second sheet of paper, or mouse click to the spot you want to insert it. Here is an example of a first draft:

✓ **TIPS**

For Drafting

1. Write as fast as you can to capture your ideas fully.
2. Leave wide margins.
3. Double space so there will be plenty of room for changes.
4. Use only one side of the paper so you can cut and paste changes.
5. Make notes in the margins—or write new material on separate sheets of paper.
6. Tape or staple additions where you want them to go.
7. Say something out loud (well, maybe in a whisper) before you write it.
8. Circle words you think you misspelled or will want to change later.

> I have a part-time job delivering pizzas for Guido's Glorious Pizzas three nights a week and on Saturday nights. I can put up with driving an old beater held together with duct tape and chewing gum, but the customers can be a pain. One woman, I'll call her Fussy Ms. Fritzy, answers the door with dozens of gold bracelets hanging from her wrist and a puffed up $90 hairdo that must be left over from the 1950's. Every time I deliver a pizza, she gives me a hard time. She says it's to cold, or it's not what she ordered, or she claimed it smells funny. Once she opened the box and told me she wanted triple extra cheeze, not double. She even demanded a discount. I had to give her the discount or eat the pizza myself. Another customer, Wobbly Wally, takes 4 minutes to anser the door after I ring the bell six times. He always has a beer can

Continued

For Drafting and Revising on the Computer

1. Write as fast as the computer will let you.
2. Save your work every five or ten minutes.
3. Use insert or cut-and-paste commands to add or move things around.
4. Print out a double-spaced copy for revisions; slow down and revise in pencil.

in his hand and sort of sways back and forth as if he's on a ship in a storm. When he talks, his breath kills. I think I could give him cheese on cardboard and he wouldn't know the diffrence. He fumbles in the pockets of his torn pants to find money, gives me a $20 bill and doesn't count the change. The fab fraternity four are another pleasure. When I arrive with the pizza, their always partying. Every time they open the door, the music from the apartment is so loud my teeth rattle. They're a lovely bunch in their teeshirts with cutoff sleeves and bellies hanging out over their pants. One of them grabs the pizza, pays me, and thank me but never gives me a tip. I hate some of the customers, the job isn't too bad. It pays well enough, and it beats digging ditches.

EXERCISE 7	Drafting a Paragraph

6. Edit
5. Revise
4. Write
3. Organize
2. Prewrite
1. Explore

Write a first draft based on the selecting and outlining you did in Exercise 6. If you compose by hand, write on one side of the page only, leave wide margins, and skip every other line so that you have room for additional changes. If you compose by computer, double- or triple-space and leave wide margins as well.

STEP 5: REVISING THE DRAFT

After completing your first draft, set it aside. Give yourself a chance to see it later with fresh eyes. It's hard to think about changing and correcting your work immediately after you finish a draft. You tend to read what you *think* you said, not what's actually on the page. If you've composed it on the computer, print out a hard copy to work on later.

Reviewing

When you come back to your writing, read it carefully. Study its organization, word choice, and details. You'll probably find some things to cut, as well as some things to add. Don't be satisfied with changing a few words here and there. Rearrange sections, rephrase sentences, and improve your word choice now. Look at the words you circled earlier and correct their spelling if you keep them in this draft. Make notes in the margins and above the lines. Write new sections and draw arrows to where they will go—or compose them on the computer. Your work at this point may be so messy that you need to make a clean copy before going any further. Here's a bit of the first draft on delivering pizza after the writer reviewed it:

> One woman, I'll call her Fussy Ms. Fritzy, answers the door with dozens of gold bracelets hanging from her wrist and a puffed up $90 hairdo ~~that must be left over~~ from the 1950's. Every time I deliver a pizza, complains that   too
> she ^~~gives me a hard time. She says~~ it's ^~~to~~ cold, or it's not what she ordered, or ~~she claimed~~ it smells funny.

Reading Aloud

Now read your work aloud. Listen hard. You'll probably hear mistakes to correct and discover improvements to make. Then read your work again—perhaps to another person—and repeat the process until you're satisfied that your writing is interesting and clear. Don't ask yourself and others, "Can this be understood?" but instead, "Can this be *mis*understood?"

Predicting

Remember, readers don't merely receive information; they actively attempt to find meaning for themselves. They *predict* what will follow from your opening sentences and then perhaps adjust their predictions as they read on. Your writing can benefit from predicting, too. Here's how to do it:

- Read the first sentence or two.
- Stop and think about (or hear) what your readers would expect to follow.
- Decide if the rest of the paragraph satisfies those predictions.
- Make notes on what to add, remove, or shift to satisfy those expectations.

Predicting is a valuable tool and should become a regular part of your revision practices.

Making a Clean Copy

You've reviewed, read aloud, and made predictions about your first draft. So you've probably come a long way toward doing a second draft. Now write it. You'll probably find more improvements to make as you write. That's good. It's evidence that you're involved in the writing process and letting the process work for you. Keep revising and copying over until you're satisfied with (or even proud of) what you've produced.

EXERCISE 8   Revising Your Paragraph

Now review the draft you composed in Exercise 7 one or more times. Make changes on the original version. Read your paper aloud so you can hear the words and rhythms of the sentences. Read the paper to someone else, too, and let the person make predictions and comments. Complete your revision by producing a clean copy incorporating all the changes and improvements you've made.

STEP 6: PRODUCING THE FINAL COPY

Once you're reasonably satisfied with your writing, you can begin the final copy. Prepare it according to guidelines your instructor gives you, or following the guidelines on pages 7 and 8. Before you're finished, however, you need to pay attention to details you've ignored while simply getting your ideas on paper and shaping them to fit your purpose and audience.

Editing

You want people to judge your ideas, not your mistakes. So edit your work carefully. **Editing** requires that you carefully examine what you've written and look for errors. This kind of attention during early stages of the writing process could freeze your creativity. In the heat of writing and revising, you probably won't want to stop and analyze sentence structure. But now in the final stages of the writing process, you can examine your work coldly and make changes. Check your work for misspelled words and words left out or repeated. Look for grammatical errors, missing word endings, incomplete sentences, and incorrect punctuation. Read the paper more than once. Copy it over or print it out again, including all your changes. This draft should be neat and legible—and represent your best effort.

Proofreading

This is the step in the writing process that students (and even some professional writers) may overlook or not treat seriously. **Proofreading** means carefully examining the last copy again, perhaps comparing it to the previous one. Did you include all your editing changes? Did you make any typographical errors? Read through the paper slowly. Place a ruler under each line to focus your eyes. Read the paper aloud. And then reread it. If necessary, make a new and completely clean copy—and then proofread that copy.

Here's the final draft of the paper on delivering pizza:

TIPS

For Preparing Final Copy

1. Use good quality standard-size paper.
2. Include your name, the date, and the assignment title according to the format your instructor requires.
3. If you write by hand, write in blue or black ink—not in pencil.
4. Leave at least an inch margin on both sides of the page.
5. Double-space on the computer; skip every other line for handwritten work.
6. Number your pages at top or bottom as your instructor requires.
7. Fasten pages together with paper clip or staple, whichever your instructor prefers.

> I work part-time three weeknights and on Saturday night delivering for Guido's Glorious Pizzas. I can put up with driving an old beater held together with duct tape and chewing gum, but the customers give me worse indigestion than the pepperoni. One regular customer, Fussy Ms. Fritzy, answers the door with dozens of gold bracelets hanging from her wrist and a puffed up $90 hairdo from the 1950s. She always throws a tantrum. She complains the pizza is too cold, or it's not what she ordered, or it smells funny. Once she looked in the box and screamed that she wanted triple extra cheese, not double. She even demanded a discount. I cut the price by $2 rather than lose the sale and eat the pizza myself. Another customer, Wobbly Wally, takes four minutes to answer the door after I ring the bell six times. He arrives with a beer

can in his hand and sways back and forth like a man on a ship in a storm. When he talks, his breath would kill just about any infectious disease. He's so delirious, I think I could give him cheese on cardboard and he wouldn't know the difference. He fumbles in the pockets of his torn pants to find money, gives me a $20 bill, and doesn't count the change. Finally, the Fab Fraternity Four are another of my least favorite regulars. They're always partying when I arrive with the pizza. Every time one of them opens the door, the loud music from the apartment makes my teeth rattle. He grabs the pizza, pays me, and gives me a thank you but never a tip. In spite of the customers, the job isn't too bad. It pays for my school tuition and books—and it beats digging ditches.

Collaborative Activity 3

Peer Editing and Proofreading

Often, other people can detect errors you may have missed. Exchange paragraphs with a classmate and check each other's work carefully. If you aren't sure of your classmate's corrections, check with another classmate or two. Then copy over your paragraph and proofread it again.

Notice that this final draft is livelier than the original. It sticks to the point. Its sentences are clear. Its examples are developed with interesting details.

You can get similar results by working your way through the steps in the writing process described in this chapter, which forms the core of the book. Return to this chapter every time you write, until the process becomes a habit—even an instinct. You, too, can write with confidence.

EXERCISE 9	Editing and Proofreading Your Work

6. Edit
5. Revise
4. Write
3. Organize
2. Prewrite
1. Explore

Look over your revised paragraph from Exercise 8 carefully. Correct mistakes in spelling, grammar, and punctuation. Copy over the paper and proofread it more than once. Keep looking for errors. Make a final clean copy and proofread it, too.

IN SUMMARY   The Writing Process

1. Consider your subject, your purpose, and your audience.
2. Discover your ideas by putting them into words through brainstorming, clustering, or freewriting.
3. Decide what to include in your writing and how to organize those details.
4. Compose a first draft (and don't worry about making it perfect).
5. Take a break and then revise the first draft several times, perhaps after getting the reactions of other people.
6. Produce a clean copy when you are reasonably satisfied with your work.
7. Edit this copy and make another if you find errors. Check your corrections and proofread the copy again until your final copy is ready for your instructor.

3 Writing a Powerful Paragraph

Building the Foundation

Now that you've seen how the writing process works, try applying it. This chapter shows you how to write a powerful paragraph. The process will also work for essays, but let's start with paragraphs—the building blocks of essays. In this chapter you'll practice

- choosing the topic
- drafting the topic sentence
- planning and writing the paragraph
- revising and strengthening the paragraph

WHAT IS A PARAGRAPH?

Throughout your college and working career, you'll sometimes need to write single paragraphs—for homework assignments, short essay answers, simple memos, and reports on various subjects. However, learning to write effective paragraphs is an important first step in learning to write an effective essay. Paragraphs break down the main idea of the essay into smaller, easily understood parts. The first part relates logically to the second part, the second part relates to the third part, and so on. Without these smaller divisions, readers would

UNIT 1	Go Electronic
Chapter 3	Use the following electronic supplements for additional practice with your writing: • For chapter-by-chapter summaries and exercises, visit the Writing with Confidence Companion Website at http://www.ablongman.com/meyers.
Writing with Confidence ©2003	• For work with the writing process, visit The Longman Writer's Warehouse at http://longmanwriterswarehouse.com (password needed). • For additional practice in grammar, use The Writer's ToolKit Plus CD-ROM.

have a hard time understanding all these ideas, and writers would have an even harder time expressing them.

In fact, you might think of the paragraph as an essay in miniature. Just as an essay is a group of paragraphs that discuss one large idea, a **paragraph** is a group of sentences that discuss a smaller idea. And, like an essay, the paragraph generally contains an introduction, a body, and a conclusion.

1. The **introduction** catches your readers' interest, and it states the paragraph's general main point in a **topic sentence**.
2. The **body** supports the main point with specific details and explanations in three, four, ten, or even more sentences.
3. The **conclusion** often summarizes or ties together the ideas of the paragraph while bringing it to a graceful end.

BLUEPRINT	For a Paragraph

Introduction: creates reader interest and states main idea

   attention-getter

   topic sentence (one sentence may do both jobs)

Body: develops the main idea

   explanations

   details

   examples

Conclusion: closes the main idea

   summary

   graceful ending

All paragraphs share several other traits.

1. A paragraph *looks like a unit*. It begins with the first line indented (usually about a half-inch or about five spaces on a typewriter). And each new sentence follows the preceding one *on the same line,* not on a new one.
2. A paragraph *is a unit.* That means each sentence is related to and develops the topic idea or point.
3. A paragraph *holds together.* That means each idea leads clearly and logically into the next.

In short, the structure of the paragraph presents its ideas in a form that's easy for readers to follow. We'll have much more to say about these traits later in this chapter.

EXPLORING AND PLANNING

Remember that the first step in writing is to explore ideas and choose a topic. And that topic has to be limited—or you'll have too much to say and too short a space to say it in.

For example, suppose you chose (or were given) the topic "the influence of television" for a one-paragraph essay. This subject can fill a long book. You could discuss television quiz shows, talk shows, cop shows, cartoon shows, comedies, documentaries, miniseries, movies, soap operas, news broadcasts, sports events, or commercials. And you could discuss the influence of any one of these on preschoolers, older children, teenagers, adults, or the elderly.

You therefore need to narrow the topic. Make a list of smaller topics, like this:

> soap operas
> Saturday morning cartoons
> the instant replay in sports
> beer commercials
> documentaries
> coverage of the Olympics

Notice that these narrowed topics are also more detailed and specific.

Then *select one topic*—perhaps "soap operas." Consider your attitude toward this topic—and write it as a question to answer in your paragraph:

> Are soap operas good or bad?

You might narrow the topic further by writing more questions:

> Is the way soap operas portray sexual relationships good or bad?
> Is the way soap operas portray sexual relationships good or bad for young people?

Your attitude will help you determine *your purpose* (probably to persuade) and *your audience* (probably people who are somewhat familiar with soaps). Now you can construct a full topic idea (you don't have to write it as a full sentence):

> how soap operas glamorize casual sex instead of lasting relationships

Collaborative Activity 1

Examining Your Topic
Choose a topic you would most like to write about from Exercise 1. With your collaborative group, discuss your focus, purpose, and intended audience. Also discuss how to limit the topic so that you can develop it fully in a single paragraph.

Notice the key terms in the topic idea: *soap operas, sex, relationships.* They're the ones to explore in the next step—prewriting—through brainstorming, clustering, or freewriting. If your ideas about the topic aren't entirely clear at this point, don't worry. They'll become clearer as you work, and you can change them later as you revise.

EXERCISE 1	Narrowing a Topic

Narrow each of the following broad topics to one that can be developed in a single paragraph.

6. Edit
5. Revise
4. Write
3. Organize
2. Prewrite
1. Explore

1. A problem in the schools   *how poor attendance in the primary grades stops children from learning*

2. Living in the city or the suburbs _____

3. A popular trend today _____

4. Women's roles and men's roles _____

5. A favorite activity _____

6. A family custom (or a custom from your native country) _____

WRITING THE TOPIC SENTENCE

You don't merely absorb ideas from a page as you read. Instead, you work at understanding the writer's ideas. You *predict* what will come based on what you've already seen. For example, suppose you see this sentence at the beginning of a paragraph:

> Slavery was not the only cause of the Civil War in 1861.

What else would you expect to find in the rest of the paragraph?_____

_____

You'd probably expect an explanation of the other causes of the Civil War.

Each paragraph often contains one key sentence—usually, but not always, at or near the beginning of the paragraph—that presents the main point and suggests how the remaining sentences will develop that point. This is called **the topic sentence**.

General and Specific Statements

A topic sentence is usually the most general statement in the paragraph, and each of the other sentences develops it specifically. For example, which of these two sentences is probably the topic sentence?

1. Stan Harris, the drummer in the rock group *The Moving Violations*, is incredibly talented.
2. He plays the cymbals well.

You probably chose the first, more general one. It leads logically into explanations and examples of the drummer's talents. The second sentence—a more specific statement—isn't a good topic sentence because it's too difficult to develop. What could you say after "He plays the cymbals well"? Perhaps "He hits them with his drumsticks." That's not exactly a brilliant observation!

Here's a full paragraph based on the topic sentence:

Stan Harris, the drummer in the rock group *The Moving Violations,* is incredibly talented. He plays the snare drums, the cymbals, the kettledrums, the bongos, the congas, and the xylophone—all in different rhythms and styles. He can set a strong tempo on the snares for hard rock, rumble on the kettledrums for big-band sounds, do fancy riffs on the cymbals, and switch over to the bongos or congas for the Latin tunes. The great sound of his xylophone blends perfectly with the sounds of the lead and bass guitars. Audiences love his solos on any instrument, and his driving rhythms keep people on the dance floor. It is no wonder that *The Moving Violations* are the most popular band on campus. Catch them when you can.

EXERCISE 2	Identifying Topic Sentences

Underline the topic sentences in the following paragraphs. Be careful: not every topic sentence comes at the beginning.

What's the Name of That Street?

Paragraph A (1) <u>*Sesame Street,* the most popular kids' show in television history, was the bright idea of one person.</u> (2) In 1966, Joan Ganz Cooney worked for a television station in New Jersey. (3) One evening, she and a psychologist friend were sitting around in her apartment after dinner, discussing TV. (4) They had just read a report that very young children watched an average of twenty-seven hours of television a week. (5) Cooney and her friend agreed that if toddlers were going to spend so much time in front of the tube, it made sense to teach them something while they were there. (6) But how could she do it?

Paragraph B (1) Shortly afterward, Cooney thought she had found the answer. (2) She left her job and started the Children's Television Workshop. (3) Her plan was to create an entertaining and fast-moving educational show for preschoolers. (4) Actually, she based her ideas for the show on beer commercials and the hit show, *Laugh-In.* (5) Cooney remembers, "Back then, kids were singing beer commercials. (6) We decided to use the idea of commercials to teach."

Paragraph C (1) A show that introduces preschool children to numbers and the letters of the alphabet might not seem like such a big deal today, but back then hardly anyone believed it would work. (2) Carroll Spinney, who plays Big Bird on the show, says that teachers "assumed preschoolers weren't ready to read. (3) So we seemed crazy, proposing to sell kids the ABCs, like other shows hustled sugarcoated breakfast cereals."

Paragraph D (1) NBC, CBS, and ABC thought the idea was too risky—especially when Cooney told them it would cost $8 million a year. (2) So Cooney looked for another way to pay for it. (3) She was in luck. (4) The federal government thought that the show would fit right in with its Headstart program and chipped in $4 million. (5) Cooney raised the rest from the public and from private foundations. (6) She needed every cent. (7) *Sesame Street* would be the most expensive program on television.

Paragraph E (1) Cooney and the show's producer, Jon Stone, wanted to create a setting that very young children from the inner city would recognize. (2) The producers didn't want the action to take place in a tree house. (3) That was because, as Stone says, "Kids learn best in a setting similar to their daily lives." (4) However, no one could think of a good set to build for the show. (5) Then one day Stone saw a commercial asking college students to be tutors in the inner city. (6) The brick and stone buildings in the commercial gave her the idea for the setting of *Sesame Street.*

Paragraph F (1) Choosing a name for the show was a much more difficult job. (2) The writers suggested *104th Street, Columbus Avenue,* and several other names, including *Sesame Street.* (3) Stone hated them all—especially *Sesame Street,* which reminded him of the corny expression used by magicians: "Open sesame!" (4) "Besides," he argued at one meeting, "*Sesame Street* will be too hard for little kids to pronounce." (5) As the time arrived to publicize the show, Cooney asked the writers what name they had come up with. (6) They hadn't thought of one. (7) "I guess we'll have to go with *Sesame Street,*" Stone sighed.

Paragraph G (1) Perhaps Cooney's most important decision was hiring Jim Henson. (2) He was a brilliant young man whose "Muppets" (part *marionette,* part *puppet*) starred in a Washington, D.C., TV show called *Sam and Friends.* (3) They had also been in commercials and had appeared on television elsewhere. (4) His first (and most famous) Muppet was Kermit the Frog. (5) When Henson was a college freshman, he made the green creature by cutting up his mother's old green coat, sewing it into a puppet, and adding the halves of a table tennis ball for eyes.

Paragraph H (1) *Sesame Street* first appeared on November 9, 1969. (2) The program received mixed reviews from the media. (3) Some critics liked it. (4) Many critics said that its fast pace would make kids restless and give them short attention spans. (5) But studies showed that preschool kids who watched *Sesame Street* were better prepared to enter school than kids who didn't. (6) Within a year, *Sesame Street* had more than 7 million regular viewers.

Making a Point

The *topic* of a paragraph is different from its *topic sentence.* The topic is what the paragraph is "about." But the topic sentence *makes a point* about the topic. The topic sentence, and the whole paragraph that develops it, should answer the question, "So what?" Compare these sentences:

| No point: | Mr. Williams teaches chemistry. (So what?) |
| Point: | Mr. Williams is an excellent chemistry teacher. (The paragraph can explain why he is excellent.) |

Expressing an Attitude or Opinion

Think of the point of the topic sentence as the attitude it expresses toward the topic. In the example you've just seen, *excellent* expresses the writer's attitude. Compare these sentences:

TIPS

For Testing Topic Sentences

Test your topic sentence by disagreeing with it. If you revise it to express an attitude.

Weak: Mr. Williams teaches chemistry. (Who can argue with that?)

Strong: Mr. Williams is an excellent chemistry teacher (but I think he's awful).

No attitude:	Most high school graduates go on to college.
Attitude:	A person without a college degree today is at a disadvantage.
No attitude:	I've had a cat for several years.
Attitude:	My cat outsmarts me all the time.

Many topic sentences follow this pattern: *subject + stated or implied attitude or opinion.* Here are examples:

Subject	Attitude or opinion
Our quarterback has some	*unusual* abilities.
I	*enjoy* fishing in the Halifax River.
Mathematics courses	*challenge* me.

Attitude or opinion	Subject
It's *dangerous*	*not to wear seat belts.*

A strong topic sentence usually helps you write a strong body of the paragraph. But don't expect to get it perfect on the first try. You'll probably revise the topic sentence several times. The point of the paragraph may become clear to you only in the late stages of the writing process. You can compose the final version of the topic sentence then.

EXERCISE 3 | **Revising Topic Sentences**

6. Edit
5. Revise
4. Write
3. Organize
2. Prewrite
1. Explore

Collaborative Activity 2

Discussing Topic Sentences

Compare your revisions of the topic sentences in Exercise 3 in your collaborative group. List the most interesting revisions and report your findings to the whole class.

Each of these topic sentences fails to make a point or express an attitude. Rewrite each one so that its point or attitude is clear.

1. This paragraph will compare living on campus with going to a commuter college.
   Living on campus offers students advantages that going to a commuter college cannot.

2. The topic that I want to discuss is popular music. _____

3. California has a lot of pet cemeteries. _____

4. An issue in the modern world is the spread of AIDS. _____

5. There are many different kinds of sports in the United States. _____

_____

6. The subject of my paragraph is drugs. _____

_____

EXERCISE 4	Writing Topic Sentences

6. Edit
5. Revise
4. Write
3. Organize
2. Prewrite
1. Explore

Assume you'd written the following paragraphs but hadn't yet decided on their topic sentences. Read each paragraph and write its opening topic sentence.

Paragraph A. *The dog has had a long and important relationship with human beings.*

_____

The dog became the first trained animal and the only creature willing to live alongside human beings. Stone Age cave paintings in Spain show that cave dwellers hunted together with trained dogs as early as 10,000 B.C. Many thousands of years before then, however, dogs were working partners with men and women in Europe. The creatures prowled around campfires, ate garbage, and guarded their human "pack."

Paragraph B. *Dogs were good at hunting other animals*

The ancient Egyptians used their big dogs to hunt antelope. Some Egyptian kings and wealthy people kept dogs as pets. They were the first nonworking animals. In fact, one Egyptian ruler made 2,000 slaves take care of his sacred dogs. Later, the early Greeks used powerful dogs to track lions in Africa. Then, with the development of agriculture, dogs were taught to guard and herd livestock.

Paragraph C. *Dogs were tamed at an early age*

Oddly enough, both dogs and cats came from the same ancestor, which lived 60 million years ago. There is plenty of evidence of the early taming of dogs. Strangely, however, there are no cave paintings or rock carvings of domestic cats. Cats did not appear in written and historical records until 2000 B.C.

Paragraph D. *Cats were like a working god and was well protected*

The Egyptians were the first to tame the African wild cat. They closely associated this animal with their cat-headed goddess, Bast. The cat was a working deity, however. It had to earn its keep by protecting food from rodents. In fact, the cat prevented famine and disease so well that the punishment for killing a feline—even by accident—was death.

Paragraph E. *Cats were at one time Treasured by humans for the work they did*

Although Egyptians would not allow anyone to take cats from the country, felines had been smuggled out to all parts of Europe by 900 B.C. There they mated with local wild cats to produce two other breeds. People treasured these animals in the fourteenth century because the felines killed rats that spread the bubonic plague. Unfortunately, later during the Middle Ages, when the cats were associated with witchcraft and other evils, people tortured and murdered these felines.

EXERCISE 5	Writing Your Own Topic Sentences

Return to the topic you chose in Exercise 1 (and perhaps discussed in Collaborative Activity 1). Or, if you don't like that topic now, list five or more lessons you have learned or been taught outside school. You don't need to be a Great Philosopher. Instead, think about some small truths about childhood or parenthood, sportsmanship, working, dating, studying, being disciplined, succeeding or failing, saving or spending money. Look over your list and choose the topic you want to explore.

Then narrow its focus and write a preliminary topic sentence. Be sure that your sentence is general (not too specific) and that it makes a point or expresses an attitude or opinion. Then brainstorm, cluster, or freewrite three to five details and examples that explain and illustrate your point.

WRITING THE BODY AND CONCLUSION

You've selected a topic and narrowed it. You've examined your attitude toward it so that you can make a point. You've drafted a topic sentence that opens the way for you to develop your ideas. Now begin to develop them.

Generating Ideas

Support your topic sentence; back it up with details. Explore your ideas through brainstorming, clustering, or freewriting. Here, for example, is a brainstorming list to support the topic sentence, "Soap operas set a terrible example for children."

Too much sex, especially between unmarried people
Too quickly into sexual relationships—boy meets girl, boy and girl take off clothes, boy and girl hop into bed
Too many quick break-ups in relationships
   Example: Tom and Terri on "General Anesthetic"
Too many bad people tricking good people
   Example: Wicked Wanda and Sucker Sam on "The Young and the Brainless"
Too much emphasis on beauty—blonde hair, flat bellies, and Barbie Doll figures
   Examples: every actress wakes up with perfect hair and fresh lipstick, bikinis are standard dress (when people wear clothes), and the men look like Greek sculptures
How will children be misled by these shows?

Selecting and Organizing Ideas

After finishing your brainstorming list, clustering diagram, or freewriting page, choose the details that support your topic sentence. Arrange them in an informal outline, as Chapter 2 illustrated. Choose only the details that relate to your purpose. Don't use those that don't fit.

Look for ways to group the details:

- Does your topic sentence mention *reasons, ways, methods,* or some similar labeling word? If so, be sure you supply three or four reasons, ways, or methods.
- Could you make any ideas clearer or more interesting through examples? Provide those examples.
- Do you need to explain any ideas? Explain them.

Then organize your material in some appropriate way.

Developing Ideas

Developing ideas involves explaining, specifying, or illustrating—or some of each.

Explanations. Because the topic sentence of a paragraph usually expresses an attitude or opinion, you might need to explain the reasoning behind your opinion. Why do you think that way? What leads to that conclusion? You might also need to explain unfamiliar ideas to readers. Suppose, for instance, that you claim soap operas set a terrible example for children. You could explain that soaps appear in the late morning and early afternoon when preschool children watch them with their caregivers. You could also argue that young people aren't emotionally prepared for the kissing and bed-hopping they see on the soaps. (Don't kids say "yuk" when that mushy stuff happens?) In fact, you could argue that these children will be influenced to become involved in sexual relationships long before they can handle them.

Specific Details. Specific information makes general ideas easier to understand and discuss. When, for example, you claim that soap operas are unrealistic, you can support that claim by describing the typical plot of *Most of My Children.* Infants are switched in the hospital at birth, brothers are presumed dead but then reappear, men learn that their sisters are actually their mothers, and every handsome married lawyer romances his beautiful young assistant.

Examples. Examples clarify and illustrate your general statements. For instance, to support your claims about casual sex on the soap operas, you might describe a scene on *One Life to Louse Up* where Trashy Trudy wears a slinky dress while she seduces Frisky Fred over a dozen oysters, a bottle of wine, and a set of silk sheets. You might discuss the episode on *Another Whirl* when Bruno the Body Builder comes home from the health club one afternoon to find his wife, Silvia, massaging the muscles of his best friend, Felix.

Looking at Paragraph Development

Let's look at a paragraph that is weak in development:

> Probably one of the biggest and most expensive meals of all time took place in 1905, when "Diamond Jim" Brady gave a party. Brady spent a lot of money to feed his guests, but, as usual, he ate the largest meal himself. His guests drank a lot of expensive champagne, and everyone agreed that it was a very nice party.

> "Caress the detail, the divine detail."
>
> —Author Vladimir Nabokov

We don't learn very much about the party, and we don't care very much about it, either. The paragraph leaves many questions unanswered, too many claims unsupported, too many ideas unexplained or not illustrated. Just how big and how expensive was this meal the topic sentence discusses? Who was "Diamond Jim" Brady, and why did he give the party? Where was it? How many people attended, and how much did the party cost? What did Brady himself eat? How much did Brady weigh? How much, how expensive, and what type of champagne did the guests drink? And why did everyone agree that the party was "very nice"?

Here's a revision of the paragraph, this time developed through explanations, specific details, and examples:

> Probably one of the biggest and most expensive meals of all time took place at a hotel in New York City in 1905, when the famous millionaire and the world's greatest eater, "Diamond Jim" Brady, gave a party in honor of his racehorse, Gold Heels. Brady invited only fifty guests, but the food bill came to $40,000. (That is $800 per person!) Since nobody could ever eat more than the 250-pound Brady himself, Diamond Jim's own meal probably came to several thousand dollars' worth. Here, for example, is what he ate—which, for him, was a typical meal. He started with three dozen oysters, followed by a half dozen crabs, two bowls of soup, seven lobsters, two ducks, two huge portions of turtle, a sirloin steak, and large helpings of assorted vegetables. For dessert, he consumed a platter of cakes, pies, cookies, and tarts, and topped it all off with a two-pound box of chocolates. Of course, all that food made him thirsty, so he guzzled a gallon or two of orange juice. Although Brady didn't drink any alcohol (he never did), he served his guests five hundred bottles of very expensive Mumm's champagne. When the meal was over, his guests said that they couldn't recall a nicer party given for a horse.

The second version of the paragraph is much longer than the first. But don't jump to the conclusion that the *quantity* of words provides the power of a paragraph. The *quality* of the information generates that power. A strong paragraph supports its central point through clear, persuasive, and lively explanations, details, and examples.

The amount of specific development to include depends on your answers to three questions:

1. How complicated is the topic idea? The more complicated it is, the more you must explain and illustrate the idea.
2. How much do your readers know about the topic? The less they know, the more information you must supply.
3. How interesting or entertaining should the paragraph be? Examples often enliven the paragraph.

Notice that the three questions relate to the three questions you should ask yourself at the very beginning of the writing process:

- What is my subject?
- What is my purpose?
- Who is my audience?

The answers will shape your writing from start to finish.

Writing a First Draft

Plunge in. There's no way to begin writing other than to write. Following your topic sentence, write one sentence, then another. Develop the topic idea with the explanations, specific details, and examples you gathered and organized. The paragraph should have seven to ten sentences, but don't pad it. And if you think of other information or better ways to present explanations, specific details, and examples, then change your plans.

Don't try to write a perfect first draft. You'll revise your draft later.

Writing a Conclusion

A paragraph's closing sentence often summarizes your point. Sometimes that means returning to the idea of the topic sentence, but don't just repeat the same words. Change the language to make the ending graceful.

Not every conclusion has to summarize, however. You might try ending your paragraph with a bang—with a quotation, a joke, a powerful example, a surprise. And, as with the first draft, expect to revise later.

EXERCISE 6	Planning Your Paragraph

6. Edit
5. Revise
4. Write
3. Organize
2. Prewrite
1. Explore

Make an informal outline of the paragraph you planned in Exercise 5. The blueprint of the outline should look like this:

- *a preliminary topic sentence that states your point*
- *explanations that clarify or expand on the point*
- *one or more examples of the point and a discussion of each example*
- *a conclusion*

Fill in the blueprint below, or, if you need more room, make your own on a separate sheet of paper.

BLUEPRINT	For a Paragraph

Topic sentence: a general statement that makes a point, has an attitude

_____

Supporting information: explanations, details, examples

1. _____

2. _____

3. _____

4. _____

5. _____

6. _____

Conclusion: summary and graceful ending

_____

EXERCISE 7	Drafting Your Paragraph

Now write the first draft. Select the strongest and most relevant details and examples you've numbered. You won't use all of them. Assume that your audience will be your classmates. Your purpose, however, will depend on the subject matter, which could be informative, entertaining (that is, amusing, shocking, or even frightening), or persuasive. The first draft should be about one handwritten page or half a computer-generated, double-spaced page.

REVISING THE PARAGRAPH

"If I am not clear, all my world crumbles to nothing."

—French Author Stendhal

You want your readers to understand, appreciate, or be convinced by your message. So make it thorough and clear and help it move logically and smoothly from one idea to the next.

As you revise your paragraph, pay attention to **unity** and **coherence**. Adjust your topic sentence and your conclusion until every part of the paragraph—the introduction, the body, and the conclusion—fit together tightly.

Unity

A good paragraph has **unity**. That means that each sentence in the body develops the topic sentence. As you revise your paragraph, examine your first draft with an eye toward dropping details that don't belong. Almost every first draft contains some information that strays off the point.

For example, the point of the paragraph "about" Diamond Jim Brady was that *his party was huge and expensive.* It doesn't mention Brady's collection of diamonds (it was large), his love affair with the actress Lillian Russell (she was large, too), or his success as a business person (yes, it was also large). These details may be interesting, but they don't belong in the paragraph. If the writer included them in early plans or drafts, they would have to be dropped later.

Key words in the topic sentence might help you test the unity in the body of the paragraph. Here, for example, is a short outline of a paragraph based on a topic sentence presented earlier in the chapter. Notice how the underlined words in the topic sentence provide a guide to the specific explanations, details, and examples that follow:

I enjoy the <u>peace</u> and <u>relaxation</u> of fishing in the Halifax River for <u>four reasons</u>.

First, it gives me a chance to get away from the pressure of my job.

    I work at a bank where I constantly . . .

    I become accustomed to a much more relaxing pace on the river . . .

    There's no clock to worry about . . .

Second, I can spend time with a friend, just talking and . . .

    We often discuss . . . while we . . .

Third, when a fish does bite, I can focus my attention only on . . .

    For example, last year, a twenty-pound bass . . .

Finally, I can go back to my tent, cook the fresh fish over a campfire, and spend a restful evening . . .

EXERCISE 8   Unifying a Paragraph

One sentence in each group strays off the point of its topic sentence. Underline the words in the topic sentence that suggest the type of support you'd expect to follow. Then draw a line through the sentence that doesn't belong.

6. Edit
5. Revise
4. Write
3. Organize
2. Prewrite
1. Explore

1. *Topic sentence:* Before the fork was widely used in seventeenth-century Italy, people picked at their food in <u>a variety of ways</u>.

   a. They speared it with an eating knife.

   b. They scooped up their food in a spoon and lifted it to their mouths.

   c. ~~They ridiculed men who used forks as fussy and unmanly.~~

   d. They held food with three fingers because five was considered impolite.

2. *Topic sentence:* Around the time of Jesus, religious law listed a great many crimes that could be <u>punished by stoning</u>.

   a. A woman accused of adultery could be stoned.

   b. A man could be stoned for stealing.

   c. Anyone could be stoned for heresy—that is, disobeying religious laws or practices.

   ~~d. The condemned person's accuser would step forward to "cast the first stone."~~

3. *Topic sentence:* The origins of <u>nursery</u> rhymes explain why some lyrics might not be suitable for young children.

   a. For centuries, the rhymes were known only as "songs" or "ditties" and were intended mainly for adults.

   b. Some rhymes were taken from crude folk ballads.

   c. In the 1820s, the lyrics of the rhymes were cleaned up because morals had changed.

   d. Many nursery rhymes started as drinking songs, jokes about religious practices, social satires, and the lyrics of romantic songs.

4. *Topic sentence:* Tecumseh (1768–1813) had all the qualities of a true leader of the Native American tribes.

   a. In the War of 1812, he was killed by a bullet through the heart from a member of the United States Cavalry.

   b. In battle, Tecumseh was fierce and fearless.

   c. In conversation, he was sophisticated and refined.

   d. In dress, he refused to wear the clothing of the whites, preferring simple buckskin with a tomahawk and a silver-handled hunting knife shoved under the belt.

5. *Topic sentence:* The superstition about bad luck on Friday the thirteenth came about for a number of reasons.

   a. Adam and Eve were supposedly expelled from the Garden of Eden on a Friday.

   b. Noah's great flood started on a Friday.

   c. Jesus was crucified on Friday.

   d. Twelve witches and the Devil—totaling thirteen—are necessary for a satanic meeting.

   e. But not all combinations of thirteen are deadly—a baker's dozen is thirteen, for example.

Coherence

An effective paragraph must also have **coherence**. The ideas in the paragraph must cohere, which literally means "stick together." So you must make the logical relationships between ideas clear.

You can strengthen coherence in a number of ways.

Logical Arrangement. Arrange your ideas in the most logical order. For example, the paragraph on fishing in the Halifax River describes the four reasons the experience is enjoyable. The paragraph also explains each reason before going on to the next; the explanation doesn't jump back and forth between ideas.

In revising, look carefully at your organization. Have you grouped together similar ideas? Should one idea come before another or follow it? What should you say first—or last?

Pronouns. Use pronouns to link ideas. **Pronouns** replace nouns and refer back to them. *It, this,* and *that* refer to a singular subject; *they, them, these,* or *those* refer to a plural subject. These references tie ideas together and help sentences mesh. But if a pronoun (*he,* for example) can refer to more than one idea in a sentence ("my *brother* borrowed the car from my *father*"), you'll need to repeat the noun to avoid confusion (*my father* or *my brother,* whichever one you mean).

Reinforcement. Repeat key words or ideas in different ways as you move from sentence to sentence. For instance, in the Halifax River paragraph, the phrase *just talking* appears in one sentence, and *we often discuss* appears in the next. Readers can see that the second sentence develops the idea of the first.

Transitions. Use transitional words and phrases to explain relationships. A **transition** shows the logical relationship between one idea and another. For example, in the Halifax River paragraph, the words *first, second, third,* and *finally* label the reasons so that readers can easily identify them. The expression *for example* in one sentence clearly introduces an illustration.

Here's a list of other transitions. Consult it often as you write and revise:

TIPS

For Achieving Coherence with Transitions

Try this test as you write. After each general statement in your paragraph, say "in other words," "for example," "to be specific," or some other transitional expression. You might not need the transition, but see if it increases the flow between ideas.

TRANSITIONS

For Counting: first, second, third, next, then, after that, finally

For Space Relationships: above, around, behind, below, beneath, beyond, close by, farther away, inside, outside, next to, over, under, underneath

For Time Relationships: after, afterward, after that, before, then, and then, finally, later (on), next, soon, as soon as, the next day, tomorrow, yesterday, a year ago, as, during, immediately, meanwhile, when, while, last night, in March, in 2004, on July 8

For Addition: additionally, also, and, furthermore, in addition, moreover, too

For Comparison: in the same way (manner), likewise, similarly

For Contrast: although, but, even though, however, nevertheless, on the other hand, yet, despite, still

For Emphasis: above all, especially, in fact, most important

For Illustrations: for example, for instance, in particular, such as

For Reasons: because, because of, due to, for, since

For Summary: and so, in other words, in short, in summary, to sum up, to summarize

EXERCISE 9	Looking for Coherence

Read the following paragraph, and answer the questions about it.

A Dark, Sweet History

(1) Although history does not prove where the chocolate chip cookie began, the cookie certainly wasn't around in 1847. (2) Before then, chocolate existed only as a liquid or a powder, not as a solid. (3) The long road to the chocolate chip cookie began in Mexico around 1000 B.C. when the Aztecs made a ceremonial drink, *xocoatl,* meaning "bitter water," from crushed cocoa beans. (4) Xocoatl later became *chocolatl* in other Mexican dialects. (5) After the Spanish had conquered Mexico about 2,600 years later, they introduced this drink to Europe, where the recipe remained unchanged until 1828. (6) That year, a candy maker in Holland tried to make a finer chocolate powder but instead created a creamy butter. (7) This discovery led to the world's first solid chocolate, produced by a British company in 1847. (8) Hard chocolate therefore became a reality, and the chocolate chip cookie a possibility. (9) From that point on, the origin of the cookie is less certain. (10) According to legend, the first chocolate chip cookie was baked around 1930 at the Toll House Inn, near Whitman, Massachusetts. (11) Ruth Wakefield, the inn's owner, was also its cook and baker. (12) One day, she added chocolate pieces to her butter cookies, creating the Toll House Inn cookie, which she sold nationally. (13) For chocolate bits, Mrs. Wakefield cut up the Nestle Company's large Semi-Sweet Chocolate Bar. (14) Nestle was impressed with her recipe and asked permission to print it on the wrapper of the bar. (15) Her reward would be a lifetime supply of free chocolate. (16) The cookie was so popular that in 1939 the company finally introduced Morsels, the packaged chocolate chips. (17) From a bitter drink of the Aztec Indians to the household delight of today, chocolate has come a long way.

1. The paragraph does not begin with the topic sentence. Where is the topic sentence? Underline it.

2. What expressions mark the passage of time? What other transitional expressions give coherence to the passage? Underline them.

3. What key words or ideas are repeated to provide coherence? Circle them.

4. What pronouns establish coherence? Put them in brackets. Look at the adjectives *this* and *that* before nouns. How do these expressions add coherence to the paragraph? _____

   _____

5. How many groups or individuals were involved in the process of discovering, transmitting, manufacturing, and producing the ingredients of chocolate

Collaborative Activity 3

Discussing Coherence
Review your answers to Exercise 9 with your collaborative group. Discuss the way the paragraph achieves unity and coherence.

chip cookies? _____ What words or phrases iden-

tify the groups? _____

_____

_____

6. Which incident does the paragraph develop most specifically? _____

_____ Why? _____

_____

Refining the Topic Sentence and Conclusion

A good topic sentence not only introduces the topic, but also provides a brief road map for readers who will journey through the paragraph. For example, suppose in collecting and examining information to support the topic sentence about Mr. Williams ("Mr. Williams is an excellent chemistry teacher.") the writer settled on three reasons. The topic sentence can include that information:

> There are *three important reasons* why Mr. Williams is an excellent chemistry teacher.

Here are other topic sentences you saw earlier, now revised with roadmapping language that helps readers predict what will follow:

> Our quarterback has some unusual abilities *as a runner, a passer, a kicker, and even a receiver.*
>
> Mathematics courses challenge me *to study, analyze, and apply what I've learned.*

You don't have to draw the road maps as you write the topic sentence. Your route may become clear to you only in the later stages of writing. The map isn't always necessary, but it does help readers predict and therefore understand a long, complex paragraph. If you can see the road you're on only after you've traveled it, go back and refine your topic sentence. Your reader will never know you circled back from the end to the beginning.

Keep adjusting your topic sentence and its supporting details until they're perfectly in sync. Then take a look at the conclusion. Can you make it summarize better or end with a stronger punch? Can you shorten the conclusion if it drags on past the logical ending point?

Using Peer Review

Your peers—your own classmates—can be a useful resource as you revise a paper. They can make suggestions and ask you questions about things you hadn't considered.

Your instructor may ask that you form groups of three or four members to review each other's work, or you and some friends may decide to form one of your own. Always begin the peer review session by stating what you like in a paper. Then focus on what could be strengthened or improved. As a writer, you don't have to agree with the group's suggestions, but do consider them. If you find yourself saying, "What I meant to say was . . . ," then stop and write it down. What you meant to say is exactly what you should say.

Collaborative Activity 4

Responding in Peer Groups

Here's a way for peer groups of three or four members to work productively. Make enough photocopies of your writing for each member of your collaborative group. The group members will do the same. Then read each other's writing during class—or, if possible, ahead of time. Use the Revision Guidelines to help you structure your comments. During discussion, take notes. These will help you improve your revision.

The Revision Guidelines that follow and appear throughout the book for specific types of writing can structure the comments you make on another writer's papers. They can also help you structure your own revisions as you work alone.

REVISION GUIDELINES   Writing a Powerful Paragraph

1. What is best about the paragraph? What are its strengths?
2. Locate the topic sentence. Does it clearly express a point or opinion? What words express that point or opinion?
3. Should any sentences or parts of sentences be restated or reworded? How could they be revised?
4. Can any general ideas be explained more? How? Would examples help? Which examples?
5. Do any statements need examples to clarify their meaning? Are there places where examples might make the paragraph livelier?
6. Look at the end of each sentence and the beginning of the next. Is there a natural flow between sentences? If not, what transitional words or phrases could be added—*therefore, however, because, when, despite, later,* and so on? Should something be deleted or shifted to another location in the paragraph?
7. Look at the beginning and ending sentences of the paragraph. Is the relationship between them clear and logical, or does the paragraph stray off the point? If so, how could the problem be corrected?
8. What would readers *do* with the information in the paragraph? That is, how does the paragraph answer the "So what?" question? Should the paragraph be rearranged or changed to answer that question better?
9. Is the conclusion effective? Does it summarize? Does it end powerfully? How could it be revised if it drags on or strays off the point?

EXERCISE 10   Arranging a Paragraph

6. Edit
5. Revise
4. Write
3. Organize
2. Prewrite
1. Explore

The following information is totally disorganized. It has no unity or coherence. Number the information in the most logical order. Then compose a paragraph based on the information. Begin with the most likely topic sentence (you can revise it later). Rewrite the other sentences as necessary to create unity and coherence. Add transitions and repeat key terms as necessary. Finally, create a topic sentence and a conclusion.

Most humans are right-handed.

② The practice dates back to the fifteenth century.

① By studying portraits and drawings of buttoned garments, historians have traced the reasons why men's clothes button from right to left while women's button from left to right.

④ Most men found it easier to have clothes that buttoned from right to left.

③ Men generally dressed themselves at home, on trips, and on the battlefield.

Buttons were very expensive at the time.

Wealthy women had female servants who dressed them.

Most maids were right-handed.

Collaborative Activity 5

Revising the Paragraph

Compare the paragraphs you wrote in Exercise 10. Have one person as "secretary" compose a paragraph that incorporates the best ideas of everyone. Submit this revised copy to your instructor.

It was easier to fasten their mistresses' garments if the buttons and buttonholes were

reversed.

Maids faced the buttons head on.

The practice has never been changed.

EXERCISE 11	Revising Your Own Paragraph

6. Edit
5. Revise
4. Write
3. Organize
2. Prewrite
1. Explore

Check for the unity and coherence in the paragraph you composed in Exercise 7. Look at the topic sentence: Is its point clear? Underline the words that make the point. Add roadmapping language to the topic sentence if it's needed. (You might need to revise the topic sentence to account for all the information in the paragraph.) Examine the supporting information. Cross out any ideas that stray off topic, and make notes in the margins about where to add sentences or phrases that develop or clarify the point.

Then examine the paragraph for coherence. Should you insert transitional words in any places? Should you repeat any key terms? Have you used pronouns effectively? Are the pronoun references clear? Record your notes above the lines and in the margins. Then rewrite the paragraph.

EXERCISE 12	Editing and Proofreading Your Paragraph

6. Edit
5. Revise
4. Write
3. Organize
2. Prewrite
1. Explore

Return to the paragraph that you revised in Exercise 11. Look it over carefully. Can any wording be strengthened? Are the grammar, spelling, and punctuation correct? Make final changes and corrections before writing a clean copy or printing a new computer copy. Then proofread. Submit the final copy to your instructor.

4 Writing an Effective Essay
Building a Larger Structure

Although you often need to write single paragraphs for school or work assignments, you'll write essays far more often. This chapter will teach you to write an essay confidently and efficiently by showing you how to

- plan and organize the essay
- compose and revise the essay

WHAT IS AN ESSAY?

After working on the paragraph, you can now turn your attention to the essay—an organized discussion of a subject in a series of paragraphs. A **paragraph** and an essay actually share many traits. The paragraph discusses a limited topic, which it introduces in a topic sentence and then explains and illustrates in separate sentences. The topic sentence unifies and shapes the content of the paragraph. The **essay** explores a much broader topic, which it introduces in a **thesis statement** and then explains and illustrates in separate paragraphs. The thesis statement unifies and shapes the content of the entire essay.

An essay is not simply a longer version of a paragraph. The content of the essay is more complex and needs more development. However, the essay is structurally similar to the paragraph, for it contains three parts:

UNIT 1	Go Electronic
Chapter 4	Use the following electronic supplements for additional practice with your writing: • For chapter-by-chapter summaries and exercises, visit the Writing with Confidence Companion Website at http://www.ablongman.com/meyers. • For work with the writing process, visit The Longman Writer's Warehouse at http://longmanwriterswarehouse.com (password needed).
Writing with Confidence ©2003	• For additional practice in grammar, use The Writer's ToolKit Plus CD-ROM.

- The **introduction**—that is, the first paragraph of the essay—attracts the reader's interest, states the point of the essay in a thesis statement, and previews what will follow.
- The **body**—usually at least three paragraphs and often more—develops the thesis by breaking it down into smaller ideas. In a well-organized essay each body paragraph
  (1) introduces its main idea in a topic sentence
  (2) develops the idea in the body sentences
  (3) and then concludes with a transition to the next paragraph.
- The **conclusion**—the last paragraph of the essay—ties all the ideas together and gracefully ends the paper.

BLUEPRINT	For an Essay

Introductory paragraph: creates reader interest and states the main point while including

an attention-getter

a thesis statement

a preview of the body

Each body paragraph (usually at least three): develops the main point

develops one idea of the thesis

usually states the idea in a topic sentence

then develops the topic sentence

ends with a transition to the next paragraph

Concluding paragraph: closes the essay

usually restates the thesis and summarizes the main ideas

gracefully ends the essay

EXERCISE 1	Analyzing an Essay

Here's an example of an essay written by Linder Anim, a student from Ghana, who attended Truman College in Chicago. Read it and then answer the questions that follow.

Michael Jordan, Superstar
by Linder Anim

* * * *

(1) Michael Jordan has played for the Chicago Bulls for years, and everyone cheers for him. Fans have filled the seats at the United Center ever since he led the team to six

NBA championships, and many millions have watched each of his games on TV. However, it is no wonder that he has attracted such admiration and fame. [**Thesis statement**] *Jordan possesses all the features of an athletic superstar: extraordinary attractiveness, incredible physical talent, and exemplary character.*

(2) [**Topic sentence**] *First of all, Jordan is a fine physical specimen of a man.* He is not only handsome, but he has a magnificent body on his 6½-foot frame. He always shaves his hair, which seems to symbolize his commitment to the game. With his broad shoulders and rippling muscles, he looks strong and formidable in his number 23 jersey.

(3) [**Topic sentence**] *Second, he is a talented athlete who has developed a game of speed, agility, and intelligence.* He quickly dodges the opposing team's defense and makes spectacular shots, sometimes as he falls away from the basket, other times when he drives toward it. As a result, he always scores a lot of points, which makes him the top scorer on the Bulls and also the rest of the NBA. The amazing part of it all is his "Air Jordan" moves, which rely on agility and leaping ability. He jumps up in the air and can stay there for a long time before coming down. He is also smart, and as the team captain he tries to keep his teammates as disciplined as he is on the court. Without Michael Jordan, the Chicago Bulls would not be where they are today.

(4) [**Topic sentence**] *Finally, Jordan is not only a great athlete, but also a gentleman on and off the basketball court.* As the team captain, he shows cool and controlled leadership and gentility. He never fights, and if any one of his teammates does fight, he immediately calms that person down. After each game, he always puts on a beautiful suit and his earring and politely answers questions from the press. He also donates money to charity for a variety of good causes. Jordan sponsors community services, too, such as basketball camps for kids.

(5) [**Conclusion**] Michael Jordan is a one-of-a-kind superstar. That is why people look up to him.

---

1. How many points does the thesis statement in the first paragraph introduce? _____ What is the function of the opening sentences of the paragraph that lead up to the thesis statement?_____

_____

2. How are the topic sentences in the body paragraphs related to the thesis statement? _____

Which words or phrases in these paragraphs are transitional? Circle them.

3. Identify the supporting details in the body paragraphs. How many details does each paragraph contain? **Paragraph 2** _____ **Paragraph 3**

_____ **Paragraph 4** _____

4. The concluding paragraph consists of only two sentences. Why? _____

_____

Reread the essay on Michael Jordan and pay special attention to its structure. The framing materials—the thesis statement, topic sentences, and conclusion—shape the whole essay. In fact, if you combined all these framing elements and removed the remaining material, you'd be left with a coherent paragraph:

> Michael Jordan possesses all the features of an athletic superstar: extraordinary attractiveness, incredible physical talent, and exemplary character. First of all, Jordan is a fine physical specimen of a man. Second, he is a talented athlete who has developed a game of speed, agility, and intelligence. Finally, Jordan is not only a great athlete, but also a gentleman on and off the basketball court. Michael Jordan is a one-of-a-kind superstar. That is why people look up to him.

Is this paragraph effective? Only as a summary. You can't develop its ideas very well in so short a space. A large topic such as Michael Jordan requires a multi-paragraph essay to explain and illustrate its ideas. At the same time, you usually can't expand a strong single paragraph into an essay.

Linder's essay is also graceful in style. Notice how she varies the word choice of her topic sentences instead of simply repeating the language of the thesis statement. Compare these versions:

> Thesis: Jordan possesses all the features of an athletic superstar: *extraordinary attractiveness, incredible physical talent, and exemplary character.*

Mechanical topic sentence	Graceful topic sentence
(1) First, Jordan is very attractive.	First of all, Jordan is a fine physical specimen of a man.
(2) Second, he has incredible physical talent.	Second, he is a talented athlete who has developed a game of speed, agility, and intelligence.
(3) Third, Jordan also has an exemplary character.	Finally, Jordan is not only a great athlete, but also a gentleman on and off the basketball court.

Linder's essay evolved from hard work in planning, writing, revising, responding to suggestions, and editing. You can do the same.

COMPOSING AN ESSAY

The process of writing an essay basically involves the same six steps you've followed for writing a paragraph:

1. **Exploring** your ideas (subject, purpose, and audience).
2. **Prewriting** to discover ideas and narrow the topic.
3. **Organizing** and writing a preliminary thesis statement and topic sentences.
4. **Composing** a first draft.
5. **Revising** the draft.
6. **Producing the final copy** through editing and proofreading.

Getting Started

Let's take a look at how Linder composed her essay. She first explored and organized her ideas, probably by brainstorming, clustering, and/or freewriting. Then she outlined her ideas, including a preliminary thesis statement, preliminary topic sentences, and possible supporting details. Here's an outline. Notice that the thesis statement and topic sentences differ slightly from the ones in the essay.

Paragraph 1 thesis: Jordan has all the qualities of a superstar.

Paragraph 2 topic sentence: Jordan is a fine physical specimen.

　　Details: muscular, 6'6" tall, shaved head, handsome

Paragraph 3 topic sentence: He is a talented athlete who is quick and smart.

　　Details: quick, great jumper with "Air Jordan" moves, best scorer, cool headed

Paragraph 3 topic sentence: Jordan is also a gentleman on and off the basketball court.

　　Details: leader on court, never fights, dresses in suit, polite to press, supports charities and community groups

Concluding paragraph: Michael Jordan is one of a kind, and everyone looks up to him.

EXERCISE 2　　　*Generating Ideas for Your Essay*

Begin work on an essay on why you admire a particular person: a public figure, a relative, a friend, a teacher, or anyone who's had a positive impact on your life or the lives of others. Compose a preliminary thesis statement—just something to get you focused. Then do some brainstorming, clustering, and/or freewriting to discover and produce ideas that develop the thesis. Remember: you're writing an essay, which is much longer and more complex than a paragraph, so generate as many ideas as you can—perhaps two pages' worth.

EXERCISE 3　　　*Selecting Details and Outlining*

Now organize your ideas. Can you select three or four main reasons why you admire the person? Can you find any details that explain or illustrate those reasons? Discard information that doesn't fit. If you don't find enough information that fits, do more brainstorming, clustering, or freewriting. Then write a rough outline of your essay, including an attention-getting opening, a thesis statement (which may have changed from your original version), topic sentences for each body paragraph, supporting details for the topic sentences (which you can merely list), and a concluding statement.

BLUEPRINT	For an Essay

Introduction

　　attention-getter: _____

　　_____

　　thesis statement: _____

　　_____

Continued

Body

1. Topic sentence: _____

_____

_____

Supporting details: _____

_____

_____

2. Topic sentence: _____

_____

_____

Supporting details: _____

_____

_____

3. Topic sentence: _____

_____

_____

Supporting details: _____

_____

_____

Conclusion: _____

_____

_____

✓ **TIPS**

For Writing a First Draft

1. Write fast and circle any parts that you want to revise later.

2. Don't worry about the exact language of the opening paragraph. You'll revise it later—after you've written the body.

3. The same advice applies to the conclusion!

4. If you get stuck for ideas in one paragraph, just make a brainstorming list. Then move on to the next paragraph.

5. Make notes in the margins about things to add or revise later.

Writing the First Draft

Now write your first draft. Include an introductory paragraph, at least three body paragraphs, and a concluding paragraph. If any body paragraphs contain only a few sentences, plan on revising them later—perhaps after you've gotten more ideas through brainstorming, clustering, or freewriting.

In your first paragraph, include an opening remark that will interest your readers, and a thesis sentence. In your concluding paragraph, return to the thesis statement of the opening paragraph—but don't just restate it. Vary the wording. And try to end with a punch: something upbeat or clever. Don't fret about writing either a perfect introduction or conclusion at this point, however. You will be revising the draft.

EXERCISE 4   Composing a First Draft

Write a first draft of your essay based on details you selected and outlined in Exercise 3. Your draft should be at least five paragraphs long, with an introduction, a body, and a conclusion.

Revising

Take a break. Then return to your essay with clear eyes and mind. Read it critically. What ideas are unclear or poorly worded? Which need more details or explanations? Do the paragraphs have unity and coherence? Does each paragraph lead smoothly to the next, or do some paragraphs seem isolated—like separate essays rather than parts of a whole? Revise the essay one or more times.

EXERCISE 5   Revising Your First Draft

Now revise the draft, according to the following Guidelines.

REVISION GUIDELINES | Writing an Effective Essay

Collaborative Activity 1

Peer Review

Read your essay aloud to your group or photocopy it for the group to read silently. Then listen to or read their responses. Use the Revision Guidelines as you critique each essay.

1. Does the first paragraph include an effective attention-getting introduction? If not, how should the opening be revised?
2. Does the first paragraph include a clear thesis statement and introduce the essay's main ideas? If the thesis isn't focused or is incomplete, how should it be revised?
3. Is the point of each body paragraph stated in a topic sentence? Is each topic sentence clear? If not, how should these paragraphs be revised?
4. Do all the details in each body paragraph support its topic sentence? Are there enough details? Are they arranged logically? It not, what should be eliminated, added, moved, or rewritten?
5. Are the transitions between paragraphs clear? Are the transitions within each paragraph clear? If not, what should be added or revised?
6. Does the final paragraph summarize the main ideas and end gracefully? If not, how should it be revised?

Editing and Proofreading

Edit the essay to correct errors in spelling, grammar, and punctuation—and to make any final adjustments in wording. Prepare a clean copy of the work according to the format your instructor specifies. Then proofread the essay more than once—and make a final copy, which you should proofread again.

EXERCISE 6   Editing and Proofreading

After revising your essay, edit it for correct spelling and punctuation, complete sentences, and clarity of ideas. Then make a clean copy and proofread it carefully for errors. Submit it to your instructor.

Write, Write, Write!

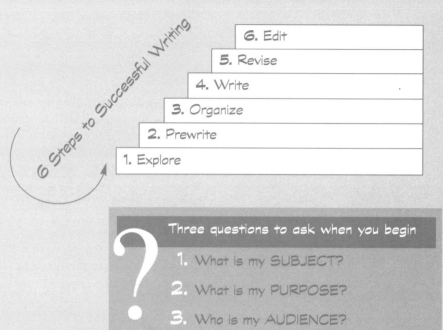

6 Steps to Successful Writing

6. Edit
5. Revise
4. Write
3. Organize
2. Prewrite
1. Explore

? Three questions to ask when you begin

1. What is my SUBJECT?
2. What is my PURPOSE?
3. Who is my AUDIENCE?

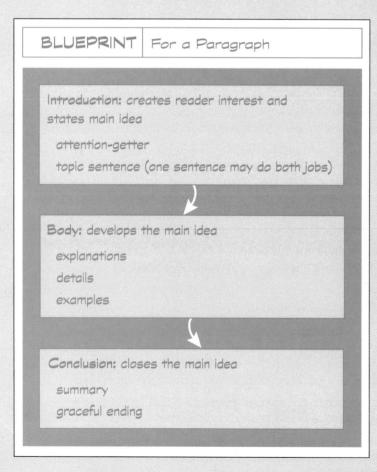

BLUEPRINT | For a Paragraph

Introduction: creates reader interest and states main idea

- attention-getter
- topic sentence (one sentence may do both jobs)

Body: develops the main idea

- explanations
- details
- examples

Conclusion: closes the main idea

- summary
- graceful ending

3 ways to generate ideas

1. BRAINSTORM
2. CLUSTER
3. FREEWRITE

The more you do it, the better you get!

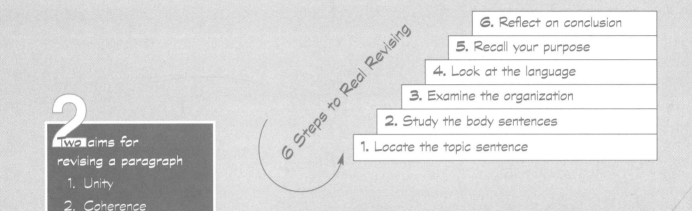

6 Steps to Real Revising

| 6. Reflect on conclusion |
| 5. Recall your purpose |
| 4. Look at the language |
| 3. Examine the organization |
| 2. Study the body sentences |
| 1. Locate the topic sentence |

Two aims for revising a paragraph
1. Unity
2. Coherence

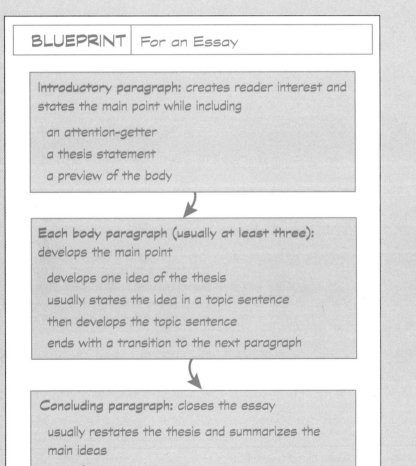

BLUEPRINT | For an Essay

Introductory paragraph: creates reader interest and states the main point while including

- an attention-getter
- a thesis statement
- a preview of the body

Each body paragraph (usually at least three): develops the main point

- develops one idea of the thesis
- usually states the idea in a topic sentence
- then develops the topic sentence
- ends with a transition to the next paragraph

Concluding paragraph: closes the essay

- usually restates the thesis and summarizes the main ideas
- gracefully ends the essay

THREE ways to develop the body of a paragraph
1. Explanations
2. Specific details
3. Examples

THREE traits of a topic sentence—or thesis statement
1. States the point
2. Expresses an attitude
3. May include a "road map"

II

Building and Repairing Sentences

The chapters in the previous unit have taken you through the writing process.

You've worked on writing and revising your ideas in the structure of paragraphs, and perhaps you've tried an essay. Now you can turn more of your attention to sentences. Developing confidence in your ability to notice and correct errors in sentence forms is important. You want readers to focus on the content of your ideas—not how you express (or misexpress) them. Eliminate the errors as you edit so that you can be judged on what you have to say, not on what the errors might say about you.

Unit II looks at ways to correct errors with incomplete sentences or improperly joined sentences, as well as a variety of ways to join them clearly, powerfully, and—above all—confidently.■

5 Recognizing Sentences and Fixing Fragments

Sentences are the basic units of expression. But if something is missing in the sentence—if it's only a fragment of a sentence—its idea will be confusing or even impossible to understand. This chapter will show you how to write complete sentences. It explains

- ■ the essentials of a sentence: a subject and a verb
- ■ ways to identify and fix sentence fragments

WHAT IS A SENTENCE?

"Begin at the beginning . . . and go on till you come to the end. Then stop."

—Lewis Carroll, *Alice's Adventures in Wonderland*

Every **sentence** makes a complete statement. That means it must contain a **subject**—*who* or *what* the statement is about. And it must contain a **verb**—that begins the statement about what the subject *does* or *is*. The subject and verb usually go together at the beginning of a group of words called a **clause**. Most often, the subject comes first, and the verb follows the subject. Here are some examples:

Subject	Verb
President Abraham Lincoln	loved
He	saved
The turkey	was

As you can see, though, the subject and verb of a sentence don't complete the statement. That usually requires additional words that follow the verb:

Subject	Verb	Remainder of Clause
President Abraham Lincoln	loved	animals.
He	saved	a turkey's life.
The turkey	was	a gift for Christmas dinner.

UNIT 2	Go Electronic
Chapter 5	Use the following electronic supplements for additional practice with your writing: • For chapter-by-chapter summaries and exercises, visit the Writing with Confidence Companion Website at http://www.ablongman.com/meyers. • For work with the writing process, visit The Longman Writer's Warehouse at http://longmanwriterswarehouse.com (password needed).
Writing with Confidence ©2003	• For additional practice in grammar, use The Writer's ToolKit Plus CD-ROM.

This combination of *subject + verb + completion of the statement* is called an **independent clause**. It creates a full sentence. You can also combine two or more clauses in the same sentence, as you'll see in this unit. But right now, we'll concentrate on identifying the main elements of a single clause: the subject and the verb.

Identifying Subjects

The easiest way to identify the subject and verb is to look for both at the same time. Let's begin, however, with the **subject**.

The subject

- tells *who* or *what* the clause makes a statement about
- usually (but not always) appears at or near the beginning of the statement—before the verb, which tells what the subject *does* or *is*
- can be a **noun**—a person, place, idea, thing
- can be a **subject pronoun**—a word used in place of a noun

---

Subject (*who* or *what*) + verb (*does* or *is*) = sentence

The following sentence, for example, makes a statement about the subject, *Tad Lincoln*. Notice that the verb *adored* follows the subject.

Tad Lincoln adored the turkey.

EXERCISE 1	Identifying Subjects

Underline the subjects **at the beginning** *of each of these sentences. Ask yourself:* Who or what *does this sentence make a statement about?*

1. Tad Lincoln was only ten years old in 1863.

2. He adored the turkey and named it Jack.

3. The bird soon followed young Tad around the White House grounds.

4. Tad and his father agreed not to kill the animal.

5. Pardoning the White House turkey has since become an annual tradition for presidents.

Are these the words you underlined? Each one demonstrates an important trait of the subjects:

1. *Tad Lincoln* A subject can be a **proper noun**–a name that is capitalized.
2. *He* A subject can be a **subject pronoun**. The complete list of subject pronouns includes *I, we, you, he, she, it,* and *they.*
3. *bird* A subject can be a **common noun**–a noun that is not a name and so is not capitalized unless it begins the sentence.
4. *Tad and his father* A subject can be two or more nouns (or subject pronouns) joined by *and.*
5. *Pardoning the White House turkey* A subject can occasionally begin with an **-ing word** (a verb turned into a noun).

Abraham Lincoln

EXERCISE 2	Identifying Subjects

Try again. Underline the subject of each sentence. You'll find at least one example of the kinds of subjects explained in Exercise 1.

1. <u>Abraham Lincoln</u> faced attacks from all sides.

2. Southerners and Democrats hated him.

3. The Republican Party temporarily split over him in the election of 1864.

4. Some Republicans refused to support him.

5. Two of his generals ran against him.

6. Nevertheless, this tall, homely fellow from Illinois achieved greatness.

7. He was indeed a self-made man.

8. Studying law on his own, becoming a lawyer, and serving in the Illinois legislature led to his election to the United States House of Representatives in 1846.

9. The future president could also tell a good story around the general store—a great asset in campaigning for office.

Identifying Verbs

Now you can turn your attention to the **verbs** in clauses.
The verb

- says what the subject *does* or *is*
- usually has a **tense**, indicating if the verb discusses the past, present, or future

- usually follows the subject and begins a statement about the subject
- may contain more than one word

Subject	Verb	Remainder of Clause
Tom	*needs*	a new hairpiece or a large, floppy hat.
Albert	*has eaten*	the whole cake and part of the plate.

EXERCISE 3	Identifying Verbs

Circle the verbs in the following sentences. Ask yourself: What word or words begin a statement of what the subject does or is?

1. Lincoln was controversial throughout his presidency.

2. By today's standards, people might even consider Lincoln a racist.

3. Lincoln didn't free the slaves at the beginning of the Civil War.

4. He wanted to bring the South back into the Union quickly.

5. However, like other great presidents, he grew in office and took courageous

positions.

6. In the fall of 1862, he drafted the Emancipation Proclamation, freeing the slaves in

the areas still in rebellion as of January 1, 1863.

Are these the words you circled? Each one demonstrates an important trait of verbs:

1. *was* A verb usually has a tense. (*Was* is the past tense of *is*.)
2. *might* (even) *consider* The parts of a two-word verb may be separated by an **adverb** such as *even*.
3. *did*(n't) *free* A two-word verb often contains a negative such as *not* or *never*.
4. *wanted* This word expresses the tense of the action. Did you circle *to bring*? See below.
5. *grew* and *took* The subject performs *two actions* in *two verbs*, which are usually joined by *and*. (Indeed, a subject can perform two, three, or even more actions.)
6. *issued* This is another past-tense verb. Did you circle *freeing*? See below.

Sentence 4: *to bring*, an action word preceded by *to*, is an **infinitive**. It's formed from a verb but doesn't function as a verb. It never has a tense—something that's infinite cannot be limited to the past, present, or future.

Sentence 6: *freeing*, an *-ing* word, which is also formed from a verb. It usually doesn't function as a verb.

Infinitives and *-ing* words, although formed from verbs, normally function as other parts of speech. (Remember "Pardoning the White House turkey" in Sentence 5 of Exercise 1? *Pardoning* serves as a noun in that sentence.) Don't confuse infinitives and *-ing* words with verbs.

Helping Verbs. Note that verbs can include two, three, or even four words. In the examples that follow, *use* is the main verb, and the words before it are **helping**—verbs which help express the complete tense or content of the verb:

Main Verb	Main Verb with Helping Verbs		
use	am using	will be using	might have been using
uses	is using	would have used	should have been using
used	has used	might be using	could have been used
	did(n't) use	must be using	must have been used
	may use	may be using	
	will use	could be using	
	had used	will have used	
	can use	should be using	
	does use	must have used	

Note the one exception to the rule about *-ing* words. They are verbs when they follow the helping verb *to be:*

is going, am going, are going, was going, were going, will be going, etc.

Linking Verbs. Most verbs express action (*works, needed, has eaten*). However, a few verbs—called **linking verbs**—simply say the subject *is* or *was* something. In other words, they give information about the subject. Here are examples:

Subject	Linking Verb	Information
Henry	is	tall and clumsy.
Horses	are	terrible house pets.
She	feels	
	sounds	sick.
	looks	
The chicken	tastes	delicious.
	smells	

The most common linking verb is *to be.* The other common linking verbs represent the five senses—*look, sound, feel, smell,* and *taste*—and the verbs *become* and *appears.*

TIPS

For Identifying Subjects and Verbs

Every clause says that someone or something does or is. Therefore, one simple question should help you locate the subject and verb of each clause: *Who* or *what does* or *is?*

Who or *what,* of course, will identify the subject of the clause. *Does* or *is* will identify the verb.

Subject Verb

Who⟍   ⟋does
or   ✕   or   something?
what⟋   ⟍is

EXERCISE 4   Identifying More Verbs

Once more, circle the verbs in the following sentences. Also, put a box around any infinitives and any -ing words that don't function as verbs.

1. Lincoln won the election in 1860, becoming the sixteenth president of the United States.

2. He was also the first president to die from an assassin's bullet.

3. He would be the second president to die as a result of the zero curse.

4. From 1840 to 1960, any president winning an election in a year ending in zero did not leave the presidency alive.

5. William Henry Harrison (election of 1840) would die in April 1841 after being in office for only thirty days.

6. President James A. Garfield (election of 1880) was shot and killed by an assassin in 1881.

7. President William McKinley (election of 1900) held office for less than a year before dying at the hands of an assassin in 1901.

8. Warren G. Harding (election of 1920) and Franklin D. Roosevelt (1940) both would not live to the end of their terms.

9. And of course, John F. Kennedy (election of 1960) would have been the first to out-live the curse, except for a gunshot coming from the sixth floor of a building in Dallas, Texas, according to the Warren Commission Report.

EXERCISE 5 | **Writing Verbs**

Complete the following passage by writing a verb in each blank space.

Lincoln (1) *faced* _____ more serious problems than any other president. Therefore, he (2) _____ some very serious and difficult decisions. While Congress was out of session, he formed an army and (3) _____ thou-sands of people in jail although he didn't charge them with crimes. Lincoln (4) _____ that this violation of the Constitution (5) _____ necessary "in cases of rebellion or invasion."

At the beginning of the war, many people in his political party (6) _____ him to end slavery. But many people (7) _____ to stop the war by any means. They (8) _____ Lincoln a tyrant. After four long years, the North finally (9) _____ the war. Lincoln's Emancipation Proclamation (10) _____ the slaves. And by 1865, the Thirteenth Amendment to the Constitution (11) _____ slavery in the United States.

Collaborative Activity 1

Classifying Verbs

In a small group, share and compare the verbs you've proposed for Exercise 5. Classify your answers into one or more of the following: (1) verbs with two or more words, (2) action verbs, and (3) linking verbs. Prepare lists for each category and share your lists with the entire class.

EXERCISE 6 | **Identifying Subjects and Verbs**

Here's a chance to apply all you've learned about recognizing subjects and verbs. In each of the following sentences, underline the subject(s) and circle the verb(s). Be certain you know why each sentence is complete.

1. Lincoln hoped to end the Civil War quickly, wanting to avoid needless bloodshed.

2. He asked one of his best military leaders, Robert E. Lee, to command the Union Army.

3. Instead, Lee resigned from the U.S. Army and accepted a commission in the Confederate Army.

4. This decision was not easy for Lee.

5. He had graduated from West Point and sworn allegiance to the United States.

6. He also hated slavery and had freed his own slaves.

7. Nor did he believe that states had the right to leave the Union.

8. But Lee was a native of Virginia.

9. "I have been unable to make up my mind to raise my hand against my native state, my relatives, my children and my home," he wrote.

10. Loyalty and duty called him to serve the Confederacy.

EXERCISE 7	Identifying Subjects and Verbs-and Incomplete Sentences

Try it one more time. In each group of words below, underline the subject(s) and circle the verb(s). If any group is missing a subject or a verb, write "incomplete" in front of the number.

1. After her husband's assassination, Mary Todd Lincoln invited several spiritualists to the White House.

2. They comforted the grieving widow.

3. Years later in Chicago, Mary going to séances under an assumed name.

4. She would test the skills of the spiritualists.

5. Once, on a trip to Boston, attended a séance.

6. Used the name "Mrs. Tundall" to avoid recognition.

7. Her dead husband appeared before her during the séance.

8. She then visited the studio of William Mumler, a "spirit photographer."

9. Mumler produced a photograph of Mary with Abraham.

10. The president in the background with his hands on Mary's shoulders.

WHAT IS A FRAGMENT?

In Exercise 7, each item you found that's missing a subject or verb is a **fragment**: an incomplete statement that's written as if it were a sentence. Many times, it lacks a subject, a verb, or both.

Fragments occur for many reasons. Here are a few:

- You might be struggling to express an idea and therefore are not paying attention to the boundaries between sentences.
- You might be punctuating by ear, without understanding how punctuation works.
- You might be omitting subjects or writing only partial verbs.
- You might be unclear about the uses of joining words such as *although* and *because*.

No matter why a fragment occurs, however, you must be able to identify and eliminate it. And that's what we'll be doing in the rest of this chapter.

FIXING SIMPLE FRAGMENTS

A simple fragment is an incomplete clause. Let's take a look at several types:

- fragments missing a subject
- fragments missing a verb or part of a verb

- fragments beginning with infinitives or *-ing* words
- fragments that add details or examples

Missing Subjects

Suppose you write a statement in which the subject performs *two actions* expressed in two separate verbs. If you end the statement after the first verb, the second verb will be left hanging, without a subject, in a fragment. Here's an example:

Sentence	Fragment
In the 1850s, many people went to séances. And supposedly communicated with their dead relatives.	

The fragment contains a verb, *communicated*, but doesn't have a subject. You could fix the fragment in at least two ways:

Combining: In the 1850s, many people went to séances and supposedly communicated with their dead relatives.

Adding a subject to the fragment: In the 1850s, many people went to séances. *These people* supposedly communicated with their dead relatives.

Missing or Incomplete Verbs

Some simple fragments result from writing incomplete verbs. Notice the missing helping verb in the following examples:

Incomplete verbs	Complete verbs
Spiritual mediums *putting* people in touch with the dead.	Spiritual mediums *were putting* people in touch with the dead.
Abraham Lincoln's wife Mary often *gone* to séances.	Abraham Lincoln's wife Mary *had* often *gone* to séances.

The most frequently omitted helping verbs are *to be* (*is, am, are, was, were*) and *to have* (*has, have, had*).

Infinitives and *-ing* Words

Infinitives and *-ing* words are formed from verbs and therefore seem to express action. However, they usually don't function as verbs but only introduce or continue a sentence. If they aren't attached to that sentence, they hang loose as fragments. Look at these examples:

Sentence	*-ing* word fragment
Mary Lincoln's young sons Willie and Eddie had died. *Sending her into deep despair.*	

-ing word fragment	Sentence
Refusing to accept her children's death. Mary told her sister that they visited her each night.	

Infinitive fragment	Sentence
To console Mary after President Lincoln's death. Several spiritualists visited her at the White House.	

✔ TIPS

For Identifying and Fixing Fragments

If you suspect that something is a fragment, try changing it to a question. You can't change a fragment into a question.

Complete sentence: The election was close. *Question:* Was the election close?

Fragment: A close election. *Question:* ????

If Your First Language Is Not English

Some languages treat the subject before the verb *to be* differently from the way English does, and that can cause some confusion:

- In Spanish, for example, one word—the verb—expresses the subject-verb combination *it is.* Be careful, therefore, not to write the sentence fragments "Is easy," or "Was a nice day" when the full sentences in English are *"It is easy,"* or *"It was a nice day."*

- Some Eastern European languages (such as Russian) omit the verb *to be* entirely from sentences. Be careful, therefore, not to write the sentence fragments "He tall," or "She a doctor" when the full sentences in English are *"He is tall,"* or *"She is a doctor."*

For Identifying and Fixing Fragments

Try changing the tense of the word you've identified as a verb. If you cannot change its tense, it may not be a verb, and the sentence may be a fragment. But also check for key helping verbs such as *must, may, could, should,* and the others listed earlier in this chapter; they cannot change tense.

You can fix the fragments by attaching them to the complete sentences:

> Mary Lincoln's young sons Willie and Eddie had died, sending her into deep despair.
>
> Refusing to accept her children's death, Mary told her sister that they visited her each night.
>
> To console Mary after President Lincoln's death, several spiritualists visited her at the White House.

Hanging Details or Examples

Some fragments are simply details that continue the idea of the previous sentence. For instance, the detail fragment that follows this sentence does not contain a verb:

Sentence	Detail fragment
At a séance, people would sit in a dark parlor.	*With their hands on the table.*

You can fix the fragment by adding it to the sentence:

> At a séance, people would sit in a dark parlor with their hands on the table.

EXERCISE 8 Fixing Simple Fragments

6. Edit
5. Revise
4. Write
3. Organize
2. Prewrite
1. Explore

Collaborative Activity 1

Writing and Correcting Fragments

Write five fragments of your own and exchange your work with a classmate who has also written five fragments. Correct each other's work and then discuss your results.

Find the fragments in this exercise. Then fix each one by supplying the missing subjects, verbs, or partial verbs, or by attaching the fragment to a complete sentence. Be careful: some sentences are complete.

1. Lincoln ^was shot at Ford's Theatre in Washington, D.C., on April 14, 1865.

2. Charles Leale the first doctor to reach the president's box.

3. Lifted Mary's head off the president's chest.

4. Mary now in a state of near collapse. Sat on a couch near her chair.

5. Leale asked a few soldiers to place the president on the floor.

6. Other doctors arrived in the president's box and were able to revive him. Using artificial respiration and some brandy and water.

7. Leale then said, "His wound is mortal. It is impossible for him to recover."

8. From the couch, Mary quietly moaned, "His dream was prophetic." (For more about Lincoln's dream, see Exercises 9 and 10.)

FIXING COMPLEX FRAGMENTS

So far, you've looked at simple sentences that contain a single independent clause. Now let's look at **complex sentences** that contain two clauses; one that depends on the other to make the meaning complete. If the two clauses are not joined together properly, one clause may be a fragment. There are two main types of these fragments:

- those beginning with words like *although* or *because*
- those beginning with words like *who, which,* or *that.*

Although and *Because* Types

Find the subjects and verbs of the following clauses:

> *Because* the doctors were trying to save the president
>
> *Although* Mary Todd Lincoln could not help her husband

Each clause contains a subject and a verb, but the clauses don't make complete statements. They're **dependent clauses**—and sentence fragments—which depend on another clause to make a full sentence. After you read them, you want to ask, "What happened?" The words *because* and *although* at the beginning of a clause make that clause incomplete. These incomplete clauses must be attached to **independent clauses** and could stand alone as a sentence.

> *Because* the doctors were trying to save the president, *they took him to the nearest house.*
>
> *Although* Mary Todd Lincoln could not help her husband, *she kissed him and begged him to speak.*

Although and *because* are only the most common words that introduce dependent clauses. There are many others:

after	if
although	once
as	since
as if	unless
as soon as	until
because	when
before	whether
even though	while

You can correct these dependent clause fragments in two ways.

1. Join the dependent clause to the sentence that precedes or follows it. This is usually the most common and best solution.

> *Fragments*
>
> A. *When President Lincoln finally passed away.* Mrs. Lincoln was waiting in the front room of the house.
>
> B. Nearly two hours passed. *Before she was in any condition to be taken back to the White House.*
>
> *Joined*
>
> C. *When President Lincoln finally passed away,* Mrs. Lincoln was waiting in the front room of the house.
>
> D. Nearly two hours passed *before she was in any condition to be taken back to the White House.*

Punctuation is very important. A comma follows a dependent clause that begins a sentence, but there's no comma before a dependent clause that ends a sentence.

TIPS

For Identifying and Fixing Fragments

As you know, writing imitates speech. In writing, the punctuation represents pauses that occur with the rise and fall of our voices. The pitch of our voices *drops* at the end of a sentence, and that's where a period belongs:

This is a complete sentence. ↓

Notice how the pitch lowers at its end. ↓

When a sentence continues, the pitch of our voices *rises* at the comma.

Because this sentence is incomplete, ↑ . . .

If we want to make it complete, ↑, . . .

Read your sentences aloud as you edit your papers. If you hear your voice rise at the end of a sentence, look closely at that sentence. It could be a fragment (unless it is a question, which also ends with our voices rising).

2. Remove the joining word before the dependent clause and write the clause as a separate sentence. However, this solution often creates choppy sentences—and sometimes it simply doesn't work. Let's return to examples C and D above. Example C could be written as two sentences by removing *when*. But notice what happens to example D if *before* is removed to create two sentences. The original meaning of the statement changes and may not even make sense.

> C. (*with* when *removed*) The doctors began their examination of the president. Mrs. Lincoln waited in the front room of the house. (*Meaning unchanged*)
>
> D. (*with* before *removed*) Nearly two hours passed. She was in any condition to be taken back to the White House. (Meaning changed)

EXERCISE 9 | Fixing Complex Fragments

6. Edit
5. Revise
4. Write
3. Organize
2. Prewrite
1. Explore

Find the sentence fragments in this exercise. Fix each one either by joining it to the clause that completes its meaning or by rewriting it as a complete sentence. Place commas where they're needed. Be careful: one of the items does not contain a sentence fragment.

Lincoln's Terrible Dream

1. On the evening of April 11, 1865, President Lincoln and Mrs. Lincoln were talking with several friends. When Lincoln suddenly began to discuss his dreams. On the evening of April 11, 1865, President Lincoln and Mrs. Lincoln were talking with several friends when Lincoln suddenly began to discuss his dreams.

2. He said that he had been unable to sleep well. Because he had had a terrible dream ten days earlier. _____

3. Since he had been waiting for important messages from the battlefront. He went to sleep very late. _____

4. In his dream, he heard soft sobs. As if a number of people were weeping. _____

5. He left his bed and wandered downstairs. When the sobbing grew louder. Although the mourners were invisible. _____

6. He kept going from room to room. Then he arrived at the East Room. _____

(For more about this dream, do Exercise 10.)

Who, That, and *Which* Types

A second kind of complex fragment includes the words *who, that,* and *which.* Look at these examples:

> . . . *who* was a famous actor at the time.
>
> "Voices" that Mary Lincoln began to hear ten years later . . .
>
> . . . *which* was a place for the mentally ill.

These are also dependent clauses. They're incomplete statements. You can complete their meaning in two ways:

1. Attach them to the words that make the statement complete, which usually immediately precede or follow them.

> *President Lincoln was assassinated by John Wilkes Booth,* who was a famous actor at that time.
>
> "Voices" that Mary Lincoln began to hear years later *were cited as evidence of her insanity.*
>
> *In 1875, she spent four months in a private hospital called Bellevue,* which was a place for the mentally ill.

2. Rewrite the clauses without *who, which,* or *that* and make them complete sentences. Again, this might not be the best solution if it creates short, choppy sentences.

> President Lincoln was assassinated by John Wilkes Booth. He was a famous actor at that time.
>
> In 1875, she spent four months in a private hospital called Bellevue. It was a place for the mentally ill.

Since the handling of *who, which,* and *that* in clauses is rather complicated, we'll return to it again in Chapter 8.

EXERCISE 10   Fixing More Complex Fragments

6. Edit
5. Revise
4. Write
3. Organize
2. Prewrite
1. Explore

Find the sentence fragments in this exercise. Fix each one by joining it to the clause that completes its meaning. Be careful: one of the items does not contain a sentence fragment.

The End of Lincoln's Dream

1. In the East Room, Lincoln saw a platform. That held a corpse wrapped in funeral clothing. *In the East Room, Lincoln saw a platform that held a corpse wrapped in funeral clothing.*

2. All around the platform were many people. Who were crying. _____

3. One of the soldiers. Who were acting as guards. Told him that it was the president. Who had been killed by an assassin. _____

_____

_____

Collaborative Activity 2

Comparing Your Solutions

In a small group, share and compare the ways in which you've fixed the fragments in Exercises 9 and 10. If you have different solutions, list them, and then share your lists with the entire class.

4. The crowd cried loudly with grief. That noise awoke Lincoln from his dream.

_____

_____

5. Mrs. Lincoln was horrified by her husband's story. Which, the president reminded her, was only a dream. _____

_____

_____

EXERCISE 11 — Fixing Fragments

6. Edit
5. Revise
4. Write
3. Organize
2. Prewrite
1. Explore

Read the Tips box on page 59. Then read each of the following groups of words aloud. Listen for the rise or fall of your voice. Then label each item either S (for sentence) or F (for fragment). Then punctuate it correctly—adding a period or a comma—and add the words to make each fragment complete.

___S___ **1.** If you think the first part of the sentence is complete, you aren't noticing the rise in pitch at the comma.

_____ **2.** When there's a rise in the pitch of your voice. _____

_____ **3.** The result should be that you can tell when a sentence is complete.

_____

_____ **4.** Your ear is a pretty good judge of these matters. _____

_____ **5.** With enough practice and repetition. _____

_____ **6.** This exercise should give you a better idea about how sentences sound.

_____

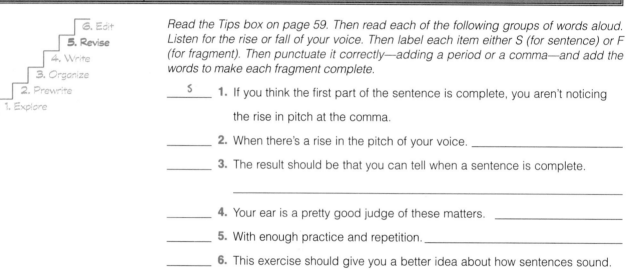

IN SUMMARY — To Recognize Complete Sentences

1. Identify the *subject* (*who* or *what* the sentence makes a statement about) usually found at the beginning of the clause.
2. Identify the *verb* (begins the statement of what the subject does or is), which usually follows the subject and has a tense—for example, past, present, or future.
3. Look for *helping verbs* to make sure the verb is complete.
4. See if the subject and verb fit logically together.
5. See if the words following the verb complete the statement.

To Fix Fragments

1. Make sure that each statement contains at least one subject and a complete verb.

2. Make sure that you do not mistake an *-ing* word or an infinitive for a verb.

3. Make sure that there are no hanging details or examples written as complete statements.

4. Make sure that a clause beginning with words such as *although* or *because* is attached to a clause that completes its idea.

5. Make sure that a clause beginning with words such as *who, that,* or *which* is attached to the words that complete its idea.

EDITING FOR MASTERY

Mastery Exercise 1

Eliminating Fragments

The following passage contains twelve fragments, excluding the example (which has been corrected for you). Find and fix them by following this procedure:

1. Identify the subject(s) and the verb(s) in every clause.

2. Make any changes necessary in sentences that are incomplete. These changes can include

  a. supplying a missing subject or a missing (or incomplete) verb

  b. joining an incomplete sentence to another sentence (usually by removing a period between the two sentences and sometimes by changing the period to a comma)

  c. rewriting the fragment

You don't have to rewrite the passage. Make all your changes above the lines.

The Death of Abraham Lincoln

(1) On Friday, April 14, 1865—Good Friday—Lincoln met with his cabinet
(2) ^to To discuss lifting the blockade of the South. (3) Now that the war was over. (4) His mood was happy, and he was telling everyone around him to look for a way to make the peace last. (5) By preparing a plan that would bring the Southern states back into the Union with very little punishment.

(6) That evening he and his wife went to see a play at Ford's Theatre in downtown Washington. (7) The Washington policeman guarding the president left his post. (8) Either to get a drink or a better view of the play. (9) When a pistol shot rang out. (10) Lincoln slumped over. (11) A man jumped from the president's box to the stage. (12) In the process breaking his leg. (13) He waved his gun and shouted something. (14) Then he escaped through a back exit and mounted a horse. (15) Which was waiting outside.

(16) Lincoln was taken to a house across the street from the theater. (17) Where he died the next morning. (18) Throwing the shocked nation into grief. (19) Although he was hated and opposed throughout the war years by many groups who criticized him for one reason or another. (20) Abraham Lincoln had finally become a hero of the entire nation.

(21) The assassin was soon discovered. (22) John Wilkes Booth, who was an actor. (23) After a huge manhunt, Booth was trapped in a barn on April 26, and shot and killed.

Collaborative Activity 3

Comparing Answers
Compare your changes in your collaborative group and report them to the entire class.

(24) A military court sentenced four other captured conspirators to be hanged. (25) Including Mary Surratt, who was the owner of a boardinghouse.

Scorecard: Number of fragments found and corrected: _____

Mastery Exercise 2

Eliminating Fragments

The passage below contains twelve fragments (excluding the example, which has been corrected for you). Find and eliminate them by following this procedure:
1. Identify the subject(s) and the verb(s) in every clause.
2. Make any changes necessary in sentences that are incomplete. These changes can include
  a. supplying a missing subject or a missing (or incomplete) verb
  b. joining an incomplete sentence to another sentence (usually by removing a period between the two sentences and sometimes by changing the period to a comma)
  c. rewriting the fragment
You don't have to rewrite the passage. Make all your changes above the line.

So What If His Name Was Mudd?

(1) Dr. Samuel A. Mudd set the broken leg of a mysterious visitor in 1865 and wound up in prison with a life sentence~~.~~ (2) ^for^ ~~For~~ assisting in the escape of President Abraham Lincoln's assassin. (3) Although four years later the White House pardoned Mudd. (4) In 1992, several of his descendants still trying to clear his name.

(5) The man who found his way to Mudd's country house on the morning of April 15, 1865. (6) He was actor John Wilkes Booth, who was wearing a false beard. (7) Booth had shot Lincoln and broken his leg when he jumped from the president's box. (8) In 1992, the Army Board of Correction of Military Records stirred up new interest in the good doctor. (9) By considering the Mudd family's appeal to remove his conviction from the books.

(10) The government's original case against Mudd has always been weak. (11) The military council had appeared to rig the trial. (12) The use of false and suspicious testimony, and the prosecution's refusal to admit evidence that was favorable to Mudd. (13) According to the evidence, Mudd was only a casual acquaintance of Booth's. (14) After the assassination when Booth looked for treatment at Mudd's house. (15) The doctor was unaware that Lincoln had been shot.

(16) The biggest supporter of Mudd's innocence was Louise Mudd Arehart, who was the youngest of Mudd's ten surviving grandchildren. (17) Arehart relied heavily on her grandmother's story of what happened. (18) When Booth came to the Mudd's house. (19) The grandmother became suspicious of Booth, who called himself Tyler. (20) When his false whiskers fell off as he left the house. (21) Mudd, who had been out, returned home. (22) He had learned of Lincoln's murder. (23) And the search for the assassin. (24) When soldiers arrived the following week, Mudd told them everything he knew and

produced the boot he had cut from the stranger's injured leg. (25) On the boot was the name "J. Wilkes."

(26) Arehart and many other of Mudd's descendants appealed Dr. Mudd's case in 1992. (27) However, William D. Clark, who was the Assistant Secretary of the Army. (28) Refused to hear their appeal. (29) Announcing that the Board had no right to "settle historical disputes." (30) The fight to clear Mudd's name still continues.

Scorecard: Number of fragments found and corrected _____

6 Joining Sentences Through Coordination

If you want to keep your readers interested—and sane—you need to create some variety in your sentences. If you don't, here is what happens:

> My sentences are short. They are simple. Each contains only one idea. They are too simple. They are choppy. They can't express complex thoughts. Short sentences get boring. They are all alike. They make me sound like a first-grader. I had better stop now. You will be glad to stop reading, too.

Sentence variety comes largely from joining sentences—clearly, logically, and correctly. This chapter will examine one way to join sentences called **coordination**. You'll learn how to

- join sentences by adding words
- join sentences by using punctuation
- use words and punctuation correctly

CONNECTING WORDS

> " . . . control yourself when, by chance, you have two things to say; say first one, then the other, not both at the same time."
>
> —Author George Polya

One way to connect sentences is to add words that join them. A joining word is called a **conjunction** (like a junction that joins two roads). Notice how conjunctions connect each of the following pairs of words:

> John *and* I (two people, or subjects)
>
> tripped *or* fell (two actions, or past-tense verbs)
>
> a fat *yet* athletic man (two describing words, or adjectives)
>
> moved quickly *but* carefully (two words describing actions, or adverbs)

UNIT 2	Go Electronic
Chapter 6	Use the following electronic supplements for additional practice with your writing: • For chapter-by-chapter summaries and exercises, visit the Writing with Confidence Companion Website at http://www.ablongman.com/meyers.
Writing with Confidence ©2003	• For work with the writing process, visit The Longman Writer's Warehouse at http://longmanwriterswarehouse.com (password needed). • For additional practice in grammar, use The Writer's ToolKit Plus CD-ROM.

The Coordinating Conjunctions

In these examples, each pair of words is grammatically equal, or *coordinate* (*co* = equal, *ordinate* = level). The joining words are therefore called **coordinating conjunctions** because they join grammatically equal structures. There are only seven coordinating conjunctions in English, which you can memorize by remembering the words *fan boys:*

For	But
And	Or
Nor	Yet
	So

JOINING SENTENCES WITH CONJUNCTIONS

Coordinating conjunctions can also join *two sentences,* which are also grammatically equal structures. Remember that every sentence must have at least one independent clause—a subject and verb combination that can stand alone. Therefore, when you join two sentences with a coordinating conjunction, you create a single sentence with two independent clauses. That single sentence is called a **compound sentence**.

EXERCISE 1   Identifying Conjunctions

Collaborative Activity 1

Analyzing Combined Sentences

Discuss with classmates the effect of each coordinating conjunction you've identified in Exercise 1. Which ones suggest an addition, an alternative, a change or qualification, or a negative? What other meanings do these conjunctions communicate as they join clauses? Which sentence with two independent clauses is incorrectly joined by a word that is not a coordinating conjunction?

Find and underline the coordinating conjunctions in the following sentences. Look carefully. One item does not contain a coordinating conjunction, so the two clauses are not correctly joined.

1. Male babies often wear blue, and female babies wear pink.

2. Years ago, people wanted to protect their infant boys from evil spirits, so they dressed the boys in blue.

3. People associated blue with good spirits, for those spirits lived in the blue sky.

4. Of course, people cared about their female children, yet people did not care enough to dress them in blue.

5. Many years later, people still dressed the males in blue, but they chose pink for the females.

6. The superstition about evil spirits had disappeared, or people might have dressed their girls in blue also.

7. Nowadays, very few parents know the reasons behind these traditional colors, nor do parents care.

8. Some parents choose yellow, then color doesn't make any difference.

Using conjunctions correctly is important. They not only join two clauses, but they also *explain the logical relationship between the two clauses:*

Conjunction	Purpose
for	shows a reason (The second clause gives a reason for the first.)
and	shows addition
nor	shows a negative alternative (It is the negative form of *or*, and it must follow a clause containing a negative word such as *not*.)
but	shows contrast
or	shows an alternative or choice
yet	shows an unexpected contrast (It is similar in meaning to *although*.)
so	shows a result (The first clause results in the second.)

PUNCTUATING COMPOUND SENTENCES

Not every coordinating conjunction requires a comma. Here are the rules:

▶ **Place a comma before the coordinating conjunction** *that joins independent clauses.*

independent clause	coordinating conjunction	independent clause
Tom likes ice cream,	*but*	he likes pizza better.

▶ *Don't use the comma* **before coordinating conjunctions that merely join two words.**

	word	coordinating conjunction	word
Tom likes ice cream		*and*	pizza.

EXERCISE 2 | Combining Sentences

6. Edit
5. Revise
4. Write
3. Organize
2. Prewrite
1. Explore

Join each of the following pairs of sentences with one of the seven coordinating conjunctions, preceded by a comma. Use each conjunction at least once.

Black Bart: Stagecoach Robber and Poet

1. It was August 3, ^1877, and a 1877. A stagecoach was traveling across California.

2. A man with a flour sack over his head stopped the coach. He pointed a rifle at the drivers.

3. The man told them to throw down their cash box. He did not harm anyone.

4. Later, someone found the box. That person was surprised.

5. The box contained an angry poem signed by "Black Bart." It also contained a note of apology saying, "Driver, give my respects to your friend, the other driver."

6. Black Bart continued robbing. He continued to leave humorous verses.

7. The stagecoach company was not amused. It offered a reward of $800 for his capture.

8. On Bart's last holdup, someone shot and wounded him. He tried to stop the bleeding with a handkerchief that he left behind.

9. Detectives learned Black Bart's real name by tracing the laundry mark on the handkerchief. The robber might have gone free.

10. He was Charles E. Bolton, an elderly gentleman with a white mustache, gold-headed cane, and fine clothes. He finally confessed to his crimes.

11. He also said, "I never robbed a passenger. I never treated a human being badly." (Use *nor*, and change the wording of the second clause.)

12. He was supposed to serve a long term in prison. His behavior was so gentlemanly that he was released four years later.

| EXERCISE 3 | Completing Sentences |

6. Edit
5. Revise
4. Write
3. Organize
2. Prewrite
1. Explore

Write a second independent clause that logically follows each coordinating conjunction.

1. The Internet has become very important today, and *many people now rely on it for e-mail and information.*

2. Nowadays, people are spoiled by the speed and convenience of e-mail, so _____

3. Many people also shop on the Internet, for it _____

| Collaborative Activity 2 |

Comparing Sentences

Discuss and compare your answers to Exercise 3 in a collaborative group. Did everyone write full and complete clauses? Do the clauses logically carry out the meaning of the coordinating conjunctions? List the best clauses, and then report your results to the class.

4. Companies without computer technology must change, or _____

5. Prices of computers continue to drop, yet _____

6. Ten years ago, hardly anyone used the Internet, but _____

7. Many people don't realize that their cars contain hundreds of computer chips, nor _____

| EXERCISE 4 | Writing Combined Sentences |

6. Edit
5. Revise
4. Write
3. Organize
2. Prewrite
1. Explore

Write seven combined sentences of your own, using a different coordinating conjunction—for, and, nor, but, or, yet, and so—in each sentence. Use your own paper.

CONNECTING PUNCTUATION

Only one punctuation mark can join two sentences into a single compound sentence without adding any words. This is the **semicolon (;).**

The Semicolon

Take a good look at the semicolon; notice that it's a combination of a period and a comma. Like a period, it signals the end of a complete statement. Like a comma, it signals that the sentence continues. But unlike a period or a comma, it joins two clauses into one sentence.

The logical connection between the two clauses is so obvious that it needs no explanation. Here are some examples of combined sentences with semicolons:

> The accident caused no serious injuries; no one involved required hospitalization.
>
> California is our country's most populous state; one out of every nine Americans lives there.
>
> Dmitri generally acts shy in a large crowd; his girlfriend Helena is more outgoing.

Follow these rules to use semicolons properly and gracefully in your writing:

Never use a coordinating conjunction with a semicolon.
Don't capitalize the first word after the semicolon.
Don't overuse semicolons; your writing will sound too choppy.

EXERCISE 5   Writing Clauses After Semicolons

6. Edit
5. Revise
4. Write
3. Organize
2. Prewrite
1. Explore

Complete each of the following sentences with a second independent clause that relates logically to the first. It may be an example, or it can present a contrast.

1. There is very little difference between "men's work" and "women's work" these days; *both sexes do a variety of jobs in all sorts of professions.*

2. Many doctors and lawyers are women; _____

_____

3. Most married women are no longer simply "housewives"; _____

_____

4. It's not unusual to see women in hard hats at construction sites; _____

_____

5. Many men work in what used to be "female" professions; _____

_____

6. Most women and men are probably happy about the changes in our society; _____

_____

Collaborative Activity 3

Discussing Your Combined Sentences

Compare your answers to Exercises 4 and 5 in a small group. Then share your results with the whole class.

Transitional Words after the Semicolon

Sometimes the logical connection between the two clauses joined by a semicolon needs a boost. Consider this example:

> Juan said he was so full that he could burst; he ate a second piece of cake. [Huh?]

That boost can come from adding a word directly after the semicolon to make the relationship clear.

> Juan said he was so full that he could burst; *however,* he ate a second piece of cake.

This additional word is called a **conjunctive adverb** because it's partly a conjunction and partly an adverb. That is, like a conjunction, it shows a link between two ideas. And, like an adverb, it explains *how* or *in what way* the ideas are related.

It's also called a **transitional word** because it establishes the transition (or movement) from one idea to another. Here's a list of common conjunctive adverbs.

Transitional word (conjunctive adverb)	Acts like this joining word (conjunction)	But in this way (adverb)
furthermore, moreover, also	and	in addition
however	but	in contrast
nevertheless	yet	in contrast
therefore, consequently	so	as a result
otherwise, instead	or	as an alternative
meanwhile, then, later, afterward	(none)	shows time relationships

Remember: the conjunctive adverb doesn't join two clauses; *the semicolon joins them.* As with the coordinating conjunctions, punctuation is important.

1. The semicolon comes first.
2. The conjunctive adverb comes next.
3. The comma comes last.

independent clause	transitional word	independent clause
Mario enjoyed quiet;	*nevertheless,*	he worked at the bowling alley.
Claudia studies during the week;	*however,*	she likes to go out on the weekends.

EXERCISE 6 | Substituting Transitional Words

6. Edit
5. Revise
4. Write
3. Organize
2. Prewrite
1. Explore

Rewrite each of the following combined sentences. Change the coordinating conjunction to a semicolon followed by a conjunctive adverb and a comma.

The Voyage of the Kon-Tiki

1. Thor Heyerdahl was born and raised in Norway, but he is most famous for his travel to Polynesia in the South Pacific. *Thor Heyerdahl was born as raised in Norway; however, he is most famous for his travel to Polynesia in the South Pacific.*

2. On an island in Polynesia in 1936, he learned the legend of a pale-skinned god Tiki who brought the ancestors of the natives from the west across the sea, so he logically concluded that they came from Peru in South America. _____

_____

_____

_____

3. He wanted to prove that such a voyage was possible, so in 1947 he built a raft like
the kind he thought the early natives used. _____

_____

_____

4. He made a forty-five-foot long raft, which he called *Kon-Tiki,* out of nine huge balsa
logs and bamboo, and he didn't use any nails or wire to hold the logs together, only
rope.

_____

_____

5. Heyerdahl and a crew of six had to be incredibly skilled and brave, or they would
never have made it on their 4,300-mile voyage across the open sea. _____

_____

_____

6. After 101 days, the raft reached the reefs off a Polynesian island, but the strong
waves there smashed the cabin and broke the mast like a matchstick. _____

_____

_____

7. The boat was destroyed and the crew thrown into the water, yet they were able to
wade their way to the palm-covered island. _____

_____

_____

8. People said that a flimsy balsa-wood raft couldn't possibly cross the Pacific Ocean,
yet Heyerdahl proved them wrong. _____

_____

_____

EXERCISE 7   **Writing Combined Sentences**

6. Edit
5. Revise
4. Write
3. Organize
2. Prewrite
1. Explore

*Complete the following sentences after the semicolon by adding a transitional word, a
comma, and a second independent clause. Use a different transitional word each time.*

1. Last summer was the hottest in many years;  therefore, I spent most weekends at
the beach.

2. The legal drinking age in most states is twenty-one; _____

_____

3. The health-care industry offers many opportunities for employment; _____

_____

4. I have developed a real talent for flipping hamburgers at my job; _____

_____

5. Mr. Gottbucks owns a seventeen-room house in Florida; _____

_____

6. I can't persuade my cat, Tubby, to go on a diet; _____

_____

| EXERCISE 3 | Combining More Sentences |

6. Edit
5. Revise
4. Write
3. Organize
2. Prewrite
1. Explore

Combine each of the following groups or sentences, creating at least two independent clauses and omitting repeated words. Use both coordinating conjunctions or semicolons (and transitional words if necessary).

The Waltz Comes to England

1. The waltz was like dirty dancing.

   ~~This was~~ in its own day.

   The older generation condemned it.

   Younger people danced it.

   ~~They danced~~ nonstop. *The waltz was like dirty dancing in its own day; the older generation condemned it, but younger people danced it nonstop.*

2. The year was 1812. ;

   The dance waltzed from Germany.

   ~~It went~~ into England.

   The newspapers called it "disgusting." *and*

   ~~The newspapers called it~~ "immodest." *The year was 1812; the dance waltzed from Germany into England, the newspapers called it "disgusting and immodest."*

3. Critics claimed that couples "embrace at the pelvis."

   They said the couples "whirl about in a posture of copulation." *Critics claimed that couples; "embrace at the pelvis, Furthermore "whirl about in a posture of copulation."*

4. In those days, people danced.

   They held each other's fingertips.

   Full-body contact was considered immoral.

   ~~Full-body contact was~~ deliciously exciting. *Full-body contact was considered immoral or deliciously exciting; In those days people danced holding each other's fingertips*

5. The waltz was becoming very popular.

   ~~It was popular~~ with lower-class people,

   They were all over Europe.

It was first danced by upper-class people at a royal ball.

The ball was in England.

The year was 1816. _____

_____

_____

6. The London *Times* wrote that the ball threatened the country's morals,

The paper warned parents against exposing their daughters to this danger, *therefore*

The warning increased the dance's popularity.,

Which
~~This increase~~ happened almost overnight. _____

_____

_____

IN SUMMARY   To Join Sentences with Coordination

1. Use one of the coordinating conjunctions (*for, and, nor, but, or, yet, so*), preceded by a comma.
2. Use a semicolon [;].
3. Add transitional words such as *however, therefore,* and *nevertheless* after the semicolon if necessary.

EDITING FOR MASTERY

Mastery Exercise 1

Combining Sentences

Ten of the following items contain two independent clauses, but they are not joined in any way. Find and fix them. Join them using either one of the seven coordinating conjunctions or a semicolon, along with a transitional word if necessary. Be careful: three of the items shouldn't be changed.

The Collyer Brothers: Strange Hermits

1. The death of Homer Collyer in March 1947 fascinated New Yorkers ^, for this blind and paralyzed ex-lawyer had starved among so much junk that the police spent several hours getting into his house.

2. Neighbors hoped to get a glimpse of the millions of dollars supposedly stashed away in the house police were more concerned with where Homer's brother Langley, a former concert pianist, had gone.

3. The Collyer brothers weren't always so strange they had lived in their house with their mother for twenty years before her death in 1939.

4. At that point the brothers gave up their careers and didn't talk to anyone in fact they allowed all the utilities to be shut off.

5. Homer went blind and became paralyzed around 1940 he never saw a doctor and was completely dependent on Langley.

6. Langley thought that he could cure his brother's blindness by feeding him one hundred oranges a week.

7. Homer never left the house Langley fetched water from the park four blocks away and roamed the streets at night looking for food and supplies.

8. Langley barricaded the house's doors and windows he was terrified of burglars.

9. He piled up mountains of junk that hid tunnels for him and booby traps for intruders.

10. After Homer's death, sanitation officers slowly cleared away the clutter in the house they removed 120 tons of material before finally reaching the second floor two weeks later.

11. They found fourteen grand pianos, the chassis of a Model-T Ford, old toys, boxes of rotting clothing, thousands of books, tons of newspapers, many bicycles, several sewing machines, a coil of barbed wire, thirty-four bank books (totaling only $3,007), many weapons, the jawbone of a horse, two large sections of a tree, and endless other items.

12. Finally, officials reached a pile of rubble only ten feet from where Homer's body had been Langley's body lay beneath it.

13. He must have been crawling through a tunnel of junk on his way to feed Homer he had been crushed by one of his own booby traps.

14. Nobody found millions of dollars the Collyers' attorney valued their property at only $100,000.

Scorecard: Number of errors found and corrected _____

Combining Sentences

Ten of the following items contain two independent clauses, but they are not joined in any way. Find and fix them. Join them using either one of the seven coordinating conjunctions or a semicolon, along with a transitional word if necessary. Be careful: four of the items shouldn't be changed.

Robert F. Stroud (1890–1963): The Birdman of Alcatraz

1. Robert F. Stroud became a self-taught expert on birds ; moreover, he ^he was the best-known example of self-improvement in the American prison system.

2. Stroud dropped out of school in third grade he drifted into Alaska in 1908.

3. Another man beat up Stroud's girlfriend there she begged Stroud to kill him, which he did.

4. With Alaska being such a wild place in those days, Stroud could have gotten off with a short sentence a new judge gave him the maximum sentence—twelve years—in a federal penitentiary.

Collaborative Activity 5

Comparing Answers
Discuss your changes in your collaborative group, and report them to the entire class.

Mastery Exercise 2

5. Stroud was transferred to the new Leavenworth, Kansas, prison in 1912, where he discovered that books could make his life in prison more bearable.

6. The hot-headed young man couldn't stay out of trouble he got into a fight with a guard and stabbed him to death.

7. When Stroud appealed the death sentence after the trial that followed, President Woodrow Wilson commuted his sentence to life imprisonment.

8. One day Stroud found two baby sparrows in the prison exercise yard, he took them back to his cell.

9. His interest in birds grew quickly he soon wrote regularly in magazines on birds and was a well-known expert on the subject.

10. Because his knowledge of curing bird diseases was greatly in demand, he wrote *Stroud's Digest on Diseases of Birds,* which is still in public libraries.

11. For a while, the prison authorities gave him an extra cell and let him fill it with birds, books, a typewriter, and a microscope, but they often threatened to take away his privileges.

12. In the twenty-sixth year of his sentence, he was transferred to Alcatraz Island he had to leave his birds behind.

13. Without real birds, "The Birdman of Alcatraz" turned to reading and research he eventually studied law and French, which he taught himself.

14. He was in prison for fifty-four years, always hoping for a parole it never came, and he died in Alcatraz in 1963.

Scorecard: Number of errors found and corrected _____

7 Joining Sentences Through Subordination

As you saw in the previous chapter on coordination, joining sentences helps you express logical relationships and achieve sentence variety. However, coordination alone cannot accomplish both these goals. For example, read the following paragraph, which relies heavily on the coordinating conjunctions *and, but,* and *so:*

> The 1912 Olympic Games were held in Stockholm, Sweden, *and* there was controversy during the pentathlon. This event involves five different skills, *and* one of them requires shooting a gun at a target. The American was competing for a gold medal, *and* he fired his gun, *but* the judges said that his bullet had completely missed the target. He didn't agree, *and* he claimed that his bullet had gone straight through a hole in the center, *and* the hole had been made by an earlier contestant. The judges did not accept his argument, *so* he lost. The contestant was an army lieutenant, *and* his name was George S. Patton.

Here's a rewritten version, which you should find clearer, more entertaining, and more graceful in style:

> At the 1912 Olympic Games, in Stockholm, Sweden, a controversy occurred during the pentathlon. Among the five different skills in this event, one requires shooting a gun at a target. After an American competing for a gold medal fired his gun, the judges said that his bullet had completely missed the target. He didn't agree, claiming that his bullet had gone straight through a hole in the center made by an earlier contestant. The judges did not accept his argument, so he lost. The contestant was an army lieutenant named George S. Patton.

UNIT 2	Go Electronic
Chapter 7	Use the following electronic supplements for additional practice with your writing:
	• For chapter-by-chapter summaries and exercises, visit the *Writing with Confidence* Companion Website at http://www.ablongman.com/meyers.
Writing with Confidence ©2003	• For work with the writing process, visit *The Longman Writer's Warehouse* at http://longmanwriterswarehouse.com (password needed).
	• For additional practice in grammar, use *The Writer's ToolKit Plus* CD-ROM.

Although the second paragraph uses some coordination, it more often joins sentences in a second way: through **subordination**. This chapter will teach you how to

- join sentences by making one clause dependent on the other
- join sentences by turning one clause into a phrase

WHAT IS SUBORDINATION?

"... be deliberate in the choice of words, in the conviction that without the right wording, without the appropriate rhythms, without design, an essential aspect of what one feels will not get communicated."

—Poet Robert Pack

Coordination joins equals, but not all ideas are equal. In the following sentence, for example, is the first idea as important as the second?

> I came home from work, and I found an eight-foot cobra snake in my living room.

If you answered yes, perhaps you live in a rather strange neighborhood! These ideas shouldn't be joined by *and*. They need to be joined in a way that expresses their inequality. Here are two possibilities:

> *When I came home from work,* I found an eight-foot cobra snake in my living room.
>
> *After coming home from work,* I found an eight-foot cobra snake in my living room.

Now the less important idea is *subordinate* (*sub* = lower, *ordinate* = level) to the more important one. This chapter explains, in detail, how you can combine sentences with subordination.

SUBORDINATING WITH CLAUSES

One type of subordination creates a **dependent clause**—which, as its name suggests, depends on an independent clause to complete its meaning. The dependent clause contains the less important idea. The independent clause contains the more important idea.

Like an **adverb**, the dependent clause often tells when, why, or where the idea in the independent clause takes place. So these dependent clauses begin with words like *when, because,* and *where.* Read the following two sentences, for example:

> Albert sits down for dinner. He can eat seven pizzas.

You could join them by subordinating the less important idea, introducing it with *when:*

> *When* Albert sits down for dinner, he can eat seven pizzas.

Now the first clause merely says when the second, and more important, action occurs. And this first clause can no longer make a complete statement:

> *When* Albert sits down for dinner, . . . (what happens?)

The joining word *when* subordinates the clause it introduces. We therefore call it a **subordinating conjunction**.

Combine the following two sentences with the subordinating conjunction *because:*

Albert had some serious indigestion.

He ate seven pizzas with sausage and anchovies.

_____

_____

And combine these two sentences with the subordinating conjunction *where:*

There is food.

You will find Albert.

_____

Are these the sentences you wrote?

> Albert had some serious indigestion *because* he ate seven pizzas with sausage and anchovies.
>
> *Where* there is food, you will find Albert.

Joining clauses with *when, why,* and *where* not only gives you more ways to express logical relationships. It also helps you helps you create sentence variety.

TIPS

For Detecting Fragments

Clauses beginning with *because* and *where* will be fragments unless they're attached to independent clauses that tell the main action.

(What happened?) . . . *because* he ate seven pizzas with sausage and anchovies.

Where there is food, . . . (what will happen?)

EXERCISE 1   Identifying Subordination

Each sentence in this exercise contains a dependent clause and an independent clause. Label them DC and IC. Then find and underline the subordinating conjunction that begins that dependent clause.

Jesse Owens

The Triumph of Jesse Owens

1. In 1936, <u>when</u> the Olympic Games began in Nazi Germany, Adolf Hitler wanted them to prove his theories of Aryan (white) superiority.

2. However, after a twenty-two-year-old African-American named James Cleveland ("Jesse") Owens had competed in the track and field events, the young man personally ripped these theories to pieces.

✔ **TIPS**

For Using *Although*

Although is a conjunction;
It joins clauses:

Although the class was
very difficult, I really
learned a lot.

But *however* is a transitional word that doesn't
join anything (notice
where the semicolon and
comma go):

The class was very diffi-
cult; *however*, I really
learned a lot.

**If Your First
Language is Not
English**

1. In some Asian languages
(especially Chinese and
Vietnamese), *although*
and *but* begin both
clauses in a combined
sentence. In English,
however, you may use
only one of the conjunc-
tions:

Correct: **Although** Albert
wasn't very hungry,
he ate nineteen
cheeseburgers.

Correct: Albert wasn't
very hungry, *but* he
ate nineteen cheese-
burgers.

2. In Spanish, the second
clause in a combined
sentence may omit a
subject pronoun because
it's part of the verb (for
example, *tengo* means "I
have"). In English, how-
ever, the second clause
must include a stated
subject:

Correct: Albert didn't eat
the last hamburger
because *he* didn't
want to be impolite.

3. At the beginning of the track and field events, Owens felt tense because a German had won a gold medal the day before and received Hitler's enthusiastic congratulations.

4. But later the same day, when one of the African-American athletes won a gold medal, Hitler did not shake his hand but hurried out of the stadium.

5. Although Hitler claimed he left to escape a light drizzle, the meaning of the German dictator's action was obvious.

6. If Hitler felt bad about a black man winning a medal, Jesse Owens would soon make him feel much worse.

7. When the track and field events were over, Jesse Owens had won four gold medals, breaking or equaling *nine* Olympic records.

Common Subordinating Conjunctions

The last exercise introduced you to many of the subordinating conjunctions. Here's a more complete list, divided into categories:

When conjunctions	
After	*After* I left, . . .
As	*As* I was walking down the street, . . .
As soon as	*As soon as* you finish, . . .
Before	*Before* the lights go out, . . .
Once	*Once* you have finished the cleaning, . . . (*Once* means *after*.)
Since	*Since* I made my first billion dollars, . . .
Until	*Until* the sun sets, . . .
When	*When* the semester is over, . . .
While	*While* the music was playing, . . .
Why conjunctions	
Because	*Because* you are improving your writing, . . .
Since	*Since* the water in the lake is so warm, . . .
Where conjunctions	
Where	*Where* there is smoke, . . .
Wherever	*Wherever* you can find a job, . . .

Other subordinating conjunctions set up a contrast or condition:

Contrasting conjunctions	
Although	*Although* you look honest, . . .
Even though	*Even though* the test was difficult, . . .
Whereas	*Whereas* many people thought the world was flat, . . .
Conditional conjunctions	
If	*If* I have the opportunity, . . .
Unless	*Unless* he stops playing that music so loudly, . . .

Punctuating Dependent Clauses

Here are the rules for using commas with adverb dependent clauses:

 Place a comma after a dependent clause *at the beginning of a sentence.*

> *subordinating conjunction*   *dependent clause,*   *independent clause*
> *When* the alarm clock rings in the morning, I put the pillow over my head.

▶ **Do not use a comma before a dependent clause at the end of a sentence (but you may use a comma before a long clause beginning with the words** *unless,* **
although, **or** *since).*

> *independent clause*   *subordinating conjunction*   *dependent clause*
> I put the pillow over my head *when* the alarm clock rings in the morning.
>
> but
>
> I always get to work on time, *although* my hair may not be combed or my shirt buttoned.

EXERCISE 2   Joining and Punctuating Sentences

6. Edit
5. Revise
4. Write
3. Organize
2. Prewrite
1. Explore

Read each pair of sentences. Then join them with a subordinating conjunction that best expresses the logical relationship between the sentences. The conjunction can come before either the first or the second sentence. Place a comma where it is needed.

Jesse Owens's Most Remarkable Day

1. No one was surprised at Jesse Owens's success in the 1936 Olympics͵^because he ̶H̶e̶ had done something even more remarkable a year earlier.

2. He competed in the Big Ten Championship on May 25, 1935. He had the greatest day in the history of modern track competition.

3. He didn't think he would even be able to participate. He had strained his back a few weeks earlier.

4. He could not even jog at the warm-up before the meet. He decided to compete in the 100-yard dash.

5. He got off to a perfect start. He finished the dash in 9.4 seconds, matching the world record.

6. His coach advised Owens to take only a single long jump. He leapt almost 27 feet and beat the world record by nearly a half-foot.

7. Owens won the 200-yard dash in 20.3 seconds. He set another world record.

8. Owens finished the 220-yard low hurdles in 22.6 seconds. He broke an 11-year-old world record.

9. Owens completed four events in forty-five minutes. He set three world records and tied another.

Collaborative Activity 1

Comparing Combined Sentences

In your collaborative group, compare your answers to Exercise 2. Did all of you use the same subordinating conjunctions? Did you agree on the placement of commas? Report your results to the whole class.

EXERCISE 3   Writing Sentences with Dependent Clauses

Each of these sentences is incomplete, so complete the sentences. Be sure that your idea contains both a subject and a verb. Add a comma wherever it is needed.

1. When you are in the neighborhood, *please come to my place and visit me.*

2. I can give you a place to stay if _____

3. Since California has many earthquakes _____

4. _____ after an earthquake happens.

5. _____ although everyone knows about the danger.

6. People live in California because _____

Subordinating with Phrases

You can also subordinate the less important idea by making it a **phrase**—a group of two or more words that don't include a complete subject and verb. Here's an example of a *when* clause changed into a phrase:

> *dependent clause*
> *After the Native American Jim Thorpe* became the most famous athlete in track
>
>   *independent clause*
> and field, *he competed* in the 1912 Olympic Games in Stockholm, Sweden.
>
> *phrase*   *independent clause*
> *After becoming the most famous athlete* in track and field, *the Native American Jim Thorpe competed* in the 1912 Olympic Games in Stockholm, Sweden.

Notice three things:

- The phrase begins with *after*.
- The verb *became* converts to an *–ing* word: *becoming*.
- The subject of the adverb clause, *Jim Thorpe*, moves to the independent clause.

Change the clause to a phrase in this sentence:

While Thorpe won all five events in the pentathlon, he also won all ten events in the decathlon.

_____

_____

Is this what you wrote?

> While winning all five events in the pentathlon, Thorpe also won all ten events in the decathlon.

You can't convert every dependent clause into a phrase—just those that begin with the conjunctions *after, while, when, since, before,* and *although.* Here are a few more examples:

Collaborative Activity 2

Writing Combined Sentences

Write two dependent clauses. Then, in your group, combine all of the clauses into a single list. Work independently for a few minutes to add independent clauses and create complete sentences. Now compare and discuss your results. Share three or four with the whole class.

TIPS

For Using Phrases
See Chapter 14 for a fuller discussion of these phrases.

TIPS

For Detecting Fragments
Notice that the dependent clauses beginning with *because* and *where* can no longer make complete statements:
(What happened?) . . . because he ate seven pizzas with sausage and anchovies.
Where there is food, . . . (what will happen?)

> *After*
> *While*
> *When*
> *Since* } *triumphing in the Olympics,* Thorpe became a national hero.
>
> *Before entering the Olympics,* Thorpe was relatively unknown.
>
> *Although coming from a poor background,* Thorpe would achieve national fame.

In fact, some phrases can drop the conjunction and begin with *–ing:*

> *Entering the Olympics,* Thorpe was relatively unknown.

▶ **Like a dependent clause beginning a sentence, a phrase that begins a sentence requires a comma.**

EXERCISE 4	Revising Sentences

6. Edit
5. Revise
4. Write
3. Organize
2. Prewrite
1. Explore

Each of the following sentences contains a dependent clause and an independent clause. Rewrite each sentence, changing the dependent clause into a phrase.

Jim Thorpe at goal-kicking exhibition

Jim Thorpe (1887–1953): A World-class Athlete

1. When ~~people~~ think about the origins of great athletes, people would never expect James Frances Thorpe to have become one of the best in history. *When thinking about the origins of great athletes, people would never expect James Frances Thorpe to have become one of the best in history.*

2. Before Jim Thorpe came to the Carlisle Indian School in Pennsylvania, he lived in Oklahoma Territory as a member of the Sac and Fox Tribe. _____

_____

_____

3. Although Thorpe planned to become a tailor at Carlisle, he attracted national attention as a track and field athlete. _____

_____

_____

4. In 1912, Thorpe won six of seven events while ~~he was~~ leading the tiny Carlisle team to an overwhelming victory over the much larger team from Lafayette. _____

_____

_____

Thorpe

5. While ~~he~~ continued to compete in track and field, he became an all-American runner, place kicker, and defensive player in football. _____

_____

_____

Thorpe Playing

6. After he enjoyed such success in football, ~~he~~ went on to play major league baseball.

_____

_____

EXERCISE 5	Combining Sentences

6. Edit
5. Revise
4. Write
3. Organize
2. Prewrite
1. Explore

Combine each of the following pairs of sentences using when, while, although, after, *or* before *plus an –ing word.*

1. Jim Thorpe breezed through the five events in the pentathlon in the Olympics. He won the decathlon so easily that it shocked the world. *After breezing through the five events in the pentathlon in the Olympics, Jim Thorpe won the decathlon so easily that it shocked the world.*

2. Thorpe received a bronze bust of himself from King Gustov of Sweden, who called him the greatest athlete in the world. Thorpe said only, "Thanks, King." *When receiving a bronze bust of himself from the King Gustov of Sweden, who called h*

3. The world later learned that Thorpe's Olympic medals had been taken away from him. The world was astonished. _____

_____

_____

Collaborative Activity 3

Comparing Combined Sentences

In your collaborative group, compare your answers to Exercise 5. Did you combine sentences in more than one way?

Now combine them with coordination, using semicolons and coordinating conjunctions. See how many ways you can devise for joining the clauses. Report your results to the whole class.

4. In 1913, the Amateur Athletic Union (AAU) took back Thorpe's Olympic medals. It claimed he had played baseball for money in 1909 and 1910. _Although in 1913, the Amateur_

5. Thorpe played for only a few dollars. He was technically a professional who should not have competed in the "amateur" Olympic Games. _While playing for a few dollars, thorpe was technically a professional who should not have completed in the "amateur —_

6. The AAU refused to change its ruling. It finally awarded Thorpe his medals—in 1973, sixty years later, and twenty years after he had died. _After the AAU refused to change its ruling, thorpe was awarded his medals in 1973, sixty years later and twenty_

IN SUMMARY | To Join Sentences with Subordination

1. Use a subordinating conjunction such as *if, when, although,* or *because* to relate a less important idea to a more important one.
2. Make the less important idea into a phrase beginning either with a word such as *when, while,* or *after* or with an *–ing* word.

EDITING FOR MASTERY

Mastery Exercise 1

Eliminating Sentence-Joining Errors

The following passage contains ten errors related to joining sentences (excluding the first error, which has been corrected as an example). Some sentences are actually fragments. Some sentences contain incorrect punctuation or are missing commas. Find and fix the errors by making any necessary changes above the line.

Jesse Owens Defeats Hitler

Collaborative Activity 4

Comparing Corrections

Appoint someone in the group to read the entire passage aloud so you can hear where errors occur. Then make corrections, discuss them in your group, and report them to the entire class.

(1) Because Adolf Hitler wanted to turn the 1936 Olympics into a gigantic show of Nazis superiority. (2) ˄The German dictator built a huge Olympic complex, including a 100,000-seat stadium just outside the city of Berlin. (3) Hitler was thrilled when in the opening parade, the Austrians gave him the Nazi salute. (4) The Bulgarians drew loud cheers. (5) When they marched like Nazi storm troopers. (6) But the German crowd jeered the Americans; because they didn't salute or dip their flag to Hitler.

(7) Hitler's joy disappeared on the second day of the track and field events when the American Jesse Owens broke into the lead in the 100-meter run. (8) Although his fellow

African-American teammate Ralph Metcalfe challenged him strongly, but no one caught Owens as he won the gold medal.

(9) The following morning as the qualifying trials were held for the broad jump. (10) Owens fouled on his first and second attempts. (11) He had only one chance left, and he was obviously tired. (12) Because he had just run the heats of the 200-meter dash.

(13) When Owens felt a hand on his shoulder. (14) He turned around to face Luz Long, a tall, blue-eyed German broad jumper. (15) Long suggested that Owens begin his jump a few inches before the starting board. (16) The grateful Owens did so and qualified with almost a foot to spare.

(17) Later that afternoon, Owens set an Olympic record on his second jump. (18) Although, Luz Long tied it on his next-to-last try. (19) Owens, however, was just warming up and lengthened the Olympic record on his fifth and sixth attempts. (20) After landing on his final jump. (21) Owens was congratulated by Long.

(22) While collecting four gold medals in all. (23) Owens didn't receive a single word of praise from Adolf Hitler. (24) Indeed, Owens and his nine African-American teammates outscored every other national team and won thirteen medals, eight of them gold. (25) Their triumph was enough to make Hitler's theory about the purity of white blood run thin.

Scorecard: Number of errors found and corrected _____

Mastery Exercise 2

Eliminating Sentence-Joining Errors

The following passage contains ten errors related to joining sentences (excluding the first error, which has been corrected as an example). Some sentences are actually fragments. Some sentences contain incorrect punctuation or are missing commas. Correct each error by making any necessary changes above the line. You may need to read the entire paragraph before you decide where to make corrections.

"Babe" Didrickson in the javelin event, Xth Olympics, 1932

Mildred "Babe" Didrikson Zaharias: The Greatest Woman Athlete

(1) Although women weren't expected to perform as well as ^men. (2) Mildred "Babe" *men, Mildred* Didrikson Zaharias could outthrow, outrun, and outhit just about anyone of any sex. (3) While standing at home plate; she could throw a baseball and hit the left-field wall on one bounce. (4) She was incredibly skilled in tennis, bowling, and basketball. (5) She won more than fifty major golf tournaments, including three women's national opens. (6) "Babe" Didrikson Zaharias was also one of the best track and field performers of all time. (7) Because she was so talented in so many ways. (8) This native of Beaumont, Texas, was named the greatest woman athlete of the first half of the twentieth century.

(9) Babe Zaharias attracted national attention in 1930 in Dallas, as she won both the baseball throw and the javelin. (10) Although she finished second in the long jump, but her jump was good enough to top a world record. (11) In 1931, she continued her record-breaking performances in New Jersey; where she threw a baseball 296 feet and won both the 80-meter hurdles and the long jump.

(12) These performances turned out to be just a warm-up for the 1932 Olympics in Los Angeles. (13) Zaharias threw the javelin more than 143 feet for a new Olympic and world record. (14) She ran the 80-meter hurdles in less than 12 seconds while setting another Olympic and world record. (15) Although, her high jump was good enough to break another world record. (16) She was disqualified for "diving" over the bar and finished in second place.

(17) After dominating women's track and field for a decade. (18) She became a world champion golfer. (19) This led to one of the greatest comebacks in sports history. (20) Even though Zaharias had a cancer operation in 1953. (21) She won the women's national open in 1954. (22) In fact, she triumphed in every contest. (23) Until she finally lost her battle with cancer and died in 1956.

Scorecard: Number of errors found and corrected _____

8 Joining Sentences with Pronouns

The previous two chapters showed you a number of ways to combine sentences in a confident, mature style. This chapter will introduce you to another option: joining sentences with **pronouns**—words that replace nouns.

We'll be looking at how to

- join sentences with pronouns that make one clause dependent on another
- join sentences by making one clause function as a noun
- join sentences by making a clause into a phrase

RELATIVE CLAUSES

"A poor relation—is the most irrelevant thing in nature."

—English Essayist Charles Lamb

The following two sentences are short and choppy, almost sounding like the writing of a child:

I talked to a counselor. She was very helpful.

These sentences are begging to be combined—in this case by replacing *she* with a different kind of pronoun, *who*:

I talked to a counselor *who* was very helpful.

We call *who* a **relative pronoun** because it *relates* the information *was very helpful* to a noun, *counselor*.

Here are two more short, choppy sentences:

Our car needs to be replaced. It is ten years old.

Join them by replacing the pronoun *it* with another relative pronoun, *which*:

UNIT 2	Go Electronic
Chapter 8	Use the following electronic supplements for additional practice with your writing: • For chapter-by-chapter summaries and exercises, visit the Writing with Confidence Companion Website at http://www.ablongman.com/meyers.
Writing with Confidence ©2003	• For work with the writing process, visit The Longman Writer's Warehouse at http://longmanwriterswarehouse.com (password needed). • For additional practice in grammar, use The Writer's ToolKit Plus CD-ROM.

TIPS

For Using Relative Pronouns

Beware of *in which*. Some writers love the expression *in which* because they think it sounds elegant. But the result often makes no sense.

Unclear: The topic *in which* we discussed today was capital punishment.

Clear: The topic *that* we discussed today was capital punishment.

Use *in which* only when *in* fits logically within the sentence:

Uncombined sentences: I want to discuss a subject. I am interested *in it*.

Combined sentences: I want to discuss a subject in which I am interested. (*In it* becomes *in which*.)

> Our car, *which is ten years old*, needs to be replaced.

Now join the following two sentences by changing *they* to *that*.

I bought three chairs. *They* look beautiful in my living room.

Combined _____

Is this what you wrote?

> I bought three chairs *that* look beautiful in my living room.

Clauses beginning with the relative pronouns *who, which,* or *that* are therefore called **relative clauses.** They are **dependent clauses** because they cannot stand alone as sentences. And they function like **adjectives** because they describe nouns or pronouns.

- *Who* describes people.
- *Which* describes things.
- *That* describes either people or things.

Placement of Relative Clauses

A relative clause most often directly follows the noun or pronoun it describes. Otherwise, the sentence may not be clear:

Poor: Bill bought a car for his daughter *that cost a fortune.* (What cost a fortune—the daughter or the car?)

Better: Bill bought his daughter a car *that cost a fortune.*

EXERCISE 1   Combining Sentences

6. Edit
5. Revise
4. Write
3. Organize
2. Prewrite
1. Explore

Combine each of the following sentences by adding the relative pronouns who, which, *or* that *above the lines to turn one sentence into a relative clause.*

The War Over a Beard

1. King Louis VII of France was married to Queen Eleanor. , who She gave her new husband two territories in southern France.

2. In 1152, the king returned from a war with a heavy beard. It bothered him, so he shaved it off.

3. Eleanor didn't like the naked face of her husband. He refused to grow the whiskers back.

4. They had a violent argument. It led to a divorce.

5. Eleanor later married King Henry II of England. He demanded that King Louis give Eleanor back the two territories in southern France.

6. When Louis refused, England and France went to war. It lasted, off and on, for 301 years and finally ended in 1453.

Commas with Relative Clauses

The way you punctuate relative clauses can determine the meaning of a sentence. Here's why.

Restrictive Clauses. Read the following sentence:

> You can't start a car *that has a dead battery.*

If you remove the relative clause beginning with *that,* what's left?

> You can't start a car . . .

The meaning is no longer the same. The original sentence with the relative clause *restricts* the meaning of the car to the one with a dead battery—and not any other car. Therefore, we call it a **restrictive relative clause.** The pronoun *that* always begins a restrictive relative clause.

Remember that commas *separate* ideas—but the information in restrictive relative clauses is essential to meaning, so it must not be separated from the words it relates to.

▶ **Don't put commas around a restrictive relative clause.**

Nonrestrictive Clauses. Many relative clauses are not essential to meaning. Remove the relative clause from the following sentence, and see if the remaining idea is unclear.

> My new car, *which I bought in October,* started every day in the coldest weather.
>
> My new car . . . started every day in the coldest weather.

TIPS

For Punctuating Relative Clauses

For more practice with punctuating relative clauses, see Chapter 26.

In this case, the basic meaning of the sentence doesn't change. The relative clause "which I bought in October" just adds a bit of extra information—the kind of information you might include in parentheses. Because that information doesn't restrict meaning in a particular way, we call the clause a **nonrestrictive relative clause.**

▶ **Put commas around a nonrestrictive relative clause, in the same place as parentheses would go:**

> My new car, *which I bought in October,* started every day in the coldest weather.
>
> My new car *(which I bought in October)* started every day in the coldest weather.

The pronouns *who* or *which* often begin a nonrestrictive relative clause. Enclose these clauses in commas. But *which* or *who* can begin restrictive relative clauses, too. So test the meaning of the clauses by temporarily removing them from the sentence. If the meaning is still clear, then use commas around the relative clause.

| EXERCISE 2 | Punctuating Relative Clauses |

Underline the relative clauses in the following sentences and then place commas around the relative clauses that need them.

The Blessing after the Sneeze

1. "God bless you" is an expression <u>that people everywhere say after someone sneezes.</u>

2. The practice of blessing someone which began in Greece in the fourth century B.C. can be traced to the philosophers Aristotle and Hippocrates.

3. They observed many people who seemed to sneeze just before dying from illness.

4. Therefore, to save sneezing people from dying, they recommended blessings that included "Long may you live!" and "May you enjoy good health!"

5. The Romans who had basically similar ideas continued the practice of the Greeks.

6. However, "God bless you" which is a Christian expression began for a different reason.

7. During the sixth century, there was a terrible plague that killed many people in Italy, so the Pope asked people to pray for the sick.

8. Therefore when people with the illness sneezed, their friends and relatives replaced "May you enjoy good health" with a stronger prayer which was "God bless you."

Collaborative Activity 1

Comparing Combined Sentences

In your collaborative group, compare your answers to Exercises 1 and 2. In Exercise 1, did you all combine the sentences in the same way? In Exercise 2, did you agree on the placement of commas? Report your results to the whole class.

| EXERCISE 3 | Completing Sentences with Relative Clauses |

Complete each of the following sentences. Some are missing only verbs; some are missing subjects and verbs. Insert commas where necessary.

1. The accomplishment that I most want to achieve in the next few years *is to finish my college education and get a good job.*

2. People who don't eat meat_____

_____

3. In July the temperature in Arizona which often reaches more than 110 degrees ____

_____

_____

4. _____ which many students major in _____

_____

5. The older chairs and desks that are falling apart _____

_____

6. _____ who live in New York _____

_____

NOUN CLAUSES

Here are two short, choppy sentences begging to be combined. Do so by using one of these pronouns: *who, which, that,* or *what.*

If Your First Language Is Not English

In English, the object pronoun always comes *after* the verb as in this example:

I heard *some news.*

I was very excited about *it.*

But if you combine these two sentences, the relative pronoun replaces the object *it*. Be careful not to remove *it* from the combined sentence:

object
I heard some news *that*
I was very excited about
it.—second object

Speakers of Eastern European languages, especially Russian, often confuse *what* with *that.*

Incorrect: I see the chair *what* I want.

Correct: I see the chair *that* I want.

I know something. You said it.

Combined: _____

Is this what you wrote?

| I know *what* you said. |

Notice that "what you said" replaces "something"—the *object* of the verb "know." An object is a noun—or, in this case, a pronoun. So we call a clause beginning with *what* a **noun clause.**

A noun clause can also be the subject of a sentence. Compare these examples:

| Sentence with a noun subject | Sentence with a noun clause |
| His behavior *annoyed me.* | *What he did* annoyed me. |

Other joining words can begin noun clauses:

He told me ⎰ *where / how / that / when / why* ⎱ I should go.

He asked me ⎰ *if / whether* ⎱ he should go.

EXERCISE 4 — Writing Noun Clauses

6. Edit
5. Revise
4. Write
3. Organize
2. Prewrite
1. Explore

Complete each of the following sentences.

1. We know what *you want* _____

2. I told you that _____

3. Do you have what _____

4. My friend asked me if _____

5. What doesn't make any sense _____

6. What will make Maria sad _____

EXERCISE 5 — Combining Sentences

6. Edit
5. Revise
4. Write
3. Organize
2. Prewrite
1. Explore

Combine each of the following groups of sentences into one sentence, using appropriate methods of both coordination and subordination.

The Origins of New Year's Day

1. Our word *holiday* comes from a word. It means "holy day." All celebrations used to be religious. *Our word "holiday" comes from a word that means "holy day," for all celebrations used to be religious.*

✓ TIPS

For Using Relative Pronouns

Beware of fragments. A relative clause doesn't make a complete statement.

Fragment: The cat that sleeps on top of the television set . . . (*does* or *is* what?).

Fragment: The instructor who gives killer assignments . . . (*does* or *is* what?)

Fragment: The watch, which Tonya gave me for graduation . . . (*does* or *is* what?)

When you write a *who, which,* or *that* clause, be sure it's attached to an independent clause.

Collaborative Activity 2

Comparing Combined Sentences

In your collaborative group, compare your answers to Exercise 5. How many different but correct ways to combine these sentences did your group come up with? Report your results to the whole class.

2. New Year's Day is the oldest "holy day." It began a long time ago. The calendar didn't exist. _____

_____

3. The first New Year's festival began in the city of Babylon. It was the capital of ancient Babylonia. Babylonia is now part of Iraq. _____

_____

4. Late in March, Babylonians had a huge festival. They wanted to celebrate the new year at a particular time. It was the beginning of spring. _____

_____

5. The Babylonians also performed a play. It was to honor the goddess of fertility. They had an enormous parade. It included music, dancing, and performers. The performers wore costumes. _____

_____

6. The idea behind the holiday began to change with the Romans. They created a calendar. It celebrated the new year on March 25. _____

_____

7. Roman rulers and government officials changed the months and years. They made the months and years longer. They wanted to lengthen time. The time was when their terms of office lasted. _____

_____

8. Members of the Roman Senate met in 153 B.C. They knew something. They had to set the date of the new year on January 1. _____

_____

9. Roman emperors continued to change the calendar. They changed it for the next century. In 46 B.C., Julius Caesar adjusted the calendar. The year now dragged on for 445 days. _____

_____

10. The Catholic Church disapproved of any "pagan" (non-Christian) festivals. These celebrated the planting of seeds. The Church eliminated the new year holiday.

_____

_____

11. The holiday came back during the Middle Ages. The British celebrated it on March 25. The French celebrated it on Easter Sunday. The Italians celebrated it on Christmas day. _____

_____

12. These differences continued until about 400 years ago. The date of January 1 was finally agreed on. _____

_____

PHRASES

How would you combine the following sentences?

> The eight-foot-tall man must be a basketball player. He is wearing Nikes and a jersey.
>
> The Rolls Royce is my second car. It is parked in the alley.

One possibility is to combine them with *who* or *that* clauses:

> The eight-foot-tall man *who is wearing Nikes and a jersey* must be a basketball player.
>
> The Rolls Royce *that is parked in the alley* is my second car.

But the combined sentences would be just as clear (and shorter) if you eliminated *who* or *that* and the verbs that follow them:

> The eight-foot-tall man *wearing Nikes and a jersey* must be a basketball player.
>
> The Rolls Royce *parked in the alley* is my second car.

These shorter versions of combined sentences now contain **phrases**—groups of two or more words—instead of clauses.

Try combining these sentences without using *who, that,* or *which:*

Many high school students have read *Great Expectations.* It is a novel written by Charles Dickens.

The book was made into a movie. The movie was made in 1998.

1. _____

2. _____

Is this what you wrote?

> Many high school students have read *Great Expectations,* a novel written by Charles Dickens.
>
> The book was made into a movie in 1998.

These combined sentences contain four types of phrases—all of which describe or rename nouns:

- phrases beginning with an *-ing* word (*wearing* Nikes and a jersey)
- phrases beginning with a *noun (a novel)*—technically called an **appositive,** which adds identifying information to the noun that precedes it
- phrases beginning with a *past participle (written* by Charles Dickens)
- phrases beginning with a **preposition** (*in* 1998).

Consider these choices when you combine sentences.

EXERCISE 6	Combining Sentences

6. Edit
5. Revise
4. Write
3. Organize
2. Prewrite
1. Explore

Combine each of the pairs of sentences, using the methods described in this chapter.

A Sticky Solution

1. The idea for Velcro began in 1941. It started with an unlucky accident that happened to the wife of Swiss manufacturer George de Mistral. *The idea for Velcro began in 1941 with an unlucky accident that happened to the wife of Swiss manufacturer George de Mistral.*

2. The zipper on her dress jammed and would not unjam. They were at a formal affair.

3. A few months later, de Mistral thought of a better way to fasten fabrics. He was on a hunting trip with his dog.

4. The dog's ear became covered with burrs. They came from brushing against some weeds.

5. De Mistral noticed tiny hooks on their ends. He was examining the burrs under a microscope.

6. Sixteen years later, this principle led to the manufacture of Velcro. It was little burr-like hooks on fabric. (*Hint:* Place the second idea after *principle* and use commas.)

IN SUMMARY	To Join Sentences Using Pronouns

1. Use the relative pronouns *who, which,* or *that* to create a dependent clause describing a noun. Enclose nonrestrictive relative clauses in commas.
2. Use *what* or *that* to create a clause that functions as a noun.
3. Turn a clause into a phrase by eliminating *who* or *that* and the verbs that follow them.

EDITING FOR MASTERY

Mastery Exercise 1   ***Eliminating Sentence-Joining Errors***

The following passage contains ten errors related to joining sentences (excluding the first error, which has been corrected as an example): incorrectly used relative pronouns, sentence fragments, incorrectly punctuated relative clauses, and incorrectly used noun clauses. Find and fix them. Correct each error by making any necessary changes above the line.

Robert Jarvik and the Artificial Heart

(1) For centuries, people have dreamed of replacing worn-out body parts, especially the ^*heart, which* ~~heart. (2) Which~~ is basically a pump for blood. (3) It seems logical, that a mechanical pump could replace this organ. (4) The dream came true in 1957; when the first total artificial heart (TAH) was developed by Dr. Willem Kolff and placed in a dog. (5) Twelve years later, Dr. Denton Cooley put the first artificial heart in a human, that was only a temporary replacement until the patient could receive a human heart transplant.

(6) The person which developed the first "permanent" TAH was Dr. Robert Jarvik. (7) He patented his mechanical device, the Jarvik-7 in 1979. (8) It was small enough to fit comfortably in the chest, but it was attached to a big air compressor that had to roll around on the floor.

(9) In December 1982, Barney Clark a retired dentist with terminal heart disease, was given only hours to live. (10) Clark's doctor recommended the Jarvik-7, and Clark awoke hours later. (11) With an artificial heart beating in his chest. (12) By 1985, seven patients had received Jarvik hearts, but three were dead, including Clark. (13) Who lived 112 days after his operation. (14) The four other patients had severe strokes; resulting from blood clots. (15) All the patients developed terrible infections.

(16) Meanwhile, human heart transplants became easier, but there have never been enough heart donors to satisfy the demand. (17) In 1988, doctors therefore recommended, that the Jarvik heart be used for a maximum of thirty days while a patient waited for a human heart.

(18) Robert Jarvik continues to improve the TAH.

Scorecard: Number of Errors Found and Corrected _____

Collaborative Activity 3

Comparing Corrections

Appoint someone in the group to read the entire passage from Mastery Exercise 1 aloud so you can hear where errors occur. Make corrections, discuss them in your group, and report them to the entire class.

Mastery Exercise 2

Eliminating Sentence-Joining Errors

The following passage contains ten errors related to joining sentences (excluding the first error, which has been corrected as an example): incorrectly used relative pronouns, sentence fragments, incorrectly punctuated relative clauses, and incorrectly used noun clauses. Correct each error by making any necessary changes above the line. You may need to read an entire paragraph before you decide where to make corrections.

Marconi and the Birth of the Radio

(1) Guglielmo Marconi was born on April 25, 1874, to Annie ^*Jameson, who* ~~Jameson. (2) Who~~ had eloped from her native Ireland and married the Italian Giuseppe Marconi. (3) His cruel father often told Guglielmo, that he was a good-for-nothing mama's boy. (4) After flunking out of high school and failing entrance exams to both the university and the naval academy.

(5) He finally got into technical school. (6) Where a blind telegraph operator taught him Morse code and a physics professor introduced him to the theory of electromagnetism.

(7) In 1894, Marconi had a brainstorm. (8) He would use electromagnetic waves to send Morse code that up to that point needed to be transmitted over wires. (9) After many months of work in a laboratory in his attic, and he then called in his mother one night. (10) Guglielmo tapped a telegraph key in which rang a bell on the other side of the attic—traveling across only air.

(11) In 1897, Marconi sent a Morse code message more than one and a half miles. (12) Nevertheless, the Italian government wasn't impressed when he demonstrated his invention. (13) So Annie took her son to London in 1896 and introduced him to Sir William Preece, chief engineer of the British postal service that immediately saw a need for the "wireless."

(14) Many scientists believed what radio waves traveled in a straight line and could not circle the earth. (15) Marconi proved the experts wrong on December 12, 1901. (16) When he sent a message from England across the Atlantic Ocean to Newfoundland, Canada. (17) Marconi was the first person which successfully transmitted wireless radio waves over long distances.

(18) The day after Marconi died on July 20, 1937. (19) Radio operators all over the would shut down their transmitters for two minutes in his memory.

Scorecard: Number of Errors Found and Corrected _____

9 Repairing Run-ons and Correcting Comma Splices

Good writing depends on strong sentences—sentences that are clear, concise, interesting, and easy to read. To write strong sentences, you need to be aware of all the options open to you for combining them. You need to recognize and avoid combinations that don't work, too.

This chapter will show you how to correct two common errors in sentence-joining:

- clauses joined by nothing at all
- clauses joined by nothing but a comma

RUN-ON SENTENCES

"I am glad you came to punctuate my discourse, which I fear has gone on for an hour without any stop at all."

—Poet Samuel Taylor Coleridge

What joins the two independent clauses in each of the following sentences?

> My friend John is a bit weird he wears six rings in his nose.
> We saw an early movie then we had a pizza later at Guido's.

Nothing joins them. The first clause simply runs on into the second. These are **run-on sentences**—two independent clauses with nothing linking them together—a very confusing and serious error.

UNIT 2	Go Electronic
Chapter 9	Use the following electronic supplements for additional practice with your writing: • For chapter-by-chapter summaries and exercises, visit the Writing with Confidence Companion Website at http://www.ablongman.com/meyers. • For work with the writing process, visit The Longman Writer's Warehouse at http://longmanwriterswarehouse.com (password needed).
Writing with Confidence ©2003	• For additional practice in grammar, use The Writer's ToolKit Plus CD-ROM.

You can repair run-ons in a number of ways. In some cases, you need only insert a conjunction or semicolon. In other cases, you need to rewrite the sentence a bit:

1. Add a coordinating conjunction:

My friend John is a bit weird, *for (so)* he wears six rings in his nose.

2. Add a semicolon:

My friend John is a bit weird; he wears six rings in his nose.

3. Add a semicolon and a transitional word:

We saw an early movie; *afterward,* we had a pizza at Guido's Glorious Pizza.

4. Rewrite the sentence to eliminate a clause:

My *weird* friend John wears six rings in his nose.

5. Rewrite the sentence and add a relative pronoun to create a dependent clause:

My friend John, *who* wears six rings in his nose, is a bit weird.

6. Add a subordinating conjunction to create an adverb dependent clause:

After we saw an early movie, we had a pizza at Guido's Glorious Pizza.

7. Rewrite the clauses as separate sentences:

We saw an early movie. Then we had a pizza at Guido's Glorious Pizza.

If you find a run-on sentence as you edit your work, experiment with different corrections until you find one that best expresses your meaning.

EXERCISE 1	Revising Run-on Sentences

6. Edit
5. Revise
4. Write
3. Organize
2. Prewrite
1. Explore

Rewrite each run-on sentence in this exercise to eliminate the error. Use a variety of solutions: coordinating conjunctions; subordinating conjunctions, semicolons and transitional words, relative pronouns, or complete revisions of the sentences.

Canine Convict Number C2559

1. Pep was a male Labrador retriever he belonged to neighbors of the governor of Pike County, Pennsylvania. *Pep, who was a male Labrador retriever, belonged to neighbors of the governor of Pike County, Pennsylvania.*

2. Pep was a friendly dog he went wild and killed the governor's cat one hot summer day. _____

Collaborative Activity 1

Comparing Combined Sentences

In your collaborative group, compare your answers to Exercise 1. Make a list of the different solutions for each item. Report your results to the whole class. Which group has the most varied solutions?

3. The governor was furious he put Pep on trial and sentenced the dog to life imprisonment. _____

_____

4. The poor beast went to the penitentiary in Philadelphia the warden gave him an ID number like the rest of the cons. _____

_____

5. The story has a happy ending Pep's fellow inmates loved him and he could switch cellmates at will. _____

_____

6. Pep spent six pleasant years in prison (forty-two dog years) then he died of old age.

_____

_____

COMMA-SPLICED SENTENCES

TIPS

For Avoiding Run-ons and Comma-spliced Sentences

Watch out for *then* and *also*. They often show up, trying their hardest to be conjunctions. But they can't be used to join sentences.

Incorrect: I took a quick shower, then I headed off to class.

Correct: I took a quick shower, *and then* I headed off to class

Incorrect: I have a quiz on Thursday, also I have to finish my math assignment.

Correct: I have a quiz on Thursday, and I have to finish my math assignment.

What joins the two independent clauses in these sentences?

> Albert wasn't satisfied with just three pizzas, he ate seven.
> Albert eats six meals a day, however, he never gains any weight.

Commas don't join the clause—because commas *separate* ideas. And *however* can't join clauses—because *however* is a *transitional* word. So nothing joins the clauses. They're **comma-spliced sentences**—two independent clauses with a comma between them but no joining word.

Just as you shouldn't splice together electrical wires with masking tape, you shouldn't splice together sentences with commas. The electrical wires should be joined securely in a *junction* box; the sentences should be joined securely with a *conjunction*.

Comma-spliced sentences occur far more frequently than run-ons. That's because writers hear a pause between ideas and mark it with a comma instead of a period. Like run-on sentences, though, comma-spliced sentences often confuse and annoy readers. Repair these damaged sentences in the same way you repair run-ons.

1. Insert conjunctions.
2. Insert semicolons (with transitional words if necessary).
3. Insert relative pronouns to create relative dependent clauses.
4. Rewrite the sentences.

EXERCISE 2   *Revising Comma-spliced Sentences*

Label each item here with CS (for comma splice) or OK (because it is correct as is). Then repair each comma-spliced sentence, using a variety of solutions.

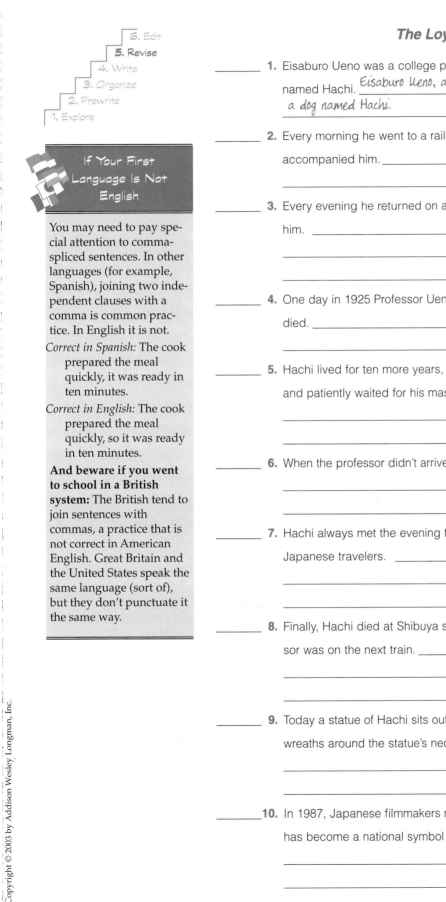

6. Edit
5. Revise
4. Write
3. Organize
2. Prewrite
1. Explore

If Your First Language Is Not English

You may need to pay special attention to comma-spliced sentences. In other languages (for example, Spanish), joining two independent clauses with a comma is common practice. In English it is not.

Correct in Spanish: The cook prepared the meal quickly, it was ready in ten minutes.

Correct in English: The cook prepared the meal quickly, so it was ready in ten minutes.

And beware if you went to school in a British system: The British tend to join sentences with commas, a practice that is not correct in American English. Great Britain and the United States speak the same language (sort of), but they don't punctuate it the same way.

The Loyal Dog

_____ **1.** Eisaburo Ueno was a college professor at Tokyo University, he had a dog named Hachi. *Eisaburo Ueno, a college professor at Tokyo University, had a dog named Hachi.*

_____ **2.** Every morning he went to a railroad station near his home, his dog always accompanied him. _____

_____ **3.** Every evening he returned on a train, Hachi was always there to greet him. _____

_____ **4.** One day in 1925 Professor Ueno had a heart attack at school, then he died. _____

_____ **5.** Hachi lived for ten more years, he went to the train station every evening and patiently waited for his master. _____

_____ **6.** When the professor didn't arrive, the dog sadly went back to Ueno's family. _____

_____ **7.** Hachi always met the evening trains, he became a familiar sight to Japanese travelers. _____

_____ **8.** Finally, Hachi died at Shibuya station, he was still hopeful that the professor was on the next train. _____

_____ **9.** Today a statue of Hachi sits outside of Shibuya station, where people put wreaths around the statue's neck and leave small gifts. _____

_____ **10.** In 1987, Japanese filmmakers made a movie about Hachi, the dog that has become a national symbol of loyalty and devotion. _____

| EXERCISE 3 | Eliminating Sentence-Combining Errors |

Each of the following items contains one or more run-ons or comma splices. Correct the errors above the lines. You don't have to rewrite the sentences.

The Death of Dian Fossey: The Lonely Woman of the Forest

1. It was a quiet morning at Karisoke Research Station in Rwanda, ^but noises suddenly broke the silence.

2. A group of men stormed into the cabin of Wayne McGuire, he was an American graduate student, they woke him up.

3. They kept on repeating in Swahili that Dian was dead, it was a language he did not know well, he finally understood them.

4. He found Dian Fossey's body lying next to the bed in her cabin, her face had been slashed from forehead to mouth.

5. It was four days later, the fifty-four-year-old woman was buried in the station's animal cemetery, in a spot next to the graves of some mountain gorillas that she loved so dearly.

6. Dian Fossey had spent her life studying the mountain gorillas, also she had saved them from extinction.

7. McGuire was accused of the crime and fled the country, however, there were other, more obvious suspects.

8. Fossey had made friends with the mountain gorillas, at the same time she had made enemies in Rwanda.

Collaborative Activity 2

Comparing Combined Sentences

In your collaborative group, compare your answers to Exercise 2. For the items that are OK, explain what these sentences complete and correct. Report your results to the whole class.

IN SUMMARY   To Repair Run-ons and Comma Splices

1. Add a coordinating conjunction (*and, but, or, for, so, nor, yet*).
2. Add a semicolon and, if necessary, a transitional word (*however, therefore, nevertheless,* and so forth), followed by a comma.
3. Use a subordinating conjunction (*because, when, if, although,* etc.) to create an adverb dependent clause.
4. Use a relative pronoun (*who, which, that*) to create a relative dependent clause.
5. Make one clause a phrase.
6. Rewrite the sentence.
7. Write the two clauses as two separate sentences.

✔ **TIPS**

For Practicing Punctuation
For additional practice with punctuating sentences, see Chapter 26.

Dian Fossey (photo by Peter G. Veit for the National Geographic Society)

EDITING FOR MASTERY

Mastery Exercise 1

Eliminating Sentence-Combining Errors

The following passage contains ten run-on or comma-spliced sentences (excluding the example, which has been corrected for you). Find and fix the errors.

Dian Fossey's Crusade to Save the Gorillas

(1) Dian Fossey's closest friends praised her as a warmhearted, completely dedicated woman, in fact, they called her "Queen of the Apes." (2) She worked most of her
life to save the East African mountain gorillas, consequently, they are a less endangered
species. (3) Today there are 650 mountain gorillas alive in the world, there were only 250
in the mid-1970s.

(4) Although people used to think that gorillas were all like King Kong, Dian
Fossey's research changed that idea. (5) She began by watching these gentle giants
from a safe distance, later on she moved among them. (6) She imitated their grunting
sounds and body language, also she nibbled on the wild celery they loved and
scratched them.

(7) Fossey's desire to live among the gorillas was understandable, she had been a
lonely child who loved animals. (8) However, she couldn't have any pets except a goldfish when it died, she cried for a week.

Collaborative Activity 3

Comparing Corrections

Appoint someone in your collaborative group to read the passage aloud so you can hear where errors occur. Make your corrections, discuss them in your group, and report them to the entire class.

(9) She saw gorillas on her first trip to East Africa in 1963, she described them as "big and imposing but not monstrous at all." (10) She left Africa, then she returned four years later and established the Karisoke Research Station in Rwanda.

(11) Fossey loved the gorillas but constantly chased after poachers, they were killing the animals. (12) When she caught the poachers, she took away their weapons and even whipped them. (13) She also fought the Rwandan authorities, who wanted to make the gorilla's home into a tourist attraction. (14) Fossey said that the gorillas were not zoo attractions, she threatened to shoot any tourist approaching her station. (15) She made many enemies among the Rwandans, and her murder has never been solved.

Scorecard: Number of Errors Found and Corrected _____

Mastery Exercise 2

Eliminating Sentence-Combining Errors

The following passage contains ten run-on or comma-spliced sentences (excluding the example, which has been corrected for you). Correct each error above the lines.

The Talking Gorilla

(1) For centuries, people have dreamed of communicating with animals, ^ *and* the most likely candidates for communication have always been apes. (2) Not surprisingly, the first animal to fulfill that dream was a female gorilla named Koko, she was born at the San Francisco Zoo on July 4, 1971. (3) In 1972, a psychology student named Francine Patterson began the gorilla's incredible education. (4) Patterson taught Koko American Sign Language, the friendly 290-pound beast quickly became a good student.

(5) Patterson and her assistants started by teaching Koko the signs for food, drink, and other things. (6) Eventually Koko was able to use language more creatively. (7) For instance, she was taught that *dirty* referred to her bowel movements, soon she used it to describe people and events as well. (8) She later chose her own meaning for certain signs, for example, *good* meant "yes" and *lip* meant "woman." (9) She learned to make jokes, also she was interviewed on television—and even on the Internet.

(10) Koko has been studying for more than twenty years, she has learned about 900 different signs. (11) Researchers wanted to see if she could pass on her language skills to another ape, therefore they began looking for a mate for her in 1983. (12) Koko didn't find a mate until 1994. (13) Then she met Ndume, he was from a Chicago zoo, and they were immediately attracted to each other.

(14) There are critics of Patterson's experiments with Koko, they complain that the gorilla has never learned grammar or how to ask a question. (15) However, there is no

doubt that Koko and other gorillas can answer questions, usually with one-word signs. (16) The human dream of communicating with animals started long ago, it has come true with a friendly ape named Koko.

Scorecard: Number of Errors Found and Corrected _____

Essentials of a sentence = an independent clause
subject + verb + completion of statement

A sentence fragment is

(NO SUBJECT) + VERB

SUBJECT + (NO VERB)

SUBJECT + INCOMPLETE VERB

SUBJECT + VERB (NO COMPLETION OF STATEMENT)

4 ways to fix a fragment

Add a missing subject.

Add a missing verb.

Complete an incomplete verb.

Complete the statement following the verb.

A run-on sentence is

FIRST SENTENCE SECOND SENTENCE
(nothing joins them)

A comma-spliced sentence is

FIRST SENTENCE , SECOND SENTENCE
(a comma incorrectly joins them)

8 ways to repair run-ons and comma splices
(correctly joining two sentences into one)

- FIRST SENTENCE , **coordinating conjunction** (*and/but etc.*)
  SECOND SENTENCE.

- FIRST SENTENCE **;** SECOND SENTENCE.

- FIRST SENTENCE **;** **conjunctive adverb** (*however/therefore etc.*), SECOND SENTENCE.

- **Subordinating conjunction** (*when/although etc.*)
  FIRST SENTENCE now a dependent clause , SECOND SENTENCE.

- FIRST SENTENCE **subordinating conjunction** (*when/although etc.*)
  SECOND SENTENCE now a dependent clause.

- FIRST SENTENCE , (*when/although etc.*) SECOND SENTENCE now a dependent clause.

- FIRST SENTENCE , **relative pronoun** (*who/which /that*) + verb
  (or subject + verb) from SECOND SENTENCE

- FIRST SENTENCE **.** SECOND SENTENCE.

Joining sentences: one question to ask

Are the statements equal or unequal?
- Equal ──▶ join by coordination
- Unequal ──▶ join by subordination

Four ways to join sentences by subordination

FIRST SENTENCE , **subordinating conjunction** (*when / although* **etc.**) SECOND SENTENCE now a dependent clause.

Subordinating conjunction (*when / although* **etc.**) FIRST SENTENCE now a dependent clause , SECOND SENTENCE.

FIRST SENTENCE + phrase (formerly SECOND SENTENCE)

Phrase (formerly FIRST SENTENCE) , SECOND SENTENCE.

Three ways to join sentences by coordination (making both sentences into one)

FIRST SENTENCE , **coordinating conjunction** (*and / but* **etc.**) SECOND SENTENCE

FIRST SENTENCE ; SECOND SENTENCE

FIRST SENTENCE ; **conjunctive adverb** (*however / therefore* **etc.**) , SECOND SENTENCE

To make a subject + verb. into a phrase, make the verb incomplete by adding —*ing* .

Comma Do's

1. before a coordinating conjunction that joins two sentences

2. after a dependent clause beginning a joined sentence

3. around a nonrestrictive clauses

Comma Don'ts

1. on either side of a conjunctive adverb

2. between two sentences

Semicolon Do's

1. between two closely related joined sentences

2. before a conjunctive adverb after the semicolon in joined sentences

COORDINATING CONJUNCTIONS

For	But
And	Or
Nor	Yet
	So

SUBORDINATING CONJUNCTIONS

although	after
if	before
because	while
when	(for more, see pp. 78)

CONJUNCTIVE ADVERBS

furthermore	nevertheless
moreover	therefore
	otherwise
also	meanwhile
however	(for more, see pp. 71)

III

Revising with Care: Building on the Framework

The previous unit focused on sentences—ways to ensure they're complete, correctly joined, and joined in ways that create variety and interest as you edit your writing. This unit looks more deeply into the parts of the sentence: the words and phrases that make sentences work—and work for *you*. It begins by showing you how to identify the elements of the sentence as you revise and edit: the subject, the verb, and the completion of the statement that follows the verb.

It then shows you how to identify and correct errors in the forms of verbs, nouns, pronouns, adjectives, and adverbs. It shows you how to place words so sentences are clear and correct. It shows you how to maintain consistency in verb tense and word order. It also shows you how to select strong verbs and adjectives while eliminating unnecessary words. In short, it shows you how to master the small matters that make a big difference in the way readers respond to your message. ■

10 Making Subjects and Verbs Agree

Readers should pay attention to your ideas, not to unexpected and confusing word forms. But readers can be confused if the subjects and verbs of sentences don't fit together. With a singular subject, you need a singular verb; with a plural subject, you need a plural verb. This agreement between subjects and verbs is sometimes difficult because English has some unusual word forms and tricky situations. This chapter will show you how to overcome the difficulties as you edit. You'll learn

- how to make subjects and verbs work together
- how to recognize exceptions that can trip you up

WHAT IS SUBJECT-VERB AGREEMENT?

"How may an author best acquire a mode of writing which shall be agreeable and easily intelligible to the reader? He must be correct, because without correctness, he can be neither agreeable nor intelligible."

–Nineteenth-Century Novelist Anthony Trollope

As you know, subjects can be nouns or pronouns. They can be **singular**: representing one person, place, or thing. Or they can be **plural**: representing more than one. In other words, nouns and pronouns have **number**. Likewise, the verbs that work with subjects can have singular or plural forms. A singular subject goes with a singular verb, and a plural subject with a plural verb. That's **subject-verb agreement**, and without it, some sentences can sound pretty odd.

Look, for example, at the following two sentences written in the **present tense**, which discusses habitual actions or states, or actions that are happening now:

I *are* reading a fascinating book.
He *am* a charming man.

They sound unnatural and unclear because the verbs don't match the subjects. This is what you'd expect to see:

I *am* reading a fascinating book.
He *is* a charming man.

UNIT 3	Go Electronic
Chapter 10	Use the following electronic supplements for additional practice with your writing: • For chapter-by-chapter summaries and exercises, visit the Writing with Confidence Companion Website at http://www.ablongman.com/meyers. • For work with the writing process, visit The Longman Writer's Warehouse at http://longmanwriterswarehouse.com (password needed). • For additional practice in grammar, use The Writer's ToolKit Plus CD-ROM.
Writing with Confidence ©2003	

Here's one more sentence:

> One of the kittens *are* awake.

How many kittens are awake? The sentence may be confusing because the verb *are* agrees with the wrong word, *kittens*—not with the actual subject, *one.* The correct subject-verb agreement clears up the confusion:

> One of the kittens *is* awake.

Subject verb agreement occurs only in tenses that deal with the present, and with just one verb in the past tense, which we'll discuss in Chapter 11. Right now, we'll focus on the present-tense agreement.

SUBJECTS

In English sentences, the subject generally comes before the verb, and the form the verb takes depends on its subject. Let's begin by looking at nouns.

Nouns as Subjects (and Objects)

A *singular* noun, which usually doesn't end in –*s*, takes a verb that ends in –*s*:

> A *jaguar is* the fastest animal on earth.
> A *professional baseball player* owns several jaguars—the driving kind.

A *plural* noun, which normally ends in –*s*, takes a verb without an –*s* ending:

> *Jaguars are* members of the cat family.
> Many professional *athletes make* millions of dollars.

The –*s* ending for plural nouns—whether they're subjects or objects—is important, for it tells readers that you mean more than one. And the –*s* ending on present-tense verbs is important, for it reminds readers that your subject is singular.

EXERCISE 1 | Choosing Correct Noun Forms

6. Edit
5. Revise
4. Write
3. Organize
2. Prewrite
1. Explore

Some of the nouns in the following sentences should be plural. Change them by adding –s or –es endings.

Facts about Zebras

1. It's not unusual to see 1,000 zebra^s together at one time.

2. They're very social animal.

3. They generally live in short grassy area or open fields.

4. A family group consists of one male (called a stallion), several female (called mares), and many infant.

5. The female are not equal; the dominant mare leads the pack and the other follow behind her in single file.

6. And the family stays together, even when they join large herds.

7. Although lion and hyenas prey on zebra, these striped horses are extremely brave, and they will often form a semicircle to protect their families.

8. The lions will sometimes come out second best, because zebras can deliver power- ful kick.

EXERCISE 2	Choosing Correct Verb Forms

✔ **TIPS**

For Hearing –s Endings

The –s ending can actually be pronounced in three different ways, determined by the following rules.

1. When the last sound be- fore the final –s does not require the use of the vocal cords (sounds such as *f*, *k*, *p*, and *t*—if you say them, you'll hear only air passing across your lips), the fi- nal –s is pronounced *s*:

    guests   walks
    chefs   hopes
    laughs   hits
    (pronounced *laffs*)

2. When the last sound be- fore the final –s requires the use of the vocal cords (sounds such as *b*, *g*, *m*, *r*, *v*, *w*, and all the vowels—if you say them, you'll hear an *uh* sound with the conso- nants), the final –s is pronounced *z*:

    robs   laws
    bugs   days
    leaves   toes

3. When the sound before the final –s resembles the sound of *s* (as in the spellings *ce*, *sh*, *ch*, *x*, *z*, *ss*, and *s*), you must cre- ate another syllable to pronounce the final –s: *es* (pronounced *ez*).

    places   wishes
    riches   buzzes
    kisses   boxes

Decide whether the subject of the sentence is singular or plural. Then write the appropriate present-tense form of the verb supplied in parentheses.

Facts about Leopards

1. Leopards normally (hunt) _____ at dusk and throughout the night.

2. These beautiful cats often (stay) _____ hidden during the day or (lie) _____ in high branches of trees.

3. A male leopard normally (live) _____ alone, and (join) _____ a female only for mating.

4. Their spotted bodies (make) _____ wonderful camouflage, so the big cats attack their prey by surprise.

5. A single bite from a leopard usually (kill) _____ the prey.

6. Then the leopard (take) _____ it up in a tree and has a leisurely meal.

Irregular Plurals

English is a very old language whose grammar was originally much more com- plicated. Singular nouns used to form their plurals in a number of ways. The regular practice of simply adding –s to the ends of nouns is actually a fairly re- cent change. But a few nouns stubbornly hold onto their ancient plural forms, without –s endings, so they are **irregular**. Here are some examples:

Singular	Plural
child	children (not childrens)
man	men (not mens)
mouse	mice
medium	media
foot	feet (not feets)
criterion	criteria

Some other nouns that name animals have the same singular and the plural form, such as these:

Singular	Plural
deer	deer
fish	fish (or fishes)
moose	moose

| EXERCISE 3 | Making Irregular Nouns Plural |

6. Edit
5. Revise
4. Write
3. Organize
2. Prewrite
1. Explore

Change the following singular nouns to plurals. Use a dictionary if you're uncertain.

1. woman _____

2. goose _____

3. louse _____

4. datum _____

5. tooth _____

6. person _____

Pronouns as Subjects

A **pronoun** takes the place of a noun. Like a noun, it can be singular or plural and can serve as the subject of a verb:

	Singular + verb		Plural + verb	
First person	I	run	we	run
Second person	you	run	you	run
Third person	he	*runs*	they	run
	she	*runs*		
	it	*runs*		

Notice that only the *third-person singular* pronouns (*he, she,* and *it*) require a verb ending in *-s*:

he
she } works, eats, itches, yawns, wiggles, giggles
it

| EXERCISE 4 | Writing Verbs with Pronoun Subjects |

6. Edit
5. Revise
4. Write
3. Organize
2. Prewrite
1. Explore

Look at the pronoun subject of each sentence. Then write the present-tense form of the verb in parentheses that agrees with the subject.

1. We (deserve) *deserve* _____ an award for talking to crazy Eddie.

2. She (wear) _____ the most attractive orange and red polka dot shoes.

3. They (own) _____ a lovely house in the suburbs of Antarctica.

4. He (scratch) _____ his ear with his salad fork.

5. It often (rain) _____ through my roof in the spring.

6. You (know) _____ how to charm people.

7. I always (write) _____ elegant and beautiful sentences in these exercises.

For Keeping Contractions Straight

You need to examine *to be* verbs carefully as you edit, for you can make two common errors when writing their contractions:

1. You might leave off the –'*s*, the –'*m*, or the –'*re*. Change, "*He* a good man," to "*He's* a good man."

2. You might confuse the contractions with sound-alike or look-alike words: *we're* with *were*, *you're* with *your*, *it's* with *its*, and *they're* with *their* or *there*.

✔ TIPS

For Remembering about Compound Subjects: The Rule of *And*

When two subjects are joined by *and*, the verb needs to be plural.

Subject *and* subject = verb without *–s*

Subjects Joined by *And*

Any combination of nouns and pronouns joined by *and* also makes a plural subject, which is called a **compound subject**. Note the following examples:

Subject	Verb without –s
a candle and a prayer	
Juan and I	*go, make, seem*
ice cream, cake, candy, and Alka Seltzer	

A compound subject, like a plural noun or pronoun, requires a plural verb.

Only the word *and* joins two subjects. *Or, nor,* and prepositions such as *with* or *in* do not make a subject compound:

The little old lady with seven dogs *is* a grandmother. (Only the woman is a grandmother—not the seven dogs.)

One in a million people *is talented* enough to play professional basketball. (Only one is talented enough—not a million.)

A roll of thunder or a flash of lightning *is* not a sure sign of rain. (*Or* signals a choice between the two subjects; it doesn't join them. The sentence means "a roll of thunder *is* not" or "a flash of lightning is not"—and the verb agrees with the second and last choice.)

Compare these three sentences:

Maria, along with her friend, *works* part-time on weekends. (Only Maria is the subject of this sentence.)

Maria and her friend work part-time on weekends. (*And* joins the two subjects of this sentence.)

Neither Maria nor her friend *works* full-time on weekends. (*Nor* signals a negative choice, and the verb agrees with the second and last choice.)

EXERCISE 5   *Writing Verbs after Compound Subjects*

6. Edit
5. Revise
4. Write
3. Organize
2. Prewrite
1. Explore

Decide whether the subject of the sentence is singular or plural. Then write the appropriate present-tense form of the verb supplied in parentheses.

1. The gold pen and the silver bullet (belong) _belong_____ to me.

2. That purple jacket and yellow tie (go) _____ together beautifully.

3. Five scoops of ice cream with only two bananas, nuts, and syrup (make)

   _____ a wonderful low-fat treat.

4. After sixty-two years of marriage, Mr. and Mrs. Wilson (look) _____ at

   each other with great affection—although they can't see too well.

5. The money in the safe, under the mattress, and on top of the refrigerator (seem)

   _____ to be mine.

6. The use of compound subjects (become) _____ quite easy to master with a little practice.

SPECIAL PRESENT-TENSE VERBS

The verbs *to be*, *to do*, and *to have* deserve special attention because they occur so often and take unusual forms. You need to know those forms well.

To Be

Collaborative Activity 1

Checking Agreement

Before the next meeting of your collaborative group, prepare five sentences with blanks for verbs. Make the subjects as varied as you can. In your group, exchange papers by passing them to the left, and fill in the blanks with appropriate present-tense verb forms. Discuss your answers.

To be (is, am, are) is the most common verb in the English language. It always precedes *–ing* words in verb phrases:

> I *am looking* for an honest man.
>
> Arnie *is looking* for a quick buck.

And it often serves as a linking verb:

> The photographs *are* beautiful.
>
> I *am* beautiful in all of them.

Here are the present-tense forms of *to be* and their **contractions** (that is, their shortened forms with apostrophes replacing omitted letters):

Subject	Verb	Contractions	Negative contractions
I	*am*	*I'm*	
he, she, it (or singular noun)	*is*	*he's, she's, it's*	*isn't*
we, you, they (or plural noun)	*are*	*we're, you're, they're*	*aren't*

EXERCISE 6	Writing To Be

6. Edit
5. Revise
4. Write
3. Organize
2. Prewrite
1. Explore

Write both the correct full form of the verb to be *and its contraction with an appropriate pronoun in each of these sentences.*

1. He *is* _____ (*he's* _____) talking to Mr. Williams.

2. I _____ (_____) intelligent, rich, and extremely modest.

3. School _____ (_____) a pleasure and a joy for me.

4. My dog _____ (_____) smarter than my brother.

5. We _____ (_____) happy to meet you.

6. You _____ (_____) in the right room.

7. They _____ (_____) going to be late.

EXERCISE 7   Correcting Errors with To Be

6. Edit
5. Revise
4. Write
3. Organize
2. Prewrite
1. Explore

Collaborative Activity 2

Discussing Your Editing

Compare your answers to Exercise 7 with the members of your collaborative group. Were any errors especially difficult to detect? Report your results to the whole class.

The following passage omits to be *in some sentences and substitutes sound-alike or look-alike words for the contractions of* to be. *Find these errors and write your corrections above the lines.*

More Facts About Leopards

(1) A leopard ^is the a very versatile hunter. (2) When its hunting in the grassland of Africa, the big cat kills adult impalas, wildebeests, kudus, waterbucks, and gazelles. (3) In the forest areas, there also small mammals such as hares, monkeys, and squirrels, as well as reptiles such as frogs and fish. (4) Its typical for a female leopard to give birth to one to three cubs. (5) There kept in isolated areas, like bushes or small caves. (6) Their much darker than adults, which are usually spotted. (7) Female Leopards very concerned mothers who leave their infants only when they. (8) When the cubs are about two years old, they leave their mother and go out on their own.

To Do

The verb *to do (do, does)* serves as a helping verb in most present-tense questions and negative statements:

> *Do* you play the guitar?
>
> He *doesn't* work on Sundays.

Here are the present-tense forms of *to do*:

Subject	Verb	Negative verb	Negative contractions
I, we, you, they	*do*	*do not*	*don't*
he, she, it	*does*	*does not*	*doesn't*

The negative forms of *do/does* create the most problems. Many people say and write, "He don't," instead of "He doesn't"—a common but very serious grammatical error. Remember that *does* is the correct form with *he, she,* or *it.*

If Your First Language Is Not English

When *do* is the helping verb in questions or negatives, it needs to agree with the subject. The main verb following *do* is the same form no matter what the subject.

Do you play . . .? You *don't* work.

Does he play . . .? He *doesn't* work.

EXERCISE 8   Writing Negative Statements with To Do

6. Edit
5. Revise
4. Write
3. Organize
2. Prewrite
1. Explore

Write the appropriate negative contraction of to do (doesn't *or* don't) *in each sentence. You'll first need to determine whether the subject is singular or plural.*

Facts about Lions

1. Lions may attack other animals, but they usually _don't_____ bother each other.

2. They're actually rather social animals. A lion _____ live alone but in a group of two to forty others called a pride.

3. However, one male rules the pride, and the rest of the animals certainly _____ share equal rights with him.

4. He is first in mating, and other lions _____ eat until he's had his portion.

5. Lionesses are chiefly responsible for hunting for food. The females

_____ receive this assignment because the male is lazy. Also, his

big mane is simply too easy for prey to recognize.

6. In the wild, a 350-pound lion will eat 45 pounds of food daily. However, a lion

_____ eat nearly as much in captivity—usually only 10 to 15 pounds

a day.

7. The biggest threat to lions _____ come from other animals; it comes

from human hunters and poachers.

To Have

You use *to have* as a simple verb:

> I *have* homework to do.
>
> In his self-portrait, the artist Vincent Van Gogh *has* only one ear.

And you use it as a helping verb:

> I *have worked* on my lab report for a week.
>
> Alfred *hasn't* ever *failed* an examination.

Here are its present-tense forms:

Subject	Verb	Contractions	Negative contractions
I, we, you, they	have	*I've, we've, you've*	*haven't*
		they've	or *don't have*
he, she, it	has	*he's, she's, it's*	*hasn't* or *doesn't have*

Don't confuse *have* and *has* with *had*—the past-tense form of the verb.

EXERCISE 9	Writing To Have

6. Edit
5. Revise
4. Write
3. Organize
2. Prewrite
1. Explore

Write the appropriate present-tense form of to have—*affirmative or negative—in each of the following sentences.*

Facts about Baboons

1. Baboons *have* _____ their homes in African forests and mountains.

2. A typical baboon colony _____ 40 to 50 members.

3. At night a baboon climbs up a tree or cliff, where it _____ a place to

sleep.

4. Baboons often travel as much as six miles from their spots, but they usually

_____ several sleeping spots within their territory.

5. Baboons (negative) _____ much protection from their predators,

especially leopards—and humans.

6. Therefore, each baboon _____ to be very careful.

7. If a predator approaches, the baboon (negative) _____ any time to lose as it runs to hide.

8. It _____ to climb a tree, but if there aren't any trees nearby, the male baboons will gather together, scream loudly to scare away their foes, and fight fiercely if necessary.

SPECIAL PROBLEMS WITH SUBJECT-VERB AGREEMENT

> "... Where order in variety we see, And where, though all things differ, we agree."
>
> —Poet Alexander Pope

Subject–verb agreement can be tricky with certain kinds of sentences or words. We'll examine those tricky situations in this section.

Questions

The subject normally comes before the verb in a sentence, alerting you to the form of the verb that follows. But in questions, the verb comes first. This can lead to errors in agreement, especially with plural subjects. Here's an example:

> *Incorrect:* Does Susan and Orlando want to go with us?

You may think that the verb agrees with *Susan,* the word that immediately follows. But then poor Orlando is left without a verb. The sentence needs to be rewritten:

> *Correct:* Do Susan and Orlando want to go with us?

As you edit, look closely at the subject following the verb in a question. Make sure they agree.

EXERCISE 10	Writing Verbs in Questions

6. Edit
5. Revise
4. Write
3. Organize
2. Prewrite
1. Explore

Fill in the proper present-tense form of to do *or* to be *in each of the following sentences.*

1. _____ Luis and Lulu practicing for the pizza eating contest?

2. _____ the seven children, three dogs, four cats, and a slightly confused goat too much to take care of?

3. _____ you love me now that I can dance?

4. _____ Mrs. Barry and Dr. Graip coming to the Orange Bowl?

5. _____ a woman with triplets have three times the fun?

6. _____ n't these sentences a pleasure to write?

✓ TIPS

For Trimming Sentences
See Chapter 16 for ways to eliminate *there is* and *there are* from sentences.

Sentences That Begin with *There*

Expressions that begin with *there* also place the verb before the subject. Use *there is* or *there are,* depending on the subject, or subjects, that follow. These sentences are correct:

> *There's a man* lying on our kitchen table.
>
> *There are two men* lying on our dining room table. [Not *there's two men . . .*]
>
> *There are no places* left for us to sleep on.

EXERCISE 11	Writing Verbs with There

Write the proper present-tense form of to be *in each sentence.*

6. Edit
5. Revise
4. Write
3. Organize
2. Prewrite
1. Explore

1. There <u>are</u> many people who want to win the lottery.

2. There _____ a band on that rickety old stage playing "Lean on Me."

3. There _____ two things that you need to know: be smart and be careful.

4. There _____ a football jersey, a can of deodorant, and a copy of *War and Peace* in the back seat of the car.

5. There _____ a few rules that no one can break.

6. There _____ no more sentences to complete in this exercise.

Collaborative Activity 3

Writing the Forms of *To Be*
Before the next meeting of your collaborative group, prepare six sentences—three questions and three statements beginning with *there.* Leave the verbs blank. Use a variety of singular and plural subjects. Then, in your group, exchange papers by passing them to the left and fill in the blanks with present-tense forms of *to be.* Discuss your answers.

Collective Nouns

A **collective noun** represents a collection of two or more persons, things, or ideas:

class	orchestra	Longman Publishers
committee	faculty	the French

Most collective nouns are singular:

> The *class is hearing* a lecture on economics.
>
> The *baseball team wins* most of its games.

A few collective nouns are always plural:

> The words *police, faculty,* and *staff:* The police patrol this area often.
>
> Team names that end in *–s:* The New York Giants actually play their games in New Jersey.
>
> All nationalities: The French are ecstatic about winning the World Cup.

EXERCISE 12	Writing Sentences with Collective Nouns

Write present-tense sentences in which the collective-noun subject agrees with the verb.

6. Edit
5. Revise
4. Write
3. Organize
2. Prewrite
1. Explore

1. The collaborative group usually reviews the material before moving <u>on to the next subject.</u>

2. My family _____

3. The New York Yankees _____

4. The police _____

5. The British _____

6. Wal-Mart_____

Indefinite Pronouns

Indefinite pronouns (pronouns that don't refer to a definite person, place, or thing) are always singular. There are four categories of indefinite pronouns:

Some	Every	Any	No
somebody	everybody	anybody	nobody
someone	everyone	anyone	no one
something	everything	anything	nothing

EXERCISE 13	Writing Sentences with Indefinite Pronouns

Complete each of the following sentences, using a present-tense verb.

1. Everybody *has a fielder's mitt, a pair of baseball cleats, a uniform, and Ace bandages.*

2. Someone _____

3. Anyone _____

4. Somebody _____

5. Nobody _____

6. There _____ no one who _____

Phrases Between the Subject and the Verb

A prepositional phrase sometimes comes between the subject and the verb. Don't let it confuse you. For example, which verbs should you use in the following sentences?

> The woman with seventeen children (need/needs) a little help.
>
> The shape and size of the ring (is/are) unusual.

Be sure you're not misled by nouns or pronouns in prepositional phrases. The choice of the correct form will be clear when you draw a line through the prepositional phrase:

> That woman ~~with seventeen children~~ needs a little help.
>
> The shape and size ~~of the ring~~ are unusual.

Check these troublesome prepositional phrases as you edit.

If Your First Language Is Not English

1. Except in a few unusual cases, **uncountable nouns** (*water, salt, homework, furniture,* and so on) are always singular. They cannot end in *–s,* and the verb that agrees with them should end in *–s.* Of course **countable nouns** (one chair or six chairs—and so on) can be singular or plural.

2. If you were educated in a British school system, be careful. British English tends to treat collective nouns as plurals: "Harrod's Department Store are having a sale." American English tends to treat collective nouns as singular: "Safeway is having a sale."

| EXERCISE 14 | Creating Correct Subject-Verb Agreement |

Cross out the prepositional phrase between the subject and the verb and then write the appropriate present-tense verb form.

1. The reason ~~for all the papers, cans, and other garbage in the park~~ (be)

   is _____ not difficult to determine.

2. A person with eleven cats (be) _____ not pussy-footing around.

3. The rules of this social club (do) _____ permit wiping watermelon

   juice from one's mouth with one's shirt tail.

4. The hard work of the engineers, drafters, contractors, and subcontractors (have)

   _____ all contributed to creating a beautiful new campus.

5. An enormous box of pizzas, french fries, garlic bread, onion rings, and nachos usu-

   ally (disappear) _____ about fifteen minutes after Mario and his

   friends see it.

6. The cause of most deaths from fires (be) _____ smoke inhalation.

Relative Clauses

In relative clauses, the pronouns *who, which,* and *that* relate to a word or words immediately before them. That means the verb in the relative clause has to agree with the same word or words:

> I want to introduce you to *the man who owns* this palace.
>
> Be sure to see *The Killers of Elephants, which* is playing at the Center Cinema.
>
> Please pick up the *banana peels, apple cores, and hamburger buns that are* rotting on your bedroom floor.

However, *whom, which,* or *that* can also function as the object in a relative clause. In this case, the the verb agrees with the subject of the relative clause:

>   O   S   V
> This is the 300-pound man *whom you are* about to wrestle. [That is, you are about to wrestle *him*.]
>
>   O   S   V
> You'll love the specialty of the house, *which Chef Alberto makes* from freshly cut grass and hay. [That is, Chef Alberto makes *it*.]

Collaborative Activity 4

Working on Agreement
Before the next meeting of your collaborative group, prepare eight sentences—two with collective nouns, two with indefinite pronouns, two with prepositional phrases after the subject, and two with relative clauses. Leave the verbs blank. In your group, exchange papers by passing them to the left, and fill in the blanks with present-tense verbs. Discuss your answers.

| EXERCISE 15 | Writing Verbs in Relative Clauses |

Complete each of the following sentences with a present-tense verb.

1. I want a car that *looks like a million dollars but costs about a thousand.*

2. Ludmilla is looking for a man who _____

3. These are my new friends, who _____

4. I need a dog that _____

5. Mrs. Vanderbucks has a new eight-carat diamond, which _____

_____

6. To eat Ralph's stew, you need a set of teeth that _____

_____

IN SUMMARY   Present-Tense Subject–Verb Agreement

1. Almost all plural nouns end in –s, but the verbs that agree with them do not; almost all singular nouns do not end in –s, but the verbs that agree with them do.
2. The pronouns *he*, *she*, and *it* and all singular nouns agree with verbs ending in –s.
3. All other subject pronouns (*I, we, you,* and *they*) and all plural nouns agree with verbs that do not end in –s.
4. All compound subjects (two or more subjects joined by *and*) are plural and agree with verbs that do not end in –s.

EDITING FOR MASTERY

Mastery Exercise 1

Correcting Noun and Verb Errors

The following passage contains fifteen errors in subject–verb agreement, noun plurals, missing verbs, and incorrect contractions with to be, excluding the first error, which has been corrected for you.

Some Facts about Cats

(1) Ever since the Egyptian^s made cats their pets 4,000 years ago, cats always been important to humans as rodent killers. (2) Today some cat still earn their living as rat exterminators, and a few others works in TV commercials. (3) However, the main job of cats these days are to be good companions—and kind owners—of their pet humans.

(4) A cat is very smart, but it don't learn the way a dog does. (5) Some tests of intelligence shows that the cat is brighter than a dog. (6) However, a cat won't allow itself to be trained. (7) As everyone know, a cat will obey its owner only when it's in the mood.

(8) There's thirty-six different breeds of cats, but all the breeds has basically the same physical make-up. (9) Their the only animals—other than camels and giraffes—that walks by moving their front and hind legs on one side, then the other. (10) And even though humans are fifteen times larger than cats, people have only 206 bones, while cats have 230.

(11) A cat is a very clean animal, and it have a strong sense of balance. (12) The cat's eyesight (especially at night) is its strongest sense, but a cat also hears well. (13) It's the only animal that purrs.

Collaborative Activity 5

Comparing and Discussing Answers

Appoint someone in the group to read the passage aloud so you can hear where errors occur. Correct the errors, discuss them in your group, and report your findings to the entire class.

(14) How much like people is the female cat and male cat? (15) A mother cat is tender to her young, but, unlike a person, she can give birth several times a year. (16) A tom cat (male cat) is like a rolling stone. (17) No matter how many kittens the mother has, he don't stick around to take care of them. (18) Maybe he's just too catty.

Scorecard: Number of Errors Found and Corrected _____

Mastery Exercise 2

Correcting Noun and Verb Errors

The following passage contains fifteen errors in subject–verb agreement, noun plurals, missing verbs, and incorrect contractions with to be, *excluding the first error, which has been corrected for you. Correct the remaining errors by writing above the lines.*

Animal Tricks and Traps

(1) Most animals are afraid of other creature^s^. (2) Therefore, many creatures protects themselves from attack by imitating frightening beasts. (3) As a result, their predators think twice before eating them. (4) Certain animals that lives in burrows (like some birds) has the ability to hiss like snakes. (5) A group of the hissing bees in the hive make a bear wonder if taking their honey is a good idea.

(6) Other animals scare their enemies. (7) Theirs a type of frog that shrieks so loudly that a predator drop it out of shock. (8) Texas horned lizards inflate themselves like balloon. (9) They also explodes the walls between sinuses and eye sockets, squirting out jets of blood from their eyes. (10) An animal that wants to eat the lizards don't find their appearance too appetizing.

(11) Many creatures fool their foes by changing shape. (12) A hawkmoth caterpillar can inflate one end of its body into a "snake head" that sway back and forth. (13) A peacock butterfly combine strategies. (14) When its threatened by a bird, the butterfly spreads its wing and exposes large spots that look like eyes. (15) At the same time, it hisses like a snake.

(16) On the other side of the coin is those animals that use tricks to get their prey. (17) A snapping turtle has a piece of flesh inside its mouth that look like a worm, which makes catching dinner easy. (18) One kind of insect called a praying mantis resembles the petals of an orchid, and insects that land on it get a big surprise. (19) And here a final— and rather disgusting trick. (20) Certain beetles look just like bird droppings; they attract flies, which expect a tasty snack but instead become one.

Scorecard: Number of Errors Found and Corrected _____

11 Using the Past Tense and the Past Participle

You often write about the past, especially if you discuss your own experiences—actions you've done, seen, or heard. In these cases, you use past tense verbs and their close relation, the past participle. These verb forms can be tricky, partly because they come in many varieties, and partly because they combine with other verbs in a variety of ways. This chapter will show you how to check all the verb forms as you edit. You'll learn about

- varieties of the past tense
- the verb forms to select in talking about the past
- other uses of these verb forms

THE PAST TENSE IN ITS USUAL FORMS

Like verbs in the present tense, past-tense verbs have a long history, and some of their forms changed over many centuries. Most verbs in the past tense share the original past-tense ending: *–ed.* However, more than one hundred verbs took irregular forms in ancient times, and they stubbornly refuse to give them up. We'll look at both regular and irregular forms in this chapter, starting with regular forms.

Regular Verbs

Here are some past-tense sentences:

Subject	Verb	
Ms. Miller	*sailed*	for Bora Bora in a canoe last week.
I	*collected*	my lottery winnings yesterday.
Jill	*tumbled*	down the hill after Jack.

UNIT 3	Go Electronic
Chapter 11	Use the following electronic supplements for additional practice with your writing: • For chapter-by-chapter summaries and exercises, visit the Writing with Confidence Companion Website at http://www.ablongman.com/meyers.
Writing with Confidence ©2003	• For work with the writing process, visit The Longman Writer's Warehouse at http://longmanwriterswarehouse.com (password needed). • For additional practice in grammar, use The Writer's ToolKit Plus CD-ROM.

Notice that each verb ends in –*ed*, no matter what its subject. As you probably know, most verbs form the **past tense** in this way. That means they are **regular verbs**:

walk + –ed = *walked*

seem + –ed = *seemed*

(or for verbs that already end in –*e*)

like + d = *liked*

smoke + d = *smoked*

EXERCISE 1   Identifying Past-Tense Verbs

Circle each verb and then identify its tense. Write Pr *for each present-tense verb and* P *for each past-tense verb.*

1. Harold bowled a perfect game. ____*P*____

2. I build houses in my spare time. _____

3. They talk for hours every day. _____

4. He stayed home. _____

5. The turtle burped. _____

6. The exercise ends with this sentence. _____

EXERCISE 2   Transforming Verb Tenses

6. Edit
5. Revise
4. Write
3. Organize
2. Prewrite
1. Explore

The following passage is written in the present tense. Change the passage to the past tense by writing the proper verb form above the line.

The Origins of the Wedding Cake

(1) Originally, the bride never ^*dined* dine on the wedding cake; the wedding guests ^*tossed* toss it at her. (2) Until the twentieth century, everyone expects children to come after marriage like night after day—and almost as often. (3) People in ancient times therefore shower the new bride with wheat, a symbol of fertility and wealth, while unmarried young women rush to pick up the grain to guarantee their own weddings. (4) Roman bakers later change the tradition. (5) Around 100 B.C. they start baking the wheat into small, sweet cakes—to be eaten, not thrown. (6) However, wedding guests continue to shower the bride with the cakes. (7) Then a new custom develops in which people crumble the wheat cakes over a bride's head. (8) And as a further guarantee of fertility, the couple consume some of the crumbs, a custom known as "eating together."

(9) The practice of eating the crumbs of small wedding cakes extends throughout Western Europe. (10) The English wash down the crumbs with a special ale. (11) They call the brew itself "bride's ale," which changes into the word "bridal." (12) The cake-eating custom also shifts during hard times in the early Middle Ages. (13) Wedding guests

bake plain biscuits to bring to the ceremony, and poor people receive the leftovers. (14) According to legend, another custom develops. (15) The guests pile the baked goods into one enormous heap. (16) The couple kiss each other over this mound of biscuits that often tumble down around them. (17) In the 1660s, a French chef visits London, watches this ceremony, and considers the practice uncivilized. (18) He therefore decides to transform the mountain of ordinary biscuits into a fancy cake with many layers and icing. (19) At first the British criticize this French creation but later adopt the practice as well.

EXERCISE 3	Writing Past-Tense Verbs

6. Edit
5. Revise
4. Write
3. Organize
2. Prewrite
1. Explore

Use one of the words in the following list to complete each of the following sentences with an appropriate past-tense verb. Don't use the same verb twice.

Verbs: play, watch, seem, behave, try, agree, share, look, feel, walk, miss, stagger, like

1. I _received_____ the award for the best-dressed student in the weight-lifting class.

2. Your son _____ like a perfect gentleman throughout the ceremony.

3. We _____ the train, so we _____ six miles home.

4. Ms. Fussfingers _____ on fourteen different pairs of socks before finding a pair she _____.

5. The glasses _____ very dirty.

6. Mr. Crier and Ms. Smiley _____ the same reactions.

7. Annie Dextrous _____ the violin, the drums, the bagpipes, and the kazoo all at the same time.

To Be

"To be or not to be, That is the question."

—William Shakespeare

The verb *to be* is irregular. In fact, it's the only past-tense verb that has subject–verb agreement. Remember that the subject of a sentence determines whether the verb is singular or plural. When the verb is *to be* and the tense is past, the verb forms must agree with their subjects. You'll need to master those forms because they occur so often.

Subject	Verb
singular nouns	
I	
he	
she	*was* or *wasn't*
it	
plural nouns	
we	
you	*were* or *weren't*
they	

Notice that the past tense of *to be* acts much like a present-tense verb. The verb takes an *–s* ending (*was*) to agree with *he, she, it,* and singular nouns, as well as with *I.*

EXERCISE 4	Writing To Be in the Past Tense

6. Edit
5. Revise
4. Write

✔ TIPS

For Hearing *–ed* **Endings**
Past-tense endings may be spelled *–ed*, but they often are difficult to hear because they're pronounced three ways:

-t When the last sound before the final *–ed* does not require the use of the vocal cords (sounds such as *s, ch, k, p, th, sh, f,* or *h*), the final *–ed* is pronounced like *t:*

	Pronounced
leaped	(leapt)
hiked	(hikt)
reached	(reacht)
raced	(ract)
wished	(wisht)
worked	(workt)

-d When the last sound before the final *–ed* requires the use of the vocal cords (sounds such as *b, g, m, n, r, v, w,* or *z*), the final *–ed* is pronounced like *d:*

	Pronounced
robbed	(robbd)
purred	(purrd)
begged	(beggd)
heaved	(heavd)
hummed	(hummd)
sewed	(sewd)

-ed When a *t* or *d* sound precedes the final *–ed*, the *–ed* is pronounced as a full syllable:

wanted	waited
pleaded	hated
needed	nodded

Write the appropriate past-tense form of to be *in each blank space.*

The Elvis Estate

1. The eighty-two-page inventory of Elvis Presley's estate, which _was_____ worth $10 million at the time of his death, _was_____ filled with information about his mansion, Graceland.

2. The house _____ piled high with statues of tigers, lions, elephants, dogs, birds, a ram, a whale, an eagle, and a dolphin.

3. In the garages and throughout the grounds _____ the many transportation vehicles of the King of Rock 'n' Roll.

4. There _____ two Stutz Blackhawks, which _____ worth at least $100,000 each.

5. His collection of other vehicles _____ quite a sight: a Ferrari, a Cadillac, an International Harvester Scout, a Jeep, a Ford Bronco, a custom-built Chevy pickup, three tractors, seven motorcycles, seven golf carts, three mobile homes, and six horses.

6. In the house itself, there _____ eighteen TV sets, including two seventeen-inch color sets in the ceiling above his nine-foot-square bed.

7. His wardrobe _____ rather simple.

8. There _____ a hundred pairs of pants, twenty-one capes, three cartons of shoes, and three jewel-studded vests.

9. Among his musical instruments _____ seven guitars; one _____ inlaid with his name in mother-of-pearl.

Could and *Would*

Can and *will* are verbs that frequently appear in your writing as you discuss the present or future. But you use them to discuss ideas in the past, too, although these verbs take different forms. The past tense of *can* is *could*, which discusses ability in the past. Compare these sentences:

You *can* kill a man, but you *can't* kill an idea.

—Myrlie Evers, after the death of her husband Medgar, the civil rights leader, in 1963

No one believed that the *Titanic could* sink.

The past tense of *will* is *would,* which refers to the future from a point in the past. Compare these sentences:

> Whether you like it or not, history is on our side. We *will* bury you.
> —Russian President Nikita Khrushchev speaking at the United Nations in 1956
>
> When you first met him, he appeared easygoing, full of humor, and nice talking. But if you stayed longer, you'd find he find he was merciless and *would* destroy anyone and anything blocking his ambition.
> —The doctor who treated former Chinese dictator Chairman Mao Zedong

As you edit your work, check for *can/could* and *will/would.* Have you used one verb form when you intended the other? If so, change the verb to the correct tense.

EXERCISE 5	Transforming Verb Tenses

6. Edit
5. Revise
4. Write
3. Organize
2. Prewrite
1. Explore

Rewrite the following sentences, changing their tense from present to past or vice versa.

Present tense

1. I know that I can pass the test on Friday.

2. He says that he will be late today.

3. _____ _____

Present tense

4. _____ today.

5. _____ _____

6. No one can answer my question.

Past tense

1. I _knew that I could_ _____ pass the test on Friday.

2. _____ the next day.

3. Bill wanted to know if he could borrow your car.

Past tense

4. His car wouldn't start yesterday.

5. Jeannette thought that she would graduate in two years.

6. _____ _____

THE PRESENT-PERFECT TENSE

> "Time present and time past
> Are both perhaps present in time future,
> And time future contained in the past."
> —Poet T.S. Eliot

Compare these two sentences:

> Igor lived in Transylvania in 1965.
> Igor has lived in Transylvania since 1965.

Put a check next to the sentence that tells you Igor still lives in Transylvania.

You should have identified the second sentence. It is an example of the **present-perfect tense,** which describes an action that began in the past but continues up to the present. You use this tense to relate the past to the present time.

Forming the Present-Perfect Tense

Circle the verbs in these present-perfect-tense sentences:

> Bruno Hamhands has played professional football since 1980.
> I have owned my collection of Porsches for quite a while.
> Ralph "Aroma" Reed hasn't bathed in a week.

You should have found two parts to the verb in each sentence: (1) the helping verb *has* or *have* and (2) a verb form called the **past participle**, which for regular verbs ends in *–ed,* just like the past-tense form. Notice that the helping verb—*has* or *have*—is present tense and changes to agree with its subject, but the past participle does not change:

> *has*
> or   } + past participle (verb ending in *–ed*) = present-perfect tense
> *have*

EXERCISE 6 | *Transforming Verb Tense*

6. Edit
5. Revise
4. Write
3. Organize
2. Prewrite
1. Explore

Change the following past-tense sentences into present-perfect-tense sentences.

1. You probably loved hamburgers all your life. *You have probably loved hamburgers all your life.*

2. They never consisted of ham. _____

3. They remained a part of American culture since 1900, when Louis Lassen invented them. _____

_____

4. They rested inside buns since the St. Louis Exposition in 1904. _____

_____

5. The original home of hamburgers, Louis Lunch in New Haven, Connecticut, served hamburgers until the present day. _____

_____

Using the Present-Perfect Tense

The present-perfect tense conveys two meanings:

1. To describe an action that began in the past but continues into the present.

Often such expressions include *since,* which signals the start of the action, or *for,* which signals the length of the action:

> Rome has been the capital of Italy only *since 1870.*
>
> California has prepared for a major earthquake *for many years.*

2. To describe an action in the indefinite past (without mentioning a specific time) that relates to the present.

When you discuss the past in relationship to the present, you usually use the present-perfect tense.

Present perfect	Present
Many people *have searched* for the Fountain of Youth,	but its location still *remains* a mystery.
The *Titanic has lain* at the bottom of the ocean since 1912,	and no one can raise its hull.

EXERCISE 7	Writing Verbs

6. Edit
5. Revise
4. Write
3. Organize
2. Prewrite
1. Explore

Supply the appropriate past-tense or present-perfect form of the verb in parentheses.

1. In the 1870s three men (inform) *informed*_____ a German named Jake Waltzer about a gold mine in a mountain that was sacred to the Apache Native Americans of Arizona.

2. Waltzer promptly (kill) _____ the men, taking the mine for himself.

3. He (protect) _____ its location until he died in 1891, leaving a map to his mistress, although she never found the mine.

4. Since then, people (call) _____ it the Lost Dutchman Mine after the "Dutchman" Waltzer.

5. For a century, at least 1,000 fortune hunters (search) _____ Arizona's Superstition Mountains looking for the sacred gold mine, but they (discover) _____ nothing.

6. To date, twenty people (die) _____ as a result of accidents or murders while seeking the gold, creating the legend that the Native Americans (curse) _____ all who might try to desecrate their mountain.

7. Others say that pygmies or an old prospector (guard) _____ the entrance to the mine, shooting anyone approaching it.

THE PAST-PERFECT TENSE

Compare these three sentences:

> Igor lived in Transylvania in 1965.
>
> Igor has lived in Transylvania since 1965.
>
> Igor had lived in Transylvania before 1965.

Put a check next to the sentence that means Igor took up residence in Transylvania before 1965.

You should have picked the third sentence. It's an example of the **past-perfect tense**, which we're about to examine.

Forming the Past-Perfect Tense

Like the present-perfect tense, the past-perfect tense is formed with a past participle and *had*, the past tense of *to have*.

> *had* + past participle = past-perfect tense

Using the Past-Perfect Tense

Unlike the present-perfect tense, the past-perfect tense is purely a *past tense*. It describes an action that occurred before a later time in the past:

Collaborative Activity 1

Switching Tenses
Write five sentences in the present tense. Then in your group, exchange papers by passing them to the left. Change each sentence into a past-tense sentence, then a present-perfect-tense sentence, and finally into a past-perfect-tense sentence. Discuss your answers.

earlier   later
Columbus had traveled to America before Amerigo Vespucci did.

later   earlier
A German geographer said that Vespucci *had arrived* first. So the geographer decided to call the New World *America*.

EXERCISE 8   Writing More Verbs

6. Edit
5. Revise
4. Write
3. Organize
2. Prewrite
1. Explore

In each of the following sentences, write the present-perfect tense or the past-perfect tense, using been *(the past participle of* to be).

1. Matthew *had been* _____ absent a lot, but then his attendance improved.

2. I _____ just _____ watching the basketball team.

3. We _____n't _____ home to see our parents this year.

4. Anna _____ active in three or four different clubs until she became ill.

5. Working and going to school this semester _____n't _____ easy.

IRREGULAR VERBS

 TIPS

For Keeping the Past-Perfect and Present-Perfect Tenses Straight

The present-perfect and the past-perfect tenses are similar, so they are easy to confuse. Remember these differences:

1. The present-perfect tense relates the past to the present. Its helping verbs are *has* and *have*.

2. The past-perfect tense relates an earlier past action to a more recent one. Its helping verb is *had*.

English is full of irregular verbs. More than one hundred verbs don't form their past tense or past participles by simply adding *–ed*. They're presented below in seven categories. You'll find you already know many of the verbs. But study all the categories and make a list of the verbs you don't know.

Category 1: *–D* to *–T*

In these verbs, the final *–d* in the present tense changes to *–t* in the past tense and past participle.

Present tense	Past tense	Past participle
bend	bent	bent
build	built	built
lend	lent	lent
send	sent	sent
spend	spent	spent

EXERCISE 9   Writing Irregular Verbs

6. Edit
5. Revise
4. Write
3. Organize
2. Prewrite
1. Explore

Write the proper past-tense or past-perfect tense of the verb in parentheses.

James Buchanan "Diamond Jim" Brady (1856–1917): The World's Greatest Eater

1. James Buchanan Brady (build) *built* _____ himself a reputation that no

one has ever (be) *been* _____ able to match: he (be)

_____ the greatest eater of all time.

2. Of course, Brady (spend) _____ huge sums of money in earning the

   title, for no one (can) _____ eat like him on a poor person's income.

3. Born to Irish working-class parents in New York, he first (work) _____

   as a baggage-handler at a railroad station. Then, a few years later, he accepted an

   offer to sell railroad equipment, and this job (send) _____ his for-

   tunes flying.

4. By putting together a series of multimillion-dollar railroad deals, he later (build)

   _____ up a large fortune.

Diamond Jim Brady

Category 2: –D and Possible Vowel Change

In these verbs, the final consonant becomes –*d*.
Some have no vowel change before the final consonant.

Present tense	Past tense	Past participle
have	had	had
make	made	made

However, some do have a vowel change before the final consonant.

Present tense	Past tense	Past participle
flee	fled	fled
hear	heard	heard

lay	laid	laid
pay	paid	paid
say	said	said
sell	sold	sold
tell	told	told

EXERCISE 10　　　　　*Writing Irregular Verbs*

6. Edit
5. Revise
4. Write
3. Organize
2. Prewrite
1. Explore

As in the previous exercise, write the proper past-tense or past-perfect tense of the verb in parentheses.

1. Jim Brady (make) *made* _____ millions of dollars when he (sell)

   sold _____ railroad equipment to major firms throughout the country.

2. He went on to use his wealth for a display of bad taste that no one (can)

   _____ ever challenge.

3. He (lay) _____ in a supply of two hundred custom-made suits and

   fifty silk hats.

4. He further decked himself out in a collection of jewelry that (have)

   _____ a net worth of at least $2 million.

5. For a single set of shirt studs, vest studs, and cuff links, Jim (pay)

   _____ $87,315.

6. People (say) _____ that his diamond rings (be) _____

   the biggest ever seen in New York, and among his more than thirty famous timepieces,

   he (have) _____ a single watch worth $17,500.

7. No one ever (hear) _____ Brady apologize for his flashy jewelry, and

   he took pride in his nickname, "Diamond Jim."

Category 3: –*T* and Possible Vowel Change

In these verbs, a final –*t* is added, and there is usually a vowel change before the final consonant.

Present tense	Past tense	Past participle
creep	crept	crept
feel	felt	felt
keep	kept	kept
leave	left	left
lose	lost	lost
mean	meant	meant
sleep	slept	slept
sweep	swept	swept

Some verbs show an additional vowel change and add –*ght* at the end of the word.

Present tense	Past tense	Past participle
bring	brought	brought
buy	bought	bought
catch	caught	caught
seek	sought	sought
teach	taught	taught
think	thought	thought

EXERCISE 11 | Writing Irregular Verbs

6. Edit
5. Revise
4. Write
3. Organize
2. Prewrite
1. Explore

Again, write the proper past-tense or past-perfect tense of the verb in parentheses.

1. Brady (leave) _left_____ none of his possessions alone but added expensive jewelry to them all.

2. He (keep) _____ twelve gold-plated bicycles with diamonds and rubies in the handlebars for his outings in Central Park.

3. For his girlfriend, the 200-pound singer Lillian Russell, Brady (buy) _____ a special bicycle with mother-of-pearl handlebars and emeralds and sapphires on the spokes of each wheel.

4. Every Sunday, Miss Russell (catch) _____ the attention of newspaper photographers when, dressed in white, she (bring) _____ this famous machine to the park for a ride.

5. However, although Diamond Jim liked women, he (feel) _____ his strongest passion for another matter: food.

6. It was in this endeavor that Brady's achievements reached such amazing heights, they (sweep) _____ away all competition for greatness.

7. The man never (lose) _____ an opportunity to eat, and stories of his accomplishments (teach) _____ the world what true dedication to a task really (mean) _____.

Lillian Russell

Category 4: Single Vowel Change

In these verbs, only the vowel changes, and the past tense and the past participle are the same.

Present tense	Past tense	Past participle
bind	bound	bound
bleed	bled	bled
breed	bred	bred
dig	dug	dug
feed	fed	fed
find	found	found
fight	fought	fought
grind	ground	ground
hang	hung	hung
hold	held	held
lead	led	led
meet	met	met
shine	shone (or shined)	shone
shoot	shot	shot
sit	sat	sat
slide	slid	slid
speed	sped	sped
spin	spun	spun
stand	stood	stood
stick	stuck	stuck
strike	struck	struck
swing	swung	swung
win	won	won
wind	wound	wound
wring	wrung	wrung

In a few cases, the past participle is the same as the present tense.

Present tense	Past tense	Past participle
become	became	become
come	came	come
run	ran	run

| EXERCISE 12 | Writing Irregular Verbs |

6. Edit
5. Revise
4. Write
3. Organize
2. Prewrite
1. Explore

Once again, write the proper past-tense or past-perfect tense of the verb in parentheses.

1. For a typical breakfast, Brady (feed) _fed_____ himself hominy grits, eggs, corn bread, muffins, flapjacks, chops, fried potatoes, a beefsteak, and a full gallon of orange juice.

2. This "golden nectar" (win) _____ Brady's love when he was younger, and he never (find) _____ any pleasure in drinking liquor.

3. Diamond Jim (become) _____ hungry during the midmorning, so this (lead) _____ to a little snack of two or three dozen clams and oysters.

4. He (sit) _____ down to a real lunch at 12:30, when he (swing) _____ into action by downing additional clams and oysters, a platter of boiled lobsters, three deviled crabs, a joint of beef, and several kinds of pie.

5. He (fight) _____ off his hunger until afternoon tea, when he (find) _____ time for a platter of seafood washed down with another of his favorite drinks, lemon soda.

6. After that, Jim (hold) _____ his appetite until the evening, when it (come) _____ time for his major meal of the day.

7. He often (wind) _____ up at Charlie Rector's—a fancy New York restaurant—where the owner bragged that Brady (be) _____ "the best twenty-five customers" he (have) _____.

8. Diamond Jim started the meal when he (slide) _____ two or three dozen Maryland oysters down his throat.

9. Crabs (come) _____ next—six of them—and then at least two bowls of green turtle soup.

10. Then Brady (dig) _____ into the main courses: six or seven lobsters, two whole ducks, two portions of turtle meat, a sirloin steak, and vegetables—followed by an entire platter of pastries for dessert.

11. As the meal (wind) _____ down, he usually (have) _____ a two-pound box of chocolate as an after-dinner treat.

12. Crowds of people (stand) _____ around the table to cheer on his progress—and to make bets on whether he (will) _____ drop dead before dessert.

Category 5: Double Vowel Change

In these verbs, the vowel changes in each form.

Present tense	Past tense	Past participle
begin	began	begun
drink	drank	drunk
ring	rang	rung
sink	sank (or sunk)	sunk
spring	sprang (or sprung)	sprung
swim	swam	swum

EXERCISE 13	Writing Irregular Verbs

6. Edit
5. Revise
4. Write
3. Organize
2. Prewrite
1. Explore

Once more, write the proper past-tense or past-perfect tense of the verb in parentheses.

1. Although Jim never (drink) _drank_____ any alcohol, his love for sweets

   (spring) _Sprang_____ as much from a desire for quality as for quantity.

2. For example, once when visiting Boston, Brady (hear) _____ about a

   local factory that (make) _____ fine chocolates.

3. He was impressed when sampling a five-pound box of bonbons, chocolate creams,

   and glazed walnuts. "Best darn candy I ever ate," his voice (ring)

   _____ out.

4. As he (begin) _____ to order several hundred boxes of candy for

   friends and acquaintances, he was told that the merchandise was in short supply.

5. "Heck," said Brady, taking out his checkbook, "tell them to build a candy factory with

   twice their capacity. Here's the money." The owner of the place nearly (sink)

   _____ to his knees when Brady (hand) _____ him a

   check for $150,000 to be paid back in candy.

Category 6: No Change

These verbs end in *–t* or *–d* and do not change for the past tense or the past participle.

Present tense	Past tense	Past participle
bet	bet	bet
burst	burst	burst
cast	cast	cast
cut	cut	cut
fit	fit (or fitted)	fit (or fitted)
hit	hit	hit
hurt	hurt	hurt

Continued

let	let	let
put	put	put
quit	quit	quit
read	read	read (the sound changes to "red")
rid	rid	rid
set	set	set
shed	shed	shed
shut	shut	shut
slit	slit	slit
spread	spread	spread
thrust	thrust	thrust

EXERCISE 14   Writing Irregular Verbs

6. Edit
5. Revise
4. Write
3. Organize
2. Prewrite
1. Explore

You know the drill. Write the proper past-tense or past-perfect tense of the verb in parentheses.

1. Brady was at Rector's when a member of his party (burst) _burst_ _____ into

   praise for a special sauce for fish prepared from a secret recipe at a restaurant in Paris.

2. Jim (let) _____ Charlie Rector know that the owner (have)

   _____ to serve the dish at his restaurant or Brady (will)

   _____ take his business elsewhere.

3. The next day, Rector pulled his son George out of college and (put)

   _____ the young man on a boat to Paris.

4. Using an assumed name, the young Rector washed pots in the kitchen of the French

   restaurant until he (fit) _____ in well enough to learn the secret of the

   fabulous sauce.

5. After more than two years, George (quit) _____ the job in Paris and

   returned home.

6. As soon as George stepped off the boat, Brady (thrust) _____ him-

   self forward and demanded, "Have you got the sauce?"

7. That night, as Jim (cut) _____ into the last of his nine portions of fish,

   he (spread) _____ some sauce on a piece of bread and (shut)

   _____ his eyes in pleasure.

8. Going back to the kitchen to congratulate George, Brady (set) _____

   the record straight: "If you poured some of the sauce over a Turkish towel, I believe I

   (can) _____ eat all of it."

Category 7: –N or –EN and Possible Vowel Change

In these verbs, the past participle is formed by adding –n or –en. Sometimes there are vowel changes as well.

Learning Verbs

Make a list of the verbs in Categories 1 through 7 that you don't know. In your collaborative group, compile a single list and then quiz each other on the problem verbs.

✓ **TIPS**

For Checking Irregular Verbs

If you aren't sure you've used the correct past-tense or past-participle form of a verb, look it up in a dictionary. The entry appears in the present tense, and the past tense and past participle are listed after it. So, for example, if you want to see if *swum* is the correct past participle, look under *swim*. You'll find all of its forms:

swim vb./ **swam** / **swum** / **swimming**

Good spellers are often bad spellers who know how to use a dictionary.

Present tense	Past tense	Past participle
beat	beat	beaten
bite	bit	bitten
blow	blew	blown
break	broke	broken
choose	chose	chosen
do	did	done
draw	drew	drawn
drive	drove	driven
eat	ate	eaten
fall	fell	fallen
fly	flew	flown
forget	forgot	forgotten
forgive	forgave	forgiven
freeze	froze	frozen
get	got	gotten
give	gave	given
go	went	gone
grow	grew	grown
hide	hid	hidden
know	knew	known
lie	lay	lain
ride	rode	ridden
rise	rose	risen
see	saw	seen
shake	shook	shaken
slay	slew	slain
speak	spoke	spoken
steal	stole	stolen
strive	strove	striven
swear	swore	sworn
take	took	taken
tear	tore	torn

Continued

throw	threw	thrown
wake	woke	woken
wear	wore	worn
weave	wove	woven
write	wrote	written

EXERCISE 15 Writing Irregular Verbs

6. Edit
5. Revise
4. Write
3. Organize
2. Prewrite
1. Explore

One more time: write the proper past-tense or past-perfect tense of the verb in parentheses.

1. For years, the 250-pound Brady (go) ___went___ on defying the medical experts, who (give) *gave* ___ him only a short time to live if he (take) ___took___ such poor care of his health.

2. Every time a doctor (speak) ___ to him about changing his eating habits, Jim quickly (forget) ___ the advice.

3. However, when his fifty-seventh birthday (draw) ___ near, Diamond Jim (fall) ___ victim to serious stomach trouble.

4. Until then, Diamond Jim (beat) ___ the odds of dying young, but he now (know) ___ he (have) ___ to listen to the doctors.

5. Therefore, he (break) ___ his old habits, (swear) ___ off rich food, and never again (overeat) ___.

6. His body eventually (wear) ___ down, and five years later the stomach illness (take) ___ his life.

7. After doctors (do) ___ an autopsy of his body, they (write) ___ up their findings, revealing that, over the years, Brady's stomach (grow) ___ five times larger than a normal person's.

8. In his will, Jim (give) ___ much of his fortune to the James Brady Urological Clinic which he (begin) ___ at Johns Hopkins Hospital in Baltimore before his death.

Collaborative Activity 3

Changing Verb Forms

Before your next collaborative group meeting, write seven present-tense sentences, using one verb from each of the seven categories. In your group, exchange papers by passing them to the left. Turn each sentence into a past-tense sentence, a present-perfect-tense sentence, and a past-perfect-tense sentence. Then exchange papers again so the student on your left can check your work. Discuss your answers.

EXERCISE 16 Writing Sentences

Choose five past-tense forms of the verbs in Category 7 and write a sentence using each form. Then rewrite each of these sentences in the present-perfect tense, rewording the sentence if necessary.

OTHER USES OF THE PAST PARTICIPLE

The past participle has many uses for expressing ideas. In addition to serving as the main verb in the present-perfect and past-perfect tenses, the past participle can appear in a variety of other places.

In Three-Word Verb Phrases

Many three-word verb phrases contain *have* plus the past participle to speculate about the past:

TIPS

For Using *Have*

Remember this simple rule: when *have* is a helping verb, the main verb after it *must* be a past participle.

could, should, would + *have* + past participle

may, might, must, will + *have* + past participle

Helping verb	+	have	+	past participle
could		have		done
may		have		seen
should		have		gone
might		have		taken
must		have		been
would		have		thought

EXERCISE 17	Writing Verb Phrases

6. Edit
5. Revise
4. Write
3. Organize
2. Prewrite
1. Explore

Complete each of the following sentences, using have *and an appropriate past participle.*

1. I didn't do well on the examination. *I should have done better.*

2. Yesterday was a holiday, and we could _____

_____

3. If I had listened to your advice, I would _____

_____

4. Mr. Fong wasn't at work yesterday. He must _____

_____

5. I don't know if Dmitri wants to have lunch with us. He may _____

_____ already.

6. Many people thought that they saw a flying saucer, but they might _____

_____

In Expressions with *To Be*

In some instances, you use the past participle after a form of *to be*, as in the following example:

> This watch *was given* to me by my grandfather.

Notice that the sentence's subject, *the watch*, did nothing, for the grandfather did the giving. In other words, the subject is *passive;* it does not act but is acted upon.

This form of expression is therefore called the **passive voice**. The passive voice always takes this pattern:

> Subject + *to be* + past participle

Here are more examples of the passive-voice in three different tenses:

Present tense:	The awards *are* always *presented* by President Gray.
Future tense:	Your grades *will be mailed* to you.
Past tense:	My wallet *was stolen.*

The passive voice often sounds awkward, so don't overuse it. Use it only (1) when the action is more important than the person who performs it; or (2) when we don't know or care who performs the action. Otherwise, use the **active voice**, in which the subject performs the action:

Passive voice:	Three home runs were hit by Sosa. (This sounds awkward.)
Active voice:	Sosa hit three home runs. (This sounds much better.)

As an Adjective

Sometimes a past participle doesn't express an action. It functions instead as an adjective describing a noun. For example, a past participle often follows a linking verb (for example, *is, seem, become,* or *sound*) and describes the subject of the sentence:

Subject	Linking verb	Past participle
I	feel	*tired.*
The eggs	seem	*done.*
The blender	was	*broken.*

Write a word ending in –*ed* to describe the subject of the following sentence:

Yolanda looked _____ when she heard the news.

Did you write *surprised, startled, excited,* or *annoyed?* These words are past participles.

A past participle can also begin an adjective phrase that follows and describes a noun:

	phrase
A woman	*named Melinda* just asked to see you.
I've always liked books	*written by Hemingway.*

Finally, past participles can also be adjectives before nouns:

> A *frightened* dog hid under the table.
>
> He's a *well-known* actor.

Look carefully at the words before or after nouns when you edit. An incorrect past-participle form can be confusing and distracting, as in this sentence:

> There's a tire man resting on the couch.

Does the sentence say that the man sells tires or that the man is tired? It probably means the latter, but we can't be sure.

EXERCISE 18   Writing Sentences

6. Edit
5. Revise
4. Write
3. Organize
2. Prewrite
1. Explore

Using the verbs provided, write two sentences that imitate the pattern of each example. Each uses a past participle.

1. We *were amazed* at the skill of the hibachi cook.

   (impress) _I was impressed with the service at the restaurant._

   (annoy) _____

2. The Screaming Eagle ride is perfectly safe, so please *don't be frightened.*

   (scare) _____

   _____

   (bore) _____

   _____

3. I *am accustomed* to getting up at 5:00 A.M.

   (use) _____

   _____

   (commit)_____

   _____

4. He *seems interested* in our book group.

   (involve in) _____

   _____

   (impress with) _____

   _____

EXERCISE 19   Writing Past Participles

6. Edit
5. Revise
4. Write
3. Organize
2. Prewrite
1. Explore

Write an appropriate past participle in each of the following sentences.

1. He sells _____ cars.

2. Do you know a man _____ Harry Leggs?

3. The police caught the man selling _____ goods.

4. When Grubbs caught the ball, 60,000 _____ fans leaped to their feet.

5. Several players were hurt during the game: Lopez had a _____

   nose; Johnson suffered a _____ leg muscle; and Hansen limped off

   with a _____ ankle.

6. You will see the new dishes _____ on the table.

7. Try not to go to places _____ by too many tourists.

8. Don't taste food _____ by Thumbs Thompson.

IN SUMMARY	Past-Tense Verbs

1. Denote events that occurred before the present.
2. Normally end in *–ed* but include more than a hundred irregular forms.
3. Include *was/were* for *be* and *could/would* for *can/will*.

Past Participles

1. Normally end in *–ed* but include more than a hundred irregular forms—which may be different from the irregular past-tense forms.
2. Appear in perfect tenses, which discuss events that occurred prior to a later time. The present-perfect tense uses *have/has* as the helping verb; the past-perfect tense uses *had*.
3. Appear after *have* in three-word verbs beginning with *could, should, may, might*, etc., and that speculate about the past.
4. Appear after *be* in the passive voice, in which the subject receives the action and doesn't perform it.
5. Function as adjectives after linking verbs or before or after nouns.

EDITING FOR MASTERY

Mastery Exercise 1

Correcting Verb Errors

The following passage contains fifteen errors in past-tense and past-participle forms, excluding two examples that have been corrected for you.

The Fountain of Youth Industry

(1) Long before Walt Disney ^had ~~has~~ even thought of opening a park in Orlando, people ^were ~~was~~ paying to see Florida's longest-running tourist attraction: the Fountain of Youth. (2) Supposedly, Juan Ponce de Leon discover Florida while searching for the fountain back in 1512. (3) But that story was just a myth.

(4) In 1512, Ponce was out of work. (5) The king of Spain has removed him as governor of Puerto Rico. (6) As a consolation prize, the king let him explore new lands in exchange for 10 percent of all the gold he can find. (7) The king didn't mentioned anything about a fountain of youth, and neither did Ponce. (8) In fact, he was not the kind of guy who looked for magical fountains. (9) In earlier voyages, he had seeked gold and slaves and developed a reputation as a ruthless character.

(10) In 1535, a Spanish historian claimed without proof that Ponce had went looking for the fountain. (11) That story reappeared in 1868, when a historian said that Ponce

was searching for a fountain to restore youth to his aging body. (12) This was just a theory, but other historians accepted it, added details, and located the fountain in various areas in Florida.

(13) In 1870, a real-estate broker in St. Augustine, Florida, named a pond on his property Ponce de Leon Spring. (14) The attraction drew a few visitors who drank its water. (15) Then in 1908, Louella McConnell tolded an amazing story about her property in St. Augustine. (16) She seen a large stone cross Ponce de Leon had put under a tree to mark a fresh water spring. (17) She also produced a map of Ponce's from a box bury near the tree. (18) When other people challenged her evidence, the map became too faded to read. (19) Then McConnell began to act crazy. (20) She wrote about conspiracies to kill women, was arrested for firing a gun, and told the judge that a police officer was trying to feed her poison apples.

(21) Meanwhile, a millionaire name Henry Flagler was building fancy hotels in St. Augustine and encouraging his wealthy friends to visit. (22) They usually wandered over to see the Fountain of Youth, where McConnell charge admission and sold bottled water and postcards. (23) McConnell sold her land to a Massachusetts developer in 1919, but then changed her mind and sued. (24) Even though the developer won the suit, it give up its plans for the property.

(25) After McConnell's death in an automobile accident in 1923, the property eventually passed to Walter Fraser, who make the Fountain of Youth into a leading tourist attraction. (26) An early Christian cemetery was discover on the property in 1934, indicating that the first Spanish town in the New World was probably located there—but this had nothing to do with Ponce de Leon.

(27) Today, Fraser's son, John, runs the park. (28) It contains a fountain (where visitors can have a drink), a Native American burial site, and a gift shop.

Scorecard: Number of Errors Found and Corrected _____

Collaborative Activity 4

Comparing Answers

Appoint someone in your collaborative group to read the passage aloud so you can hear where errors occur. Make your corrections, discuss them in the group, and report your findings to the entire class.

Mastery Exercise 2

Correcting Verb Errors

The following passage contains fifteen errors in past-tense and past-participle verb forms, excluding one example that has been corrected for you. Write your corrections of these errors above the lines.

The Dolphin Pilot

(1) He was a fourteen-foot dolphin, who, for more than two decades, ^help *helped* steamships avoid being shipwrecked off New Zealand. (2) He was the first dolphin in

history whose life was protected by a special government law. (3) Pelorus Jack, name for Pelorus Sound, become famous in 1888 when he guided steamships through a six-mile stretch of rough, swirling water in Cook Strait, New Zealand. (4) He was love by both sailors and passengers who watched him playfully leaping above the waves toward their ships. (5) He will often scratch his back against the ship's hull and then swiftly glide out in front to guide a steamer along. (6) After getting one ship safely through, the dolphin would immediately leave to wait for another vessel.

(7) Passengers aboard ships described him as silvery white, with eyes that looked "almost human." (8) He always traveled alone and cutted through the waves with the greatest of ease. (9) When two ships needed his services at the same time, Pelorus Jack always choose the faster steamship.

(10) In 1903, a drunken sailor on the *SS Penguin* shooted at Pelorus Jack with a rifle. (11) Luckily, the shot missed. (12) Jack didn't showed up again for two weeks, but then he came back. (13) However, he never again accompanied the *Penguin,* which was wreck in 1909 in Cook Strait, killing seventy-five people. (14) In September 1904, the government of New Zealand passed a law to protect Pelorus Jack, for he had became an international celebrity. (15) A movie was make about him. (16) There was postcards that featured his picture. (17) There were many songs wrote about him. (18) A chocolate bar was named after him. (19) Sightseers, including Mark Twain, came great distances to see him, and when they seen him leaping toward them, someone would always shout, "Here comes Pelorus Jack!"

(20) In 1912, Pelorus Jack disappeared. (21) A local newspaper printed a tentative obituary, concluding, "If he is dead, more's the pity; if he has been slaughtered, more's the shame." (22) Pelorus Jack never appear again.

(23) Incidentally, no one will ever know, but he may have been a she.

Scorecard: Number of Errors Found and Corrected _____

12 Using Pronouns

The word *pronoun* literally means "for a noun," and **pronouns** are in fact substitutes for nouns. They're valuable substitutes, too. They help you avoid repetition, create unity, add emphasis, and combine sentences gracefully. You really couldn't write well without pronouns, so checking them as you edit is important. We'll take a look at a variety of ways to use them

- to replace nouns
- to make comparisons
- for clarity and unity
- for emphasis

SELECTING THE RIGHT PRONOUN

> "No word or phrase should be ambiguous."
>
> —Poet Robert Graves

Like nouns, pronouns serve a variety of functions in a sentence. Let's take a look at those pronouns and the functions they serve.

For Subjects and Objects

Unlike nouns, pronouns take different forms according to the role—or **case**—they fulfill in a sentence. For review, here are the subject-case and object-case pronouns:

First person	Subject	Object
singular	I	me
plural	we	us

Continued

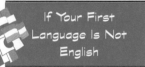

If Your First Language Is Not English

In many languages, the pronoun is included in the verb, but not in English. In Spanish, for example, the verb *está* means "it is." But English requires the pronoun.

Therefore, while editing your work, make sure you haven't omitted a pronoun in a clause and created a fragment.

Second person singular and plural	you	you
Third person (represents people or things) singular	he	him
	she	her
	it	it
plural	they	them

You probably realize that subject-case pronouns can only be subjects, but you might wish to review where object-case pronouns occur. Remember that **objects** follow verbs, words formed from verbs, or prepositions:

After verbs:	Tom helped *them.*
After –ing words:	I wrote to Ms. Sanchez before meeting *her.*
After infinitives:	You must memorize the multiplication tables to know *them* well.
After prepositions:	between *you* and *me,* from *him,* to *her*

In clauses with just one subject or object, choosing the right pronoun case is usually no problem. For example, the pronouns in these sentences are obviously in the wrong case:

> *Me* want a banana!
>
> Nancy talked to *I.*

But determining pronoun case is trickier in clauses with more than one subject or object:

> *Me and her* had a great time.
>
> People have been very kind to *my friend and I.*

The simplest way to determine the pronoun case to use in these clauses is to *remove all but one* subject or object for a moment:

Incorrect	Correct
Me . . . had a great time.	*I* . . . had a great time. [*My friend and I* had a great time.]
. . . very kind to . . . *I.*	. . . very kind to . . . *me.* [People have been very kind to *my friend and me.*]

Choosing the correct pronoun case can also be confusing when *we* or *us* appears before a noun. Note these pronoun errors:

> Before the lake became polluted, *us kids* always swam in it.
>
> For *we folks,* nothing is too good.

Again, you can check the pronoun case by temporarily removing the noun:

Incorrect	Correct
. . . *us* . . . always swam in it.	*we* . . . always swam in it. [. . . *we kids* always swam in it.]
For *we* . . . , nothing is too good.	For *us* . . . , nothing is too good. [For *us folks,* nothing is too good.]

EXERCISE 1 | Using Correct Pronoun Case

Some, but not all, of the following sentences contain errors in pronoun case. Write the correct forms above the lines. If a sentence is already correct, make no further changes.

1. ^~~Her and me~~ She and I have always said that for ^~~she and I~~ her and me nothing is too good.

2. Can you keep a secret between you and I?

3. Only four other students and him scored above 90 on the test.

4. Our pet boa constrictor is very close to LaVelle and I.

5. Me and him shared a pizza, a milk shake, and a diet cream pie.

6. Just send your money orders to her and me, but make them out to "Cash."

7. Some people feel that them are the best kind.

In Comparisons

Choosing the right pronoun can be difficult when you make comparisons. Notice in the following comparisons that a subject pronoun and a verb come after *than* or *as*:

Harvey is a better swimmer *than I am.*

But I dive as well *as he does.*

You can often leave out the verbs, but you should keep the same subject pronouns:

Harvey is a better swimmer than *I (am).*

But I dive as well as *he (does).*

If you compare objects instead of subjects, an object pronoun follows *than* or *as*:

Ms. Blake treats him as well *as (she treats) me.*

Note carefully how the idea of this sentence changes if the pronoun is in the subject case.

Ms. Blake treats him as well as *I (do).*

Now *I* treat him well, but who knows how Ms. Blake treats *me!*

If the meaning of the comparison is unclear with words omitted, don't omit them.

Collaborative Activity 1

Comparing Your Comparisons

Write ten sentences using pronouns, but for each pronoun slot, offer three choices—one of which is right. Be sure to include some comparisons. In your group, exchange papers by passing them to the left and then select the correct pronouns. Pass your completed paper to the left again and let a third student check your answers. Discuss any difficulties or debatable choices.

EXERCISE 2   Combining Sentences to Make Comparisons

Write a sentence making a comparison based on the information provided. Use than *or* as *in the sentence.*

1. Guy is 200 pounds, but she is 112 pounds. *Guy is heavier than she (is).*

2. Gloria is very pretty. Her mother is also very pretty. _____

   _____

3. Sam works hard. We don't work too hard. _____

   _____

4. Mr. Williams has three part-time jobs. She has only one job. _____

   _____

5. The counselor talks to you quite often. She hardly ever talks to me. _____

   _____

6. Albert ate fourteen hamburgers for lunch. I ate two. _____

   _____

AVOIDING PRONOUN CONFUSION AND BIAS

Because a pronoun often replaces—or refers back to—a noun, your readers need to know which noun. The word or words a pronoun refers back to are called **antecedents.** Here are some examples of antecedents and the pronouns that go with them:

Antecedent	Pronoun	Possessive before noun	Possessive
the team	it	its game	its
a person	he or she; him or her	his or her book	his or hers
John and I	we	our car	ours
John and me	us	our car	ours
John and she	they	their party	theirs
John and her	them	their party	theirs

Agreement in Number

To be clear and consistent, pronouns should agree in **number** with their antecedents. That is, a singular pronoun must have a singular antecedent, and a plural pronoun must have a plural antecedent. The following sentence, for example, may be confusing because the antecedent and pronoun don't agree:

>   plural antecedent   singular pronoun
> I stay away from *drugs* because *it's* nothing but trouble.

Rewrite the sentence to avoid the confusion: _____

_____

 **TIPS**

For Distinguishing Between Contractions and Possessives
Whenever you aren't sure about using an apostrophe with a pronoun, look at the meaning you're trying to express. Remember

1. *possessives* don't use apostrophes: That is *your* hat. The dog hurt *its* leg.
2. *contractions* need apostrophes. *You're* in good shape. *It's* a nice day.

Did you change *it's* to *they're?* If not, note this carefully:

> *Singular:* one drug = it
>
> *Plural:*   drugs = they

But suppose a pronoun could have more than one antecedent. The pronoun's reference may be unclear. For example, what does *he* refer to in the following sentence?

> Roberto told his father that *he* had been wrong.

The answer can be either *Roberto* or *his father,* so the sentence needs to be revised. Here are two possibilities:

> Roberto told his father, "I was wrong."
>
> Roberto accused his father of being wrong.

And suppose a pronoun doesn't have an antecedent. Then the meaning of the pronoun may also be unclear. What does *he* refer to in this sentence?

> After I honked my horn at the cab that was blocking my way, *he* just honked back and refused to move.

The writer apparently means the *cab driver* but doesn't mention one, so the sentence needs to be revised to include the specific noun:

> . . . *the cab driver* just honked back and refused to move.

Here's a third common problem. In speaking, people sometimes use *they* or *we* without an antecedent:

> At work, *they* are receiving double-time pay.

Readers expect meanings to be more exact because you can't clear up their confusion. So the sentence needs to be revised:

> At work, *the employees* are receiving double-time pay.

EXERCISE 3 | Correcting Pronoun Agreement

Some—but not all—of the items contain an error in agreement between pronoun and antecedent. Circle the antecedent and underline the pronoun that refers to the antecedent. Then correct any errors you find.

1. The first bubble gum was invented by Frank Fleer in 1906, but ^it ~~they~~ never ^was ~~were~~ sold.

2. The gum was so sticky that only hard scrubbing with turpentine would remove them.

3. Fleer spent more than twenty years until they could fix the problem.

4. In 1928, stores everywhere began selling a "new, improved" gum named Dubble Bubble gum. They were pink because Fleer had only pink food coloring available in the factory.

5. None of the other penny candies could compete with Dubble Bubble, which outsold it all.

6. Other manufacturers copied Dubble Bubble, including its color.

7. Now pink bubble gum is everywhere; it's the industry's standard color.

EXERCISE 4 | Clarifying Sentences

6. Edit
5. Revise
4. Write
3. Organize
2. Prewrite
1. Explore

Insert nouns in place of pronouns whose antecedents are unclear or completely missing in the following sentences.

1. In the last twenty years, the microelectronics industry has made better and less expensive products. ^Companies ~~They~~ manufacture cellular phones, digital watches, computers, video games, CD-ROM players, DVD, and minidisc players.

2. Pocket calculators used to cost $50 to $100, but now they sell them for $5.

3. Nowadays they don't repair calculators and many watches; they just throw them away.

4. Twenty years ago, nobody would have thought that computers would be in so many homes, but they are so inexpensive now that many families own them.

5. The electronics industry is changing so fast that you have to wonder: What will they think of next?

EXERCISE 5 | Clarifying Sentences with Multiple Antecedents

6. Edit
5. Revise
4. Write
3. Organize
2. Prewrite
1. Explore

Pronouns in the following sentences can refer to more than one antecedent. Underline each problem pronoun and substitute a noun that will clarify the sentence's meaning.

Odds and Ends about Famous People

1. At the beginning of the century, George Eastman wanted to make inexpensive cameras for children. He called ^these cameras ~~them~~ Brownies and sold them for a dollar.

2. Six-shot rolls of film sold for fifteen cents, but Eastman made hardly any profit from the cameras. They were the real money makers.

3. Because the king of Bavaria from 1886 to 1913 liked to shoot poor people for sport, his attendants purposely deceived him. One attendant dressed as a peasant, and the other gave a rifle filled with blank bullets to the king. He then strolled into view and fell dead at the sound of a gunshot.

4. Hans Christian Andersen, the famous writer of fairy tales, was terrified that he would pass out and be found by a policeman. Then he would bury him alive.

5. Andersen almost always carried a note in his pocket telling anyone who might discover him unconscious that he must not assume that he was dead.

Collaborative Activity 2

Discussing Pronouns

Review your answers to Exercises 3, 4, and 5 in your collaborative group. Report areas of disagreement to the whole class and try to reach some conclusions on the best ways to avoid pronoun confusion.

6. King Charles II, the ruler of Great Britain from 1660 to 1685, sometimes took powder

from the mummies of Egyptian kings and, in hopes of acquiring "ancient greatness,"

would rub it on himself.

Pronouns Referring to Pronouns

Some pronouns don't refer to a specific person, place, or thing. So these are called **indefinite pronouns.** Here's a list of indefinite pronouns for people.

everyone	someone	each
everybody	somebody	every
anyone	no one	either
anybody	nobody	neither

All these indefinite pronouns are singular, so they present a special challenge. For example, which word (*their, his,* or *her*) should refer to *everyone* in the following sentence?

Everyone in the class has done _____ homework.

Did you answer *their?* This plural word is a common choice, but it creates some problems. Remember that *everyone* is grammatically singular (its verb is *does*), even though it seems like a plural.

Another choice for agreement with *everyone* might be *his.* It's certainly singular, but seems to leave the women out of the discussion. Of course, *his* works fine when an indefinite pronoun represents only males, and *her* would likewise be correct to represent females:

Everybody in the men's gym class has done *his* exercises.

Each of the women on the tennis team must practice *her* backhand.

As you can see, when an indefinite pronoun represents both sexes, there's no easy choice. Some people use *their,* but not in formal writing. Some people use *his* because they believe its meaning is neuter—neither male nor female—in this situation. Other people use *his or her,* as in "Everyone in the class has done his or her homework." Still others use the female pronoun, as in "Everyone in the class has done her homework." And others tend to rewrite the sentence with a plural subject:

All of the students in the class have done their homework.

This last solution is probably the best, but it won't work in every situation. As you revise, pay special attention to pronouns. If they suggest a sexual bias you don't intend, change them or rework the sentence until it says what you mean.

Pronouns Referring to Collective nouns

Like pronouns referring to pronouns, pronouns referring to collective nouns can give you trouble. A **collective noun**—a team, a band, an audience—represents a group of people or things, and almost all collective nouns are singular. Make sure the verb form you choose agrees in number.

TIPS

For Identifying Singular Indefinite Pronouns

Here's a handy way to remind yourself that indefinite pronouns are singular. Look at the root words that most contain—*one* and *body.* It's simple arithmetic: *one* = one and *a body* = one body. If you're writing in the present tense, look at the verb, which should also be singular:

Everybody *has* . . . , no one *does* . . . , someone *is* . . . , and so on.

TIPS

For Learning Subject-Verb Agreement

See Chapter 10 for more discussion of subject-verb agreement.

> The *class has* met for half the term.
> The *band* at the football game *is* loud but not very good.

And any pronouns you use should be singular, too.

> The *orchestra* reaches *its* greatest heights when Rudolfo Parachuti conducts *it*.
> The *team* has already won more games than *it* (not *they*) won all last year.

EXERCISE 6   Removing Sexual Bias

6. Edit
5. Revise
4. Write
3. Organize
2. Prewrite
1. Explore

Rewrite the sexually biased sentences by changing the male singular pronouns to plurals or use he *or* she, *or find another solution. Adjust the remainder of the sentence to reflect your changes. Replace pronouns with nouns, if necessary.*

1. It's a common superstition that when a person breaks a mirror, he will have seven years of bad luck. It's a common superstition that when people break mirrors, the people will have seven years of bad luck.

(Note that, for consistency, the word *mirror* also becomes plural.)

2. However, the belief goes back to a time before someone even had a glass mirror that he could break. _____

   _____

3. The superstition about bad luck started in the sixth century B.C., when a person would gaze at his image and see his future in a shallow glass bowl filled with water.

   _____

   _____

Collaborative Activity 3

Working with Pronouns
Write ten sentences—five with indefinite pronouns as subjects and five with collective nouns as subjects. Make the sentences complex enough to require pronouns that refer to the subjects, but leave the pronoun spaces blank. In your group, exchange papers by passing to the left, and then complete the sentences. Pay attention to case, number, and potential sexual bias. Exchange papers again by passing to the left, and correct—or entirely rewrite—any sentences that have problems. Discuss the problems and solutions in your group.

4. A "mirror seer" would predict the future from the reflection of anyone who held the bowl in his hands. _____

   _____

5. If someone dropped and broke the bowl, that meant he would soon die, and the gods were sparing him the view of his horrifying future. _____

   _____

   _____

6. The modern superstition developed in the first century, when the Romans began to use a bowl called a *miratorium.* A person could predict his future by looking at his reflection in it. _____

   _____

7. They believed that a person's health changed every seven years and that he could determine his condition from the mirror. _____

   _____

8. Thus, seven years of bad health and bad luck came to the man who broke a mirror.

   _____

   _____

EXERCISE 7	Writing Collective Nouns

6. Edit
5. Revise
4. Write
3. Organize
2. Prewrite
1. Explore

The subjects are supplied in these partial sentences. Complete each sentence, referring back to the subject with an appropriate pronoun.

1. The band *plays its best when Elvis Bernstein is the conductor.*

2. The jury _____

_____

3. A good department store _____

_____

4. The police _____

_____

5. The team _____

_____

6. The class _____

_____

SPECIAL PRONOUNS

Pronouns do more than simply replace nouns. They can emphasize your ideas and help you be specific. In this section, we'll look at three additional types of pronouns: reflexive pronouns, demonstrative pronouns, and relative pronouns.

Reflexive Pronouns

Sometimes the same person or thing is both the subject and the object in a sentence:

> *I* admired *myself* in the mirror.
>
> *He* loves *himself,* because nobody else does.

The object pronouns in these sentences are special kinds, called **reflexive pronouns**, because they reflect back to their subjects like mirrors. Here's a full list of these pronouns:

	Singular	Plural
First person	myself	ourselves
Second person	yourself	yourselves
Third person	himself (not hisself)	themselves (not theirselves)
	herself	
	itself	

Notice that the singular pronouns end in *–self,* while the plural pronouns end in *–selves.*

A reflexive pronoun can also repeat (but not replace) a subject or object for emphasis:

> Albert ate seven whole pizzas, but I *myself* had only three.

However, people sometimes incorrectly use reflexive pronouns as subjects, especially when a sentence contains more than one subject:

> *Incorrect:*   John and myself are grateful for your help.
>
> *Incorrect:*   . . . myself am grateful for your help.
>
> *Correct:*   *John and I* are grateful for your help.

Again, the best way to determine the correct case is to remove the other subjects or objects temporarily. The correct form will then be clear.

EXERCISE 8	Writing Reflexive Pronouns

6. Edit
5. Revise
4. Write
3. Organize
2. Prewrite
1. Explore

Write a pronoun in each sentence. Not every sentence requires a reflexive pronoun.

1. I like to carry on intelligent conversations with __myself_____.

2. Brian has taught _____ several languages just by listening to the student conversations between classes.

3. You folks should help _____ to some food.

4. We like to spend some time by _____ once in a while.

5. Shorty thinks very highly of _____.

6. Many students support _____ while going to school.

7. My brother, my sister, four cats, three dogs, and _____ still live at home.

Demonstrative Pronouns

The pronouns *this/that* and *these/those* actually make nouns more specific. They're called *demonstrative* words because they demonstrate what you're discussing. They serve as **demonstrative adjectives** before nouns (*this woman, that story, these women, those stories*) and as **demonstrative pronouns** by themselves (*this* is a nice place, but *that* is not).

Demonstratives have both singular and plural forms:

Singular	Plural
this	these
that	those

In general, use *this* or *these* to refer to things physically close and *that* or *those* to refer to things farther away—whether they're subjects or objects.

> *These cookies* (close by) look fresh, but *those* (over there) don't look as appetizing. So I'll take *this one*—and on second thought, I'll take *that* one, too.

✓ TIPS

For Handling Demonstratives

Don't use demonstratives pronouns as subjects of sentences. They almost never have clear antecedents.

EXERCISE 9 | Writing Sentences with Demonstratives

6. Edit
5. Revise
4. Write
3. Organize
2. Prewrite
1. Explore

Using the words supplied, write two sentences with demonstrative pronouns that imitate the pattern of each of the following sentences.

1. *These women* lost their handbags on the bus.

   (people) *These people found a young child in the park.*

   (gorillas) _____

2. Do you want any of *these desserts* to take home?

   (compact discs) _____

   (hundred-dollar bills) _____

3. I'll take some of *this pasta* and a little of *that sauce.*

   (rice/sushi) _____

   (fruit/vegetables) _____

Relative Pronouns

When you use **relative pronouns**, which begin relative clauses, to refer to people, there are two choices: *who* and *whom.* The first choice, *who* serves as the subject:

> relative clause
> Please return this snake to the person *who* lent it to you.

> relative clause
> The man *who* lent the snake to me took my skunk in exchange.

In formal writing, many people insist that *whom* serves as the object. But you can usually drop *whom* from a clause, unless the pronoun directly follows a preposition:

> object   subject   verb
> Mr. Slither was the man *(whom)* you borrowed the snake from.
>
> but
>
> preposition + object
> Mr. Slither was the man *from whom* you borrowed the snake.

Collaborative Activity 4

Writing Special Pronouns

Working in pairs in your collaborative group, write two sentences that need reflexive pronouns, two that need demonstrative words, and two each that need *who* or *whom*—but leave the pronoun spaces blank. Then present your sentences to the group and ask the members to supply the correct words. Be sure that everyone in the group agrees and understands. Report disagreements to the entire class.

EXERCISE 10 | Combining Sentences with Relative Pronouns

6. Edit
5. Revise
4. Write
3. Organize
2. Prewrite
1. Explore

Combine each pair of sentences into one sentence, using who, whom, *or no relative pronoun.*

1. The identity of the person is unknown. The person created the first bagel. *The identity of the person who created the first bagel is unknown.*

2. Somebody probably created the bagel by accident. The person dropped a piece of dough into hot water. _____

   _____

3. However, we do know the identity of the man. He first called a bagel a "bagel."

_____

_____

4. And, believe it or not, the person wasn't even Jewish! We give this person credit for

inventing the word. _____

_____

5. In 1683, the first coffeehouse in Vienna was opened by a Polish man. He introduced

a new bread called the *beugel*. _____

_____

6. Americans changed the name of the round bun to *bagel*. The foreign word was too

difficult for them to pronounce. (*Hint:* Begin the clause with *for* or *because*.)_____

_____

_____

IN SUMMARY   To Use Pronouns Correctly

1. Choose subject pronouns for subjects, object pronouns for objects.
2. Make sure pronouns agree with their antecedents.
3. Rewrite pronouns that do not refer to antecedents.
4. Rewrite pronouns that show sexual bias.
5. Use *this* and *that* before singular nouns, *these* and *those* before plural nouns.
6. Use *–self* for singular reflexive pronouns, *–selves* for plurals; do not use reflexive pronouns as subjects.
7. Use *who* as a subject, *whom* as an object.

EDITING FOR MASTERY

Mastery Exercise 1

Correcting Pronoun Errors

The following passage contains ten errors related to pronoun use, excluding the first error, which has been corrected as an example.

Thomas Alva Edison (1847–1931): An Unlikely Genius

themselves

(1) People all over the world find^ ~~themself~~ living better lives because of the inventions of one man, Thomas Alva Edison. (2) This man started three large laboratories where it invented and patented 1,097 different products—including the electric light bulb, the phonograph, and the motion picture camera and projector. (3) However, there never was a more unlikely genius.

(4) When Edison was in first grade, his teacher told him to drop out of school because he was hopelessly stupid. (5) Edison soon did leave school, and at the age of twelve he

was working full-time selling candy and newspapers on passenger trains. (6) Scarlet fever had already harmed his hearing, and when someone playfully lifted him by the ears, they made his hearing worse. (7) Although he didn't have much formal education, Edison began educating hisself by experimenting with new inventions. (8) Unfortunately, one of this experiments set a train on fire, and they fired him.

(9) Soon afterward, he saved the life of a stationmaster's son, and the stationmaster gave Edison a job as a telegraph operator. (10) His first invention, in 1868, was a business failure, but Edison soon quit his job as a telegraph operator and devoted his time to inventing. (11) In 1871, he built a machine shop in Newark, New Jersey, that eventually became the General Electric Company. (12) In the next few years, Western Union and Automatic Telegraph paid him $70,000 for the rights to inventions that his assistants and himself had perfected. (13) Soon another of his inventions—the phonograph—were earning him national fame. (14) Everyone was buying one for themselves. (15) With this sudden changes in his fortunes, Edison built another laboratory in Menlo Park, New Jersey. (16) There he invented most of his most important products, including the electric light bulb. (17) In Menlo Park, many more of Edison's dreams became reality—for he and the rest of the world.

Scorecard: Number of Errors Found and Corrected _____

Correcting Pronoun Errors

The following passage contains ten errors related to pronoun use, excluding the first error, which has been corrected as an example. Correct these errors by making your changes above the lines.

Edison's Electric Light

(1) For years, Edison never stopped working, until ^*he* ~~him~~ and his family finally took a vacation in the summer of 1878. (2) They traveled to Wyoming to view a total eclipse of the sun, but it was hardly relaxing. (3) He spent the entire time talking with a traveling companion about electrically generated light. (4) When Edison returned to his laboratory, they put aside all their other projects and began working on a practical and dependable light bulb.

(5) Edison needed money to pay for the project, so he went to New York. (6) There on Wall Street, an important conversation took place between he and the banker J. P. Morgan. (7) Edison told him that the company could produce a reliable electric light in six weeks. (8) As a result, Morgan talked other bankers into forming the Edison Electric Light Company. (9) They issued 3,000 shares, but they did not sell. (10) Therefore, to stimulate business, Edison lied to the newspapers, saying that they had already perfected the invention. (11) Everyone quickly bought stock for theirselves, and Morgan gave Edison $50,000 to conduct his research.

Mastery Exercise 2

(12) For the next year, Edison's five assistants and himself worked twenty hours a day. (13) One of the most difficult problems was that the filament (the part that glowed) inside the bulb always burned up or melted after only a few minutes. (14) Edison tried to solve it by putting the filament in a glass bulb and creating a vacuum inside of it. (15) They also tested a variety of materials as filaments, including several types of bamboo.

(16) Finally, Edison manufactured cotton threads, that were coated with carbon and used them as filaments. (17) This kinds of filaments worked, and Edison switched on his light bulb on October 21, 1879. (18) It glowed with a reddish light for over forty hours and quit only when Edison increased the voltage to test the filament's strength. (19) That small piece of thread in Menlo Park, New Jersey, turned night into day throughout the world.

Scorecard: Number of Errors Found and Corrected _____

13 Placing Modifiers

Modifiers—adjectives and adverbs—are important tools. They add variety, live-liness, and specific information to your writing. They're also versatile tools, for they can describe more than one idea in a sentence. They therefore need to be placed correctly, next to the idea you want them to describe. This chapter will show you how to check your modifiers as you edit. It explains

- how to identify modifiers
- how to know where they belong
- how to avoid misplacing or misusing them

WHAT ARE MODIFIERS?

A **modifier** is a descriptive word, phrase, or clause that makes another word or phrase specific. In a sense, a modifier sets limits. For example, the modifier *same* before *thing* in the quotation from *Alice's Adventures in Wonderland* on page 162 rules out any other *thing*. And the modifier *hastily* before *replied* in the same se-lection rules out replying at any other speed.

Modifiers can be **adjectives,** which describe nouns. Adjectives also can be placed in a variety of positions. Single-word adjectives precede nouns such as *vase:*

a *large* vase

an *interesting red* vase

UNIT 3	Go Electronic
Chapter 13	Use the following electronic supplements for additional practice with your writing: • For chapter-by-chapter summaries and exercises, visit the Writing with Confidence Companion Website at http://www.ablongman.com/meyers. • For work with the writing process, visit The Longman Writer's Warehouse at http://longmanwriterswarehouse.com (password needed).
Writing with Confidence ©2003	• For additional practice in grammar, use The Writer's ToolKit Plus CD-ROM.

> "Then you should say what you mean," the March Hare went on. "I do," Alice hastily replied; "at least—at least I mean what I say—that's the same thing, you know."
>
> "Not the same thing a bit!" said the Hatter. "Why, you might just as well say that 'I see what I eat' is the same thing as 'I eat what I see'!"
>
> —Lewis Carroll, *Alice's Adventures in Wonderland*

Adjective phrases come after a noun:

> a vase *with red flowers*
>
> a vase *broken into many pieces*
>
> a vase *sitting on the table*
>
> a vase *to hold the roses*

Or, as you may recall from Chapter 8, adjective (or relative) clauses also follow a noun:

> a vase *that we received as a wedding present*
>
> a vase, *which holds a great many flowers,*

Modifiers can also be **adverbs**. They describe verbs or words formed from verbs, such as *–ing* words or past participles, explaining *when, where, why, how,* or *how often* an action occurs or occurred. Like adjectives, they can appear in many places. For example, single-word adverbs, which usually end in *–ly*, can come before or follow a verb:

> I ran *quickly*.
>
> I ran *quickly today*.
>
> *Today*, I ran *quickly*.

Adverb phrases can also come before or can follow a verb:

> I ran *for thirty minutes*.
>
> I ran *accompanied by my friend Juanita*.
>
> *Trying to build up my endurance*, I ran *for thirty minutes*.
>
> I ran *to try to build up my endurance*.

And so can adverb clauses:

> *Because I wanted to build up my endurance*, I ran *three times a week*.
>
> I ran *before I had eaten breakfast*.

Notice that adjective and adverb phrases are a lot alike. Both types can begin with any of these:

- a preposition (*with* red flowers, *for* thirty minutes)
- an *–ing* word (*sitting* on the table, *trying* to build up my endurance)
- a past participle (*broken* into many pieces, *accompanied* by my friend Juanita), or
- an infinitive (*to hold* the roses, *to try to build* up my endurance)

Notice, too, that adjective clauses can begin with words such as *that, which, who,* or *whose*, while adverb clauses begin with such words as *before, if,* and *because*.

EXERCISE 1	Writing Adjectives and Adverbs

Change the adjectives in the left-hand column into adverbs in the right-hand column.

1. The train is slow.   **1.** The train moves _slowly_.

2. The motor sounds quiet.   **2.** The motor runs _____.

6. Edit
5. Revise
4. Write
3. Organize
2. Prewrite
1. Explore

3. The sea looks peaceful.

4. The towels are very neat.

5. She has bad eyesight.

6. The band is very loud.

3. The waves roll in _____.

4. The towels are folded _____.

5. She sees _____.

6. The band plays _____.

EXERCISE 2   Identifying Prepositional Modifiers

Underline each prepositional phrase and draw an arrow to the word(s) the phrase describes.

John Chapman (1774–1845): Johnny Appleseed

1. Young John Chapman had a lifelong love for <u>flowering plants and trees</u>—especially apple trees.

2. Chapman planted apple seeds throughout the Midwest, and he walked barefoot through his orchards.

3. This man in simple clothes was also deeply religious, so he preached from the Bible as he traveled.

4. He supposedly wore a tin pan on his head for protection against sun and rain and for use as a cooking pot.

5. Settlers on the frontier began calling him Johnny Appleseed in a spirit of humor or ridicule.

6. Native Americans, however, respected Chapman for his ability to cure their illnesses with herbs.

7. He is buried today in Johnny Appleseed Park, near Fort Wayne, Indiana.

EXERCISE 3   Identifying -ing Modifiers

Underline the –ing phrase modifiers in each of these sentences and then draw an arrow to the word or phrase the modifiers describe.

1. Benjamin Franklin performed the first successful electrocution, <u>killing several chickens and a ten-pound turkey with electric shocks in 1773.</u>

2. Up until 1785 in New England, engaged couples wearing clothes could share the same bed if they were separated by a board.

3. Guests to the White House were often amazed to be greeted by President Thomas Jefferson wearing plain working clothes—a shabby brown coat, corduroy pants, and old slippers.

4. Dropping the *u's* in words like *colour* and *labour,* Noah Webster's *American Spelling Book* in 1783 "Americanized" the spelling of many English words.

5. In 1791, when carpenters in Philadelphia went on strike, they formed their own organization, offering their services for *25 percent less* than their employers had charged.

6. In 1821, Emma Hart Willard opened the Troy Female Seminary, the first institution in the United States offering a high school education for girls.

EXERCISE 4	Identifying Past-Participle and Infinitive Modifiers

Underline each past participle or infinitive and draw an arrow to the word or phrase it describes.

1. Many people believe that the Liberty Bell was rung for the first time on July 4, 1776, to celebrate the colonists' Declaration of Independence.

2. We also know that the bell has a long crack, caused by its ringing on that fateful day.

3. The cause of the crack is a wonderful story, but it's a myth, invented by writer George Lippard in his 1847 book, *Legends of the American Revolution.*

4. The actual bell was installed in 1753, twenty-two years before the American Revolution, and it rang many times to awaken people, call them to church, and so on.

5. Its nickname, "Liberty Bell," was coined in 1839 to refer to the hoped for end of slavery in America.

EXERCISE 5	Identifying Clause Modifiers

Collaborative Activity 1

Checking Your Answers
Review your answers to Exercises 1 through 5 in your collaborative group. Has everyone in the group determined the word or words each modifier describes? Which modifiers function as adjectives, describing nouns? Which function as adverbs, describing verbs, or words formed from verbs? Discuss your areas of disagreement with the entire class.

Underline each adjective clause and draw an arrow to the noun it describes.

1. "Yankee Doodle" is a Revolutionary War song that inspired General Washington's troops.

2. However, its composer was a British Army surgeon who wanted to make fun of the Americans.

3. Dr. Richard Shuckburgh, who wrote the first version of "Yankee Doodle," was camped with some British and American troops during the French and Indian War.

4. The Americans, who wore all sorts of clothes but no uniforms, looked sloppy compared to the uniformed British troops.

5. Shuckburgh wrote a crude song that made fun of the colonials' appearance.

6. The song insulted the Americans, who decided to change its lyrics and make it their own defiant song.

PLACING MODIFIERS CORRECTLY

Although modifiers can appear in many positions, that doesn't mean their placement is unimportant. It's very important.

Misplaced Modifiers

A misplaced modifier can't do its job. Notice, for example, how the meaning of the following sentence changes when you move the word *only:*

> I *only* want to give Biggie Schnozzle a nose job.
>
> *Only* I want to give Biggie Schnozzle a nose job.
>
> I want *only* to give Biggie Schnozzle a nose job.
>
> I want to give *only* Biggie Schnozzle a nose job.
>
> I want to give Biggie Schnozzle *only* a nose job.

Because so many meanings are possible, you must place *only* exactly where it expresses the right meaning. It usually—but not always—belongs directly before or after the word it describes.

Placing longer modifiers also affects meanings. Look at how incorrectly placed modifiers say something different from what you might mean.

> *Poor:*   The passengers were safe from the sharks in the boat. (What were the sharks doing in the boat?)
>
> *Better:* The passengers in the boat were safe from the sharks.
>
> *Poor:*   Ralph gave a puppy to his girlfriend with brown spots and white whiskers. (What did Ralph give to his other girlfriend, who doesn't have these skin problems?)
>
> *Better:* Ralph gave his girlfriend a puppy with brown spots and white whiskers.

EXERCISE 6 | Placing Modifiers Correctly

6. Edit
5. Revise
4. Write
3. Organize
2. Prewrite
1. Explore

Indicate where each modifier most logically belongs in the following sentences by drawing an arrow to that location.

The Real Uncle Sam

1. (modifier) in striped pants and top hat

(sentence) The man who symbolizes the United States Government is based on a meat packer and politician from upstate New York who came to be known as Uncle Sam.

2. (modifier) now known as Arlington

(sentence) Uncle Sam was Samuel Wilson, who was born in Massachusetts, on September 13, 1766, in the town of Menotomy.

3. (modifier) at the age of eight

(sentence) Sam Wilson served as a drummer boy and was on duty the April morning in 1775 when Paul Revere made his famous ride.

4. (modifier) by banging the drum at the sight of the redcoats

(sentence) In fact, young Sam alerted local patriots, who prevented the British from entering Menotomy.

5. (modifier) with the Treaty of Paris in 1783

(sentence) After independence had finally been settled, Sam moved to Troy, New York, and opened a meat-packing company.

Collaborative Activity 2

Composing Sentences

Rewrite the following sentences, attaching as many modifiers as you can—prepositional phrases, gerund phrases, past participles, infinitives, relative clauses, and *before/if/because* clauses.

> The cowboy rode his horse.
>
> The woman twirled her lasso.

Then share your sentences with your collaborative group members, who may suggest ways to place the modifiers more effectively.

6. (modifier) with great affection

(sentence) People in the town called him Uncle Sam because of his cheerful manner and complete honesty.

7. (modifier) which was also fought against Britain

(sentence) Another war caused Sam Wilson's nickname to be heard around the world.

8. (modifier) stamped with the abbreviation "U.S." for "United States"

(sentence) During the War of 1812, Sam Wilson won a military contract to provide beef and pork to soldiers.

9. (modifier) when asked by government inspectors what the "U.S." stood for

(sentence) One day, a meat packer joked that it represented the initials of his employer, Uncle Sam.

EXERCISE 7 Eliminating Misplaced Modifiers

6. Edit
5. Revise
4. Write
3. Organize
2. Prewrite
1. Explore

Each of the following sentences contains a misplaced modifying phrase or clause. Underline the problem phrase, and then draw an arrow to the spot where it belongs.

1. The second president of the United States, <u>after living to be ninety,</u> John Adams, died at home in his Braintree, Massachusetts.

2. This lifelong hypochondriac lived longer than any other president, who always feared an early death.

3. Adams complained to everyone at the age of thirty-five that his health was poor.

4. During the eighty-ninth year of his life, his son John Quincy Adams's inauguration as our sixth president gave John Adams great pleasure.

5. Ironically, John Adams died on the fiftieth anniversary of the signing of the Declaration of Independence, which he helped write at 6:00 in the evening.

6. Earlier that same day, July 4, 1826, the other author of the Declaration of Independence, Thomas Jefferson, unknown to Adams, had died.

✓ **TIPS**

For Testing Modifier Placement

If a sentence starts with an *-ing* word, examine it carefully. Draw an arrow from the *-ing* word to the subject. If the *-ing* word does not express an action that the subject performs, then the *-ing* word is probably dangling or misplaced. Rewrite the sentence.

Dangling Modifiers

Sometimes a modifier describes nothing at all. It dangles unattached because the word it should describe is not in the sentence:

Walking down the street on a windy day, my hat blew off. (Who was walking down the street? It wasn't your hat—which is the only noun the phrase could describe in this sentence.)

Talking to Mr. Smith, he said that the problem was serious. (Who talked to Mr. Smith? The sentence suggests that he talked to himself.)

Since the modifier doesn't describe anything in the sentence, moving a dangling modifier won't eliminate the problem. Instead, you must rewrite the sentence and add the word the modifier describes:

> *As I was walking down the street on a windy day,* my hat blew off.
>
> Mr. Smith *told me* that the problem was serious.

EXERCISE 8	Eliminating Dangling Modifiers

6. Edit
5. Revise
4. Write
3. Organize
2. Prewrite
1. Explore

Each of the following sentences contains a dangling modifier. Underline the problem phrase and then rewrite the sentence. If necessary, you may change a phrase to a dependent clause.

More Facts About John Adams

1. After graduating from Harvard University at the age of nineteen, a job of teaching at a school became available. <u>After John Adams had graduated from Harvard University at the age of nineteen, a job of teaching at a school became available to him.</u>

2. After teaching for a few years, his parents thought that a career as a minister would be more appealing. _____

3. Unhappy with both teaching and the clergy, the law became his true love.

   _____

   _____

4. With a sharp mind and total honesty, the law practice became very successful.

   _____

   _____

5. His reputation could have been damaged by defending the British soldiers who shot some Massachusetts citizens in the Boston Massacre. _____

   _____

6. By proving that the British soldiers had fired in self-defense, the citizens of Boston greatly respected his courage and integrity. _____

   _____

EXERCISE 9	Combining Sentences

6. Edit
5. Revise
4. Write
3. Organize
2. Prewrite
1. Explore

*Combine each of the following groups of sentences, changing full clauses into modifying phrases. Use both coordinating conjunctions (*for, and, nor, but, or, yet, so*), and subordinating conjunctions (*although, because, when, after, and so on) as needed. Check your combined sentences for misplaced or dangling modifiers.*

1. Noah Webster saw something.

   There was a need.

   The need was for a dictionary.

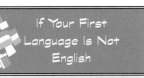

**If Your First
Language Is Not
English**

1. Word order is crucial to meaning in English. But many other languages use a different word order than English uses. In Spanish, for example, an object often comes *before* a verb, while in English an object always comes *after* a verb. This verb–object combination usually cannot be separated by a modifier. Compare these sentences:

   Incorrect: I found in my book the answer.

   Correct: I found the answer in my book.

2. A similar problem occurs when two objects follow a verb. The first object receives the action of the verb and the second (in a prepositional phrase) receives the first object. The prepositional phrase cannot separate the verb from its object:

   Incorrect: Tom lent   to me   the book.

   Correct: Tom lent   the book   to me.

The dictionary was for the American language.

He saw this need for a long time.

Then he began working on one.

Noah Webster saw the need for a dictionary of the American language long before he began working on one.

_____

2. He began his work.

Americans were independent of the British.

English-language dictionaries ignored American words.

The dictionaries used English spellings.

The dictionaries used English pronunciations.

There were very few exceptions.

_____

_____

3. He was a brilliant young man.

He was also very patriotic.

He was sure of something.

A national language would unify the country.

He began his research.

He started in 1803.

_____

_____

4. Webster put in a great deal of effort.

He worked for three years.

He published *A Compendious Dictionary of the American Language.*

_____

_____

5. Webster then began to work again.

He worked on a dictionary.

It was much longer.

He finished his work.

It was two decades later.

_____

_____

6. He published the *American Dictionary of the English Language.*

The year was 1828.

The dictionary was in two volumes.

It had 70,000 words.

_____

_____

7. Webster died.

He died in 1843.

George and Charles Merriam bought something.

It was the rights to Webster's dictionary.

_____

_____

8. They continued his work.

They updated his work.

They did these things over many years.

They published *The Merriam-Webster Unabridged Dictionary.*

They published *The First International Dictionary.*

They published *The First Collegiate Dictionary.*

_____

_____

Collaborative Activity 3

Playing with Modifiers

Before the next meeting of your collaborative group, write three sentences that deliberately contain misplaced or dangling modifiers. (It's hard to do!) Then exchange papers in your group by passing to the left. Rewrite the sentences to correct the problems. Exchange papers to the left again so a third student can check your work. Discuss any problem sentences with the whole group.

IN SUMMARY   To Eliminate Misplaced or Dangling Modifiers

1. Locate each modifier: adjectives, adverbs, prepositional phrases, *–ing* phrases, past participles, infinitives, relative clauses, and adverb clauses.
2. See if the modifier comes directly before or after the word or phrase it describes.
3. Move the modifier to another place in the sentence if necessary.
4. Rewrite the sentence entirely if necessary.

EDITING FOR MASTERY

Mastery Exercise 1

Eliminating Errors with Modifiers

Eight sentences in the following passage contain misplaced or dangling modifiers, aside from the first sentence, which has been corrected as an example. Find and revise the sentences with the errors.

More About Uncle Sam

1. At first, when thinking of Uncle Sam, only a name came to mind, until illustrations first appeared in New England newspapers in 1820. *At first when people thought of Uncle Sam, only a name came to their minds, until illustrations first appeared in New England newspapers in 1820.*

2. Wearing a solid black hat and topcoat, the first pictures of the old gent showed a man without a beard. _____

_____

_____

3. Because of the work of many illustrators over more than a century, today we recognize a familiar image of Uncle Sam. _____

_____

_____

4. The first pictures of him were introduced in a red hat in the 1830s. _____

_____

_____

5. The flowing beard appeared during Abraham Lincoln's presidency, which was inspired by the president's own chin whiskers. _____ .

_____

_____

6. Uncle Sam was such a popular figure that cartoonists decided he should appear more patriotically dressed in the late nineteenth century. _____

_____

_____

7. His red pants were decorated with stripes, and his top hat with both stars and stripes, making him a sort of living American flag. _____

_____

_____

8. Pictures of a tall, thin man came from the pen of Thomas Nast, the famous cartoonist from the Civil War period, resembling the original Uncle Sam, Sam Wilson.

_____

_____

9. However, the most famous portrait of Uncle Sam was painted in this century by James Montgomery Flagg, the one most often reprinted and most widely recognized. _____

_____

_____

Collaborative Activity 4

Checking Your Answers
Appoint someone in your collaborative group to read the sentences aloud so you can hear where errors occur. Make your changes, discuss them in the group, and report your findings to the entire class.

10. With a serious face and a finger pointing directly at the viewer on World War I posters, this figure said, "I Want You for the U.S. Army." _____

_____

_____

11. The poster sold four million copies during the war, and more than half a million during the Second World War that showed Uncle Sam dressed in his full flag costume.

_____

_____

12. Flagg's Uncle Sam, however, is not a copy of Abraham Lincoln's face, but is a self-portrait of the artist, contrary to popular belief. _____

_____

_____

Scorecard: Number of Errors Found and Corrected _____

Mastery Exercise 2

Eliminating Errors with Modifiers

Eight sentences in the following passage contain misplaced or dangling modifiers, aside from the first sentence, which has been corrected as an example. Find and revise the sentences with the errors.

The Real Dr. Jekyll and Mr. Hyde

1. A real man named William Brodie, who lived in Edinburgh, Scotland, became the inspiration for the fictional Dr. Jekyll and Mr. Hyde between 1741 and 1788. *A real man named William Brodie, who lived in Edinburgh, Scotland, between 1741 and 1788, became the inspiration for the fictional Dr. Jekyll and Mr. Hyde.*

2. Robert Louis Stevenson wrote *The Strange Case of Dr. Jekyll and Mr. Hyde,* using Brodie as his model, in a three-day period in 1885. _____

_____

_____

3. Brodie inherited a large estate and a profitable business from his father, who then became a member of the town council. _____

_____

_____

4. However, at night Brodie was the opposite of a respectable citizen with a few beers in his belly. _____

_____

_____

5. He kept company with thieves and gamblers, and he supported two mistresses and their children. _____

_____

_____

6. After running up huge debts from gambling losses and supporting three households, money became an obsession for Brodie. _____

_____

_____

7. Hanging inside their doors on a hook, Brodie's shopkeeper friends usually left their keys. _____

_____

_____

8. He copied these keys and burglarized the shops, and several times he was almost caught by the police. _____

_____

_____

9. In July 1786, after several small break-ins, the plans for committing bigger robberies entered his thoughts. _____

_____

_____

10. He robbed several stores along with a gang of three convicts. _____

_____

_____

11. After one of his partners confessed to the police hoping to escape, Brodie left the city. _____

_____

_____

12. Found hiding in a cupboard in Amsterdam, the police brought him back to Scotland for trial, where he was convicted and hanged. _____

_____

_____

Scorecard: Number of Errors Found and Corrected _____

CHAPTER

14 Making Comparisons

Whenever you compare people or things, you use words like *taller, tallest,* or *more gracefully, most gracefully* to describe them. The forms of these expressions show the comparisons, but sometimes the forms can be tricky. This chapter will help you check for correct use of comparative forms as you edit. You'll examine

- ways to compare people and things that are alike
- ways to compare people and things that are different
- special forms of comparative words

COMPARING WITH ADJECTIVES AND ADVERBS

> "Learn, compare, collect the facts."
>
> —Psychologist Ivan Pavlov

One way to compare people or things is with **adjectives**. You'll recall that adjectives describe nouns, and that one-word adjectives usually go before the nouns they describe:

> a *silly* mistake
>
> a *delicious* cake

One-word adjectives may also come after linking verbs and describe the subjects of those verbs:

> Mr. Gottbucks is *generous.*
>
> Your plan to save the universe sounds *interesting.*

Another way to make comparisons is with **adverbs**, which, as the name suggests, usually describe verbs. One-word adverbs usually end in *–ly*.

> Bruno dresses *casually*.
>
> Professor Tedium talked *slowly*.

Adverbs can also describe adjectives or other adverbs, usually to explain *how much* or *how often*:

> a *really* cool day
>
> a *slightly* crooked nose
>
> Silvia Shout talks *very* loudly.

Now let's look at these adjectives and adverbs as they actually work in comparisons.

ADJECTIVE FORMS

There are several methods for making comparisons with adjectives: in their simple form, comparative form, or superlative form.

The Simple Form

In one type of comparison, you explain that two people or things are the same in some way. Here are two examples:

> Stubby is *as short as* Tina [is].
>
> Billy Bob is *as strong as* an ox [is].

Note that this type of comparison uses *as . . . as,* and the adjective shows up in its usual form.

For Distinguishing *Then* and *Than*

Don't confuse *than* after a comparative adjective with *then,* which means "at a later time." (First he asked her father's permission. *Then* he proposed to her.)

One way to remember the difference is to remember that *then* is like *when*—and both refer to time.

The Comparative Forms

When you want to explain that two people or things are different in some way, you can do so by adding *–er* to the end of an adjective, or by placing *more* or *less* before it. This is the **comparative form**. Here are some examples:

> Tomas is *smarter* than his dog [is].
>
> Walter is *thinner* than a cracker [is].
>
> My new Rolls Royce is *more expensive than* the last car I bought. The Honda was *less expensive*.

The following rules describe when to use *–er, more,* or *less*:

▶ **Add *–er* to one-syllable adjectives (or *–r* to adjectives ending in silent *e*).**

Simple	Comparative
bright	brighter
cute	cuter

If the adjective ends in a single vowel plus a consonant, you usually double the consonant before adding *–er*.

Simple	Comparative
thin	thinner
big	bigger

 Add *–er* to two-syllable adjectives ending in *–y:* or *–ow:*

Simple	Comparative
pretty	prettier
narrow	narrower

Place *more* before most other two-syllable adjectives and all adjectives of three or more syllables:

Simple	Comparative
awful	more awful
beautiful	more beautiful
interesting	more interesting

Place *less* before any adjective, no matter what its spelling or number of syllables:

less tall	less intelligent
less thin	less pretty

With every comparative form, you usually need to complete the statement with *than:*

After cleaning the basement, the barn, and the pig pen, Bill is dirtier *than a mud wrestler.*

EXERCISE 1	Writing Comparisons

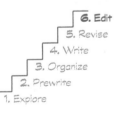

Fill in the correct form of each adjective in parentheses.

Some Notable Noses

1. Michelangelo was a (talented) _more talented_____ artist than a fighter. A fellow

artist broke Michelangelo's nose in a fist fight one day, and as a result, he had a (flat)

_____ nose than he had before.

2. The famous entertainer Jimmy Durante had a (profitable) _____

nose than any other person in show business. Durante's famous long-hooked nose

made him (recognizable) _____ and (rich) _____

than most other comedians.

Collaborative Activity 1

Looking at Comparative Forms

Collaborative Activity 1

Looking at Comparative Forms

In your collaborative group, list as many adjectives as you can think of. Aim for fifty. (Just think of words before these nouns: *person* and *car*—as in tall person, beautiful person, new car, and red car.) Then next to each adjective on your list, write the comparative form. Show which adjectives add –*er* and which need *more.*

3. The sixteenth-century Danish astronomer Tycho Brahe had a (shiny)

_____ nose than anyone else. He lost the tip of it in a sword fight

and replaced it with a gold one—probably a (expensive) _____ nose

than anyone else's.

4. Thomas Wedders, who worked in a circus in the eighteenth century, had a (long)

_____ nose than anyone else in recorded history. It measured 7 1/2

inches.

5. Albert Weber's nose was (useful) _____ than most people's noses.

He worked as an official smeller for the U.S. Food and Drug Administration.

6. Finally, a Czech composer named Josef Myslivecek had a (noticeable)

_____ problem with his nose than other people have. When his nose

became diseased, a doctor cut the nose off. That left him (healthy)

_____ but a lot (sad) _____

EXERCISE 2 | *Writing More Comparisons*

6. Edit
5. Revise
4. Write
3. Organize
2. Prewrite
1. Explore

If Your First Language Is Not English

Some languages form all comparatives in only one way: by adding a word. (For example, *mas* in Spanish means *more.*) But in English, you cannot use *more* and –*er* with the same adjective:

Incorrect: Bill is more bigger than I am.

Correct: Bill is *bigger* than I am.

Compose five statements based on the information provided:

	Egbert Egghead	Bruno Masher
height	5'6"	6'6"
weight	140 pounds	330 pounds
age	45 years old	23 years old
education	Ph.D.	B.A.
job	college professor	pro football player
income	$50,000 yearly	$6 million yearly

1. *Egbert Egghead is shorter than Bruno Masher.* _____ (or)

   Egbert Egghead is less tall than Bruno Masher. _____

2. _____

3. _____

4. _____

5. _____

The Superlative Forms

When you compare three or more things, you usually use the **superlative form** of adjectives:

Len Lanky is the *tallest* player on the basketball team.

Jarrett is the *most articulate* person I have ever heard.

These superlative forms differ from comparative forms in three ways: the –*er* ending becomes –*est* in the superlative, *more* becomes *(the) most,* and *less* becomes *the least.* Note that *the* usually appears before the adjective:

Collaborative Activity 2

Looking at Superlative Forms

Return to your list from Collaborative Activity 1 and write the superlative forms for each adjective in the third column.

Simple	Comparative	Superlative
long	longer	(the) longest
fat	fatter	(the) fattest
pretty	prettier	(the) prettiest
beautiful	more beautiful	(the) most beautiful
generous	less generous	(the) least generous

EXERCISE 3 Writing Superlatives

6. Edit
5. Revise
4. Write
3. Organize
2. Prewrite
1. Explore

Write the correct superlative form of the adjective in parentheses.

1. Most people agree that Michael Jordan is (great) _the greatest_ basketball player in history.

2. The city with (long) _____ name is probably Krung Thep Mahanakhon Borvorn Ratanakosin Mahintharayutthaya Mahadilok pop Noparatratchathani Burirom Udumratchanivetmahasathan Amornpiman Avatarnsathit Sakkathattiyavisnukarmprasit, which is the poetic, full name for the capital of Thailand. Foreigners call it Bangkok.

3. Probably (unusual) _____ painting in recent years was executed by John Banvard, who covered three miles of canvas with a view of 1,200 miles of the Mississippi shoreline.

4. (small) _____ country on earth is Vatican City, only 16 square miles in area, with a population of less than 1,000. It is located inside Rome, Italy.

5. (silly) _____ play ever performed is probably Samuel Beckett's "Breath," which lasts 30 seconds, has no actors, and contains no dialogue.

6. (large) _____ country in the world in population is the People's Republic of China.

EXERCISE 4 Writing Less and the Least

6. Edit
5. Revise
4. Write
3. Organize
2. Prewrite
1. Explore

Complete the following sentences, using less *or* the least.

1. Fred Fumbles is not very careful, but his brother is even _less careful_.

2. Professor Drab never gives a very interesting lecture, but today's was even _____ than it normally is.

3. Of all the artists in the world, Thumbs Thomas is probably _____.

4. I thought that *Halloween XXVII* was _____ than the first twenty-six movies.

5. Mrs. Twigg's older children hardly eat a thing, but little Tina eats even _____.

EXERCISE 5	Writing Statements of Comparison

6. Edit
5. Revise
4. Write
3. Organize
2. Prewrite
1. Explore

Compose a statement using a superlative form of an adjective to describe one of each group in parentheses.

1. (three fish) _The salmon is the largest of the three fish._

2. (three clowns) _____

3. (three birds) _____

4. (three suits) _____

5. (three watches)_____

6. (three witches) _____

ADVERB FORMS

TIPS

For Keeping Adjectives and Adverbs Straight

Don't confuse adjectives with adverbs. An adverb describes a verb, not a noun:

Incorrect: The road work is going *slower* (adjective) than planned.

Correct: The work is going *more slowly* (adverb) than planned.

Regular adverbs always end in *–ly* and do not change form in the comparative or superlative. Use the same patterns for comparing *–ly* adverbs that you use when comparing three- and four-syllable adjectives: *as . . . as, more than,* and *the most:*

The simple form
She dances *as gracefully* as a ballerina.

The comparative form
Prunilla did her work *more carefully* than Maria [did]. (Maria did her work *less carefully* than Prunilla did.)

The superlative form
Toni sang *the most beautifully* of all. (Terry sang *the least unpleasantly* of the group.)

EXERCISE 6	Comparing Adverbs

6. Edit
5. Revise
4. Write

Collaborative Activity 3

Looking at Adverbs in Comparisons

In your collaborative group, list as many adverbs as you can think of. Aim for twenty-five. Next to each adverb on your list, first write the comparative form, then the superlative form.

Supply the correct comparative or superlative form of the adverb in parentheses.

1. With more than 160 biographies published about him, William Shakespeare has been written about (extensively) _more extensively_ than any other person.

2. Calamity Jane, with twelve husbands, was at the altar (frequently) _____ than Pancho Villa, with nine wives.

3. In the United States, the name Johnson appears (commonly) _____ than the name Jones.

4. People have bought the Bible (faithfully) _____ than they have bought any other book.

5. According to the FBI, a murder is (likely) _____ to happen between 6:00 P.M. and 6:00 A.M. than during the working hours of the day.

IRREGULAR ADJECTIVES AND ADVERBS

So far, you've seen the regular, comparative, and superlative forms of adjectives and adverbs—the forms that follow consistent rules. But several adjectives and adverbs don't follow these rules; they have irregular forms.

Adjectives and Adverbs That Are the Same

A few words can serve as both adjectives and adverbs. Here is a partial list:

early   hard   low   fast   late   straight

> The *early* bird arrives *early*.
>
> *Fast* Eddie runs really *fast*.

The comparative and superlative forms of these words are the same whether you use them as adjectives or adverbs:

Simple	Comparative	Superlative
early	earlier	(the) earliest
fast	faster	(the) fastest
hard	harder	(the) hardest

Note how they function as adjectives or adverbs:

> **adverb**
> The first train *came earlier* than I thought, so I missed it and had to take *a*
> **adjective**
> *later train*.
>
> **adjective**
> My little brother is *the slowest eater I've ever seen*. Everyone *finishes dinner*
> **adverb**
> *much faster* than he does.

Good and *Well*, *Bad* and *Badly*

Good is an adjective, and *well* is an adverb (or an adjective when it means "in good health").

Adjectives	Adverbs
Freddie did a *good* job.	Freddie did the job *well*.
The motor is in *good* shape.	The car runs *well*.
I feel *well*.	

However, the comparative and superlative forms of *good* and *well* are the same:

Simple	Comparative	Superlative
good	better	(the) best
well	better	(the) best

Continued

(adjectives) The salad is *good*. The soup is *better*. But the dessert is *the best* of all.

(adverbs) Juan sings *well*. Lourdes sings *better*. But Sixta sings *the best* of the three.

Likewise, *bad* is an adjective and *badly* is an adverb:

Adjectives	Adverbs
Frederico Falsini is a *bad* actor.	Frederico Falsini performs *badly*.
Toni felt *bad* about losing his teeth.	Toni took a *badly* needed vacation.

Bad and *badly* also share identical comparative and superlative forms:

Simple	Comparative	Superlative
bad	worse	(the) worst
badly	worse	(the) worst

(adjectives) The soup is *bad*. The salad tastes *worse*. And the fish tastes *the worst* of all.

(adverbs) Tom sings *badly*. His brother sings *worse*. But their father sings *the worst* of anyone in the whole family.

EXERCISE 7   **Writing Good/Well and Bad/Badly**

6. Edit
5. Revise
4. Write
3. Organize
2. Prewrite
1. Explore

Circle the correct adjective or adverb in parentheses in the left-hand column. Then supply the correct comparative or superlative form of that word in the right-hand column.

1. Susan swims (good/well).
1. But Maria swims _better_____.

2. His painting looks (good/well).
2. But Renoir's painting looks _____ of all.

3. Nobody does it half as (good/well) as you.
3. Nobody does it _____.

4. I have seen some (good/well)-trained dogs.
4. But Prince is _____ -trained dog that I have ever seen.

5. The light in this room is (bad/badly).
5. In fact, of the light in all the rooms, it is _____.

6. The old schoolhouse looks (bad/badly).
6. But it looks _____ than it actually is.

7. He fell and broke his arm (bad/badly).
7. It was _____-looking break that the doctor had seen in years.

Collaborative Activity 4

Using Adverbs as Similes
Return to the sentences you completed in Exercise 1 in Chapter 13. Rewrite them so that each contains a simile, such as, "The train moves as slowly as an elephant in mud." Then in your group, brainstorm ways to make everyone's sentences even more lively or humorous. Compile a list of the best ones and share them with the entire class.

Lively Comparisons

Comparisons with adjectives and adverbs can enliven your writing, especially if you employ them creatively in similes. A **simile**, a common poetic device, is a comparison using *like* or *as*. Here are several examples with *as . . . as:*

Otto is *as strong as a bull on steroids.*

Albert eats *as sloppily as a hog in a barrel of mush.*

At 3:00 A.M., Zeke sneaked into his room *as quietly as a cat in slippers.*

And here are a few similes with *like:*

Otto walks *like a bull.*

Albert eats *like a hog.*

Zeke sneaked into his room *like a cat in slippers.*

IN SUMMARY   To Make Comparisons

With regular adjectives

1. Between equals (simple form): use *as (adjective) as.*
2. Between two unequal adjectives (comparative forms):
   a. Add *-er* to short adjectives and place *more* (or *less*) before long adjectives.
   b. Follow the adjective with *than* (not *then*).
3. Among three or more unequals (superlative forms):
   a. Add *-est* to short adjectives or place *most* (or *least*) before long adjectives.
   b. (Usually) place *the* before superlatives.

With regular adverbs

1. Between equals (simple form): use *as (adverb) as.*
2. Between unequals (comparative form): place *more* (or *less*) before the adverb and follow the adverb with *than.*
3. Among three or more unequals (superlative form): place *(the) most* (or *least*) before the adverb.

With irregular adjectives and adverbs

1. For *good/well:* use *better, (the) best.*
2. For *bad/badly:* use *worse,* and *(the) worst.*

EDITING FOR MASTERY

Mastery Exercise 1   ***Correcting Adjective and Adverb Errors***

The following passage contains ten errors in the use of adjectives and adverbs, aside from the first error, which has been corrected for you.

The Passenger Pigeon's Rise and Fall

(1) One of the ^~~most saddest~~ saddest stories of modern times is the story of the extinction of the passenger pigeon in North America. (2) Never have so many animals disappeared so quick. (3) The story is filled with incredible statistics and eyewitness accounts that are even more harder to believe.

(4) Very few birds were as attractive and graceful as the passenger pigeon, with its light blue feathers and pink breast. (5) However, its greatest claim to fame was the giant size of its populations; there might have been more passenger pigeons than any other bird in history.

(6) The numbers are amazing. (7) One expert on birds watched for two days as one 150-mile-long flock passed over his home. (8) The famous naturalist John James Audubon said 300 million birds blotted out the sun for three days as they flew overhead. (9) Another flock of perhaps 2 billion birds caused a completer solar eclipse than the moon could achieve. (10) A single rifle shot into a flock could supposedly kill at least 200 birds.

(11) For centuries the passenger pigeon lived happy and created no problems to humans. (12) In fact, the bird saved the Pilgrims from starvation when a terrible winter hurt their crops bad in 1648. (13) And the bird became one of the mostest important parts of the diet of the settlers. (14) The pigeon tasted about the same like chicken but was a little more tough.

(15) During the 1700s and early 1800s, hunters found clever ways of killing the birds. (16) One method involved waiting until a flock of pigeons roosted in tree branches for the night. (17) The men set the grass on fire, and its dense smoke suffocated the pigeons. (18) Another device that worked good was to attract the birds through a decoy—a live passenger pigeon whose eyes had been sewn shut. (19) When it was placed on a perch called a stool, the bird called very loud and attracted an enormous flock, which the hunters then shot. (20) The term *stool pigeon*—for one person who sets up another—comes from this practice.

Scorecard: Number of Errors Found and Corrected _____

Collaborative Activity 5

Comparing Your Answers
Have someone in your collaborative group read the passage aloud to help you hear errors. Make your corrections, discuss them in the group, and report your findings to the entire class.

Mastery Exercise 2

Correcting Adjective and Adverb Errors

The following passage contains ten errors in the use of adjectives and adverbs, aside from the first error, which has been corrected for you. Make your corrections above the line.

The Extinction of the Passenger Pigeon

most

(1) The ^mostest remarkable part of the disappearance of the passenger pigeon was how it happened. (2) A number of factors caused the extinction. (3) As the human population grew more large, the people cut down forests of trees and shrunk the pigeons' food supply. (4) The railroad brought hunters to the West, and they killed the birds and sent them back east. (5) Passenger pigeons also became live targets in shooting galleries at city and county fairs. (6) By the 1880s, the baddest damage had been done. (7)

There were no more passenger pigeons on either coast and only a few flocks in other places.

(8) The passenger pigeon's most big flock was in Michigan, where the lastest great pigeon hunt took place in 1878. (9) Hundreds of people began shooting as many as a billion pigeons in an area about five miles long by a mile wide. (10) Some pigeons flew away but then returned to the same trees, where the hunters killed them easy. (11) It took the hunters thirty days to wipe out the entire pigeon population. (12) Every day, they packed the birds into five railroad cars for shipment to Boston and New York.

(13) Although the hunters did their job good, the passenger pigeon was not yet extinct—but it was getting there quick. (14) On the morning of March 24, 1900, a teenager in Ohio shot the last passenger pigeon in that state. (15) Maine reported that its only remaining bird was shot by a hunter in 1904. (16) Arkansas recorded the end of the species in 1906.

(17) The pigeons that a hundred years more early had represented about 35 percent of birds in the United States were now reduced to a total of three, all in the Cincinnati Zoo. (18) When two of the birds in the zoo died, a pigeon named Martha was the only one left. (19) Martha lived to be real old—twenty-nine years—but died on September 1, 1914. (20) Its body was sent to the Smithsonian Institution in Washington, D.C., where it was stuffed and mounted. (21) It can be viewed today in the Smithsonian's collection of the most rarest birds.

Scorecard: Number of Errors Found and Corrected _____

CHAPTER

15 Being Consistent

> As you read, you are annoyed if the writer confuses us.

Did that sentence seem confusing? It should have, for it contained an inconsistency. Here is the same sentence with the problem corrected:

> As you read, you are annoyed if the writer confuses you.

At best, inconsistencies are annoying; at worst, they are frustrating, for they make the meaning unclear. But in either case you should try to eliminate them as you edit. This chapter helps you avoid inconsistencies

- in pronouns
- in verb tense
- in structures that build sentences

KEEPING PRONOUNS STRAIGHT

"Use the right word and not its second cousin."

—Mark Twain

Consistency in **person** (first, second, or third) and in **number** (singular or plural) helps make writing clear and coherent. For example, here are the subject pronouns arranged according to person and number:

	Singular	Plural
First Person	I	we
Second Person	you	you
Third Person	he, she, it	they

As you edit, look for and correct accidental shifts in person and number. The common shift is from first person (*I, we*) or third person (*he, she, it,* or *they*) to second person (*you*). Read the following sentence, for example:

> *I* go to Sam's Sanitary Sandwich Shop because *you* always get a good meal there.

The sentence may be slightly confusing because it talks about two people: *I* and *you*. It should be revised:

> *I* go to Sam's Sanitary Sandwich Shop because *I* always get a good meal there.

This next sentence is not only confusing but unintentionally funny:

> There is such a wide selection of dresses at Wendy's Fashion Farm that *anyone* can find one that looks good on *you*.

Male readers will certainly appreciate the advice! The sentence should be revised:

> There is such a wide selection of dresses at Wendy's Fashion Farm that *any woman* can find one that looks good on *her*.

Here is another muddled sentence:

> *Any student* can make the dean's list if *they* study hard.

The subject shifts from singular (*any* is grammatically singular) to plural (*they*), *perhaps* to avoid the sexual bias problem, discussed in Chapter 12:

> Any student can make the dean's list if *he* studies hard.

This sentence, while technically correct, seems to ignore women. But what alternatives are available? One is to rewrite the sentence with plurals:

> *All students* can make the dean's list if *they* study hard.

A second alternative is to rewrite the sentence with both male and female singular pronouns. And a third alternative, which some people in academics prefer, is to use the female pronoun—and gently work against the male bias in language:

> *Any student* can make the dean's list if *he or she* studies hard.
>
> *Any student* can make the dean's list if *she* studies hard.

To be clear, be consistent. Choose the pronoun that makes the most sense in the writing—for example, *we, you,* or *everyone*—and stick with it all the way through your paper. Don't switch unless you have a logical reason to do so.

EXERCISE 1   Establishing Consistency in Person and Number

6. Edit
5. Revise
4. Write
3. Organize
2. Prewrite
1. Explore

Replace the underlined word with the correct pronoun that maintains consistency in a sentence. When you must use a third-person-singular pronoun, use a female pronoun, she or her.

Beyond Our Wildest Dreams

1. We spend nearly one-third of our lives sleeping, and now scientists are beginning to understand what happens when <u>you</u> (*we* _____) sleep.

2. A sleeping person's brain waves often increase in strength and speed, and with the increase, <u>their</u> (_____) eyes begin to move quickly behind the eyelids.

3. Our *rapid eye movement*, or *REM*, occurs about every ninety minutes and indicates that <u>you</u> (_____) are dreaming.

4. Experiments have shown that dreaming is important to mental health. If someone is awakened during REM, <u>they</u> (_____) will be short tempered the next morning.

5. But when the same person goes to sleep the following night, <u>their</u> (_____) dream activity will greatly increase.

6. If you take sleeping pills regularly, <u>it</u> (_____) may do more harm than good, for after a month or so, <u>our</u> (_____) REM activity will decrease and make <u>someone</u> (_____) irritable.

Collaborative Activity 1

Rewriting Sentences

Write one sentence for each of the following subjects: *everyone, you,* and *people.* Refer back to the subject with an appropriate pronoun. In your group, exchange papers by passing to the left. Correct errors in consistency if you find any. Then rewrite each sentence, changing its number or person. Exchange papers to the left again and check for errors.

EXERCISE 2   Revising Sentences

6. Edit
5. Revise
4. Write
3. Organize
2. Prewrite
1. Explore

Each of the following groups of sentences contains a shift in person. Cross out the inappropriate pronoun(s), and write in the appropriate one(s) above the line. Or, if necessary, rewrite the entire sentence.

1. I find psychology class fascinating. ^I ^~~You~~ learn so much about ^*myself* ^~~yourself~~.

2. When I come back to my dormitory after class, you never know what kind of funny things you will find happening.

3. People who like Asian food should eat at the new Thai restaurant. You will really enjoy the unusual tasting food.

4. Everyone should try the new diet in which you eat only leaves and twigs. It will really give you an attractive figure.

5. A student who wants to enjoy themselves ought to take Dr. Johnson's class. You'll laugh a lot and learn a lot, too.

6. One should be cautioned against trying to write in a formal style if you are unsure how to use it.

EXERCISE 3	Rewriting Sentences

6. Edit
5. Revise
4. Write
3. Organize
2. Prewrite
1. Explore

Complete each of the following sentences, maintaining the same person and number. If the subject is third-person singular, use either the female pronoun (she, her) or a combination of both male and female: he or she, him or her, his or her.

1. When a teenager is at a party with people using drugs, *he or she will have to work hard to resist the peer pressure to try them.*

2. The average billionaire _____

3. Every parent should _____

4. A person who wants to start a business _____

5. Most students _____

6. One should be consistent or _____

KEEPING TENSE CONSISTENT

✔ **TIPS**

For Keeping Verb Tenses Straight

If you tend to omit verb tense endings or have trouble with consistency of tense, try this as you edit your work: Place a ruler under each line in your paper to focus your eyes on the verbs, underline each verb, and check the verbs for consistency.

In the early stages of the writing process, you may accidentally shift from one tense to another—especially when you discuss literature, movies, or plays:

> The movie *"Scream 16"* **begins** just like the other ones, with actress Never Soupcan having to protect herself from a mad slasher. He **threatens** to attack her time after time. But as in the previous movies, Never **escaped** unharmed.

Although this passage begins in the present tense, it ends in the past, a logical tense for storytelling, but not logical in this context. Here are some other examples of tense inconsistencies:

> I *was* positive that I *will* get an A. (This past-tense sentence should use *would*—the past tense of *will*.)
>
> Every day my mother *came* home and *would cook* dinner. (This past-tense sentence should use *cooked*.)

Look carefully at each verb as you edit. Is the tense consistent with the other verbs? If you've shifted tense, have you done so logically? Correct any illogical shifts in tense. And if you're not sure of the appropriate form of the verb, look up the verb in your dictionary or consult Chapter 12 of this book.

EXERCISE 4 | Transforming Tenses

6. Edit
5. Revise
4. Write
3. Organize
2. Prewrite
1. Explore

Change the following sentences from present to past action or from past to present action.

Present time	**Past time**
1. He _can_____ answer you.	1. He _____ answer you.
2. It _____ fine.	2. It seemed fine.
3. He is supposed to come.	3. He _____ supposed to come.
4. I _____ been there before.	4. I had been there before.
5. I think it is all right.	5. I _____ it _____ all right.
6. I wonder if he will come to work later.	6. I _____ if he _____ come to work later.
7. I know they can do it.	7. I _____ they _____ do it.

EXERCISE 5 | Writing in Consistent Verb Tenses

6. Edit
5. Revise
4. Write
3. Organize
2. Prewrite
1. Explore

Complete each of the following sentences, using verbs in logically appropriate tenses.

1. When I was five years old, *I could ride a bicycle without training wheels.* _____

2. Every day when I do my homework, _____
_____

3. I told you that _____
_____

4. Willie smiled as _____
_____

5. You'll receive an award when _____
_____

6. You'd better be careful or _____
_____

Collaborative Activity 2

Writing More Sentences

Working in pairs, compose a second sentence for each completed sentence in Exercise 4 that follows up on its idea. Write in the appropriate tense. Then examine and discuss the sentences.

EXERCISE 6 | Editing for Consistent Verb Tense

6. Edit
5. Revise
4. Write
3. Organize
2. Prewrite
1. Explore

The following passage contains eight illogical shifts in tense, excluding the first error, which has been corrected for you. Correct these errors above the lines.

Alexandra David-Neel (1868–1969): Explorer, Writer, and Adventurer

(1) Alexandra David, who was born in Paris in 1868, dreamed of traveling to faraway

places, and she soon ^left ~~leaves~~ home as a young person to explore the world. (2) Although

only five feet tall, Alexandra is physically tough and completely independent. (3) She

traveled to Vietnam, Greece, and North Africa as an opera star, but she will eventually

If Your First Language Is Not English

1. Some languages do not use past-tense forms of *can, will,* and *is/are*—especially languages spoken in the Philippines and in parts of Africa. As a reminder, here are the forms:

   Present tense: am, are, is; can; will

   Past tense: was, were; could; would

2. Also, many Asian languages do not indicate time through verb tense, but only through adverbs. So someone might mistakenly write, "I am sick yesterday" instead of "I was sick yesterday."

become a journalist to support herself. (4) However, she always kept in mind her goal of exploring Central Asia.

(5) In 1904, Alexandra married her distant cousin Philippe-Francois Neel. (6) Alexandra said that marriage and motherhood are threatening to her independence, so she never had children and didn't live with her husband. (7) But the couple always claimed to love one another, and Philippe Neel gave his wife money so she can explore Tibet without him for fourteen years.

(8) Alexandra became a Buddhist in 1911 and was the first European woman to meet privately with the spiritual ruler of Tibet, the Dalai Lama. (9) Afterward, Alexandra would become fluent in the Tibetan language. (10) A fifteen-year-old boy named Yongden aids her on many journeys through northern India, China, and Tibet. (11) He remained with her until he had died in France in 1955.

(12) Because Alexandra wanted passionately to learn more about the Tibetan way of life, she decides to undergo training as a Buddhist priest. (13) For two years, she lived as a hermit in a cave on top of a 13,000-foot mountain. (14) She loved the hardships of cold, hunger, and isolation. (15) The holy men of Tibet blessed her after she emerged from the cave in 1916.

KEEPING STRUCTURES PARALLEL

The following sentences will probably make you stop and puzzle for a moment:

> The movie star Barry Biceps is 6 feet 4 inches tall, weight 220 pounds, and piercing brown eyes.
>
> They loved telling stories, to dance, and sang.

The sentences move along as if they have lost their balance. In fact, they are unbalanced; they join similar ideas but use different grammatical structures. The sentences would be clearer if they repeated the same structures:

> The movie star Barry Biceps is 6 feet 4 inches tall, *weighs* 220 pounds, and *has* piercing brown eyes. (three present-tense verbs)
>
> They loved *telling* stories, *dancing*, and *singing*. (three *—ing* words)

This repetition of grammatical structures is called **parallel construction**, or **parallelism**. You can use it to balance subjects with subjects, verbs with verbs, phrases with phrases, clauses with clauses—or balance any other grammatical structures. Notice how parallelism establishes clarity in the following sentences:

> We could have *gone* and *seen* it. (two past participles following *could have*)
>
> "It is true that you may *fool all the people some of the time; you can even fool some of the people all of the time;* but *you can't fool all of the people all of the time.*" (Abraham Lincoln)

EXERCISE 7 — Identifying Parallel Structures

6. Edit
5. Revise
4. Write
3. Organize
2. Prewrite
1. Explore

Underline the structure that is different from the others in each group.

1. shifting gears
   avoid the accident
   keeping control
   swerving to the left

2. cooperation
   admiring
   respect
   reliability

3. cute
   friendly
   a good student
   athletic

4. works by night
   plays by dawn
   eats junk food
   sleeps by day

5. overtired
   swollen feet
   sore muscles
   aching back

6. sewn by hand
   decorated with ribbon
   embroidered in red
   an odd color

7. gone there
   done it
   ran back
   been finished

EXERCISE 8 — Using Parallel Structures

6. Edit
5. Revise
4. Write
3. Organize
2. Prewrite
1. Explore

Choose four groups of parallel phrases from Exercise 7 and write a sentence for each group. Be sure to keep all the phrases in a group parallel.

1. As the car began to skid, Ralph was able to avoid a collision by shifting gears, keeping control, and swerving to the left.

2. _____

3. _____
   _____

4. _____
   _____

5. _____
   _____

Collaborative Activity 3

Examining Parallelism

In your collaborative group, compare the responses you prepared in Exercise 8. List the best ones and present them to the entire class.

EXERCISE 9 — Writing Parallel Structures

Complete each of the following sentences by maintaining the pattern it establishes.

1. The kids talked about hiking, sailing, and swimming. _____

2. She was spoiled by her mother, bored by school, and _____
   _____

6. Edit
5. Revise
4. Write
3. Organize
2. Prewrite
1. Explore

3. You could have called me, written me, or _____

_____

4. The movie has no story, only scenes. It has no believable characters, only _____

_____

5. We have been working hard, paying attention, and _____

_____

6. The food was too ordinary, the portions too small, the price _____

_____

EXERCISE 10 | *Editing for Parallel Structures*

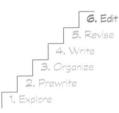

6. Edit
5. Revise
4. Write
3. Organize
2. Prewrite
1. Explore

Each of the following contains an error in parallelism. Underline the section with the error and then rewrite it to make it parallel.

The Further Adventures of Alexandra David-Neel

1. Alexandra David-Neel set her sights on another accomplishment: <u>to journey through China,</u> climbing the Himalaya Mountains, and reaching the forbidden Tibetan city of Lhasa, which had never before been seen by a white woman.
Rewritten: journeying through China _____

2. Over the next year, Alexandra and her companion, Yongden, traveled in disguise as a Tibetan peasant woman and his disguise was her Buddhist monk son.
Rewritten: _____

3. They would have been killed if they were discovered. But they were saved time and again by Alexandra's complete knowledge of the Tibetan people, their language, and also the customs they had.
Rewritten: _____

4. Along the way, they also faced deep piles of snow, bitter cold, and they had to deal with mountains 20,000 feet high.
Rewritten: _____

5. Once, after struggling for nineteen hours along a snow-covered mountain pass, Yongden could not light a fire. He realized that they could not live through the night and calling on Alexandra to try an ancient Buddhist art of creating internal warmth through will power.
Rewritten: _____

6. Alexandra refused to worry about warming herself, concentrated on drying out the materials, and a fire was started by her before Yongden had returned from his search for more wood.
Rewritten: _____

7. After they finally reached Lhasa in 1923—Alexandra was fifty-five years old—the two remained in their disguises and undetected.

Rewritten: _____

8. Several months later, she and Yongden journeyed first to India and then returning to Europe, where she stayed for the next ten years.

Rewritten: _____

9. In the mid-1930s, her urge to travel made her return to Tibet and lived there until she had to flee on foot when the Japanese invaded in 1944. She was seventy-six years old.

Rewritten: _____

10. Alexandra David-Neel then spent the rest of her life in France as a writer and famous. She died in 1969, just seven weeks shy of her 101st birthday.

Rewritten: _____

IN SUMMARY | To Maintain Consistency

1. Check your pronouns—don't shift person or number illogically.
2. Check your verbs—don't shift tense illogically.
3. Check items in a series—don't lose parallelism.

EDITING FOR MASTERY

Mastery Exercise 1

Editing for Consistency

The following passage contains twelve errors in parallelism, shifts in person, and shifts in tense—aside from the first error, which has been corrected as an example.

The Eruption of Mount Vesuvius

(1) August 24, 79 A.D., began like any other day in the resort town of Pompeii, Italy: people opened their window shutters, shopkeepers ^got ~~would get~~ ready for business, and the townspeople discussed the upcoming elections. (2) However, at 1:00 p.m., you could hear a mighty roar and then a big explosion. (3) The volcano Mount Vesuvius is awakening from 1,500 years of sleep. (4) A black cloud rose to cover the sky and blotting out the sun. (5) Melted rock shot from the volcano's mouth, cooled quickly in the air, and then it would fall back into the volcano. (6) The volcano exploded a second time and raining stones all over the mountainside.

(7) A few people ran from the city, reached the sea, and had escaped in their boats. (8) He or she lived to tell about the disaster. (9) However, most people tried to find safety

in their homes, temples, or they went to the public baths. (10) These people weren't as lucky as those who left by sea. (11) They died as hot stones piled on roofs, collapsed some roofs, and setting others on fire. (12) Poison gases killed many people, while thirty to fifty feet of volcanic ash buried the city, and the rest were suffocated.

(13) Within 24 hours, 30,000 people were dead. (14) Their bodies and homes will be preserved in the ash for almost 1,700 years. (15) At that point the city was excavated, and you could visit the city near the sleeping killer volcano.

Scorecard: Number of Errors Found and Corrected _____

Editing for Consistency

The following passage contains twelve errors in parallelism, shifts in person, and shifts in tense—aside from the first error, which has been corrected as an example. Correct these errors above the lines.

The Great Influenza Epidemic (March–November 1918)

(1) It all started one spring day during World War I when a United States Army fort was hit with the first cases of Spanish Influenza. (2) Before the epidemic ^had ~~has~~ run its course, almost 22 million people died throughout the world.

(3) The disease struck first in Fort Riley, Kansas, in 1918; it quickly spreads throughout other military camps from coast to coast. (4) Soon, so many sailors in Norfolk, Virginia, and Boston, Massachusetts, had such high fevers that you couldn't go to sea. (5) In California, one-third of the prisoners in the San Quentin jail became ill.

(6) The influenza soon reached Europe. (7) Scotland reported 15 to 20 deaths daily, London reported 300 deaths a week, and large numbers of ill and dead were reported in Germany and France. (8) Then the killer disease hit China and India, hopped the Pacific to Hawaii, and Alaska, Puerto Rico, Iceland, and Norway were attacked. (9) It finally hit Spain, where doctors call it Spanish Influenza.

(10) All across North America, the influenza struck millions of people and killing hundreds of thousands of them. (11) There were not enough coffins and graves, and there aren't enough undertakers. (12) To prevent the spread of the disease, churches closed on Sundays, businesses and stores went on half-day schedules, and theaters would shut down.

(13) No one knew what caused the disease or how you could cure it. (14) One official blamed it on a tiny poisonous plant, and one doctor blamed it on too much clothing. (15) Another doctor suggested that a person could cure it by putting towels soaked in hot vinegar on your stomach.

(16) By early October, the disease was completely out of control. (17) U.S. military camps reported one death every hour, and Britain recorded 2,000 deaths a week.

Collaborative Activity 4

Comparing Answers
Compare your corrections with those of the members of your collaborative group and report the results to the whole class.

Mastery Exercise 2

(18) India lost 12.5 million people; the United States lost 500,000. (19) Finally, in November, the war ended, the disease came to an end, and the virus will disappear almost completely. (20) Where did it come from and what location is the place where it went to? (21) No one knows.

Scorecard: Number of Errors Found and Corrected _____

16

Writing Concretely and Concisely

Good writing is direct and concise; it puts each word to work. It is specific, concrete, and lively. You should speak to readers in a strong voice, and much of the muscle that you add to your voice can be built up during revising and editing. This chapter looks at ways to strengthen your voice through

- choosing strong verbs and adjectives
- eliminating unnecessary words and meaningless expressions

CHOOSING WORDS THAT WORK

> "What makes me happy is rewriting . . . it's like cleaning house, getting rid of all the junk, getting things in the right order, tightening things up."
>
> —Newspaper columnist Ellen Goodman

Don't be content to limp along on flabby word choice after your first draft. Put a little muscle into your verbs and adjectives. We'll show you how.

Strong Verbs

Look carefully at **verbs**—the words that carry the action. Are they strong and lively? Commonly used (and overused) verbs such as *is/are/am, go, get, have, make, do, run, put, take, see, use,* and *talk* are weak, vague, lifeless. The verb *take,* for example, can express countless meanings:

> take medicine, or a powder
>
> take a nap, a walk, a shower, or a vacation
>
> take up, down, off, in, on, over, from, to, away, or back
>
> take your time, your pick, or your punishment

But let's take a break from these examples!

Obviously, you can't eliminate all common verbs, but don't overuse them. Replace them with more precise, interesting verbs whenever you can.

UNIT 3	Go Electronic
Chapter 16	Use the following electronic supplements for additional practice with your writing: • For chapter-by-chapter summaries and exercises, visit the Writing with Confidence Companion Website at http://www.ablongman.com/meyers. • For work with the writing process, visit The Longman Writer's Warehouse at http://longmanwriterswarehouse.com (password needed).
Writing with Confidence ©2003	• For additional practice in grammar, use The Writer's ToolKit Plus CD-ROM.

If Your First Language Is Not English

In most languages only one verb expresses the different ideas of the English verbs *do* and *make*.

- **Make** means to create something in the physical world, in our imagination, or in our minds: make a dress, make a cake, make a decision
- **Do** means *to perform an action or a job*: do homework, do (wash) the laundry, do (the work on) a paper

Therefore: A teacher makes an assignment; the students do it.

We make the dishes dirty when we eat; then we do (clean) them.

To strengthen your verbs:

- circle common and repeated verbs
- consider replacing them with less common verbs that more precisely express your meaning.

Original	Revision
Black Bart *took* the money.	Black Bart $\begin{cases} accepted \\ snatched \\ ran\ off\ with \end{cases}$ the money.

Look especially at the verb *have*. Does it simply express possession? If so, perhaps you can replace it with a **possessive** such as *my, his, her, their, our, your,* or *Ralph's.* You may then be able to combine the ideas from two sentences into a single sentence.

To eliminate unnecessary uses of *have:*

- circle *have, has,* or *had* when these words express possession
- substitute a possessive word if possible, and combine ideas

Original	Revision
I *have* an old car. It barely runs anymore.	*My old car* barely runs anymore.

EXERCISE 1   Choosing Strong Verbs

6. Edit
5. Revise
4. Write
3. Organize
2. Prewrite
1. Explore

Replace each of the following common verbs with a strong and vivid verb. (Notice, incidentally, that you are replacing two words with one.)

1. get on _board_____
2. go up _____
3. do again _____
4. do over _____
5. go over _____

6. go in _____
7. do in _____
8. go on _____
9. take off _____

EXERCISE 2   Finding Alternative Verbs

6. Edit
5. Revise
4. Write
3. Organize
2. Prewrite
1. Explore

Write three or more different verbs or phrases that express each idea in parentheses, but don't rely on common verbs.

1. (fast movement) The big cat _shot, darted, raced, tore, scooted_____ into the room.

2. (talk angrily) The woman _____ at the salesperson.

3. (build) The workers _____ a garage in just a few hours.

4. (slow movement) The sheriff _____ through the saloon, staring at each man at the poker tables.

5. (remove) The man in the dark suit _____ the
   wallet from the shopper's backpack.

6. (give) Waldo _____ the stinking fish to (or at)
   the waiter.

EXERCISE 3 | Revising Sentences

6. Edit
5. **Revise**
4. Write
3. Organize
2. Prewrite
1. Explore

Collaborative Activity 1

Comparing Changes

In small groups, compare and discuss your revisions to the sentences in Exercises 1, 2, and 3 and then appoint a spokesperson to report your results to the whole class.

Streamline each of the following sentences (if there are two, combine them) by eliminating the verb have.

1. Ralph has a cat. It seems to think that it's human. *Ralph's cat seems to think it's human.*

2. I have a car. It belongs in an exhibit of ancient, worthless machines. _____
   _____

3. The university has a library that has every book you can imagine. _____
   _____

4. The city has some laws that are very unfair. _____
   _____

5. That dog has fleas. They are bigger than grapes. _____
   _____

6. Fred has a hair that looks as if it was combed with an electric mixer. _____

EXERCISE 4 | Eliminating Common Verbs

6. Edit
5. **Revise**
4. Write
3. Organize
2. Prewrite
1. Explore

Collaborative Activity 2

Comparing Changes

In small groups, compare and discuss your revisions in Exercise 4. Make a list of the best ones and then appoint a spokesperson to report your results to the whole class.

The following passage relies too much on the verbs do *and* get. *Rewrite it, supplying more exact and vivid verbs and making any other changes that will strengthen the passage. (Don't be afraid to rewrite a sentence completely.)*

When I get home from school each day, I have a lot of chores to do. I do the laundry and the housecleaning, I do the dishes from breakfast and lunch, and I get dinner ready for my family. We eat dinner at around 5:30, and after we get finished, I do the dishes again. I usually don't get any help from my children or husband, so I have to do everything myself. I get the kids into bed around 9:00, which is when I can do my homework. I do my math assignments first because I can do problems while the TV is on. Then I do the rest of the assignments I've got for the next day. I usually get to bed around midnight so that I can get up at 6:00 the next morning.

Vivid Adjectives and Details

Examine your **adjectives** as you revise. If you find flat, imprecise, and too common adjectives such as *good, bad, nice, great, different,* or *happy,* consider replacing them. Think of more lively adjectives that more precisely express your meaning.

To strengthen your adjectives:

- circle overused and imprecise adjectives
- substitute more lively words or phrases
- or completely rewrite the sentence using more specific detail

Original	Revision
The Stephen King novel was *very interesting*.	The Stephen King novel was { *riveting.* *fascinating.* *terrifying.* }

(*Or:* Some especially frightening parts of the Stephen King novel made the hair on my arms curl.)

EXERCISE 5   *Choosing Fresh Adjectives*

Circle the adjective in each of the following sentences and replace it with a more precise, animated word. Or, if you wish, rewrite the sentence to include much more specific detail. The first item contains four examples.

1. The view of the Grand Canyon is ⌃(pretty). *breathtaking (astonishing, magnificent) The jagged walls, deep and varied colors, and incredible size of the Grand Canyon create an overwhelmingly beautiful sight.*

2. The movie *Gladiator* was interesting. _____
   _____

3. Mother Theresa was a nice woman. _____
   _____
   _____

4. Ms. Wilson is a good instructor. _____
   _____

5. Mt. Everest is tall. _____
   _____

6. The afternoon talk shows on TV are stupid. _____
   _____

DISCARDING WORDS THAT DON'T CONTRIBUTE

Wordiness is easy to spot. Compare these sentences:

1. In the modern-day world of today, there are many important problems that concern each and every one of us, and one of the most important of these problems is the problem concerning the danger of biological and chemical warfare.
2. Everyone fears biological and chemical warfare.

You probably prefer the second sentence, which states its point in just six words. The first sentence, all forty words of it, is bloated with repetition. Let's examine it further:

Copyright © 2003 by Addison Wesley Longman, Inc.

For Pruning Deadwood

Read your work aloud.

- Listen for vague and dull expressions, for repeated words and ideas.
- Listen to the sounds and rhythms of your sentences.

Then strike down and discard the deadwood.

1. In the modern-day world of today . . . (Isn't *today* a day, and isn't it modern? Why mention *the world* unless we expect a discussion of the moon instead?)
2. there are many important problems that concern each and every one of us . . . (Don't we know that? And what is the difference between *each* and *every*?)

In short, sentence 1 is filled with *deadwood:* lifeless and useless language. Don't worry about such language as you compose your first draft. But as you revise, try to prune the deadwood.

In fact, revising your sentences at this stage can be fun. You've already done the hard work of capturing your ideas in words. Now you can take pleasure in shaping those ideas more gracefully and powerfully.

Empty Sentence Starters

There is and *there are* often are merely sentence starters: empty words that add bulk without meaning. Eliminate these empty sentence starters by turning statements around. If the result is awkward, try another way to express your idea.

To eliminate *there is/are* (or *was/were, will be,* etc.)

- circle these expressions
- delete them from the sentence
- if possible, begin the sentence with the last words of the original

Original	Revision
1. <u>There are</u> two important points that you must know.	You must know two important points.
2. <u>There is</u> a man at the next table who is eating a sandwich with green meat.	A man at the next table is eating a sandwich with green meat.

EXERCISE 6 | *Cutting Empty Sentence Starters*

Rewrite each of the following sentences, eliminating there is *or* there are.

1. There are three important rules that everyone should follow.

   Rewritten: Everyone should follow three important rules.

2. There is a woman on the street corner who is talking to herself.

   Rewritten: _____

3. There were seven men that were sleeping on the floor at the end of the party.

   Rewritten: _____

4. There are many people in this country who speak both English and Spanish.

   Rewritten: _____

5. There will be a train arriving from Philadelphia in a few minutes.

   Rewritten: _____

6. There must be a final sentence that ends this exercise.

   Rewritten: _____

Vague Expressions

Vague, general words and expressions such as *things, ways, stuff, type of, methods,* and *factors* often add very little meaning to a statement.

To replace these expressions:

- find and circle them
- express the same ideas through more specific details or information

Original	Revision
Everybody likes Susan because of *all the funny things she does.*	Susan makes everyone laugh when she says, "This test will be no problem," and then fakes a heart attack.

EXERCISE 7	Increasing Clarity and Liveliness

6. Edit
5. Revise
4. Write
3. Organize
2. Prewrite
1. Explore

Rewrite each of the following sentences in more vivid and exact language.

1. Tom's behavior is annoying. When Tom borrows my clothes and returns them dirty, eats half a gallon of ice cream from my freezer without asking, or calls me at 2:00 a.m. to find out the next day's homework assignment, I seriously consider turning him over to the proper authorities for prosecution and imprisonment.

2. What the acrobat did was interesting. _____

3. Pedro has a nice personality. _____

4. My friend sometimes does odd things. _____

5. The dog acts really silly. _____

6. The rock concert was great. _____

Repetition

A word or sound accidentally repeated, even in a different form or with a different meaning, can be annoying, confusing, or dull.

To avoid weak repetition:

- read your work aloud, listening for words or sounds accidentally repeated
- circle repeated words or sounds, including those used in different forms or with different meanings
- rewrite the passage, substituting for or eliminating the weak repetition

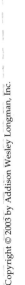

For Testing Repetition
A simple way to distinguish between weak and strong repetition is the "oops and ah" test. If, when reading a repeated word or idea you react with "Oops, I didn't mean that," the repetition is weak. If you react with "Ah, that sounds good," feel proud of yourself!

Original	Revision
Ball State *University* is a *university* that provides a complete program of undergraduate and graduate study.	Ball State University provides a complete program of undergraduate and graduate study.
He had a *reasonably* good *reason* to be absent.	His absence was justifiable.
I just read a fascinating *book*. The *book* was about the U.S. space program.	I just read a fascinating book about the U.S. space program.

Not all repetition is weak, however. Sometimes writers intentionally repeat words or sounds to build to a climax or tie ideas together:

[Climax] Each day Brian *studies* the sports section, *studies* the movie listings, and occasionally even *studies* his assignments.

[Coherence] We waited for an explanation, an excuse, or any kind of answer, but *no answer* ever came.

EXERCISE 8   Cutting Repetition

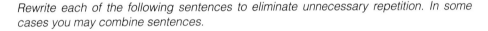

6. Edit
5. Revise
4. Write
3. Organize
2. Prewrite
1. Explore

Rewrite each of the following sentences to eliminate unnecessary repetition. In some cases you may combine sentences.

1. Some of the algebra problems gave me problems. *Some of the algebra problems were difficult.*

2. Our new house is a beautiful house. _____

3. Bus fare is fairly high in this city. _____

4. Jill's teacher is not like my teacher. My teacher is very understanding. _____

5. I always read the directions on an examination first. After I read the directions, I know exactly what is expected of me. _____

6. Stretch Everest, the center on our basketball team, is always the center of attention when he comes on the floor. _____

Wordiness

Good writing is clear, simple, and direct. Why say in ten words what you can say in four or five? Moreover, bad writing is not only tiresome but may needlessly explain what is already implied. Why say, "My mother is a woman who" unless we have reason to believe your mother is a man? Even the best writers create wordy early drafts, so tighten your language as you revise and edit.

To tighten your sentences:

- circle words whose meanings are already included in other words
- circle vague words and expressions such as *thing, type of, kind of, way, area,* and *method*
- eliminate these unnecessary words
- or rewrite a statement to express its idea more directly

Original	Revision
1. *As far as looks are concerned,* Maria is very pretty.	Maria is beautiful.
2. I can't talk to you *at this point in time.*	I can't talk to you now.
3. He *has the ability to* swim.	He can swim.
4. She shouted at him *in a very loud voice.*	She screamed at him.
5. Calculus *is a branch of mathematics that presents different types of challenges* to students.	Calculus challenges many students.
6. *The reason why* rock music is so popular *is because* it appeals to the rebel in all of us.	Rock music appeals to the rebel in all of us.

EXERCISE 9 — Tightening Sentences

6. Edit
5. Revise
4. Write
3. Organize
2. Prewrite
1. Explore

Rewrite and tighten each of the following sentences.

1. The pie had an unusual taste to it. *The pie tasted unusual.*

2. Celia Gonzalez is the kind of student who studies hard and gets good grades. _____

3. The reason why I like art is because it allows me to be creative. _____

4. The car was large in size and blue in color. _____

5. Anita seems to have a lot of self-confidence in herself. _____

6. When my instructor returned back my paper to me today, I saw that it had several different types of errors that were mistakes that came from being careless. _____

EXERCISE 10	Combining Sentences

6. Edit
5. Revise
4. Write
3. Organize
2. Prewrite
1. Explore

Find the weak repetition and unnecessary words in each of the following groups of sentences. Then combine each group into one graceful sentence. Omit repeated words or ideas whenever possible.

The Origin of the Teddy Bear

1. It was November 1902. Theodore (Teddy) Roosevelt was president. The president visited the South. He went to settle an argument. The argument was between Mississippi and another state. The name of the state was Louisiana. *In November 1902, President Theodore (Teddy) Roosevelt visited the South to settle an argument between Mississippi and Louisiana.*

2. Roosevelt had an official duty. His duty was to "draw the line" between the states. He took time off from his duty. He went bear hunting. _____

3. His host showed him an easy target. The target was a baby bear. A baby bear is also called a cub. The president refused to shoot it. _____

4. A cartoonist drew a picture. The picture was of the president. The president was refusing to kill the cub. The picture had a caption. The caption was underneath the picture. The caption said, "Drawing the line." _____

5. Morris Michtom was the owner of a toy store. The toy store was in Brooklyn, New York. He was inspired by the cartoon. He and his wife made a bear. The bear was soft. The bear was brown. _____

6. They put the bear in the window. They put a copy of the cartoon in the window. They put a sign in the window. The sign said "Teddy's Bear." _____

7. The bear sold quickly. Then many more bears sold quickly. A fad developed. The fad became very popular. _____

_____

_____

8. Michtom wrote to the president. He wanted to use the president's name. His purpose was to sell stuffed animals. He wanted to sell them all across the country. ____

_____

_____

_____

9. The president sent a note to Michtom. The note was handwritten. It granted the permission. _____

_____

_____

10. Many imitators of Teddy's bear appeared. They came from manufacturers. The manufacturers were all across America. The manufacturers were also from Europe. They created an extremely popular toy._____

_____

_____

_____

Tired Expressions

In your first rush to put words on paper, you may find yourself using familiar expressions such as "last but not least." These expressions—called **clichés**—are often *too* familiar. They're so overused and tired that they've lost both power and meaning. Here are a few examples:

one in a million	over and done with
as cold as ice	selling like hotcakes
stick like glue	bored to tears
barely scratches the surface	tried and true
easier said than done	up at the crack of dawn
few and far between	it goes without saying

Expect to write clichés in early drafts—everyone does. But when you revise, try to substitute fresher expressions.

To avoid clichés:

- circle tired expressions as you revise
- substitute fresh, original language

Original	Revision
It was *raining cats and dogs*.	The rain covered the streets and flooded basements.
I opened my umbrella *as quick as a wink*.	I instantly opened my umbrella.
Jamie's mind is *as sharp as a tack*.	Jamie's mind is sharp as a laser cutter.

EXERCISE 11   Eliminating Clichés

6. Edit
5. Revise
4. Write
3. Organize
2. Prewrite
1. Explore

Find the clichés in each of the following sentences. Then replace each cliché with a fresh expression.

1. The Moving Violations' new album is selling like hotcakes. *The Moving Violations' new album is extremely popular.*

2. He was as happy as a lark. _____

3. Getting rid of every cliché is easier said than done. _____

4. The day of the exam I was up at the crack of dawn so I'd be good and ready. _____

5. In this day and age, honest politicians are few and far between. _____

6. This exercise barely scratches the surface of eliminating clichés; you must work like a horse to get rid of them in your writing. _____

Collaborative Activity 3

Listing Clichés

In your collaborative group, brainstorm and list as many clichés as you can. Then add to your own list each time the group meets. Include all the clichés you encounter in each other's writing throughout the term. Aim for a list of one hundred and share your discoveries with the other groups in the class periodically. The lists will help make you aware of expressions to avoid.

IN SUMMARY   To Eliminate Weak or Unnecessary Words

1. Identify overused common verbs such as *do, get, make, put, go,* and *have;* then replace them with more specific and stronger verbs.
2. Identify and replace common and imprecise adjectives.
3. Identify and eliminate any unnecessary uses of *there is* and *there are.*
4. Identify and replace vague and tired expressions with more specific and vivid language.
5. Identify and eliminate unnecessary repetition.
6. Identify wordiness and revise wordy passages with more concise expressions.
7. Identify and eliminate any clichés.

EDITING FOR MASTERY

Mastery Exercise 1   ***Writing Concretely and Concisely***

Each of the items in the following passage contains empty language, unnecessary repetition, and weak verbs or adjectives. Rewrite the items to eliminate the problems.

A Desperate Situation in World War I

1. It was on October 4, 1918, when a division of American soldiers was fighting the Germans in the Argonne Forest that was in France. *On October 4, 1918, a division of American soldiers was fighting the Germans in the Argonne Forest in France.*

2. The thing that the Germans did was surround the Americans and attack them. ____

3. Another bad thing was that the American division also was getting "friendly fire" from their own army. _____

4. The division had a commander. His name was Major Charles W. Whittlesey. He knew that his many of his men had been killed or hurt, and they had almost run out of rations and medical supplies._____

5. There was more "friendly fire" that was coming at the division. To stop this friendly fire from coming, Whittlesey decided to do something. He wrote a note to his superiors at division headquarters at Rampont. _____

6. He asked them to do something. They had to stop bombing the division. _____

7. There was only one way to get the message to headquarters. The location of the headquarters was twenty-five miles away. It was to send the message by carrier pigeon._____

8. Whittlesey had five pigeons that he sent up with the message. But German marksmen killed each and every one of them in the blink of an eye. _____

_____

_____

9. There was only one pigeon left. His name was Cher Ami, which means "dear friend" in French, and the message was put inside a capsule, and the capsule was attached to his leg. _____

_____

_____

10. Cher Ami made a short flight, and as quick as a wink he landed on the branch of a tree that was nearby. Cher Ami decided that the thing to do was to start grooming his feathers. _____

_____

_____

11. Major Whittlesey knew that this was a situation that was bad, so he had to do something. What he decided to do was make the bird fly. _____

_____

_____

Scorecard: Number of Errors Found and Corrected _____

Collaborative Activity 4

Comparing And Discussing Answers

Meet in your group to compare and discuss the change you made to each item in Mastery Exercise 1. Report your findings to the entire class.

Mastery Exercise 2

Writing Concretely and Concisely

Each of the items in the following passage contains empty language, unnecessary repetition, and weak verbs or adjectives. Rewrite the items to eliminate the problems.

The Pigeon Hero

1. Major Whittlesey and the unit's pigeon handler, who was named Sergeant Richards, tried to get Cher Ami to take off. What they did was shout and wave their hands.
   Major Whittlesey and the unit's pigeon handler, Sergeant Richards, tried to get Cher Ami to take off by shouting and waving their hands.

2. They even tossed stones at the pigeon, but there was nothing that worked. Because nothing else worked, Richards got the idea that he would climb up in the tree where the pigeon was and then he would shake the branch that that pigeon was on. _____

_____

_____

3. The action that Richards did made Cher Ami finally get off of the tree and fly. As soon as Cher Ami began to get into the air, he was shot and fell to the ground. ____

_____

_____

4. The pigeon stayed on the ground for a few minutes. What he did next was to start to fly again. As quick as a wink, he was shot, but even though he was shot, he continued to his way "home" to Rampont. _____

_____

_____

_____

5. When all was said and done, Cher Ami made it to Rampont. What had happened to the bird before he made it there was that he had lost one eye and he had also lost one leg, and he had been shot in the breast. _____

_____

_____

_____

6. It was good that he still had the message in the capsule that was put on his leg. __

_____

_____

7. The soldiers at Rampont made the decision to stop the bombing right then and there, and when they did that, the division that belonged to Major Whittlesey was saved. _____

_____

_____

8. The United States had a medal that called the Distinguished Service Medal that they gave to heroes, and it was Cher Ami that received it. He also got a medal from France._____

_____

_____

9. The pigeon spent a lot of time getting well, and after he got well, he took a trip to Washington, D. C. When he got there, United States Signal Corps took good care of him. _____

_____

10. The thing that happened to Cher Ami was that he became famous, and the other thing that happened to him was that he lived for another year._____

_____

_____

11. It was in 1919 that the pigeon died, and after he died, the government decided that the best thing to do was to put him on display at the Smithsonian Institute. That is where the famous pigeon is at today _____

_____

_____

_____

WHERE TO PUT THE S

With subject-verb agreement (see pg. 110-111)

Singular noun or third-person pronoun	Singular verb ← s
The boy, he, she, it	goe**s**, play**s**, walk**s**, know**s**
Plural noun ← s	Plural verb
The boy**s**	go, play, walk, know

But not with irregular plurals
(children, men, women, etc.)

With possessives (see pg. 315-317)

Singular noun	Plural noun
the boy'**s** room	the two boy**s**' room

With contractions (see pg. 115)

he is = he'**s**
she is = she'**s**
it is, it has = it'**s**

But not with possessive pronouns

his car
its tires

WHAT TO MAKE AGREE

Subjects and verbs in number (see pg. 110)

Pronouns and antecedents in person and number (see pg. 150)

WHAT FORMS ARE IRREGULAR

Plural nouns not ending in -s (see pg. 112)

Verbs that form past tense and past participles without -ed (see pg. 131)

Adjectives and adverbs that form comparisons with word changes (see pg. 173)

WHERE TO PUT THE -ED

On regular verbs (see pg. 124)	Past tense	Past participle
work, play, want	work**ed**, play**ed**, want**ed**	has work**ed**, has play**ed**, has want**ed**
But not on irregular verbs (see pg. 131-140)		
bend, build	ben**t**, buil**t**	has ben**t**, buil**t**
pay, has	pai**d**, ha**d**	has pai**d**, ha**d**
feel, lose, bring	fel**t**, los**t**, brough**t**	has fel**t**, los**t**, brough**t**
find, sit, stand	f**ou**nd, s**a**t, st**oo**d	has f**ou**nd, s**a**t, st**oo**d
become, come, run	bec**a**me, c**a**me, r**a**n	has bec**o**me, has c**o**me, has r**u**n
begin, drink, swim	beg**a**n, dr**a**nk, sw**a**m	has beg**u**n, has dr**u**nk, has sw**u**m
bet, cut, read	bet, cut, read	has bet, cut, read
break, eat, see	br**oke**, **ate**, saw	has br**oken**, eat**en**, seen
Or BE (see pg. 126)		
I am, he is	I, he **was**	I have **been**, he has **been**
they are	they **were**	they have **been**

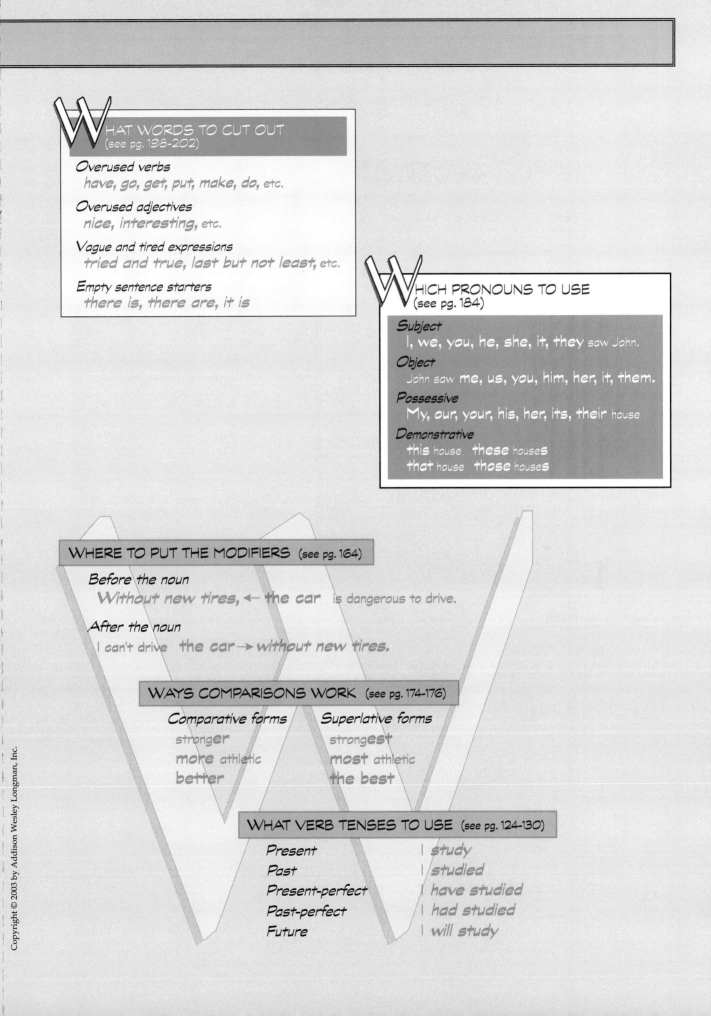

WHAT WORDS TO CUT OUT (see pg. 198-202)

Overused verbs
have, go, get, put, make, do, etc.

Overused adjectives
nice, interesting, etc.

Vague and tired expressions
tried and true, last but not least, etc.

Empty sentence starters
there is, there are, it is

WHICH PRONOUNS TO USE (see pg. 184)

Subject
I, we, you, he, she, it, they saw John.

Object
John saw me, us, you, him, her, it, them.

Possessive
My, our, your, his, her, its, their house

Demonstrative
this house   these houses
that house   those houses

WHERE TO PUT THE MODIFIERS (see pg. 164)

Before the noun
Without new tires, ← the car is dangerous to drive.

After the noun
I can't drive the car → without new tires.

WAYS COMPARISONS WORK (see pg. 174-176)

Comparative forms   Superlative forms
stronger   strongest
more athletic   most athletic
better   the best

WHAT VERB TENSES TO USE (see pg. 124-130)

Present   I study
Past   I studied
Present-perfect   I have studied
Past-perfect   I had studied
Future   I will study

IV

Writing Types of Paragraphs: Shaping the Structure

The chapters of Unit I introduced you to the writing process and applied that process to composing both paragraphs and essays. You saw that you write for many different purposes and audiences. You explored the six steps in the writing process while learning to shape and develop your ideas clearly, emphatically, and convincingly.

Unit IV looks at these things in more detail. Although the steps in the process of writing remain basically the same for each purpose and audience, this unit shows that different purposes and audiences affect the structure of a paragraph or essay. This unit introduces nine organizational structures—from narrative through definition. Each one is different because each aims at accomplishing a different goal.

That's what writing is all about. When you write with a goal in mind, you write with confidence.■

17 Describing a Scene

A good description of a scene creates a sharp, specific image that looks (and often sounds—or even feels and smells) like the place you describe. Through careful word choice, strong details, and clear organization, you create a mental motion picture for your readers. Instead of just *telling* them that a place is pretty, unusual, or horrible, you *show* them the place so they can see its beauty, uniqueness, or ugliness for themselves.

A clear and lively description doesn't require a large vocabulary or any special talent. It just requires a good eye and ear—and attention to the whole writing process. We'll work on that process in this chapter, by

- examining a model paragraph of description
- analyzing what makes a paragraph effective
- thinking through ways to organize the paragraph
- writing a description of a scene

A MODEL PARAGRAPH: DESCRIBING A SCENE

A **description** of a scene must concentrate on specific details, use several of the five senses, and arrange the details in some logical way. Some scenes are views of nature, but most scenes involve the actions of people, animals, or things. You should therefore first describe the physical setting and then tell what goes on within the setting. As you describe the setting and actions, make it easy for readers to locate things by arranging the details in **spatial order**. That involves first providing an overall picture of the scene, then locating each important part in a consistent arrangement from top to bottom, right to left, or nearest to farthest.

UNIT 4	Go Electronic
Chapter 17	Use the following electronic supplements for additional practice with your writing: • For chapter-by-chapter summaries and exercises, visit the Writing with Confidence Companion Website at http://www.ablongman.com/meyers.
Writing with Confidence ©2003	• For work with the writing process, visit The Longman Writer's Warehouse at http://longmanwriterswarehouse.com (password needed). • For additional practice in grammar, use The Writer's ToolKit Plus CD-ROM.

A blueprint of a typical descriptive paragraph might include most or all of these elements:

BLUEPRINT | For Describing a Scene

Topic sentence: overview of scene

Body: elements of scene, arranged in spatial order

Specific detail or activity 1

Specific detail or activity 2

Specific detail or activity 3

Conclusion: general impression of scene

Not every description includes all these parts. Some descriptions of nature don't include a lot of action or may not have any action at all. Other descriptions include people or animals, so they contain a great deal of activity. We'll look at examples of both types.

This first example, from a novel by Amy Tan, is almost pure physical description. Here's the situation: The narrator, a man named Simon, and the narrator's sister, Kwan, have come from the United States to China and are about to get their first glimpse of Changmian, a small village where Kwan grew up but has not seen in many years. As you read the example, notice how Tan first gives a general picture of the village, then provides more specific details. Notice, too, how Tan sharpens her focus on the village by contrasting it to others the narrator has already seen. Incidentally, the word "detritus" means junk *or* rubbish.

Excerpt from *The Hundred Secret Senses*
Amy Tan

* * * *

We approach a stand of trees, arid then, as soon as Kwan announces, "Changmian," I see it: a village nestled between two jagged peaks, their hillsides a velvety mossgreen with folds deepening into emerald. More comes into view; crooked rows of buildings whitewashed with lime, their pitched tile roofs laid in the traditional pattern of dragon coils. Surrounding the village are well-tended fields and mirrorlike ponds neatly divided by stone walls and irrigation trenches. We jump out of the car. Miraculously, Changmian has avoided the detritus of modernization. I see no tin roofs or electrical power lines. In contrast to other villages we passed, the outlying lands here haven't become dumping grounds for garbage; the alleys aren't lined with crumpled cigarette packs or pink plastic bags. Clean stone pathways crisscross the village, then thread up a cleft between the two peaks and disappear through a stone archway. In the distance is another pair of tall peaks, dark jade in color, and beyond those, the purple shadows of two more. Simon and I stare at each other, wide-eyed.

Questions for Analysis

1. The description begins with the countryside surrounding Changmian and then moves into the village itself. Why? What transitions help you see this movement? What transitions help you locate things in the picture?

2. The narrator contrasts Changmian to other villages. What transitions introduce those contrasts? What *doesn't* Changmian have? How does the narrator feel about the other villages?

3. Make a list of nouns—words that name the features of the surrounding countryside and of the village itself. Then list adjectives that make the nouns more specific and interesting. What do you learn about the village from these lists?

4. Also make a list of the verbs—words that express actions. Which ones are most lively? Which ones show the most specific actions?

5. Could you draw a rough sketch of the village based on the description? What would surround the village? What would be its interior?

This second example, from Frank McCourt's book, Angela's Ashes, *includes physical description, people's activities, and even some dialogue.* Angela's Ashes *tells the story of McCourt's childhood in terrible poverty and is set mostly in Limerick, Ireland. In the scene that follows, McCourt describes a day he and his brother Malachy entered their house, located next to an outdoor latrine where people from every house on the street emptied their buckets. The reference to the Pope is to a painting of Pope Leo XIII, whom McCourt's dad worships as a hero. As you read the description, note how it begins by showing people in action even while establishing the setting. Note the specific details about the house, both the kitchen downstairs and the room upstairs. And note how McCourt combines description, action, and dialogue throughout the scene.*

Excerpt from *Angela's Ashes*
Frank McCourt

* * * *

Two weeks before Christmas, Malachy and I come home from school in a heavy rain and when we push in the door we find the kitchen empty. The table and chairs and trunk are gone and the fire is dead in the grate. The Pope is still there and that means we haven't moved again. Dad would never move without the Pope. The kitchen floor is wet, little pools of water all around, and the walls are twinkling with the damp. There's a noise upstairs and when we go up we find Dad and Mam and the missing furniture. It's nice and warm there with a fire blazing in the grate, Mam sitting in the bed, and Dad reading *The Irish Press* and smoking a cigarette by the fire. Mam tells us there was a terrible flood, that the rain came down the lane and poured in under our door. They tried to stop it with rags but they only turned sopping wet and let the rain in. People emptying their buckets made it worse and there was a sickening stink in the kitchen. She thinks we should stay upstairs as long as there is rain. We'll be warm through the winter months and then we can go downstairs in the springtime if there is any sign of a dryness in the walls or the floor. Dad says it's like going away on our holidays to a warm foreign place like Italy. That's what we'll call the upstairs from now on, Italy. Malachy says the Pope is still on the wall downstairs and he's going to be all cold and couldn't we bring him up? but Mam says, No, he's going to stay where he is because I don't want him on the wall glaring at me in the bed. Isn't it enough that we dragged him all the way from Brooklyn to Belfast to Dublin to Limerick? All I want now is a little peace, ease and comfort.

Questions for Analysis

1. The description begins with the kitchen. What details do you learn about it? What sentence serves as a transition, leaving the kitchen?

2. How many of the five senses does the description use? What words refer to or suggest each of those senses?

3. McCourt describes the scene in the present tense even though it occurred long ago. This is a device that professional writers sometimes use. What effect does this use of the present tense have on you?

4. McCourt also uses another device of a professional writer: he includes dialogue but does not put it in quotes. How do you know who is speaking? Based on the dialogue, how old would you guess Frank and Malachy are?

5. Based on the action and dialogue, how do you think McCourt feels about this scene? Is he sad? Angry? Amused? How do you think he feels about his parents?

WRITING ASSIGNMENT FOR DESCRIBING A SCENE

Write a one-paragraph advertising brochure that would interest students in enrolling at your college. Describe one area—an attractive, unusual, or lively gathering place, the library, the weight room in the gym, the student center, the counseling center, the cafeteria, the quadrangle, or any other place you find attractive—and the typical activity that goes on there.

Gathering, Generating, and Arranging the Materials

The best way to gather material for the paragraph is to visit the place for about half an hour and take notes on what you see and hear—and even smell. Record as much information as possible. Although you probably won't use it all, it's better to have more than you need than not enough when you compose the first draft.

Then arrange the details in some consistent spatial order. A brainstorming list or clustering diagram may help as you generate details and decide how to arrange them.

The following questions should guide your note taking:

1. Where is the location? (And what is its name?)

2. What are its dimensions and most important features? Where is each feature—on the right, in the middle, above something else, close, or far away?

3. How large or small are the objects you see? How are they shaped? What are their colors?

4. How many people are in the scene, and where are they? What do they look like? What are they doing?

5. What are the names of things and important people? Use them.

Here is an example of the kind of brainstorming notes you might gather in a half-hour visit to the student center.

located on Wright Avenue in the center of the campus
one-story building, modern, lots of glass
hundreds of students inside
pool tables on the north end—six of them

Continued

> room on the south end with large screen TV, maybe 50 chairs, busy during soap opera time
>
> lots of sofas and upholstered chairs
>
> lots of noise
>
> students reading, talking, eating donuts, drinking sodas
>
> table tennis room next to the pool room, four games at once
>
> music room with radio on
>
> a lot of tables in the music room
>
> some card games at the tables
>
> some students on the east side of room sitting in circle talking about an assignment
>
> two or three couples talking, kissing, etc.
>
> a lot of coming and going throughout the center
>
> guys greeting each other with friendly insults
>
> size and shape: a square building, large open area in the center filled with tables, sofas, and chairs
>
> four rooms—one on each end of center: pool, table tennis, music, TV, study areas

These notes would probably fill more than one paragraph, so you need to *select the details that are most important,* and that *directly support the main idea* of the description. You can accomplish this task in one of two ways—or both of them:

1. Write the topic sentence and then select the materials to develop and support it.
2. Select and arrange material through additional brainstorming, clustering, freewriting, or perhaps an informal outline. Then write the topic sentence.

The final draft of the topic sentence might look like this:

> At almost any time of the day, you'll find the student center a place where you can enjoy yourself, meet people, or study in pleasant surroundings.

6. Edit
5. Revise
4. Write
3. Organize
2. Prewrite
1. Explore

The rest of the paragraph would probably be organized as follows:

1. A general description of the setting
2. More specific details about the scene, arranged in spatial order
3. Transitional sentences or phrases that introduce the activities in the scene
4. A description of those activities, including a few specific examples

Composing the Paragraph

After arranging your material, write a first draft. Don't assume that your arrangement is final. You'll probably shift around details each time you revise.

At some point in the composing process, examine the beginning of each sentence. Do you include transitional words or phrases that show the reader the

spatial relationship between objects or people in the scene? Also examine your organization. Is it consistent, moving from front to back, left to right, top to bottom, or some other way? Do transitions show those locations? If not, rearrange the materials and add transitions so the organization is clear. Finally, do you include a transition that marks the shift from describing the place to describing the activity within it? If not, add one.

Revising Your First Draft

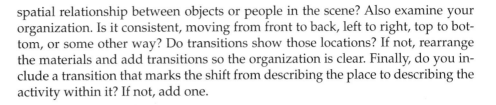

The following questions should guide your revision of the paragraph. Answer them yourself, or collaborate with a group of three or four classmates. If you collaborate, photocopy the draft for the group, or read it aloud twice so the members of your group can hear its content first, and then focus on specific issues.

REVISION GUIDELINES   Describing a Scene

1. What are the strengths of the paragraph?
2. Does a topic sentence clearly state the point? If not, what should the sentence say?
3. After reading the first few sentences, stop to predict the spatial organization of the description. How will the details be introduced? Then read on. If the paragraph doesn't follow a logical spatial pattern, discuss how to rearrange the information and what transitions to include.
4. Should more (or fewer) details be included? Which ones? Where?
5. Look carefully at the nouns and verbs, for they're the real building blocks of any description. Does the paragraph have vivid nouns and strong verbs? Or does it rely too heavily on adjectives and adverbs?
6. Is there a clear transition between description of the place and the people?
7. Is the language awkward or unclear at any point? If so, how might it be improved?

Take notes of these responses and let them guide your revision. Rewrite the paper later when you can examine it with fresh eyes and a clear head.

Further Revising and Editing

Return to your paragraph and revise it again, this time paying special attention to specific details and strong word choice. Make sure you haven't overused adjectives and adverbs. They'll make your writing sound flowery and unnatural. Then edit and proofread your paper, checking for misspelled words, words accidentally left out (or left in—especially if you've composed and revised your paper on a computer), and any other errors you notice. Hand in a clean copy of your work.

ADDITIONAL WRITING ASSIGNMENT

Assume you're writing a brochure for visitors to an exhibit at an art museum. Write a description of the painting that follows, making clear why visitors should stop to see this painting. For example, your topic sentence might say that the painting shows a shocking or humorous scene. Compose, revise, and edit the paragraph following the advice provided throughout this chapter.

William Hogarth, *The Engaged Musician,* **1741, British Museum**

A STUDENT MODEL PARAGRAPH

The paragraph that follows was written by Tuyet-Ahn Van, a Vietnamese student now living in Chattanooga, Tennessee. The scene begins with a general discussion of the larger setting, moves to a specific location, and then describes places and activities within it.

The Happiest Place of My Life
Tuyet-Ahn Van

* * * *

The place that I love the most is in the small country where I was born and spent my childhood. It was a small village in the middle of a rather large area surrounded with green bamboo hedges. In front of the village was my house with a yard where wet clothes were dried and which was also storage for the rice crop in harvest-time. Not far from there was a beautiful garden full of pretty flowers and fruit trees. It was my favorite place. In the afternoon, I used to run merrily along its flower-bordered walks, chasing gorgeous butterflies or catching shining beetles. In doing so, I sometimes trod on a flowering plant, and I was scolded by my mother for being so careless. At the corner of the garden, there was a small arbor with a seat where I spent much time reading some fairytales or doing my homework. Every morning, I also watched the farmers go by with their horses on their way to the fields. Now and then, their merry laughter broke the momentary silence of the countryside. From some cottages nearby, a slender thread of smoke curled upward, announcing the first activities of the hamlet. Certainly, my home was only a humble village, but I still love it very much. It was the place where I had the happiest memories of my life.

Questions for Analysis

1. What is the topic sentence of the paragraph? What general details about the village does Tuyet-Ahn provide? What place within the village does she focus on most specifically?
2. What words and phrases establish the location of things? What words or phrases establish the times of activities?
3. Aside from visual description, does Tuyet-Ahn call on any of the other five senses, either directly or indirectly? If so, where?
4. What main impression does the writer wish you to take from her description?

FINAL WRITING ASSIGNMENT

Think about a place that you loved or hated when you were younger, or visit a place that you love or dread now. Describe it so your classmates can experience the feelings it creates in you: excitement, affection, fear, disgust, calmness—or whatever. Make that point clear in your topic sentence and support the point with relevant physical details and actions.

18 Describing a Person

Good writers notice things. They pay close attention to details and how the details are arranged. They use words to paint a mental picture with clear outlines, colors, and shadings.

But good writers aren't necessarily born with special talent. They develop their skills through practice and patience. If they want to describe someone, for example, they observe all they can about the person's height, weight, physique, facial features, and behavior. They take the time to arrange the details logically. Then they put their observations into clear and specific language that results from many drafts and careful editing.

This chapter will help you write an effective paragraph describing a person by

■ examining a model paragraph describing a person

■ analyzing what makes a description effective

■ thinking through ways to organize a description

■ writing a description of a person

A MODEL PARAGRAPH: DESCRIBING A PERSON

Just as with the description of a place in Chapter 17, your description of a person uses **spatial order** so readers can form a clear mental picture. Sketch the general outlines first and then add specific details in a pattern that moves from top to bottom, right to left, or near to far. A blueprint for this descriptive paragraph might include all or most of the following parts:

UNIT 4	Go Electronic
Chapter 18	Use the following electronic supplements for additional practice with your writing: • For chapter-by-chapter summaries and exercises, visit the Writing with Confidence Companion Website at http://www.ablongman.com/meyers.
Writing with Confidence ©2003	• For work with the writing process, visit The Longman Writer's Warehouse at http://longmanwriterswarehouse.com (password needed). • For additional practice in grammar, use The Writer's ToolKit Plus CD-ROM.

BLUEPRINT | For Describing a Person

Topic sentence: overview of size and shape of person

Body: most noticeable features, arranged in spatial order

Specific feature 1

Specific feature 2

Specific feature 3

Conclusion: general impression of person

As you read the following description, notice the arrangement of details. Are they presented from top to bottom, right to left, or some other way? Pay attention to its word choice, especially the nouns and adjectives.

Diego Velázquez, Sebastian de Morra, 1643–44, Museo del Prado

A Giant of a Dwarf

Although the royal family in seventeenth-century Spain treated dwarfs cruelly, Diego Velázquez portrayed them with great dignity in his paintings, as the portrait of

Sebastian de Morra demonstrates. In it, a well-dressed man sits on the ground, staring directly at the viewer. His face is handsome, with its square jaw and neatly trimmed black hair, sideburns, full goatee, and handlebar mustache. His deep-set eyes gaze darkly beneath arched eyebrows as if he is studying us with great intelligence. He wears elegant clothing: a green jacket that skirts out at the waist, with a delicate white fabric at the sleeves and wide collar. A long, heavy orange cape covers the front and back of his shoulders but not his arms. His fists are clenched at his belt, almost like a sheriff preparing for a gunfight. Only the man's tiny legs, pointing directly at us, reveal that de Morra is a dwarf. This is a portrait of a nobleman, not a ridiculous figure, and it is a tribute to the heart and talent of the artist.

Questions for Analysis

1. What is the topic sentence—the sentence that states the main point of the paragraph?
2. What is the purpose of the second sentence? How does it relate to the sentences that follow?
3. What specific details develop the point of the topic sentence? What words or phrases are especially descriptive?
4. How is the description arranged spatially? Why do you think the writer chooses this arrangement? Why doesn't the writer use phrases like "at the top" or "on the left" to help you locate what is being described?
5. An effective description also reveals something about the person's character. What details show the dignity of Sebastian de Morra?
6. The writer establishes a contrast between the royal family's treatment of dwarfs and the treatment by Velázquez. Why?

WRITING ASSIGNMENT FOR DESCRIBING A PERSON

Write a one-paragraph description of a person for a popular magazine read by adults. Base your description on the photograph that you find most interesting. Include details that describe the person clearly—and details that reveal something about his or her character.

For Describing Clearly
The following adjectives may help you express your observations: oval, round, circular, square, broad, narrow, wide, oblong, piercing, intense, protruding, upturned, sloping, straight, hooked, bumpy, lumpy, bushy, almond-shaped, high, full, soft, hard, deep, shallow, indented, thick, thin, massive, tiny, weak, receding, attached, detached, close-set, large, long, well-defined, bulging, slack, light, dark, numerous, dimpled.

Library of Congress

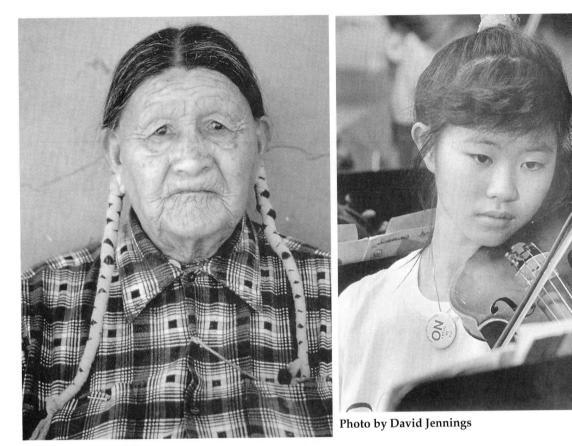

Photo by Dan Morrill

Photo by David Jennings

Photo by David R. Frazier, Photolibrary

6. Edit
5. Revise
4. Write
3. Organize
2. Prewrite
1. Explore

Gathering, Generating, and Arranging the Materials

Begin by jotting down your strongest reaction to the photograph you've chosen. Let this reaction guide you in deciding what to include and how to arrange the information. What do you think the picture reveals about the person? What feeling does the picture create in you? Follow these steps in composing the paragraph:

1. Examine the picture closely and take notes on the details you observe. What shape is the face? Are the person's eyes large or small, round or oval, wide or narrow? How could you describe the eyebrows? Is the nose big or tiny, broad or narrow, straight or crooked? How could you characterize the cheekbones and ears? Describe the person's hair—its thickness, shade, and style. Could any short comparisons ("His eyes are like . . . ") help to clarify the description?

   Also, if the photograph shows only the upper body of the person, note its size and shape, the width of the shoulders, or any other important feature. Consult the Tips box for possible adjectives to use, but don't rely too much on adjectives or the paragraph will sound unnatural.

2. Using brainstorming or clustering, put your ideas down on paper. Here is part of the clustering diagram for the description of Sebastian de Morra you just read:

3. Now consider if the details support—or change—your reaction to the photograph. Does your first reaction still hold up, or should you revise it? What details would further support that reaction? Are any ideas unimportant or off the topic?

4. Then organize your materials in an informal outline. You'll probably think of more details while composing and revising the paragraph. Here's an outline for the description of Sebastian de Morra, revised several times until the spatial arrangement of information is clear:

Overall view of the dwarf-well-dressed man sitting on ground
  Top-to-bottom description of man
    Face
      Neat black hair, beard, sideburns, mustache
      Eyes-deep set, intense
    Clothes
      Jacket, green with white collar and sleeves
        long, skirted at waist
      Cloak over shoulders
    Arms
      Short, with fists clenched at waist
    Legs
      Short
      Only real clue that he is a dwarf

Writing the Paragraph

6. Edit
5. Revise
4. Write
3. Organize
2. Prewrite
1. Explore

State your reaction in a topic sentence. It should make your point about the person and maybe suggest how you'll arrange the details in the paragraph. Here are some examples:

The face of Abraham Lincoln is certainly not handsome, but it reveals a serious and intelligent man.

Princess Diana was incredibly beautiful, and her kindness showed in her smile.

The body and face of Nelson Mandela show both his dignity and his grace.

6. Edit
5. Revise
4. Write
3. Organize
2. Prewrite
1. Explore

Then write the first draft. Relax and let the words flow. Say your sentences aloud so you can hear what sounds natural and clear. After finishing the draft, put it aside for a while unless you immediately think of ways to rearrange, restate, or further develop your ideas.

Revising Your First Draft

Revise the paragraph, paying special attention to the following questions. You may answer them yourself or collaborate with three or four classmates. If you work with classmates, photocopy your paper or read it aloud twice.

REVISION GUIDELINES | Describing a Person

1. What are the strengths of the paragraph?

2. Is the point of the paragraph clear? If not, what would make it clear?

3. Stop after reading the first sentence or two and predict what information might follow. Then continue reading. If the predictions aren't met or the organization isn't clear, consider how to correct these problems.

4. If the description includes the body of the subject as well as the face, what should be described first? Where is the most specific development? Does it appear in a logical place?

5. What principle of spatial organization does the description follow—top to bottom, bottom to top, center to sides? Should any details be rearranged to follow that organization?

6. Should more details be included, especially details that reveal the character of the person? What kind of details? Where?

7. Is the language unclear at any point? Are there too many adjectives or too few? How might the language be improved?

8. Are the connections between ideas clear? If not, how could they be strengthened?

Take notes of these responses to guide your revision. Rewrite the paper when your mind is clear and you can attend to word choice, clarity, and conciseness.

Further Revising and Editing

Return to your paragraph. Revise it again, this time paying special attention to clear transitions.

Then edit and proofread your paper, checking for misspelled words, words accidentally left out (or left in—especially if you've composed and revised your paper on a computer), and any other errors you notice. Hand in a clean copy of your work.

ADDITIONAL WRITING ASSIGNMENT

Suppose you're working as a teacher's aide in a sixth-grade classroom in a local school, and the class is studying the Great Depression, which began in 1929 and lasted until about 1941. The teacher and you want students to study the faces of people from that time to see their suffering, their strong character, and their dignity. Choose one of the following photographs and write a description that will highlight one of those qualities. Revise and edit the paragraph, following the guidelines discussed in this chapter.

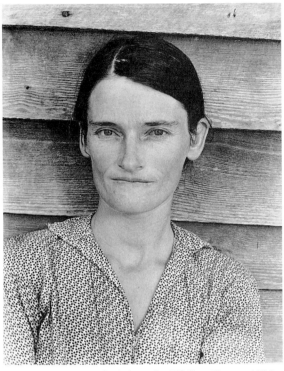

Allie Mae Burroughs, photo by Walker Evans, 1936.

Othel Lee Burroughs, photo by Walker Evans, 1936.

Walker Evans, Subway Portrait, 1941.

Walker Evans, Subway Portrait, 1938–1941.

A STUDENT MODEL PARAGRAPH

The following description was written by Iman Rooker, a student at Chattanooga State Community College. As you read it, notice how she blends physical description with details and observations that reveal both the character of the subject and her attitude toward him.

A Man I Love
Iman Rooker
★ ★ ★ ★

Once, there was a man so strong that his muscles showed with every move he made. He was so healthy and kind that when people met him, they looked at him with respect. Now age and disease have caught up with him, leaving him blind and sick. There he sits silently on his chair, looking at me with his deep brown eyes. Patience and experience have settled in, and the expression on his face looks as if life has carved a chapter in every line. Even his hair has started to get gray by the passing of each minute, but it still looks full and shiny. He sits in his favorite chair, wearing his blue and white-striped pajamas. His hands shake and tremble, trying to keep the cup in his hands from falling. With long legs and broad shoulders, he still looks bigger than he is. A man like him should always be respected and loved, especially because he is my father.

Questions for Analysis

1. The paragraph actually describes the subject at two stages in his life. Which sentence actually introduces the main part of the description?
2. What transitional expressions establish the contrast between the descriptions of the younger and older man?
3. What details establish the man's former physical power? Iman claims the man should be respected because he is her father. What physical details suggest that he should be respected even if we don't know who he is?

FINAL WRITING ASSIGNMENT

Describe a person you know well so your classmates can see the person's most important character traits and perhaps your attitude toward the person. State the point in the topic sentence and then support it with revealing physical details.

19

Writing Narration

Narration is simply telling a story. Think of the story as a movie in which you let readers see people in action and hear them speak. You set the scene, and then let the action progress until it reaches a conclusion. This chapter will help you to write an effective narrative by

■ examining a model of narration

■ analyzing what makes a narration effective

■ thinking through ways to organize a narration

■ writing a narration

A MODEL OF NARRATION

A good narrative paragraph or multiparagraph essay usually takes all of the following into account:

1. It must be unified, with all the action developing a central point.
2. It should introduce the **four Ws** of a setting—*who, what, where,* and *when*—within the context of the action.
3. It must be detailed enough for readers to feel as if they're on the scene, observing and listening to the events.
4. It must be *coherent,* with transitions indicating changes in time, location, and characters.
5. It should begin at the beginning and end at the end. That is, the narrative should follow a **chronological order**—with events occurring consecutively in a time sequence. Only the most skillful storyteller can jump back and forth in time without confusing readers.
6. It should build toward a **climax**, which brings the action to a close. This is the moment of most tension or surprise—a time when the ending is revealed or the importance of events becomes clear. But even if the climax is surprising,

UNIT 4	Go Electronic
Chapter 19	Use the following electronic supplements for additional practice with your writing:
	• For chapter-by-chapter summaries and exercises, visit the Writing with Confidence Companion Website at http://www.ablongman.com/meyers.
Writing with Confidence ©2003	• For work with the writing process, visit The Longman Writer's Warehouse at http://longmanwriterswarehouse.com (password needed).
	• For additional practice in grammar, use The Writer's ToolKit Plus CD-ROM.

it should still be logical. Readers may feel cheated when the story ends with: "Then I woke up to discover it was only a dream."

The following narration is taken from James McBride's The Color of Water, *the remarkable story about his white mother who raised twelve black children in New York—all of whom received college degrees and became highly successful adults. In the four-paragraph excerpt you're about to read, young James is fourteen years old, and his stepfather, Hunter Jordan, has just had a stroke. As you read the excerpt, notice how the four Ws of setting are introduced within the context of the action. Notice the specific detail. And notice how McBride handles the conversations between the characters.*

Excerpt from *The Color of Water*
James McBride

* * * *

1   [Daddy] came home from the hospital about a week later and seemed to get better. His speech, though slurred, returned. He sat in his basement headquarters, recuperating, while we crept around the house and Mommy walked about silently, eyes still red-rimmed, on edge. One day he summoned me downstairs and asked me to help him dress. "I want to take a drive," he said. I was the oldest kid living at home by then, my other siblings being away at school. He put on his sweater, wool pants, hat, and blue peacoat. Though ill and thin, he still looked sharp. Slowly, he mounted the stairs and stepped outside. It was May and brisk, almost cold outside. We went into the garage and stepped into his gold-colored Pontiac. "I want to drive home one more time," he said. He was talking about Richmond, Virginia, where he grew up. But he was too weak to drive, so he sat there behind the wheel of the car, staring at the garage wall, and he began to talk.

2   He said he had a little money saved up for Mommy and a little land in Virginia, but it was not enough. He said that since I was the oldest living at home, I had to watch out for Mommy and my little brothers and sisters because "y'all are special," he said. "And just so special to me." It was the only time I ever heard him refer to race in any way, however vaguely, but it didn't matter, because right then and there I knew he was going to die and I had to blink back my tears. I wanted to tell him that I loved him, that I hoped with all my heart that he would get better, but I could not formulate the words in my mouth. We had never spoken that way to one another. We joked and talked, but his chief concern had always been my "schoolin'" and "church raising" as he called it. He was not a man for dialogue. That was Mommy's job.

3   Two days later he suffered a relapse. An ambulance came and got him. About four in the morning the phone rang. My sister Kathy and I lay upstairs and listened, and through what seemed to be a fog, I heard my older brother Richie telling Mommy, "It's all right, Ma. It's all right."

4   "It's not all right! It's not all right!" Ma cried, and she wailed and wailed, the sound of her cries circling the house like a spirit and settling on all the corridors and beds where we lay, weeping in silence.

Questions for Analysis

1. Where and when does the action take place? What month was it? Who was involved? What are their names?

2. What transitional words indicate changes in time, location, or participants in the action? Look especially at the beginnings of each paragraph.

3. Locate the proper nouns—the nouns that are capitalized. Aside from the people, what else does McBride name specifically? Why?

4. McBride handles dialogue in two ways: by quoting and by indirectly reporting what people say. What, specifically, do you notice about these

techniques—the use of quotation marks, use of punctuation and capitalization, and the handling of tenses?

5. There are four paragraphs in this narration. Give each of them a "title" or a label so you can see what determines the paragraph divisions.

6. Describe how this excerpt builds toward a climax. What is the climax? Where is it first hinted at?

WRITING ASSIGNMENT FOR NARRATION

Even if we think our own lives have not been dramatic, tragic, or fun-filled, all of us still have personal stories worth telling. Write a paragraph (or more than one paragraph) about one event that affected you greatly and would probably interest your classmates. Your main purpose will be to entertain, but you may also wish to make a larger point about a lesson in life. "Firsts" often serve as excellent subjects for such narratives: your first day at school, your first date, your first job, the first time you drove a car, or the birth of your first child.

Gathering, Generating, and Arranging the Materials

Specific details create the realism and drama of a story. But if you choose too large a topic to discuss, one of two problems might result.

1. You will find yourself writing a book.
2. You will write a short paragraph filled with generalizations because you can't possibly develop each one.

You should begin, therefore, by choosing a subject that is small enough for you to explore. List three or four topics to write about and record any details that occur to you about each one. If possible, consider the point your story might make. That will help you decide which details to include. For example, don't describe your uncle and aunt's little store if that information doesn't develop the point of the story. But if you want to emphasize the great loss your uncle and aunt suffered when the building burned down, then take your readers on a short tour of the store.

Explore your topic through freewriting, brainstorming, or clustering, and then arrange your ideas chronologically. A revised brainstorming list about a first day at school, arranged in chronological order, might look like this:

> Arrived at school, holding Mom's hand
>
> Met lady who said she was my teacher
>
> Cried when Mom told me good-bye
>
> Ran after her, but teacher stopped me
>
> Told me that I would meet all sorts of new friends
>
> Led me into a classroom filled with toys, bright posters, and assorted treasures
>
> Became interested in all this new stuff
>
> Maybe school wouldn't be too bad

Composing the Paragraph or Essay

Now compose a first draft of the paragraph or essay. The story should include these elements:

1. A topic sentence that makes the point of the narrative clear, such as: "My first day at school was frightening." This topic sentence—and its point—could evolve in later drafts of the story—or it might be omitted altogether if revealing the main idea at the beginning will destroy the climax. In either case, its point should be clear by the end of the story.
2. Information to establish the setting: *who, what, where,* and *when*
3. Enough detail to develop the topic idea convincingly and clearly
4. An arrangement of the details in chronological order
5. A progression to a climax or dramatic conclusion.

If the first draft of your paragraph turns out to be only five to seven sentences long, you're probably summarizing events rather than developing them specifically. Try one or more of the following procedures to generate more details:

1. Look for the verbs *used to* or *would.* Look also for expressions such as *always, usually, often,* and *sometimes.* These verbs and expressions introduce habitual actions—that is, generalizations. Omit them if you can. Then compose sentences beginning with expressions such as *once, one day, one evening,* or a specific hour or day. These sentences should lead you through a sequence of more specific actions.
2. Close your eyes and put yourself back into the experience. What did you do first, next, and then next? What did other people do, and how did they respond to each other's actions? As events enter your mind, write them down quickly so that you capture them. When you revise later, you can eliminate the unnecessary details and smooth out your language.

A blueprint of such a paragraph of narration might look something like this:

TIPS

For Establishing Transitions in Narration

Say words such as *first, second, third* or *next, then, afterward* aloud as you explore the sequence of actions. You don't have to include these words in the paragraph if the sequence is clear—but use them if they add coherence.

BLUEPRINT	For Writing Narration

Topic sentence: overview of subject and point of the story

Setting: who, what, where, when

↓

Body: action and dialogue of story, arranged in climax order

Action 1

Action 2

Action 3

↓

Conclusion: climax of action, surprise, revelation, reflection

Revising Your First Draft

Return to the paragraph after a few hours or days and revise it further, clarifying your point, adding (or removing) details, and checking for coherence.

Let the following questions guide you in revising your paragraph. Answer them yourself or collaborate with a group of three or four classmates. As usual, photocopy your paper, or read it aloud twice.

REVISION GUIDELINES | Writing Narration

1. What are the strengths of the paragraph(s)?

2. Does a topic sentence clearly state the point? If not, is the point of the story clear without it?

3. After reading the first few sentences, stop to predict what will follow. Then read on, noting what predictions aren't met and what further information, if any, should be added to meet these predictions.

4. Should more (or fewer) details be included? Which ones? Where?

5. Determine the climax of the story—the most dramatic moment at or near the end. Does it end the story logically? Does it genuinely surprise? Does it reveal the importance of events? If the climax isn't strong enough, could it be strengthened through additional details or more polished sentences?

6. Is the language unclear at any point? If so, how might it be improved?

7. Is there clear movement between ideas in the paragraph? If not, how could it be improved?

Take notes of these responses to guide your revision. Rewrite the paper later when you can examine it with fresh eyes and a clear head. Pay special attention to word choice, clarity, and conciseness.

Further Revising and Editing

Review and revise your paragraph again. Then edit and proofread, checking for misspelled words, words accidentally left out (or left in—especially if you've composed and revised your paper on a computer), and any other errors you notice. Hand in a clean copy of your work.

ADDITIONAL WRITING ASSIGNMENT

When many families get together on holidays or special occasions, they hear the same stories year after year. Write an account of one of the legends from your family. (You may wish to write a story of perhaps four or five paragraphs in length.)

Assume that your audience is a group of people who don't know you, and shape the story so it reveals something important about your family or one of its members. If you can't recall a family legend, write a story about a pleasant event from your childhood, perhaps one that you'll pass on as a legend to the next generation. Assume again that your primary purpose is to entertain. At the beginning or end of the story, make its significance clear.

A STUDENT MODEL ESSAY

Christine Mueller was a student at Truman College in Chicago. As you read her story, notice that she begins with the ending and then goes back in time to the beginning. Notice, too, how she introduces information about the setting: Who? What? When? Where? Finally, notice how the end returns to beginning, and consider why Christine chose to arrange the story in that way.

The Butterfly Is Free
Christine Mueller

* * * *

1   "The butterfly is free to fly

2   She spread her wings and . . ."

3   This was part of the eulogy I wrote and read at my best friend's funeral when we were eighteen. She had attempted suicide twice and failed. Her doctor had given her three bottles of anti-depressants which she took her last day.

4   Her name was Sonya Rodriguez but we all called her "Stone." Stone was a modern-day Cinderella, a ward of the state at the age of four. She lived with her wicked step-mother and two wicked stepsisters. She was expected to clean, cook, shop, and do the laundry for the entire family. Her free time was to go to studying, to maintain a straight "A" average. At fifteen, she did all this but looked for more. She created a life-like dummy to lay in her bed, and we'd crawl out the bedroom window to hang out and party all night. When we were together they called us Orange and Yellow Sunshine for the colors of our hair.

5   The week her stepmother took a vacation, Stone and I, another girl named Sonny, and some guys we hung around with went wild. We took Stone horseback riding, partying, to shows, concerts, and everywhere we could get to.

6   Shortly after turning eighteen she stopped by my house with a suitcase and asked if she could stay. My mother left the decision up to me. Sure, why not?

7   I introduced her to B.S. Phil and they laughed, danced, and romanced. But he broke her heart one weekend and she was still very fragile. Unfortunately, the same weekend I went off camping. The following Tuesday I came home from work to find Stone had O.D.'d on pills for depression her doctor had prescribed.

8   Phil and I were pretty blown away. After the funeral we were sitting in my mother's backyard. We saw one hundred butterflies or more only in the yard, none to the right, none to the left. We both knew then that the dead could communicate. We knew she came to say, "Until we meet again."

9   Once when we were fifteen, I asked Stone, "If you believed in reincarnation, what would you want to be?"

10   She answered quickly, "A butterfly, because butterflies are free."

Questions for Analysis

1. This story isn't told in chronological order. It begins with Stone's funeral and then flashes back to the beginning. Why?
2. The story describes a tragedy, but were you sad after you read it? Why or why not?
3. What transitions in the story signal the passage of time? Where are they placed and why?
4. This story is divided into ten paragraphs. What seems to determine where the paragraph divisions occur?

FINAL WRITING ASSIGNMENT

Write about a time when you lost a loved one or a prized possession—or a time when a prized possession of yours was broken. Establish the circumstances (Who? What? Where? When?) at or near the beginning, and then let the action unfold. You may wish to include a bit of dialogue as Christine Mueller did.

Your narrative will probably be more than one paragraph long.

CHAPTER

20 Writing a Report

A **report** is a summary of the decisions taken at a meeting, the details of some incident, a set of observations, or the results of an experiment. It's an important way to communicate facts and information. Managers, teachers, scientists, students, and business people care about and want to know the information. But these readers are often busy, so they want a brief summary in the report: what happened, how it happened, and why. Like a narrative, the report often follows chronological order, but unlike a narrative, the report is objective. It sticks only to the facts.

Writing a report isn't difficult, especially after you've learned to compose topic sentences and write narratives. This chapter will show you how to write one type of report by

- examining a model paragraph of a report
- analyzing what makes a report effective
- thinking through ways to organize a report
- writing a report

A MODEL PARAGRAPH: A REPORT

In some ways, a report is like a narrative. Both tell when and where something took place, who was involved, and what happened. But the report doesn't try to entertain; its purpose is to inform. It therefore begins with a topic sentence that states the most important conclusions or results of the event. Then it supplies supporting details and explanations in chronological order.

UNIT 4	Go Electronic
Chapter 20	Use the following electronic supplements for additional practice with your writing: • For chapter-by-chapter summaries and exercises, visit the Writing with Confidence Companion Website at http://www.ablongman.com/meyers.
Writing with Confidence ©2003	• For work with the writing process, visit The Longman Writer's Warehouse at http://longmanwriterswarehouse.com (password needed). • For additional practice in grammar, use The Writer's ToolKit Plus CD-ROM.

A blueprint of a typical narrative report looks like this:

BLUEPRINT | For a Report

Topic sentence: main results

Body: explanations, arranged in chronological order

Explanation 1

Explanation 2

Explanation 3

Conclusion: summary, interpretation, call for action

As you read the following report about a strange—but true—fad in the United States, note that the statement of conclusion comes first, and then its narrative structure. Notice how the conclusion introduces several points. Look for them as you read on.

The Pet Rock Phenomenon

The pet rock was the perfect fad: an item that was useless, pointless, and extremely profitable—and its success was short-lived and impossible to explain. In 1975 more than a million Americans who were fed up with feeding cats and walking dogs chose a pet that cost five dollars, needed no maintenance, did absolutely nothing, and looked exactly like the rocks in any garden. This multimillion-dollar scheme began after Gary Dahl, a thirty-eight-year-old unemployed advertising executive from California, spent an evening in a bar with friends who complained about the costs and inconveniences of owning a pet. Soon afterward, Dahl joked that he had the perfect maintenance-free pet and gave his friends some smooth beach rocks. They loved the gag, and Dahl was inspired. He ordered nearly three tons of rocks from a Mexican beach and wrote a clever owner's manual for the "care and training of your Pet Rock." The manual explained that, with a little push, the rock could "learn to roll over," and with hardly any training, it would "play dead." It knew how to roll down a hill. And, like a guard dog, the rock also could protect its owner from an assault. "Reach into your pocket or purse as though you were going to comply with the mugger's demands. Extract your pet rock. Shout the command, 'Attack!' and bash the mugger's head in." When pet rocks were introduced just before Christmas of 1975, they soon sold out at card shops and department stores throughout the country. The original pet rock was just a plain stone, but later versions were painted brightly with sly smiles, wise grins, and devilish sneers—as if to say, "Yes, we all know I'm a joke." About 5 million pet rocks were sold, bringing Dahl a profit of ninety-five cents for each. Dahl was featured in *Newsweek* and *Time,* and he soon introduced additional products like Pet Rock Food—a chunk of rock salt.

Questions for Analysis

1. What are the main conclusions of the report? Which sentences further summarize events? Which sentence introduces the supporting details?

2. What words or phrases in the report indicate the location and time of the events?

3. Examine the treatment of quotations in the report. How are they introduced? How are they punctuated?

4. Where does the report end and further summary of results continue? What is the purpose of the final sentence of the paragraph?

WRITING ASSIGNMENT FOR A REPORT

Write a report on a lecture for one of your classes for a student who could not attend. State the main points or results of the lecture first, followed by the most important supporting points, which you explain and interpret. You may include short quotations from the lecture that clarify or illustrate important ideas.

Gathering, Generating, and Arranging the Materials

Begin by taking notes of the lecture. What are its subject matter and its thesis? If your instructor outlines its main points (or even some supporting points)—either at the beginning or during the class period—write them down. Take notes on what the instructor says, especially examples that will clarify ideas. And note the comments and questions of classmates, too, if you find them important.

After the class, organize your notes, perhaps in an outline. What points should you state at the beginning of the report, probably in a topic sentence? What details support those main points? Use these as the basis for your organization.

Brainstorming may help you generate and organize the details, and freewriting may help you state your ideas. For example, a revised brainstorming list for the pet rock report (which, of course is not a classroom lecture!) might look like this:

6. Edit
5. Revise
4. Write
3. Organize
2. Prewrite
1. Explore

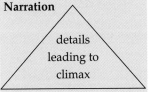

TIPS

For Distinguishing Between a Narration and a Report

Most narratives lead up to a climax, with the most important information at the end. You can visualize a narrative as a triangle:

Narration

> details
> leading to
> climax

A report, however, reveals the result at the beginning of the paragraph. The details leading up to that result follow. You can visualize the report as an upside-down triangle:

Report

> results (or climax)
> followed by
> details

---

inventor Gary Dahl
   from California
   advertising man, no job
   thirty-eight
idea started in a bar
friends complained about problems with pets
gave his friends "pet rocks" as joke
friends loved it, inspired him
ordered about three tons of rocks from Mexican beach
wrote owner's manual ("care and training of your Pet Rock")
quotes from the manual: when you push the rock,
   it can "learn to roll over"
   could "play dead" with training
   could roll down a hill
   could protect owner from assault (quote this explanation from manual)
sold out during Christmas season
later versions: brightly painted with smiles, grins, etc.

Continued

> about 5 million rocks sold
> Dahl's profit on each: 95 cents
> Dahl featured in Newsweek and Time
> additional product: rock salt as food

Composing the Paragraph

Now write a draft of the paragraph, and after you finish, compare the opening statement with the supporting details. Adjust both if necessary so that you support every main point with details. This process of adjusting will probably carry you through several revisions.

End the paragraph with a return to the beginning, restating its main ideas in different terms.

Revising Your First Draft

Let the following questions guide your revision of the paragraph. You may answer them yourself or collaborate with three or four classmates who will discuss them. If you work with classmates, photocopy your paper, or read it aloud twice.

REVISION GUIDELINES   Writing a Report

1. What are the strengths of the paragraph?
2. Does the report make the purpose clear?
3. Does a topic sentence clearly state the main points? If not, what should be added or omitted? Are the points presented in a clear and consistent organization? If not, how could the organization be improved?
4. Use predicting to analyze the organization and development of ideas. Read the first few sentences of your paper aloud, and then stop so the group may predict what will follow.
5. Is more specific information needed? Should any information be dropped?
6. Is any language unclear? If so, how might it be improved?

Take notes of these responses to guide your revision. Rewrite the paper later when you can examine it with fresh eyes and a clear mind. And pay special attention to word choice, clarity, and conciseness.

Further Revising and Editing

Return to the paragraph and revise it again. Edit and proofread your paper, checking for misspelled words, words accidentally left out or left in, and any other errors you notice. Hand in a clean copy of your work.

ADDITIONAL WRITING ASSIGNMENT

Write a report of a discussion you were involved in that led to a simple decision. It could have taken place within your family, among your friends, at work, in a club, or in a class. Limit the topic to one that you can examine specifically in one paragraph. Begin by stating the decision you reached, and then explain how you reached it.

A STUDENT MODEL PARAGRAPH

The following report was written several years ago by Veronica Fleeton, a former member of the armed forces and a student at Truman College. The report was sent to the school administration and resulted in some improvements in the cleanliness of washrooms. As you read the report, notice that it summarizes the results of a plan the students themselves devised. Notice that it explains how the plan was carried out, as well as what each part of the plan revealed. Notice, too, that it concludes with a call to action, which—in this case—was actually accepted.

Let's Keep It Clean
Veronica Fleeton

* * * *

If the manager of the janitorial department at this college wants to score a few "brownie" points with students, he or she might discuss what to do about improving the cleanliness and sanitation practices in the restrooms. They are filthy and foul smelling, and there is very little evidence that they are being cleaned often enough. During several visits to various restrooms on different floors this semester, a group of students found the doors propped open, the maid carts in the restrooms, but no one actually cleaning the rooms. At other times, we have checked the trash cans, sinks, commodes, floors, corners, and soap and towel dispensers. The results of these inspections were not positive. In our opinion, some restrooms had not received any form of cleaning whatsoever. The trash cans were overflowing, and the towel and soap dispensers were empty. As a further test, we intentionally planted objects in conspicuous areas such as corners or stall areas. We revisited the restrooms the next day to see if they had been removed. In most cases, they were right where we had planted them. This situation is both frustrating and unsafe. In our society today, there are many different types of germs and bacteria present, especially in public facilities such as restrooms. The college has a large population, and the restrooms are constantly being used. Since they are receiving heavy usage, how often are they being cleaned? We would like to think the frequency of cleaning is at least once a day, but it should be twice a day to accommodate students in both day and night classes. We come to the college to learn and pursue our educational goals. We should not have to worry about the quality of the cleaning done in the restrooms.

Questions for Analysis

1. What is the topic sentence of this paragraph—the sentence that summarizes the conclusions of the report?

2. According to the report, what specific problems were found in the restrooms?

3. What did the group of students do to uncover these problems? Did the students do more than one thing?

4. Although the activities the report describes are not exactly in chronological order, there are a number of transitions that make references to time. Locate them.

FINAL WRITING ASSIGNMENT

Observe and report on something that's happening in your school or surrounding community: at a student meeting place, the library, the cafeteria, the parking lot, a park, an off-campus student hangout, even a place that serves small children. You don't have to uncover a scandal or file a complaint. In fact, your report may discuss how well the event turned out. You may wish to collaborate with other students on this report, especially if it involves events happening at different times or locations. Divide the visits among the members of the collaborative group. Do not disturb the people you observe. Take notes of your findings.

If you collaborate, each person in the group may write a separate report, or the group may collaborate on a single report. The audience for the report should be the person or persons who would find it most useful. End the report with praise of the activities, or recommendations for improvements, if either seems appropriate.

21 Describing a Process

When you write a **process analysis**, you explain how to do something or how something works. A description of how an egg develops into a mature chicken is a process analysis. A description of how an automobile's fuel injector mixes gasoline with air is a process analysis. So are the recipes in a cookbook and the instruction books that come with new stereos and appliances. Of course, every process analysis ought to provide information or instruction that readers want or need to know. This chapter will help you write a process analysis paragraph by

- examining a model paragraph of process analysis
- analyzing what makes a process analysis effective
- thinking through ways to organize a process paragraph
- writing a process analysis

A MODEL PARAGRAPH: PROCESS ANALYSIS

Many process analysis paragraphs provide a set of instructions for their readers. The instructions must therefore be complete—including all the information necessary to perform or at least understand the process. They must also be well organized—breaking down the process into a series of steps. The typical organization usually includes two parts:

1. It introduces the process and lists the materials (tools, parts, or ingredients) that the process requires.
2. It presents each step in the process in a sequence so that readers can visualize the process or perform it themselves.

UNIT 4	Go Electronic
Chapter 21	Use the following electronic supplements for additional practice with your writing: • For chapter-by-chapter summaries and exercises, visit the Writing with Confidence Companion Website at http://www.ablongman.com/meyers.
Writing with Confidence ©2003	• For work with the writing process, visit The Longman Writer's Warehouse at http://longmanwriterswarehouse.com (password needed). • For additional practice in grammar, use The Writer's ToolKit Plus CD-ROM.

A blueprint of such a paragraph would look like this:

BLUEPRINT | For Describing a Process

Topic sentence: process name and importance

Body: steps in the process, arranged in sequential order

Listing of tools and/or materials

Step 1

Step 2

Step 3

Conclusion: summary, restatement of importance

The following example of a process analysis comes from Laura Ingalls Wilder's Little House on the Prairie, *a classic story for young readers based on the Ingalls family's experiences as settlers in Kansas in the mid-nineteenth century. The selection you're about to read describes the father's making of a wooden door for their log cabin. The process is actually in two parts: constructing the door and then creating its hinges. As you read, pay attention to the introductions, summaries, and transitions that mark each step in both processes.*

Excerpt from *Little House on the Prairie*
Laura Ingalls Wilder

* * * *

1   Pa said he would make a door that very day. He wanted more than a quilt between them and the wolves, next time. . .

2   With the saw he sawed logs the right length for a door. He sawed shorter lengths for crosspieces. Then with the ax he split the logs into slabs and smoothed them nicely. He laid the long slabs together on the ground and placed the shorter slabs across them. Then with the auger he bored holes through the crosspieces into the long slabs. Into every hole he drove a wooden peg that fitted tightly.

3   That made the door. It was a good oak door, solid and strong.

4   For the hinges he cut three long straps. One hinge was to be near the top of the door, one near the bottom, and one in the middle.

5   He fastened them first to the door, in this way: He laid a little piece of wood on the door, and bored a hole through it into the door. Then he doubled one end of a strap around the little piece of wood, and with his knife cut round holes through the strap. He laid the little piece of wood on the door again, with the strap doubled around it, and all the holes making one hole. Then Laura gave him a peg and the hammer, and he drove the peg into the hole. The peg went through the strap and the little piece of wood and through the strap again and into the door. That held the strap so that it couldn't get loose.

6   "I told you a fellow doesn't need nails!" Pa said.

Questions for Analysis

1. In the explanation of making the door, how many steps are involved? What transitions help you identify the steps?
2. Which sentences summarize the process of making the door?
3. Before explaining how the hinges were made, a short paragraph tells where the hinges will be placed. Why?
4. What tools and materials did the father use in making the door and hinges? This process analysis shows you how the father made the door, not how to make a door yourself. If the purpose changed to actual instructions for making a door, where should the tools and materials be mentioned?
5. Using the information from this process analysis, could you draw a sketch of the door and its hinges? Try it.

WRITING ASSIGNMENT FOR DESCRIBING A PROCESS

Write an entertaining description of the steps you, a friend, or a relative goes through in performing some daily, weekly, or less frequent ritual. Keep the topic simple so you can describe it in one paragraph. For example, you could describe dressing for a date or formal event, getting ready to write a paper, doing stretching and warm-up exercises, studying for a big examination, combing hair over a bald spot, or straightening up the mess in a bedroom. Assume your readers are adults who might find your article in a popular magazine.

Gathering, Generating, and Arranging the Materials

After choosing a topic, brainstorm or cluster several lists of details to include in the paragraph. Add to these lists as more ideas occur to you. Include the following:

1. All the materials needed to perform the task (for example, shampoo, conditioner, towel, blow-dryer, comb, brush, hair spray, curlers, curling iron, wall mirror, handheld mirror, and chewing gum)
2. Any terms that need to be defined and explained (such as *mousse, gel,* or *tantrum*)
3. All the steps in the process (for instance, washing, drying, setting, combing out, teasing, further combing, primping, crying—and then resetting, combing out, and so on)

Now make an outline in which you list all the steps in the order you will present them. Include explanations of each step. The outline might look like this:

I. Introduction and topic sentence
   a. What the process is
   b. Why the process is worth knowing about
II. Preliminary information
   a. Tools needed
   b. Definitions of terms
II Steps in the process
   a. Step one
   b. Step two
   c. Step three, and so on
IV. Conclusion

6. Edit
5. Revise
4. Write
3. Organize
2. Prewrite
1. Explore

✔ TIPS

For Making the Steps Clear

The transitions need to be explicit so readers recognize each step. Here are some examples:

first, to begin, at the start

second, next, then, after that, following that, later, third, fourth, fifth, finally, last, to finish

Here are transitions for simultaneous steps:

meanwhile, during, at the same time, while

Composing the Paragraph

Now compose a first draft of the paragraph that includes all of these elements:

1. A topic sentence that identifies the process and suggests or outlines the steps, such as "My teenage son goes through an elaborate ritual in preparing his hair for a date."
2. One or more sentences that list the materials used in the process and define any specialized terms.
3. A step-by-step description of the process, arranged in sequential order.

Revising Your First Draft

The following questions should help you in revising the paragraph. You may answer them yourself or collaborate with three or four classmates. If you collaborate, photocopy the paragraph or read it aloud twice.

REVISION GUIDELINES | Describing a Process

1. What are the strengths of the paragraph?
2. Does a topic sentence identify the process and then outline or suggest the steps involved in performing the process?
3. Does the paragraph identify the tools or materials needed to perform the process?
4. Does the paragraph define any usual or specialized terms? Are the definitions clear?
5. Is each step in the process clearly identified? Are any important steps omitted? Does the paragraph *explain* the steps—not just list them?
6. Aside from entertaining readers, what is the goal of the paragraph—to let readers understand the process, or to teach them how to perform it? Is that goal clear? What, if anything, should be added to achieve the goal?

Further Revising and Editing

Return to the paragraph and revise it again. Edit and proofread it before handing in a clean, proofread copy of your work.

ADDITIONAL WRITING ASSIGNMENT

Write instructions that accompany the following diagram to explain and clarify the process it illustrates. Assume that your purpose is to inform readers who want to understand the process. They will be looking at the diagram as they read your instructions.

Begin by clustering or by making several brainstorming lists. Then write a full description of the process, explaining each step or series of related short steps. Revise the paper until it clearly follows a logical format such as the following:

1. An opening sentence that introduces the subject, summarizes the process, and mentions the materials or parts involved.
2. A middle section (7–10 sentences) that describes each step in the process.
3. A final paragraph that summarizes the process and ends the essay gracefully.

Be sure to include appropriate transitional words to show the movement between steps. Revise and edit your paper and hand in a clean final draft.

Cartoon by Rube Goldberg

A STUDENT MODEL PARAGRAPH

Here's a process analysis by Sara Sebring, a student at Chattanooga State Community College. As you read it, notice her goal in writing the paragraph—that is, what she wants readers to do with the information. Also note the number of steps involved in the process and the explanations of each step.

Practicing Good Sales Techniques
Sara Sebring

* * * *

Good salespeople are successful when they put the customers first. When customers trust and feel comfortable with the person who waits on them, they are likely to want to stay in a store, examine the merchandise, and make one or more purchases. Therefore, salespeople should follow these simple steps to be effective. First, they must make a good impression by greeting the customers as they enter the department or certainly no later than within the first two minutes. This shows customers that a salesperson is happy to assist them in finding what they are looking for. Second, if the customers want to browse, the salesperson must extend the courtesy of allowing them that freedom. At the same time, a conscientious salesperson should assure customers that he/she is available to help as quickly as the customers are ready. When customers have questions or are trying to make decisions, the salesperson should answer the questions completely and honestly and present the customers with options to choose from. Once customers have decided on their purchase, the salesperson can try to get add on sales by suggesting other items. Customers often purchase more from a salesperson who has been helpful and pleasant. Finally, at checkout time, the salesperson must tell customers that it was a pleasure serving them and that he or she looks forward to serving them again. This reinforces the impression that the salesperson has been willing to help, and it reflects well on the business, leading to repeat customers. If salespeople follow these simple steps, they will be highly effective.

Questions for Analysis

1. Who is the likely audience for this paragraph? What sentence or sentences attract the reader's interest?
2. What is the topic sentence of the paragraph?
3. How many steps does Sara Sebring present? What transitions introduce each step? What transitions show when the steps are performed?
4. Sara Sebring doesn't simply list steps; she explains them and explains the importance of each one. Find examples.
5. What, according to Sara, are the traits of a salesperson that will lead to the largest number of sales?
6. What words in the conclusion restate (but vary) the main point of the paragraph?

FINAL WRITING ASSIGNMENT

As Sara Sebring does, write a paragraph of advice to people your age on how to succeed in some task. Your audience should be people who want or need to know this advice.

The subject matter could relate to a job, to schoolwork, or to family or social life. You might, for example, discuss how to be effective in a particular field. You might discuss how to share responsibilities at home—or how to resolve a typical conflict between siblings or roommates. In any case, choose a subject you know well and feel confident explaining.

Your instructor may ask you to make an oral presentation, followed by a question and answer period, to your collaborative group (or the whole class) prior to submitting your final draft of the paragraph. Explaining the process aloud and hearing responses often reveal issues that need further clarification or rewording.

22 Writing about Causes and Effects

A **causal analysis** is an explanation of why something happened or is happening. When a car won't start, for example, you or a mechanic will look for the cause or causes of the problem. Is the battery dead? Is the starter broken? Is a wire loose or worn out? Is the fuel tank empty? It could be any one of these causes, or a combination of several.

An **analysis of effects** does just the opposite of a causal analysis. It explains or predicts the results of some action. If a college student takes five courses while working full-time, what will happen as a result? Will he be able to complete all the homework? Will he fail some courses? Will he lose sleep, and will his health suffer as a result? Will he lose his job?

This chapter will show you how to write paragraph on causes or effects by

■ examining a model paragraph of causal analysis

■ analyzing what makes an effective paragraph on causes or effects

■ thinking through ways to organize the paragraph

■ writing a cause or effect paragraph

A MODEL PARAGRAPH: CAUSAL ANALYSIS AND ANALYSIS OF EFFECTS

A *cause* is the reason an event happens, while an *effect* is the *result* of the cause. So, for instance, the cause of someone's gaining weight may be overeating, while the effect of overeating may be gaining weight. You can examine either causes or effects in your paragraph.

UNIT 4	Go Electronic
Chapter 22	Use the following electronic supplements for additional practice with your writing: • For chapter-by-chapter summaries and exercises, visit the Writing with Confidence Companion Website at http://www.ablongman.com/meyers.
Writing with Confidence ©2003	• For work with the writing process, visit The Longman Writer's Warehouse at http://longmanwriterswarehouse.com (password needed). • For additional practice in grammar, use The Writer's ToolKit Plus CD-ROM.

Keep in mind, though, that many things have more than one cause. For example, a person may gain weight because of giving up smoking, substituting food for cigarettes, and not exercising. Likewise, many things have more than one effect. For example, the decision to begin an exercise program can lead to losing weight, increasing strength, and achieving a greater sense of self-esteem or self-confidence.

If you trace several causes or effects in your paragraph, you may organize it somewhat like you'd do with a narration or a process analysis. You can tell the story of how or why something happened, either in chronological order or in a series of steps arranged in climax order. Blueprints of a paragraph discussing causes and a paragraph discussing effects might therefore like these:

BLUEPRINT	For Writing About Causes

Topic sentence: statement of effect and overview of causes

Body: causes, arranged in chronological or climax order

Cause 1

Cause 2

Cause 3

Conclusion: restatement of effect, summary of causes, call for action

BLUEPRINT	For Writing About Effects

Topic sentence: statement of cause and overview of effects

Body: effects, arranged in chronological or climax order

Effect 1

Effect 2

Effect 3

Conclusion: restatement of cause, summary of effects, call for action

Here's an example of a short essay that explains the probable causes of an effect. Because the causes need to be explained in detail, the essay devotes an entire paragraph to each. As you read the essay, notice that the first paragraph introduces the effect—the result of the causes—while the body paragraphs of the essay explore those possible causes of—or reasons for—the effect. Examine the conclusion to determine its effectiveness.

The Mystery of Custer's Last Stand

* * * *

1   Probably no single battle in U.S. history has created more controversy than the Battle of Little Bighorn River. On June 25, 1876, General George Armstrong Custer made his famous last stand against members of the Great Sioux Nation. After dividing the 700 troops of the Seventh Cavalry into three groups that would surround and attack a Native American village, he took command of one group and rushed them into the battle alone. As a result, 3,000 Sioux, led by their chief, Sitting Bull, killed Custer and every one of his 250 men. No one will ever know why Custer ordered his men into such a one-sided fight in which they had no chance for survival. No one will ever know why he didn't retreat once the battle had begun. No one will know the answers because no one from Custer's side lived to tell the story. However, some information about the battle, gathered from scouts, messengers, and the members of the other two groups, suggest four reasons.

2   First, Custer ignored the orders of his commanding officer. He was supposed to bring his troops to the valley of the Little Bighorn River and wait there until one of the other two divisions could join him. Custer decided to attack alone. He rode his troops all night and well past dawn, and his men and horses were exhausted when they entered the valley.

3   Second, Custer apparently ignored the advice of his own Native American scouts. The two men, Mitch Bouyer and Bloody Knife, warned him that there were too many Sioux warriors to be captured even by all of the soldiers in the three divisions. Custer probably thought that his Seventh Cavalry could whip any Native American party and didn't take the warnings of the scouts seriously.

4   Third, Custer probably misinterpreted the movements of the Sioux. After one of the three divisions, led by Major Marcus Reno, charged the village, a messenger told Custer that it contained far more warriors than they had expected. Custer apparently assumed that the number of Sioux didn't matter because they were fleeing. He and his men therefore rushed to the far end of the campsite to cut off the escape. He rode hard and fast, further wearing down his men and their horses.

5   Fourth, after the three groups of Custer's men had separated, they probably soon lost communication with each other. Major Reno attacked the campsite, expecting Custer to follow him from the rear. But Custer was trapped at the far end of the camp. Reno finally retreated to the woods near the village, where he was forced to make a stand. His Native American opponents not only outnumbered him, but they had better weapons. By the time the third division of the Seventh Cavalry arrived, many of Reno's men were dead, and this last division was trapped as well. Meanwhile, Custer and every single one of his men were being slaughtered.

6   To this day, when people think of Custer, they think of headstrong behavior and stupidity. Although no one knows exactly why Custer and his men lost their lives, that headstrong behavior and that stupidity are the likely reasons.

Questions for Analysis

1. Why doesn't this essay give definite causes (reasons) for Custer's defeat and the death of his soldiers?

2. How many causes does the essay suggest? What in the organization makes these causes easy to locate?

3. What is the function of the first paragraph of the essay? What specific details do you learn from it? What is the function of the last paragraph?

4. What words and phrases show a lack of certainty? Why are they necessary?

5. When does the essay depart from past-tense explanation? Why?

6. Is the final paragraph a logical conclusion, based on the evidence presented? Why or why not?

WRITING ASSIGNMENT FOR A CAUSAL ANALYSIS

Write a paragraph analyzing the reasons behind an important decision you've recently made: for example, to major in a particular field, to work part-time, to move, or to buy a car. Assume you're writing to explain your decision to an academic advisor, your parents, or a friend.

Gathering, Generating, and Arranging the Materials

Explore your ideas by clustering or brainstorming a list of the causes. Then choose three reasons for your decision—the most important, most distinct reasons—to develop in your paragraph. List the reasons either (1) chronologically if they happened in a time sequence, or (2) from the least to most important if they happened at or near the same time. This method, called **climax order**, builds to the strongest point:

> "Finally, and most importantly, I realized . . ."
>
> "But these reasons alone wouldn't have been enough. The strongest reason came . . . "

Using a simple grid may help you organize ideas:

> Possible Causes (or Possible Effects)
>
> 1.
> Example:
> 2.
> Example:
> 3.
> Example:

✓ TIPS

For Making the Causes and Effects Clear

To guide your readers through a paragraph on causes or effects, the following transitions might be useful.

For identifying causes: *reason, cause, because, since*

For labeling causes or effects: *first, second, finally*

For qualifying causes or effects that aren't definite: *maybe, possibly, probably*

Composing the Paragraph

As you begin work on your first draft, write a topic sentence to introduce or summarize the causes you'll discuss:

> "I decided to major in computer sciences *for several reasons*."
>
> "I decided to major in computer sciences *because of my interest in business, my good grades in computer classes, and the great job opportunities in this field*."

Explore three reasons in the body of the paragraph, but don't just list them. Explain them, and, if you can, support them with specific examples.

Revising Your First Draft

The following questions should help you in revising the paragraph. You may answer them yourself or collaborate with three or four classmates. As usual, if you collaborate, photocopy the paragraph or read it aloud twice.

REVISION GUIDELINES | Writing about Causes and Effects

1. What are the strengths of the paragraph?
2. Does the topic sentence state the effect (the decision) and clearly introduce or summarize the causes (reasons)? If not, how could the sentence be improved?
3. After reading the topic sentence, stop to predict what will follow. Does the remainder of the paragraph fulfill reasonable predictions? Is the organization of the paragraph clear, tight, and predictable? If the paragraph uses climax order, are the three reasons arranged to build to the most important? What changes in organization, if any, does the paragraph need?
4. Are examples needed? If so, where?
5. Are the transitions between ideas graceful and clear? If not, what transitions might be added?
6. Is any language unclear? If so, how might it be improved?

Take notes of these responses to guide your revision. Rewrite the paper later, paying special attention to word choice, clarity, and conciseness.

Further Revising and Editing

Revise the paragraph again. Edit and proofread it, and, as always, hand in a clean, proofread copy.

ADDITIONAL WRITING ASSIGNMENT

Choose another important event in your life, one resulting in three or more important effects—changes in your living conditions, changes in your behavior, or changes in your attitudes. Here are a few examples:

gaining a younger sibling

losing a loved one or caregiver

losing a job

being involved in an accident

moving to a new neighborhood, city, or country

Assume that your audience is a group of people who know you now but didn't know you at the time of the event. Your purpose should therefore be to let these people understand you better. If you prefer not to write about yourself, choose an event in the life of someone you know well.

List at least three effects of the experience, perhaps by brainstorming, and then arrange them from weakest to strongest. Consider examples of each. Freewriting may be useful here. Explain and illustrate each effect.

A STUDENT MODEL PARAGRAPH

The following paragraph was written by Sara Sebring at Chattanooga State Community College, who also wrote the student model in Chapter 21. In this paragraph, she describes an allergic reaction to a medicine—in other words, the effects of a cause. As you read it, notice first the cause (or reason she took the drug), the immediate results of taking it, and then the longer-term results.

A Reaction to Medicine
Sara Sebring

* * * *

Some people can take medicines without having a problem. Others react mildly to some medicines. However, I had one terrible reaction to an antibiotic, one that taught me that I would never take it again. I went to the doctor to get treatment for my right eye, which had been swollen shut for the previous two days. He told me my eye was infected and gave me a prescription for Duricef and Polymeral. I then left the doctor's office, had the prescription filled, and went home to take the medicine. I took the Polymeral and had no problems; however, after taking the Duricef, I experienced an allergic reaction. First I fell asleep and slept for fourteen hours. When I finally woke up, my speech was slurred; I couldn't catch my breath; my neck broke out in a rash; and my face was swollen all over. In addition, I kept running into walls because my balance was off. As a result, I called the doctor's office and reported my condition to the nurse, who said the doctor would return my call in two minutes. Four hours later, the doctor returned my call and said he would phone the drug store and order a new prescription to stop my swelling. To my dismay, the new prescription was never called in, and three days later my symptoms were still present. Finally, after four days of misery, the symptoms disappeared, and I found out that Duricef was a type of penicillin to which I have an allergic reaction. From this entire episode, not only did I learn that I cannot take Duricef, but I also learned that some doctors do not respond quickly enough to their patients' medical needs. This was truly the worst experience I have ever had.

Questions for Analysis

1. What is the topic sentence of this paragraph? Underline it.
2. What was Sara Sebring's first reaction to the medicine? Following that, what symptoms did she exhibit? What was the last allergic reaction she mentions, and what transition introduces it?
3. The allergic reaction caused her to take additional actions. What were they? What results did they bring?
4. What transitional expressions show time relationships? How much time passed between Sara's initial infection and her recovery from the allergic reaction?
5. Two changes in Sara Sebring's attitude and behavior occurred as results of this experience. What were they? What transition introduces them? How—and why—do these changes relate to the topic sentence?

FINAL WRITING ASSIGNMENT

Like Sara Sebring, you or someone you know has probably suffered from an illness or had a medical emergency. Write a paragraph in which you describe what happened—the causes—and the results of the illness or emergency—the effects. Your subject matter will determine which part receives the most development. For example, if the illness or emergency resulted in important changes in health, behavior, or attitude, you may wish to stress those changes.

23 Classifying Information

We classify all the time: busy streets versus shortcuts, easy classes versus hard classes. And usually we think of more than two categories. For example, we look for items in a supermarket according to the sections they're in: frozen foods, produce, dairy products, paper goods, and so on. We can store information in a computer database by categories: accounts paid, accounts unpaid, new customers, and so on. We can learn about animals in a biology course by examining their types: reptiles, mammals, fish, and so on.

This chapter will show you how to write a classification paragraph by

■ examining a model paragraph of classification

■ analyzing what makes a classification effective

■ thinking through ways of organizing a classification

■ writing a classification paragraph

A MODEL PARAGRAPH: CLASSIFICATION

Classification is a way of dividing a group of people, objects, or ideas into categories based on some **criterion**, or standard for judging them. In fact, you've already seen an example of a paragraph that places people into categories. The model paragraph in Chapter 2 is a classification of pizza customers.

There are many ways to classify a group. You could divide cars into categories based on size: full-size cars, mid-size cars, compact cars, and subcompacts. But you could just as easily classify cars by cost, gas mileage, or color. You could classify college students into four categories according to the number of credit hours they've completed: first-year students, sophomores, juniors, and seniors. But you could just as easily classify students by age, grade-point average, or religion.

UNIT 4	Go Electronic
Chapter 23	Use the following electronic supplements for additional practice with your writing: • For chapter-by-chapter summaries and exercises, visit the Writing with Confidence Companion Website at http://www.ablongman.com/meyers.
Writing with Confidence ©2003	• For work with the writing process, visit The Longman Writer's Warehouse at http://longmanwriterswarehouse.com (password needed). • For additional practice in grammar, use The Writer's ToolKit Plus CD-ROM.

Therefore, once you've chosen a topic for a paragraph on classification, follow these guidelines for creating clear and consistent categories:

1. *Use only one criterion for classifying.* You can group people according to their income, intelligence, or ambition—but not according to income *and* intelligence or intelligence *and* ambition. Otherwise, you might discover that a person fits into more than one category. A rich student can also be bright; a bright student can be either lazy or hardworking. Besides, if the classification gets too complicated, you'll never be able to discuss it fully in a single paragraph.

2. *Create categories that allow room for everyone or everything you are classifying.* Suppose, for example, that you're grouping your classmates according to age. If the youngest category includes people between the ages of eighteen and twenty, it excludes a classmate who is only seventeen. A better category might be students seventeen to twenty years old or students twenty years old and younger.

3. *Illustrate the categories through examples.* The categories will be clearer, and more interesting, if you provide specific examples. Show a hardworking waitperson scooting from table to table, balancing four trays on one hand while pouring water in cups with the other.

Above all, don't oversimplify, or you might be guilty of stereotyping people. There are too many negative and misleading stereotypes in the world already, and they tend to create and reinforce prejudices.

A blueprint of a typical paragraph of classification might look like this:

BLUEPRINT	For Classifying Information

Topic sentence: overview of categories and statement of criterion

Body: explanation of categories, with examples, arranged in some logical order

Category 1

Category 2

Category 3

Conclusion: restatement of overview and interpretation of categories

Here's an example of a paragraph that classifies people into three categories. As you read it, notice the criterion for determining the categories. Notice the explanations of each category. And notice the examples that support each explanation.

Every Body Has a Place

* * * *

If you are looking for ways to describe fat, muscular, and wiry bodies, William H. Sheldon has created a handy vocabulary for doing so. In 1940, he invented a system of classifying body types that corresponds to the three layers of cells in an unborn child:

endoderm—the inner layer, which later becomes the stomach and intestines; meso-derm—the middle layer, which forms the skeleton, muscles, and veins; and ectoderm—the outer layer, which develops into the skin, hair, nails, and nervous system. He believed that these layers emerge differently in each adult. In some people, the layers are evenly balanced, but in many people, one layer dominates the others and forms one of Sheldon's three main body types. The first is the *endomorph,* a person with a soft body and many bulges. He or she may have strong muscles, but they are hard to find beneath the body fat. Famous endomorphs include comedians John Belushi and Chris Farley, and other examples are easy to spot at any ice cream or pizza parlor. The second body type is the *mesomorph,* a person with big bones and rock-hard neck, shoulders, chest, stomach, buttocks, arms, and legs. You see mesomorph body types often in ads for health clubs or as action heroes like, for instance, the movie star and former Mr. Universe, Arnold Schwarzenegger. The third type is the *ectomorph,* a person with a wiry body, small bones, thin chest, a flat stomach, and small buttocks. An ectomorph tends to have long arms and legs, and is generally very active. Just about any marathon runner is a typical ectomorph. Although Sheldon's classifications aren't perfect, they provide a useful way to describe the hulks, hunks, and scarecrows who populate the planet and compete in the rings and on the fields, courts, and tracks of the world.

Questions for Analysis

1. Which sentence introduces Sheldon's classifications of body types? Why isn't it the first sentence in the paragraph?
2. What criterion determines the classifications?
3. What is the stated purpose for classifying body types?
4. Does the paragraph include any examples? If so, what words or phrases identify them as such?
5. Examine the conclusion. What attitude toward Sheldon's classifications does it express?

WRITING ASSIGNMENT FOR A CLASSIFICATION PARAGRAPH

For a popular magazine that specializes in entertainment and humor, write a paragraph of classification on one of these topics. They'll be familiar to your audience (your classmates), so have some fun and try to be entertaining.

1. types of people on a crowded bus, in a library, in a department store during a blowout sale, or at a party
2. types of people at movie theaters or concerts
3. types of grandparents
4. types of customers you serve
5. types of pets (or dogs)

Gathering, Generating, and Arranging the Materials

Begin by thinking of a single criterion for classification—such as the amount of noise that fans at a sporting event make—and then brainstorm or cluster at least three categories, along with examples that fit within each. If you can't think of a criterion, start by generating categories, see what criterion holds them together, and eliminate or reshape the categories that don't fit the criterion.

Organize your ideas into a chart like the following one. Notice that the main categories, on the left, are arranged from most to least noisy. The examples of each type haven't yet been placed in any order.

TIPS

For Making the Categories Clear

Use transitional expressions to introduce each transition. Here are some examples: *first, another, still another, in addition, finally, last*

Types of fans at a sports event

Criterion:	Amount of noise they make
Category	Example
Loudmouth	The "expert" commentator, the insulter, the screamer, and the person who talks about everything but the game
Semi-talker	The occasional cheerer, the groaner, and the question-asker
Quiet mouth	The watcher, the silent scorekeeper, and the sleeper

6. Edit
5. Revise
4. Write
3. Organize
2. Prewrite
1. Explore

Composing the Paragraph

Write a first draft of the paragraph. Discuss the examples in some detail so your paragraph is lively and entertaining, and not merely a list. Then put your paper aside.

6. Edit
5. Revise
4. Write
3. Organize
2. Prewrite
1. Explore

Revising Your First Draft

The following questions should help you in revising the paragraph. You may answer them yourself or collaborate with three or four classmates. As usual, if you collaborate, photocopy the paragraph or read it aloud twice.

REVISION GUIDELINES   Writing a Classification Paragraph

1. What are the strengths of the paragraph?
2. What is the criterion for classification? Is the criterion clear? Is there more than one criterion? If so, what should be changed?
3. Are the categories big enough to include all the examples? If not, should the categories or examples be changed?
4. Does the paragraph explain and illustrate each category? If not, what could be added?
5. Does the paragraph include transitions that label the categories? Do other transitions establish logical connections between each category, explanation, and illustration? If not, what could be added or changed?
6. Does the arrangement of categories move from most to least, least to most, or in some other consistent order? If not, how should the categories be rearranged?
7. Is the language clear and graceful? If not, how could it be improved?

6. Edit
5. Revise
4. Write
3. Organize
2. Prewrite
1. Explore

Further Revising and Editing

Return to the paragraph and revise it again. Edit and proofread it before handing in a clean, proofread copy of your work.

ADDITIONAL WRITING ASSIGNMENT

Write a classification of any of the following:

1. favorite places at your college
2. types of movies
3. types of music
4. nightclubs, restaurants, or other gathering places

No matter what subject you choose, assume again that you're writing for a popular magazine, that your audience is already somewhat familiar with your topic, and that your purpose is mainly to entertain.

Be sure to use only one criterion for classifying and create at least three different categories within the classification. Include at least one interesting or humorous example for each category.

A STUDENT MODEL ESSAY

Jane Smith is a student at Danville Community College in Danville, Virginia. As you read her essay, notice that the first paragraph introduces three categories and that each category is discussed in a separate paragraph in the body of the essay. Notice, too, how her concluding paragraph summarizes the discussion and ends on a positive note.

Chamber Volunteers
Jane Smith

* * * *

1   My first volunteer experience was when I joined the Burnes County Junior Woman's Club twenty-five years ago. Since that time I have become so involved in this activity that a group of my friends has dubbed me a professional volunteer. According to my husband John, this is defined as any job that offers no pay, demands lots of time, and requires the donation of supplies from our office. Over the years, I have learned a great deal about the different types of people who work in volunteer organizations. Although most organizations consist of similar types of members, as president of the Burnes County Chamber of Commerce, I have observed that the chamber has a unique membership because these people are representing their businesses, industries, and professions. Therefore, they have distinct motives for offering their time and talents. The majority of these volunteers can be divided into three main categories: the bossy executives, the glory seekers, and the backbones.

2   The bossy executives are always right. If you don't believe it, just ask them! They have grand ideas and are very willing to tell you how to carry them out. The problem is they expect everyone else to do all the work. When someone else comes up with a different idea, the bossy executives will discuss only its negative aspects even if the idea is much better than theirs. If the committee decides to proceed with the new idea, the executives will still do it their way. No matter what the outcome of a project is, you can be sure of one thing: if anything goes wrong, it is not the bossy executives' faults because they are always right.

3   Unlike the bossy executives who like to be heard and obeyed, the glory seekers participate so that they can be seen. They are the first ones to volunteer for a project that is high profile and involves a lot of free publicity. If they happen to think of a good idea, everyone will know because they will be sure to take all of the credit. However, if anything goes wrong, they react like the bossy executives and are never at fault. When the time comes to begin working, they somehow feel that their presence is not

necessary. They leave all of the planning and activities to the third type of volunteers, the backbones.

4   In any committee, if you can have at least one backbone, you can be sure that the work will be done because the backbones believe that actions speak louder than words. Whether these backbones are chairing committees or are members of the team, you know that they will follow through with their responsibilities and pitch in to complete the unfinished tasks of the bossy executives and the glory seekers. Their only motivation is the satisfaction they receive from supporting the organization, and their aim is to follow through and complete every project. When the cameras are flashing and the credits are given, the backbones are content to take the pictures and give the credits to the other team members.

5   Even though the backbones are the ideal chamber members, the bossy executives and the glory seekers do contribute in their own special ways to the goal of the Burnes County Chamber of Commerce. That goal is to deal with issues that affect the economic well-being of our community, and, through the unified efforts of everyone, this goal continues to be achieved.

Questions for Analysis

1. Jane Smith begins the first paragraph by discussing her experience in volunteer organizations and her role as president of a local chamber of commerce. How do those experiences qualify her to classify volunteers?

2. What are three categories of volunteers introduced in the first paragraph? Underline them. What words identify and repeat categories in the three body paragraphs? Underline them, too. How is the language similar? How is it different?

3. Examine the first sentence of the third paragraph, beginning with "Unlike the bossy executives." Why does Jane Smith make this contrast? What role does it have in unifying the essay?

4. How are the first two categories similar? How are they different? Which of the three categories does Jane Smith respect the most?

5. Jane Smith doesn't say which category she belongs to. Which one is the most likely? Why?

6. How does the structure of this essay resemble the structure of a single paragraph? How is the structure different? Why wouldn't this essay work as only one paragraph?

FINAL WRITING ASSIGNMENT

Like Jane Smith, classify people in an organization into three types—saving the best type for last. You can discuss types of students in a class, members of a club, or players on a team. Arrange the categories so the best appears at the end. According to the directions of your instructor, you may write a single paragraph or an essay.

24 Writing Comparisons and Contrasts

Each day you make comparisons: this lesson was easier than the last one; traffic this morning ran more smoothly than traffic the day before; the test in biology was the hardest yet. Comparisons and contrasts examine the similarities and differences among people, ideas, or things. Sometimes you make comparisons and contrasts in order to evaluate: that is, to decide which is best, most valuable, or most fun. Other times, you compare and contrast in order to clarify ideas. The contrast control on a television set makes the picture sharper, and a contrast between people or things often sharpens the focus of your ideas. This chapter will show you how to write a comparison or contrast paragraph by

- examining a model paragraph of comparison and contrast
- analyzing what makes a comparison and contrast effective
- thinking through ways to organize a comparison–contrast paragraph
- writing a comparison–contrast

A MODEL PARAGRAPH: COMPARISON–CONTRAST

A comparison shows how people or things are similar. A contrast shows how they are different, usually when evaluating them. And a **comparison–contrast** paragraph discusses both similarities and differences. To do so, it must also organize, explain, and illustrate the similarities and differences in ways that make sense.

There are two main strategies for organizing the comparisons and contrasts:

1. **Whole-to-whole.** In this organization, you describe Movie X completely, and then Movie Y completely. You draw the comparisons and contrasts while describing Movie Y, or after describing Movie Y.

UNIT 4	Go Electronic
Chapter 24	Use the following electronic supplements for additional practice with your writing: • For chapter-by-chapter summaries and exercises, visit the Writing with Confidence Companion Website at http://www.ablongman.com/meyers.
Writing with Confidence ©2003	• For work with the writing process, visit The Longman Writer's Warehouse at http://longmanwriterswarehouse.com (password needed). • For additional practice in grammar, use The Writer's ToolKit Plus CD-ROM.

2. **Part-to-part.** In this organization, you describe one part of Movie X, such as its plot, and then compare it to the plot of Movie Y. Then you return to Movie X to describe its acting, followed by a comparison to the acting in Movie Y. You continue in this way until you have drawn all the comparisons between the two movies. If you discuss point A about one subject, then your readers must see its relationship to point A about the other.

Keep these additional guidelines in mind as you compose and revise the paragraph:

1. *Don't oversimplify.* Very few issues are as simple as black versus white or good versus evil. So be careful as you evaluate—deciding if something is better than something else. It's is fine to say that Movie X is better than Movie Y, but don't automatically assume Movie Y is a waste of time. Movie Y may be entertaining, but not as good as Movie X.

2. *Don't use circular reasoning.* When explaining why Movie X is better than Movie Y, give specific reasons to support your claim. Don't say that Movie X was better because it was better. For example, the statement, "Movie X was interesting because it held my attention" is circular reasoning because "interesting" and "held my attention" mean the same thing. Say instead, "Movie X was interesting because it was fast-moving, full of surprises, and well acted."

3. *Be consistent in your organization.* Make your comparisons and contrasts easy for your readers to understand. If you discuss the acting, directing, photography, and editing of Movie X, you must discuss all these matters in Movie Y. You should also present the points in the same order for both movies.

A blueprint of a paragraph using the whole-to-whole organization might look like this:

BLUEPRINT	For Comparison (Whole-to-Whole)

Topic sentence: introduction of two topics to be compared

Body: examination of topics, first one and then the other

Topic 1:

   Point A

   Point B

   Point C

Topic 2:

   Point A

   Point B

   Point C

Conclusion: evaluation of topics compared

And a blueprint of a paragraph using part-to-part organization might look like this:

```
┌─────────────────────────────────────────────────────────────┐
│  BLUEPRINT  │  For Comparison (Part-to-Part)                  │
├─────────────────────────────────────────────────────────────┤
│                                                               │
│   Topic sentence: introduction of two topics to be compared   │
│                              ↓                                │
│   Body: examination of each point, first with one topic       │
│   and then with the other                                     │
│                                                               │
│   Point A:                                                    │
│     Topic 1                                                   │
│     Topic 2                                                   │
│                                                               │
│   Point B:                                                    │
│     Topic 1                                                   │
│     Topic 2                                                   │
│                                                               │
│   Point C:                                                    │
│     Topic 1                                                   │
│     Topic 2                                                   │
│                              ↓                                │
│   Conclusion: evaluation of topics compared                   │
│                                                               │
└─────────────────────────────────────────────────────────────┘
```

The following paragraph compares and contrasts two subjects. As you read it, notice that it begins with a comparison of white and dark meat. Then notice that a comparison between two types of birds follows.

The Light and the Dark of It

* * * *

Why do chickens and turkeys have both dark and light meat, while most other birds we eat (such as quail, duck, or pigeon) have dark meat only? The reason is that there are two types of fibers in the muscles of birds: red and white. The red fibers contain a muscle protein that makes animals able to work for much longer periods than do white fibers, which are designed for short, powerful bursts of activity. You can therefore guess which birds have the most red-fibered muscles—and the most dark meat. They are the creatures that must fly long distances to migrate or to find food—the geese, ducks, and quails. But chickens and turkeys live a less strenuous life. They move around by walking or running, so only their legs and thighs contain dark red fibers. These land birds don't use their wings and breasts very much, so these parts contain light white fibers. In fact, the absence of red fiber in wings and breasts is an advantage. When chickens and turkeys are threatened, their wings and upper bodies must deliver a lot of power quickly but for only a short time. The next time you pay an extra 50 cents for an order of all-white-meat chicken, remember that these parts of birds racked up fewer trips in the air than you may have taken in an airplane.

Questions for Analysis

1. What is the topic sentence of the paragraph?
2. Is the main purpose of the paragraph to inform, persuade, or entertain?
3. What is the paragraph comparing or contrasting?
4. List the points of comparisons and contrasts in the paragraph. Which does the paragraph mainly discuss—similarities or differences?
5. Is this primarily a whole-to-whole or part-to-part comparison?
6. What words or phrases signal contrasts? Do any words signal similarities?

WRITING ASSIGNMENT FOR COMPARISON–CONTRAST

Write a paragraph for a feature section of a newspaper or magazine. Compare two subjects you know well. Conclude by recommending one or both of them to your readers. You might choose two movies, two rock groups (or songs), two books, two performances, two types of sports (or two games in the same sport), two celebrities, or two cars.

Gathering, Generating, and Arranging the Materials

6. Edit
5. Revise
4. Write
3. Organize
2. Prewrite
1. Explore

Use a simple grid to help you generate and organize the points of comparison and contrast. As you list one point about the first subject, you must consider the corresponding point about the second subject. Continue until your grid covers every point. Here, for example, is a grid for two movies:

Beach Blanket Bozos		Crash and Burn
Type	comedy	action
Actors	no-name actors	major stars
Plot	not much plot	suspense leading to a climax
Contents	slapstick humor and silly dialogue	action more important than clever dialogue
Rating	R	R
Length	90 minutes	two hours
Cost	low budget, no unusual locations, and hardly any special effects	high budget, with plane crashes, car chases, and many special effects
Audience	appeals to teenagers	appeals to teenagers

After you've completed the grid, construct a second grid with the items grouped according to similarities and differences:

Beach Blanket Bozos		Crash and Burn	
Similarities			
Rating	R	R	
Audience	teenagers	teenagers	
Dialogue	weak	weak	
Differences			
Type	comedy	action picture	
Actors	no-name actors	major stars	
Plot	not much plot	suspense leading to a climax	
Contents	slapstick humor	action	
Length	90 minutes	two hours	
Cost	low budget, no unusual locations, and hardly any special effects	high budget, with plane crashes, and many special effects	

TIPS

For Indicating Comparisons and Contrasts

Help your readers recognize the comparisons and contrasts by supplying appropriate transitions. Here's a list:

For comparisons (similarities): *like, as, likewise, similarly, also, too, moreover, in a similar way or fashion*

For contrasts (differences): *in contrast, on the one hand . . . on the other hand, however, unlike, but*

Then decide on the type of organization to use in your comparison. Read down both columns of the grid for a whole-to-whole approach. Read across the columns for a part-to-part. As you continue planning, select examples of each point of comparison or contrast, and consider what explanations to provide.

Composing the Paragraph

Now compose a first draft. Write a topic sentence that states the main idea of the paragraph. Use either the whole-to-whole or part-to-part organization. If the organization you choose doesn't work well when you compose the draft, switch to the other organization. Add transitions to introduce the points of comparison and to emphasize the similarities and differences. Try to conclude with a statement that sums up the main points of the paragraph, or that packs a punch.

Revising Your First Draft

As usual, the following questions should help you in revising the paragraph. You may answer them yourself or collaborate with three or four classmates. If you collaborate, photocopy the paragraph or read it aloud twice.

REVISION GUIDELINES   Writing Comparison–Contrast

1. What are the strengths of the paragraph?
2. Is the main purpose of the paragraph to show comparisons or contrasts—or both? Does the paragraph include a topic sentence that states the main idea?

3. What form of organization is used—whole-to-whole or part-to-part? Is the organization consistent? If not, what needs to be changed?

4. Do any points of comparison need explaining or illustrating? If so, what could be added?

5. Does the paragraph include transitions that introduce the comparisons and contrasts? Do the transitions establish logical connections between each point of comparison, explanation, and example? If not, what could be added or changed?

6. Does the conclusion follow logically from the points of comparison and contrast in the paragraph? If not, how should it be changed?

7. Is the language clear and graceful? If not, how could it be improved?

Take notes of these responses and begin work on your first revision. Then put it aside.

Further Revising and Editing

Return to the paragraph and revise it again. Edit and proofread it before handing in a clean, proofread copy of your work.

ADDITIONAL WRITING ASSIGNMENT

Assume you're a newspaper or magazine columnist who often expresses opinions on matters of interest to you and your readers. Write a paragraph of comparison and contrast on one of the following topics:

1. small or large families
2. studying liberal arts or studying business administration
3. marrying young or marrying later in life
4. working part-time to pay for college or borrowing the money
5. doing high-impact activities such as running or low-impact activities such as walking

Choose a subject you know well. If you used whole-to-whole organization in the earlier assignment in this chapter, then use part-to-part here—or vice versa. Explain any ideas that are unfamiliar to your readers. Tell little stories or cite examples to support your main points if possible. Recommend or suggest which of the two things you're comparing is best—or perhaps best for some people, while the other thing is best for other people.

A STUDENT MODEL ESSAY

Here's an essay written by Mirham Mahmutagic, a student at Truman College who grew up in Bosnia. It compares how Bosnians and Americans think about how to use their time. As you read it, notice how Mirham makes a part-to-part comparison between time spent in school in the two countries and then, later, between time spent with families.

Examining the Differences: Old Tradition vs. New World
Mirham Mahmutagic

* * * *

1   When I first came to the United States, I remember wondering why Americans have fast-food restaurants, or why they spend so much time eating out, instead of cooking their meals at home, like we did in Bosnia. Well, after spending six years here in Chicago, I have learned that besides food, everything else also seems to be "on the go," here in the States. That, simply said, is the biggest difference between the "old world" of tradition and history, where I came from, and this "new world" of high rises and big money.

2   In the United States, time, or should I better say the lack of it, has a direct impact on people and their decision on how to use that time throughout the entire course of their lives. People in the States spend a lot of time in their schools, which starts as early as the first grade of elementary school. On the average, children here attend eight to nine hours of school every day, five days a week, while children in Bosnia, on the average, attend five to six hours of school every day. After graduating from high school, American youth are facing five to eight years till their professional degrees, while in Bosnia that translates into four to five years of college. Finally, at the age of twenty-three, a young doctor starts practicing medicine in Bosnia, while at the same age of twenty-three the American future physician is finishing his first year of medical school and heading toward the next three. Ironically, the American doctor will spend the rest of his life chasing that time "lost" in school by working endless hours and 48-hour shifts year after year, while the doctor in Bosnia will work forty to fifty hours a week, enjoying most of his Saturdays and Sundays off.

3   This seemingly simple time grid suggests that children in Bosnia do have more time, outside of school, to spend with their families and their friends while children in the States don't. Accordingly, children in Bosnia do grow up closer to their families, and as adults they adjust their lives so that they can spend more time in their homes and less time at work. On the other hand, children in America probably grow up with a different set of values, where their career and work will come first and the time for their families and friends will come second. As a result of their dedication to their careers and their work, young Americans appear to be more independent, ambitious, efficient, and prosperous compared to youth in Bosnia. As adults, they seem to have much stronger work ethics than Bosnians do, which ultimately leads to the current immeasurable economic difference between the two countries. Today, those Americans are able to give their children modem toys and video games, expensive cars, and the latest technological inventions, which is something most of the children in Bosnia grow up without.

4   I can still remember just how beautiful my childhood was growing up in Bosnia. My friends, with whom I have spent endless hours playing games like tag, riding a bike or playing ball, constantly surrounded me. Unlike many fathers in the States, my father always had time to play with me, help me with the homework, and simply be around whenever I needed him. Now that I think how important his presence in my life was, I keep wondering if I will have enough time to spend with my child to be able to show him how important the family is, just like my parent showed to me.

Questions for Analysis

1. What sentence or sentences in the first paragraph introduce the comparison? Underline the sentence(s). What are the topic sentences in the remaining paragraphs? Underline them as well.

2. How many comparisons does Mirham make in the second paragraph? Number them, and circle the words that serve as transitions between comparisons.

3. In the third paragraph, and then later in the final paragraph, Mirham begins to discuss how the two cultures he compares seem to have differing values. What differences does he see? Do you agree with his observations? Which values, in your opinion, are most important?

4. How does the conclusion relate to ideas earlier in the essay?

5. Construct a grid of the comparisons or contrasts Mirham makes in his essay. Are they consistent and complete?

FINAL WRITING ASSIGNMENT

Like Mirham Mahmutagic, write a paragraph (or an essay) in which you contrast one set of values you have learned with another set that other people seem to think are important. You might consider any one of the following issues: the relationship between parent and child, neatness, study habits, manners, behavior in school, behavior at parties, showing off, the use of language (including slang or profanity), or the importance of money or material possessions.

25 Defining Terms

One of your most important concerns when you write is to be as clear as possible, so you have to anticipate the moments when readers might ask, "What do you mean?" This question often occurs when you use an unfamiliar term or a term with several meanings. In those cases, you need a **definition**—that is, an explanation of what you mean when you use the term. This chapter will show you how to write a paragraph of definition by

- examining model paragraphs of definition
- analyzing what makes a definition effective
- thinking through ways to organize a definition
- writing a definition

MODEL PARAGRAPHS: DEFINITION

Definition seems like a simple matter, and sometimes it is. You can merely define a term with a **synonym** (another word that means the same thing) or a short dictionary definition. But at other times defining is not so simple. A word may have several meanings, or you may want to define the word in a special way. Your definition may therefore require a full paragraph in which you discuss and illustrate exactly the meaning you intend—or do not intend.

Consider the word *mother*. It usually just represents a person, but it can also represent a concept. With adoption, artificial insemination, donor eggs, and even cloning, what does it mean biologically—or legally—these days? And what, personally, does the term mean to us? Most of us can provide a clear and concrete definition by describing the mother we knew (or didn't know) as we were growing up. And we can supply examples that make the description come alive. For some, she could be the woman whose natural environment was the kitchen and the PTA meeting. For others, she could be the woman who rose early and got her children dressed, fed, and packed off to school before she left for her full-time job. She wasn't home to greet us after school, but she nevertheless prepared or brought home dinner each night. For still others, neither definition would fit. In any case, we could define the word *mother* by including stories and examples of her typical behavior and by contrasting those stories and examples to the behavior of other people.

Here's a blueprint of one way a definition paragraph might be organized, assuming that the definition includes three important traits. Note that it arranges the traits in climax order—going from the least important to the most:

BLUEPRINT | For Defining Terms

Topic sentence: the main idea of the definition

Body: examination of traits, with examples, arranged in climax order

Trait 1
Trait 2
Trait 3

Conclusion: interpretation or evaluation

The following personal definition of a mother comes from James McBride's The Color of Water. *As you may recall from Chapter 19, McBride is one of twelve black children raised by his mother, a white woman born in the South to Jewish parents (you'll see that she could speak Yiddish—a Germanic language spoken by Jews, usually written in Hebrew characters). She married two black men (each died), and she became the leader of a Baptist church in New York. As you read this definition, notice the opening topic sentence, each supporting statement of the topic sentence, and each example for the supporting statements.*

Excerpt from *The Color of Water*
James McBride

* * * *

As a boy, I always thought my mother was strange. She never cared to socialize with our neighbors. Her past was a mystery she refused to discuss. She drank tea out of a glass. She could speak Yiddish. She had an absolute distrust of authority and an insistence on complete privacy which seemed to make her, and my family, even odder. My family was huge, twelve kids, unlike any other family I'd ever seen, so many of us that at times Mommy would call us by saying, "Hey James—Judy–Henry–Hunter–Kath—whatever your name is, come here a minute." It wasn't that she forgot who we were, but there were so many of us, she had no time for silly details like names. She was the commander in chief of my house, because my stepfather did not live with us. He lived in Brooklyn until near the end of his life, staying away from the thronging masses to come home on weekends, bearing food and tricycles and the resolve to fix whatever physical thing we had broken during the week. The nuts and bolts of raising us was left to Mommy, who acted as chief surgeon for bruises ("Put iodine on it"), war secretary ("If somebody hits you, take your fist and *crack* 'em"), religious consultant ("Put God first"), chief psychologist ("Don't think about it"), and financial adviser ("What's money if your mind is empty?"). Matters involving race and identity she ignored.

Questions for Analysis

1. James McBride says in the topic sentence that he considered his mother "strange." In what ways was she strange? What examples illustrate these ways?

2. In one sentence, McBride lists a number of "occupations" his mother had. What were they? Does McBride mean them literally?

3. How does McBride seem to feel about his mother?

4. McBride also briefly mentions that his stepfather didn't live with the family during the week but would come home on weekends. Does McBride suggest his stepfather didn't care about the children?

Here's a definition—of a black mother—taken from Maya Angelou's Heart of a Woman, *a memoir of her extraordinary life, filled with a variety of experiences, much unhappiness, and much joy. Her definition of a black mother is controversial, and some people may find it disturbing, even offensive. Other people will find it accurate, even if brutally so. As you read it, notice the topic idea, the specific development of each point of the topic idea, and the descriptions of the circumstances under which the definition applies.*

Excerpt from *Heart of a Woman*
Maya Angelou

* * * *

The black mother perceives destruction at every door, ruination at each window, and even she herself is not beyond her own suspicion. She questions whether she loves her children enough—or more terribly, does she love them too much? Do her looks cause embarrassment—or even more terrifying—is she so attractive her sons begin to desire her and her daughters begin to hate her? If she is unmarried, the challenges are increased. Her singleness indicates she has rejected, or has been rejected by her mate. Yet she is raising children who will become mates. Beyond her door, all authority is in the hands of people who do not look or think or act like her and her children. Teachers, doctors, sales clerks, librarians, policemen, welfare workers are white and exert control over her family's moods, conditions and personality; yet within the home, she must display a right to rule which at any moment, by a knock at the door, or a ring of the telephone can be exposed as false. In the face of these contradictions, she must provide a blanket of stability, which warms but does not suffocate, and she must tell her children the truth about the power of white power without suggesting that it cannot be challenged.

Questions for Analysis

1. The topic sentence introduces three parts in its definition. What are they? Does the paragraph discuss each one? If so, where?

2. The definition explores a number of problems that a black mother faces. What are they? What transitions introduce them?

3. The concluding sentence begins with "In the face of these contradictions . . ." What are the contradictions Maya Angelou refers to?

4. Although this definition says a lot, it also leaves out a lot—matters that are explored in the entire book. Can you explain some of the assumptions that lie underneath her claims about the worries a black mother faces?

WRITING ASSIGNMENT FOR A DEFINITION PARAGRAPH

Terms such as *New Yorker, Chicagoan, suburbanite,* and *country folk* suggest a variety of traits about the people they describe. Assume that you're writing a letter to a friend who's thinking about moving to your community, neighborhood, or town but doesn't know if he or she would be happy living in the area. Describe some typical traits of people who live there, but be careful not to stereotype the people. Define, explain, and illustrate not only what you mean, but also what you do not mean. For example, are the people friendly but not too nosy, informal but not rude?

Any large group of people possesses a number of traits, and the people are as different as they are alike. Remember: concepts can be hard to understand. So don't let your definition become too vague—or much too detailed. As you select examples for the traits you want to discuss, think about one person in one incident that best illustrates the point. Limit that illustration to a sentence or two.

For example, James McBride uses quotations from his mother: "If somebody hits you, take your fist and *crack* 'em." He describes his father returning home on each weekend carrying food and tricycles. And Maya Angelou uses the details of a "knock at the door, or a ring of the telephone" to show what undercuts a mother's "right to rule."

Don' t think about everybody, every action, every time. Think about *only one,* and describe it.

Gathering, Generating, and Arranging the Materials

Brainstorm a list, or make a clustering chart, of the most important or easily seen traits of the people you are defining. You should mention at least three traits, or narrow your list to the three most important. Consider examples you can cite for each of those characteristics. Then write a preliminary topic sentence that states the general definition, as well as sentences that state each of the traits you've chosen.

You may wish to outline your paragraph, using as a guide the diagram of a definition paragraph from earlier in the chapter.

Writing the Paragraph

Look over your materials and write a draft of the full paragraph. Begin with the topic sentence. Include the statements of each main trait. And follow each statement with an example.

Revising Your First Draft

Once again, the following questions should help you in revising the paragraph. You may answer them yourself or collaborate with three or four classmates. If you collaborate, photocopy the paragraph or read it aloud twice.

REVISION GUIDELINES   Writing a Definition Paragraph

1. What are the strengths of the paragraph?

2. Is the topic sentence clear? Is it general enough to account for all the information in the paragraph, but not too general as to be almost meaningless? If not, how could the sentence be improved?

3. Do the main traits fit within the definition? Should any be reworded to avoid stereotyping? Are more examples needed? If so, where?

4. Does any one example stand out as a powerful illustration of a trait? If not, how can one example be focused and heightened to be more effective?

5. Is the organization of the paragraph clear? If not, what could be shifted, expanded, or deleted?

6. Is the movement between ideas graceful and clear? If not, what transitions might be added?

Take notes of these responses to guide your revision. Rewrite the paper later when you can examine it with fresh eyes and a clear head. And pay special attention to word choice, clarity, and conciseness.

Further Revising and Editing

6. Edit
5. Revise
4. Write
3. Organize
2. Prewrite
1. Explore

After waiting a few hours or days, return to the paragraph and revise it again. Edit your work, and hand in a clean, proofread copy.

ADDITIONAL WRITING ASSIGNMENT

Write your own personal definition of *father*, similar to the ones you've seen in the model paragraphs. You can discuss your own father or a male caregiver, or the father of someone you know. Include several traits in the definition, introduce each one with a clear transitional expression, and, if possible, illustrate each one.

A STUDENT MODEL ESSAY

The following definition essay was written by Amra Skocic, a student at Truman College who came from Bosnia. In it, she defines the term courageous act *by examining the behavior of one person. Notice that she includes several criteria in her definition and then discusses each one in a separate paragraph.*

True Courage
Amra Skocic

* * * *

1   It is not very often that we hear about, read about, or experience a truly courageous act. Indeed, do we really even understand what a courageous act is? According to *Webster's Dictionary*, *courage* is defined as "the ability to control fear when facing danger or pain." But there is much more involved. A courageous act is an unselfish gesture taken on a voluntary basis which involves some risk. An example

is Oscar Schindler, the real-life hero of the movie *Schindler's List,* who performs a courageous act by saving thousands of Jewish lives during the Second World War.

2   Oscar Schindler is a German factory owner who employs Jewish people and later rescues them from death in the concentration camps. In the beginning, he is primarily motivated by the opportunity to start production and earn a high profit using forced labor. As time goes by, Schindler's motivation changes from greed to selflessness. As he witnesses the mass execution and torture of the Jews in Poland, he realizes that he has the ability to save innocent lives. Gradually this realization overcomes his desire for money. Led by unselfish motivation, his action meets the first criterion for courage.

3   A courageous act must be voluntary, meaning that the person performing the act must have the full opportunity to walk away and avoid risk. Schindler understands his choices, but the one that he makes is to employ Jewish people. He could just as well have employed German workers or used other options without taking any risk. The voluntary nature of employing Jewish people in his factory meets the second criterion for courage.

4   A courageous act involves risk and sacrifice. How much the goal is worth determines the price of risk. From the moment Oscar Schindler decides to save those innocent lives, he is aware of the danger to his own life. If discovered by the Nazis, he will inevitably be killed. This risk completes the third and the final criterion for a courageous act.

5   Is there anything worth risking our own lives for? For most of us, probably not, but for a courageous person like Oscar Schindler, obviously there is. This points out the great difficulty of true courage, which the world rarely sees. Today it is more common for people to act out of selfishness, to avoid any danger, and to let others volunteer. Schindler sets himself apart when he accepts a great risk without potential reward, and without hesitation. Schindler stands as a beacon of courage in a world that still has many dark corners. We would all do well to emulate the courage of Schindler.

Questions for Analysis

1. Amra Skocic includes a dictionary definition in her first paragraph. Why? What sentence in the first paragraph introduces the three criteria she uses to shape her essay?

2. In the second, third, and fourth paragraphs, what sentences refer to each of the three criteria for the definition? Where does she place these sentences and why?

3. Would the definition be strengthened if she had discussed the actions of more than one person? Why or why not?

FINAL WRITING ASSIGNMENT

Define an abstract term such as *love, friendship, maturity, beauty,* or *success.* Establish your criteria for the definition, and use one person as an example. Don't try to be "the great philosopher." Just think carefully about the definition and base it on your common sense. You may write one paragraph or a whole essay, such as the one by Amra Skocic.

Types of paragraphs

- description: a scene, a person
- narration
- report
- process analysis

- cause and effect
- classification
- comparison and contrast
- definition

What to include in introductions
(see pp. 44, 47)

attention-getter

overview or preview

topic sentence (or thesis statement)

What conclusions might include
(see pp. 44, 47)

general summary or impression

call for action

climax of action: surprise, revelation, reflection

interpretation or evaluation

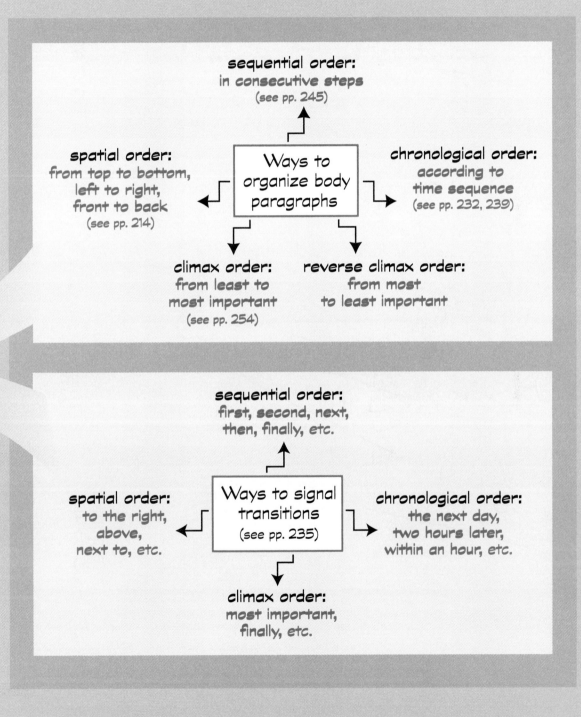

sequential order:
in consecutive steps
(see pp. 245)

spatial order:
from top to bottom,
left to right,
front to back
(see pp. 214)

Ways to
organize body
paragraphs

chronological order:
according to
time sequence
(see pp. 232, 239)

climax order:
from least to
most important
(see pp. 254)

reverse climax order:
from most
to least important

sequential order:
first, second, next,
then, finally, etc.

spatial order:
to the right,
above,
next to, etc.

Ways to signal
transitions
(see pp. 235)

chronological order:
the next day,
two hours later,
within an hour, etc.

climax order:
most important,
finally, etc.

V

Editing for Grammar and Mechanics: Finishing the Job

Previous units of this book have discussed the writing process as well as ways of organizing, developing, and strengthening paragraphs. This final unit offers you additional help in editing for grammar, punctuation, and the mechanics of written presentation. Some parts of this unit—especially Chapters 29 and 30—may be particularly helpful if your first language is not English. You may want to study the whole unit, some chapters in the unit, or only the parts of the chapters that address your individual concerns. You may even wish to use the unit as a reference as particular issues arise.

Specifically, the chapters discuss the following topics:

1. punctuation—including the rules for all the punctuation marks
2. spelling and matters related to spelling
3. look-alike and sound-alike words
4. verbs and the arrangement of words that accompany verbs
5. articles and prepositions

Take what you need from the unit so your work will exhibit the polish and clarity that calls forth confidence.■

26 Punctuating Sentences

As you've seen in Chapters 5 to 9, punctuation marks—commas, periods, semi-colons—are signals that help readers understand your sentences and avoid confusion. Incorrect punctuation can announce the end of a sentence that hasn't ended, join ideas that shouldn't be joined, or separate ideas that shouldn't be separated.

To punctuate correctly, you must know the rules. This chapter will help you

- identify where punctuation is needed
- know which punctuation marks to select: commas, periods, question marks, exclamation points, semicolons, colons, dashes, parentheses, or quotation marks

> "Take care of the sense, and the sounds will take care of themselves."
>
> —Lewis Carroll, Alice's Adventures in Wonderland

THE COMMA [,]

If you tend to place a comma wherever you hear a pause, be careful. You might be mispunctuating. **Commas** have six specific uses—some to separate ideas and others to enclose them.

Items in a Series

▶ **Separate three or more items with commas.**

A **coordinating conjunction**—usually *and*—ends the series. A comma before the conjunction is optional; you can include the comma or not. But be consistent; include it or omit it each time:

Subjects:	Anna, Maurice, *and* I
Verbs:	They came late to the party, threw their coats on the bed, *and* made a dash for the refreshments.

UNIT 5	Go Electronic
Chapter 26	Use the following electronic supplements for additional practice with your writing: • For chapter-by-chapter summaries and exercises, visit the Writing with Confidence Companion Website at http://www.ablongman.com/meyers. • For work with the writing process, visit The Longman Writer's Warehouse at http://longmanwriterswarehouse.com (password needed).
Writing with Confidence ©2003	• For additional practice in grammar, use The Writer's ToolKit Plus CD-ROM.

> *Adjectives:*   The field was wet, muddy, *and* slippery.
>
> *Phrases:*   They looked on top of the dresser, in the drawers, behind the nightstand, *and* under the bed.

EXERCISE 1   Editing for Comma Use

6. Edit
5. Revise
4. Write
3. Organize
2. Prewrite
1. Explore

Place commas along with and *where they are needed in the following sentences.*

1. Benjamin Franklin was a printer⌃writer⌃philosopher⌃inventor⌃scientist⌃politician⌃ *and* diplomat.

2. Franklin was so successful that he was able to retire at the age of forty-four. He had started a newspaper begun a club for tradespeople founded the first American subscription library become clerk to the Pennsylvania legislature established the first fire company become postmaster of Philadelphia begun the American Philosophical Society begun his famous *Poor Richard's Almanac*—a collection of wit wisdom financial advice he continued for twenty-five years.

3. King Henry VIII of England (1491–1547) had six wives: Catherine of Aragon Anne Boleyn Jane Seymour Anne of Cleves Catherine Howard Catherine Parr.

4. He divorced the first Catherine beheaded Anne lost Jane in a childbirth death canceled his marriage to Anne executed the second Catherine stayed married to the last Catherine.

Independent Clauses

Place a comma before the coordinating conjunction joining two independent clauses.

> The Cherokee Indians were an agricultural people, *and* they lived in villages in the southern part of the United States.
>
> Their homes at first were made of mud, *but* later the Cherokees built themselves log cabins.
>
> They established their own courts and schools in the early 1800s, *and* they had a higher standard of living than their white neighbors.

Only the coordinating conjunction joining two independent clauses requires a comma. Don't use a comma between two nouns or verbs.

> *Incorrect:*   The Cherokees also had a written constitution, and published their own newspaper.
>
> *Correct:*   The Cherokees also had a written constitution and published their own newspaper.

| EXERCISE 2 | Editing for Comma Use |

Place the commas where they're needed before coordinating conjunctions that join independent clauses. There are six missing commas in the passage.

Sequoyah (c. 1770–1843): Inventor of an Alphabet

(1) Young Sequoyah called the white people's books "the talking leaves"^ʌ and he and his fellow Cherokees of Tennessee were fascinated with their mysterious power. (2) They had seen the white settlers reading books and writing messages on paper. (3) Sequoyah's friends said that the Great Spirit had given this magic to whites but hadn't given it to the Indian peoples. (4) Sequoyah thought their arguments were nonsense for the white man had himself invented "the talking leaves."

(5) Sequoyah came from the Native American village of Taskigi (later Tuskegee) and his mother was a member of the emperor's family. (6) As he grew older, he became a master silversmith, a talented storyteller, and a skilled participant in dances, foot races, and ball games. (7) He was illiterate like everyone else in his tribe.

(8) A hunting accident left Sequoyah slightly handicapped or his life might have taken a different path. (9) After the injury, he had more free time and more chances to think about how his people might also come to get "the talking leaves." (10) He began wandering off into the woods and there he spent hours alone, avoiding everyone, playing like a child with pieces of wood, or making odd little marks with one stone or another. (11) His wife and friends encouraged and sympathized with him for they were sure that he was either going mad or communicating with spirits. (12) Months became years and the sympathy turned to ridicule and disrespect. (13) Nevertheless, Sequoyah was overpowered with his dream.

Scorecard: Number of Errors Found and Corrected _____

Interrupters

Place two commas around words, phrases, or clauses that interrupt a sentence. These interrupters can be temporarily removed without changing the basic meaning of a sentence—as in these examples:

With interrupter:	A Cherokee newspaper, *the Phoenix,* began publication in 1828.
Interrupter removed:	A Cherokee newspaper began publication in 1828.
With interrupter:	Many Cherokee, who live in Oklahoma and North Carolina today, originally lived in what is now Tennessee.
Interrupter removed:	Many Cherokee originally lived in what is now Tennessee.

Note on the TIPS box:

✓ TIPS

For Using the Coordinating Conjunctions

To help you recall the co-ordinating conjunctions, think of the phrase FAN BOYS.

For	But
And	Or
Nor	Yet
	So

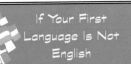

If Your First Language Is Not English

Speakers of Spanish need to be careful about trying to join two complete sentences with a comma. The practice is correct in Spanish but not in English. Commas don't join—they separate. Two sentences joined by a comma create an error called a **comma-spliced sentence.**

Think of the interrupter as something you'd place in parentheses. Although commas and parentheses are not the same, the two commas enclose the interrupter like parentheses (You'll see how to use parentheses on p. 295).

> The main branches of the Cherokee (who live in Oklahoma and North Carolina today) trace their ancestors back to what is now Tennessee.
>
> The main branches of the Cherokee, who live in Oklahoma and North Carolina today, trace their ancestors back to what is now Tennessee.

One sentence interrupter is called an **appositive**, a word or phrase that renames a noun. Appositives after proper (that is, capitalized) nouns usually need commas, but appositives after common (uncapitalized) nouns do not:

> Will Rogers, *a famous actor*, was a Cherokee Indian.
>
> The famous actor Will Rogers was a Cherokee Indian.

Be sure to enclose an interrupter in two commas, even if you think you hear just one pause. Otherwise, the sentence may be confusing:

> *Incorrect:*   Sequoyah, whom many people know was a famous leader of the Cherokee. (This looks like a sentence fragment.)
>
> *Correct:*   Sequoyah, whom many people know, was a famous leader of the Cherokee.

Remember, too, that commas enclose **relative clauses** (*who, whom, that, which* clauses) only when they are **nonrestrictive**—that is, they don't provide essential information. The clause in the previous example is nonrestrictive. A **restrictive relative** clause provides information essential to understanding the idea, so it isn't enclosed in commas. You may wish to review the discussion of these clauses in Chapter 8.

Introductory or Concluding Expressions

 Place a comma after most introductory phrases or clauses.

Long introductory (or transitional) phrases require a comma, but many short phrases don't:

> *For many centuries*, the Cherokee lived in the hills of Tennessee.
>
> *Perhaps* the first European contact with the Cherokee happened in 1540.

An introductory dependent clause requires a comma:

> *When Fernando de Soto came from Spain to the New World in search of gold*, he had many conflicts with the Cherokee.

A sentence can also end with a transitional word or phrase:

> He never found gold, *however*.
>
> He died instead, *having searched throughout Florida and along the Mississippi River for three years*.

✔ **TIPS**

For Using Commas with Interrupters

If you're unsure about punctuating interrupters, remember this simple rule: When in doubt, leave the commas out.

You can usually hear when no comma is needed:

> De Soto's body was sunk in the Mississippi *to prevent the Cherokee from mutilating it.*
>
> His companions floated down the river to the Gulf of Mexico, *from where they returned to Spain.*

EXERCISE 3 | Incorporating Transitional Expressions

6. Edit
5. Revise
4. Write
3. Organize
2. Prewrite
1. Explore

Include transitional expressions in the sentences that follow and punctuate the expression with commas when necessary.

Sequoyah's Attempt at Developing an Alphabet

1. at first Sequoyah tried to give every word of Cherokee its own separate character.

At first, Sequoyah tried to give every word of Cherokee its own separate character.

2. however He eventually found that approach too difficult and decided to assign a character to each sound. _____

3. when his friends and neighbors talked He no longer heard what they were saying.

4. (1) instead (2) trying to separate the sounds and identify new ones He carefully listened to their sounds. _____

5. with eighty-six characters representing all the sounds of spoken Cherokee What he eventually achieved was not so much an alphabet as a *syllabary.* _____

6. when combined These characters produced a clear and remarkably effective written language. _____

7. in all The task took Sequoyah twelve years. _____

EXERCISE 4 | Punctuating Interrupters and Transitional Expressions

6. Edit
5. Revise
4. Write
3. Organize
2. Prewrite
1. Explore

Correctly punctuate the following passage. You should add twelve commas.

Sequoyah's Fame

(1) Many stories ^ true or false ^ have been told of how Sequoyah presented his "alphabet" to the Cherokee people. (2) According to one legend his little daughter read

aloud what the chiefs had privately told him to write on a paper, instantly amazing and convincing everyone. (3) Sequoyah's alphabet was so simple that it could be learned in a few days. (4) Moreover those who learned it then taught it to others. (5) Within a few months a group of almost entirely illiterate people suddenly became literate. (6) Furthermore the odd little man who had been ridiculed by his people was now treated as almost a god.

(7) In 1828 Sequoyah and other Cherokees arrived in Washington, D.C., to settle a dispute over the federal government's failure to honor its treaties. (8) Because Sequoyah had already become famous he received a great deal of attention in the capital. (9) Charles Bird King a famous painter asked him to sit for a portrait, and many newspaper reporters asked for interviews.

(10) During their negotiations the Cherokees signed another treaty to exchange their lands for new ones in Oklahoma. (11) Although most Cherokees refused to leave Tennessee and Alabama Sequoyah's group from Arkansas moved westward to Oklahoma. (12) Sequoyah now over sixty years old built himself a new cabin, took care of his small farm, and traveled through the woods to the salt springs from time to time. (13) He lived there for days or weeks, filling his kettles, tending his fires, scooping out salt, and talking to anyone who came to see and speak with the famous Cherokee philosopher.

Scorecard: Number of Commas Added _____

Two or More Adjectives

 Place a comma between adjectives before a noun if *and* could go between the adjectives.

Sometimes to sharpen a description or make it more specific, you pile up several adjectives before a noun. If you can join them with *and* or reverse their order, that means they're equal. You should separate them with a comma:

> an ugly, disgusting wart (a disgusting, ugly wart)
>
> a thick, juicy steak (a thick and juicy steak)

If you cannot reverse the adjectives, don't separate them by commas:

> a bright red rubber ball (not a rubber red bright ball)
>
> a large frozen pizza (not a frozen large pizza)

EXERCISE 5 | Punctuating Adjectives

Place commas where they are needed in the following phrases.

1. a clever ˄ resourceful man

2. a beautiful large birthday cake

6. Edit
5. Revise
4. Write
3. Organize
2. Prewrite
1. Explore

3. an old red wagon

4. a torn worn faded pair of jeans

5. an awkward tall basketball player

6. a skillful old worker

✔ TIPS

For Punctuating Adjectives

If both adjectives describe the *noun,* they're equal and need a comma to separate them. But if the *first* adjective describes the *second adjective,* then they're not equal. You cannot separate them with a comma: a shiny blue car (*shiny* describes *blue,* not *car*)

Dates, Places, and Addresses

Place a comma between parts of dates, places, and addresses.

Put commas after the day and year for full dates. Also put a comma between a city and state in a sentence—and after the state, too, if the sentence continues. When you address an envelope, however, don't put a comma between the abbreviation for the state and the zip code:

> On August 9, 2004, the building should be completed. (No comma separates the month and day, but a comma follows the year.)
>
> Brookline, Massachusetts, is a lovely town. (Note the comma after the state.)
>
> 324 W. Juneway Street, Brookline, MA 01506 (No comma comes before the zip code.)

EXERCISE 6   Punctuating Addresses

6. Edit
5. Revise
4. Write
3. Organize
2. Prewrite
1. Explore

Place commas in the following dates or places.

1. (on envelope) 1522 E. Hartford Street꜔ Elizabethtown꜔ New York 12932

2. Have you been to Columbus Ohio before?

3. After December 5 2005 Kathy will be an attorney.

4. We expect 2005 to be a good year—after we pay our income taxes.

5. The Declaration of Independence was signed on July 4 1776 in Philadelphia Pennsylvania.

EXERCISE 7   Editing for Commas

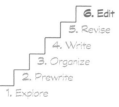

6. Edit
5. Revise
4. Write
3. Organize
2. Prewrite
1. Explore

Place commas where they're needed in the following passage. You should add nineteen commas.

Sequoyah's Final Deeds

(1) Although Sequoyah lived in a peaceful forest around Lee's Creek꜔ Oklahoma꜔ the Great Spirit did not allow him to end his life that way. (2) The federal government which had for so long wanted to grab the Cherokees' land in Tennessee and Alabama decided to remove them from the area. (3) Consequently a large battalion of well-armed hostile soldiers drove some 17,000 Cherokees from their homes. (4) The Native Americans began a long hard journey westward and suffered for many months. (5) About 4,000

Collaborative Activity 1

Looking at Commas

In your collaborative group, review your answers to Exercises 2, 3, 4, and 7. Discuss areas of disagreement with the entire class.

Collaborative Activity 2

Correcting Comma Errors

Write ten sentences in which you deliberately omit necessary commas. Include at least one error representing each of the six rules in this chapter. In your group, exchange papers by passing to the left, correct the errors, and then exchange papers to the left again so a third student checks your work.

Cherokees died before the Native Americans arrived in the Oklahoma Territory in the spring of 1839. (6) Because they greatly outnumbered the Cherokees who were already there problems immediately started. (7) The groups argued over the land over the members of local government and over many other matters.

(8) Sequoyah who wished to stop the conflict among his people persuaded them to be reasonable. (9) At a meeting of the entire tribe all the groups agreed to live in peace. (10) Consequently the Cherokees of Alabama Tennessee Arkansas and Oklahoma joined together to become the Cherokee Nation.

(11) However Sequoyah still could not rest. (12) He wanted to find a band of Cherokees who had come out west many years before. (13) Where were these lost Cherokees who did not know of his alphabet or the new Nation? (14) Sequoyah who was now an old man headed south with nine horsemen. (15) He supposedly found the lost Cherokees and died somewhere in Mexico. (16) Not long afterward in California a type of redwood that included the largest trees in the world was named "sequoyah" after the only man in history to invent an entire alphabet.

Scorecard: Number of Commas Added _____

THE PERIOD [.]

Periods have two functions: to signal the end of sentences and to mark abbreviations.

Statements

End every complete statement with a period.

Sentences that aren't statements need a different mark of final punctuation. End questions with a question mark, exclamations with an exclamation point:

> It looks like a nice day.
>
> *but*
>
> Do you think it will rain?
>
> Get out of here!

Abbreviations

Use periods for most abbreviations.

The following abbreviations require periods:

> Mr., Ms., Mrs., Dr., Rev.
>
> A.M., P.M.
>
> etc., i.e., e.g.

✓ TIPS

For Using Abbreviations Correctly

Most words in compositions shouldn't be abbreviated, for example:

lb. (use *pound*)	w/ (use *with*)
& (use *and*)	Va. (use *Virginia*)
ft. (use *feet*)	hr. (use *hour*)
Feb. (use *February*)	yr. (use *year*)
St. (use *Street*)	

Abbreviations require periods, but acronyms do not. Each letter of an acronym represents a word. Here are some common examples:

1. government agencies (*CIA*—the **C**entral **I**ntelligence **A**gency—and *FBI*—the **F**ederal **B**ureau of **I**nvestigation)

2. well-known organizations (Operation *PUSH*—**P**eople **U**nited to **S**ave **H**umanity)

3. television or radio stations (*WGN*—owned by the *Chicago Tribune,* which modestly calls itself the **W**orld's **G**reatest **N**ewspaper)

4. and words such as *scuba*—**s**elf-**c**ontained **u**nderwater **b**reathing **a**pparatus—which have become so well known that the acronym is now a word

Consult your dictionary when you aren't sure whether the word is an abbreviation or an acronym.

| EXERCISE 8 | Including Periods |

6. Edit
5. Revise
4. Write
3. Organize
2. Prewrite
1. Explore

Place periods where they are needed in the following groups of words.

1. I don't care what you say^ I am not going to speak in front of all those people^

2. (on envelope) 121 W Third Ave, New York, N Y

3. N B C

4. Mr and Mrs Jones

5. The Environmental Protection Agency is called the E P A

6. Get your scuba gear we're going to dive off the coast

THE QUESTION MARK [?]

Place question marks only after direct questions.

Question marks, like periods, end sentences—in this case, sentences that ask a question.

A **direct question** always ends with a question mark:

| *Direct questions:* | When was the Cherokee War? |
| | Who fought in the war? |

But don't use a question mark with an **indirect question,** which is contained within a larger statement and uses the word order of a statement:

| *Indirect questions:* | I asked when the Cherokee War occurred. |
| | Please tell me who fought in the war. |

| EXERCISE 9 | Punctuating Direct and Indirect Questions |

Place a period or a question mark at the end of each of the following sentences.

1. When did Sequoyah die^

2. No one knows for sure where Sequoyah died

3. Sequoyah asked his people if they could live in peace with each other

4. I want to know how many letters are in Sequoyah's alphabet

5. How many Sequoyah trees are in the national forest

6. Where do the Cherokee live today

THE EXCLAMATION POINT [!]

Collaborative Activity 3

Using End Punctuation
Prepare ten sentences—simple statements, direct questions, statements with indirect questions, and exclamations. Omit all the end punctuation marks. Pass your papers to the left and supply the missing punctuation marks and revise as necessary.

Use exclamation points after expressions of strong emotion.

An **exclamation point** signals excitement, anger, fear, or other strong emotions, whether in a full sentence or simply in a partial sentence:

> This is the last time I'll tell you!
>
> Don't, please!
>
> Help! Police!

Don't overuse exclamation points! Too many of them will bombard your readers! (As do the sentences you have just read.)

EXERCISE 10 | Supplying End Punctuation

Punctuate the following sentences with a period or an exclamation point.

1. The Cherokee have survived terrible losses to their people^

2. In just a few years after de Soto arrived in 1540, European diseases wiped out at least 75 percent of the Cherokee population

3. During the Civil War, the Cherokee lost 25% of their population.

4. No other group of Americans suffered as much during the conflict

5. With as many as 370,000 persons, Cherokee are the largest Native American group in the United States today

6. Amazingly, at least 15,000 are full-blooded Cherokee

THE SEMICOLON [;]

A **semicolon** is a combination of a period and a comma. Like a period, it makes the reader stop. Like a comma, it urges the reader to go on. The semicolon has two uses: to join independent clauses and to separate items in a series containing internal punctuation.

Independent Clauses

Join independent clauses with a semicolon.

A semicolon may join independent clauses whose ideas are closely related:

> The name Cherokee comes from a Creek Indian word; it means "people of a different speech."

Don't use a conjunction after the semicolon. But you may use a transitional word (a conjunctive adverb) after the semicolon. The transitional word is followed by a comma:

> Most Cherokee today accept this name; *however,* some call themselves *Tsalagi,* which comes from their own language.

EXERCISE 11 | Using Semicolons

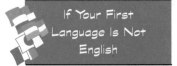

Insert semicolons and commas in each of the following sentences. Be careful. One sentence doesn't require a semicolon.

1. The early Cherokee village had about sixty houses ^;^ it also had a large council house.

2. A house looked like an upside-down basket it was made of branches and the outside was plastered with mud.

3. The houses where the Cherokee lived were sunken into the ground however their council house was usually located on a raised mound.

4. The Cherokee had settled on land used by earlier tribes therefore they did not build the mounds themselves.

5. Each council house was used for meetings and religious ceremonies each contained a sacred fire, which the Cherokee always kept burning.

6. Cherokee villages usually had their own governments, although the villages came together for ceremonies or war councils.

If Your First Language Is Not English

Spanish begins a question with an inverted question mark [¿] and an exclamation with an inverted exclamation point [¡]. English uses only the end punctuation. Don't confuse the different practices and check for errors in your editing.

Items in a Series

▶ **Use semicolons to separate items with internal punctuation.**

Remember that commas separate three or more items in a series. But if the items themselves contain commas, separate the items with semicolons:

> According to the 2000 census, the only cities in the United States with a population of more than one million are New York, New York; Los Angeles, California; Chicago, Illinois; Houston, Texas; Philadelphia, Pennsylvania; San Diego, California; Phoenix, Arizona; San Antonio, Texas; and Dallas, Texas.

> According to a list compiled by ten (male) members of an advisory board to the Modern Library in 1998, the five best novels in the English language are James Joyce, *Ulysses;* F. Scott Fitzgerald, *The Great Gatsby;* James Joyce, *A Portrait of the Artist as a Young Man;* Vladimir Nabokov, *Lolita;* and Aldous Huxley, *Brave New World.* Of the one hundred best novels, only eight were written by women.

6. Edit
5. Revise
4. Write
3. Organize
2. Prewrite
1. Explore

Place semicolons and commas where they are needed in the following sentences.

1. The novels you will read in the American literature course are Nathaniel Hawthorne *The Scarlet Letter* Mark Twain *Huckleberry Finn* Herman Melville *Moby-Dick* William Faulkner *The Sound and the Fury* F. Scott Fitzgerald *The Great Gatsby* and Ernest Hemingway *For Whom the Bell Tolls*.

2. The winners of the Academy Awards for 2000 were as follows: Best Picture *Gladiator* Best Director Steven Soderbergh for *Traffic* Best Actor Russell Crowe in *Gladiator* Best Actress Julia Roberts in *Erin Brockovich* Best Supporting Actor Benicio Del Toro in *Traffic* and Best Supporting Actress Marcia Gay Harden in *Pollock*.

3. If you are going south on your vacation, be sure to visit Bear Wallow Kentucky Pewee Kentucky Bulls' Gap Tennessee Difficult Tennessee Hot House North Carolina Improve Mississippi Scratch Ankle Alabama and Dime Box Texas. (They are all on the map.)

4. Among the most important dates in World War II were September 1 1939 when Hitler invaded Poland December 7 1941 when the Japanese attacked Pearl Harbor Hawaii September 3 1943 when Italy agreed to suspend fighting May 7 1945 when Germany surrendered unconditionally and September 2 1945 when Japan signed formal terms of surrender.

THE COLON [:]

Colons are like equal signs. They indicate that the last words of a grammatically complete statement are equal to the words that follow the statement.

Use a colon after a complete introductory statement.

When you introduce a list or a long quotation, end the introduction with a colon:

> Please bring the following items: a package of doughnuts, a case of soda pop, a picnic blanket, and a four-foot dueling sword.

> Here is part of a letter written by James H. Harris, warden of the United States Jail, written on January 6, 1906: "This is to certify that Mr. Harry Houdini at the United States Jail today was stripped stark naked, thoroughly searched, and locked up in cell No. 2 of the South Wing—the cell in which Charles J, Guiteau, the assassinator of President Garfield, was confined during his incarceration, from the date of his commitment, July 2nd, 1881, until the day on which he was executed, June 30th, 1882. Mr. Houdini, in about two minutes, managed to escape from that cell and then broke into the cell in which his clothing was locked-up. He then proceeded to release from their cells all the prisoners on the ground floor."

Be sure to place a colon only after a complete statement:

> Please bring a package of doughnuts, a case of soda pop, a picnic blanket, and a four-foot dueling sword. (*Please bring* is not a complete statement because the verb requires an object, so don't use a colon here.)

Never place a colon after any form of *to be*:

> *Incorrect:*   Albert's favorite foods are: tacos, enchiladas, and chop suey.
>
> *Correct:*   Albert's favorite foods are tacos, enchiladas, and chop suey.

EXERCISE 13 | Using Colons

Place colons and commas where they are needed in the following sentences.

1. For our trip to Central America, we took only the essentials^ suntan lotion^ some light clothing^ and a great deal of money.

2. For any dance at which *The Moving Violations* play you need three important items comfortable shoes comfortable clothes and comfortable earplugs.

3. Sally's appearance follows all the latest fashions a neon T-shirt jeans torn at the knees orange and green spiked hair and seventeen pierces in her left ear.

4. The three winners of the contest were Rolando Rodriguez Lavelle Wilson and John Jacobs.

5. You can take one from column A two from column B and your choice of two from column C or D.

6. Don't forget to add mustard, mayonnaise, ketchup, tomatoes, pickles, peppers, garlic salt, relish, and onions to make a great hot dog, if you can still find it under all that stuff.

THE DASH [—]

Dashes separate—and enclose—items in a sentence. They usually come in pairs.

Enclose an emphasized sentence interrupter in two dashes.

Use dashes (—) in pairs, just like the two commas that enclose sentence interrupters. Unlike the commas, however, the dashes call attention to the interrupter:

> Some—but not all—of the work was easy.
>
> The answer—I think—is obvious.

Use only one dash for an interrupter at the end of a sentence.

Of course, when an interrupter comes at the end of a sentence, it needs only one dash:

> The answer is obvious—I think.

Dashes are especially useful to set off an interrupter that contains commas.

> Punctuation marks—commas, periods, semicolons, and the like—help readers understand your sentences.

PARENTHESES [( )]

Parentheses enclose an item that isn't essential to a sentence's meaning. They always come in pairs.

Enclose a deemphasized sentence interrupter in parentheses.

Using Punctuation

Prepare ten sentences that use semicolons, colons, dashes, or parentheses. But omit all these punctuation marks. Then exchange papers by passing to the left and supply the missing punctuation marks. Then pass to the left again so a third student can check your work.

Dashes call attention to a sentence interrupter; parentheses draw attention away from it. They enclose information that's merely incidental to a sentence (usually short explanations, definitions, or examples—such as the material you're reading right now). Think of parentheses as footnotes within a sentence; almost anything that can go into a footnote can go into parentheses:

> The wallaby (a small- or medium-sized kangaroo) is found only in Australia and New Zealand.
>
> George Washington Gale Ferris (1859–1896) built the Ferris wheel for the World's Columbian Exposition in Chicago in 1893.

The parentheses are part of the sentence in which they appear, so a period follows the second parenthesis (like this).

EXERCISE 14   Using Dashes and Parentheses

6. Edit
5. Revise
4. Write
3. Organize
2. Prewrite
1. Explore

Punctuate each sentence interrupter with two dashes (or one dash) or with parentheses.

1. Sizzling hot meteors ^ some huge fireballs, others tiny specks ^ bombard the earth's atmosphere at the rate of one million per hour.

2. Five planets Mercury, Venus, Mars, Jupiter, and Saturn are visible to the naked eye.

3. Uranus the first planet beyond normal eyesight to be observed was discovered accidentally by William Herschel, who thought it was a comet.

4. The best candidate among the planets for having life other than Earth, of course was Mars.

5. Since the moon's gravity is too weak to hold atmosphere, there is no weather at all on the moon in fact, there is no wind, no sound, no life.

6. The surface temperature of the sun is approximately 6,000 degrees Kelvin 11,000 degrees Fahrenheit.

QUOTATION MARKS [" "]

In speaking, when you want to tell someone *exactly* what another person said, you gesture with your hands or imitate the other person's voice to emphasize that fact. **Quotation marks** function much like that gesture or change in voice.

They come in pairs, enclosing and identifying the exact words of another speaker or writer.

Quotation marks can also identify the exact words that you've taken from other sources—including titles, words being defined, or words used in a special way. We'll begin with those uses.

Titles

▶ **Use quotation marks for titles of poems, songs, articles, and chapters.**

Use quotation marks around the titles of short works or works contained within longer ones:

> "Coming of Age" (chapter title within a book)
>
> "Raging Fire Kills Three" (newspaper headline)
>
> "Michelle" (song title contained within an album)
>
> "Ode on a Grecian Urn" (poem contained within a book of poems)

Underline (or set in italics if you are using a computer) the titles of complete books, the names of magazines, the names of newspapers, and other longer works:

> *Time* (magazine)
>
> The *Chicago Tribune* (newspaper name)
>
> *The Simpsons* (television series)
>
> *Writing with Confidence* (book title)
>
> *The Mummy Returns* (movie)
>
> *Rent* (play)

✔ TIPS

For Quoting Titles

Don't put quotation marks around the titles of your own writing or writing assignments. But if, in another assignment, you refer to the title of another work (including another of yours), then place the title in quotation marks.

My Summer Vacation (title of assigned essay)

My Reaction to Being Asked to Write about "My Summer Vacation" (journal entry)

EXERCISE 15 | Punctuating Titles

Use underlining or quotation marks where appropriate.

1. Life magazine

2. The New York Post (newspaper)

3. Cold Mountain (novel)

4. The Fight Against AIDS (title of article) in Newsweek (magazine)

5. The Producers is a very popular Broadway production.

6. My favorite song from the album Rappin' with the Dudes is Gimmee Gimmee Some Heartburn.

Definitions

▶ **Underline (or italicize) words you define, and quote the definitions.**

> *Agnostic* literally means "without knowledge" (of God), while *atheist* means "without belief in God."

> *Recalcitrant* means "unwilling"; it comes from a Latin word, *recalcitrare*, which means "to kick back."

Words Used in a Special Way

Use quotation marks for words used in unusual ways.

When you use a word or phrase in an original or unusual way, enclose it in quotation marks:

> When the famous temperance leader Carry Nation was smashing saloons and crusading against the use of liquor, Kansas was technically a "dry" state—that is, liquor was illegal.
>
> The world's most famous eater, "Diamond Jim" Brady, never touched a drop of alcohol but instead drank his "golden nectar," orange juice.

Don't overuse quotation marks, especially to quote slang words. If you feel you must excuse your word by placing it in quotes, use another word instead:

> *Poor:*   Sam is a real "loser."
>
> *Better:*   Sam is always in trouble.

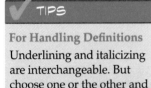

TIPS

For Handling Definitions
Underlining and italicizing are interchangeable. But choose one or the other and then be consistent.

EXERCISE 16	Replacing Slang Words

6. Edit
5. Revise
4. Write
3. Organize
2. Prewrite
1. Explore

Substitute another expression for each item in quotation marks or remove any unnecessary quotation marks.

1. I really "have a knack" for science. *I'm really good at science.* _____

2. Mark McGwire "blasted" a home run into the third deck. _____

_____

3. Let's go and "boogie" tonight. _____

_____

4. I can't stand the "hassle" of registration. _____

_____

5. Thomas is always "putting down" the people he meets. _____

_____

6. Juan is "as cool as a cucumber" when he meets some "tough dudes." _____

_____

_____

Speech

Use quotation marks for the exact words a person says or writes.

Quotation marks signal a **direct quotation**—the exact words of a speaker or writer. Never use quotation marks with **reported speech**—a retelling in your own words of what the speaker or writer says or said:

Direct quotation:	Harry said, "I need to rest for a while."
Reported speech:	Harry said that he needed to rest for a while.
Direct quotation:	Patty asked, "Are you studying for the exam with anyone?"
Reported speech:	Patty asked if I was studying for the exam with anyone.

Note that the words *that* or *if* (or *whether*) introduce reported speech. Notice, too, that with direct quotes, the words identifying the speaker are not within the quotation marks.

EXERCISE 17 | Writing Quotations and Reported Speech

6. Edit
5. Revise
4. Write
3. Organize
2. Prewrite
1. Explore

Change each of the following direct quotations into reported speech or vice versa.

Direct quote

1. Tomas said, "I know what I am doing."

2. My mother always asks me, "What do you want for supper?"

3. _____

   _____

4. The doctor told me, "You can make an appointment for tomorrow."

5. Mr. Joseph asked, "Where is the registrar's office?"

6. The man asked us, "Have you seen a kangaroo carrying a pogo stick?"

Reported speech

1. Tomas said that he knew what he was doing.

2. _____

   _____

3. Martha told me that she had been working late.

4. _____

   _____

5. _____

   _____

6. _____

   _____

Follow these rules when punctuating and capitalizing quotations:

a. Capitalize the first word of a complete quoted sentence, but don't capitalize the first word of a partially quoted sentence.

b. Place a comma after the introductory words that identify the speaker.

c. Place a comma, question mark, or exclamation point inside the end quotation mark, followed by the words identifying the speaker, which do not begin with a capital letter.

d. Enclose the entire quote—whether one word, one sentence, or more than one sentence—in a single set of quotation marks.

Collaborative Activity 5

Writing Dialogue

In your collaborative group, compose a short dialogue between two people on a humorous subject—a first date, a trip to the barber or beauty shop, someone giving advice to a friend, or whatever you wish. Have everyone in the group contribute and appoint one person to write out the dialogue. Check it over for correct use of quotation marks, punctuation marks, and paragraphing. If you encounter any problems, discuss them with the entire class.

If Your First Language Is Not English

Speakers of Russian should note that the opening quotation mark goes at the head of the word, like this—

"Word—not at the bottom of the word, as in Russian.

e. However, you may interrupt a quotation to identify the speaker and then resume the quotation.

Note these examples:

> In a letter to a friend, Thomas Jefferson asked, "What country before has ever existed a century and a half without a rebellion?" (A comma follows the identification of speaker; the quotation begins with a capital letter; and the question mark comes before the final quotation mark.)

> "Give me liberty," said Patrick Henry, "or give me death!" (The quotation ends to identify the speaker and then resumes without capitalization. The exclamation point is the end punctuation of the sentence and appears inside the quotation mark.)

> Carry Nation was famous for her crusades against alcohol. Once, after she had smashed tables, chairs, and the bar inside a saloon, a police officer came to arrest her for defacing property. She protested, "Defacing? I am defacing nothing! I am destroying!" (The three sentences are treated as a single quotation.)

When you write dialogue, begin a new paragraph each time you change speakers. Here's an example:

> When author Sam Clemens, alias Mark Twain, proposed marriage to Olivia Langdon, her upper-class father asked the young suitor for character references, which the latter provided. However, the letters Langdon received gave Clemens a unanimous and enthusiastic thumbs down. Two even predicted that the author would fill a drunkard's grave.
>
> "Haven't you a friend in the world?" Langdon asked.
>
> "Apparently not," Clemens replied.
>
> "I'll be your friend myself," Langdon said. "Take the girl. I know you better than they do."
>
> His instincts were correct, since Clemens proved a loyal and loving husband to Olivia.

EXERCISE 18 | Punctuating Quotations

6. Edit
5. Revise
4. Write
3. Organize
2. Prewrite
1. Explore

Correctly punctuate and capitalize the following quotations. Indicate paragraph breaks with this symbol: ¶.

Famous Last Words

1. As Ethan Allen, the famous Revolutionary War soldier, lay dying, his doctor said to him˄"General I fear the angels are waiting for you.˄ ˄"are they?˄ he answered. ˄"Waiting, are they? Well—let'em wait!"˄

2. It is very beautiful over there said Thomas Edison as he lay in a near-coma.

3. Well, I must arrange my pillows for another weary night murmured Washington Irving, the famous American author when will this end?

4. As Marie Antoinette, the French queen, was being led to her execution, she stepped on the executioner's foot. Monsieur she exclaimed I beg your pardon!

5. Marie Antoinette's husband, King Louis XVI, bravely asked his servants why do you weep? Did you think I was immortal?

6. I have a terrific headache complained Franklin D. Roosevelt.

7. Please mumbled Theodore Roosevelt put out the lights.

IN SUMMARY   To Punctuate Sentences

Using commas

1. Separate three or more items in a series with commas.
2. Separate two independent clauses joined by *and, but, or, for, so, nor,* or *yet* with a comma.
3. Enclose a sentence interrupter with commas.
4. Separate introductory words or phrases from the rest of the sentence with a comma.
5. Separate two or more adjectives preceding a noun with a comma if the adjectives could be reversed.
6. Separate elements in dates, places, or addresses with commas.

Using periods

1. Use periods after sentences that make a statement.
2. Use periods after abbreviated words, except those that stand for government and other well-known organizations, television and radio stations, and acronyms.

Using question marks

Question marks follow all direct questions but not indirect questions.

Using exclamation points

Use exclamation points after all sentences or sentence fragments expressing strong emotion.

Using semicolons

1. Semicolons join two independent clauses whose ideas are closely related but are not joined by *and, but, yet, or, nor, so,* or *for.*
2. Semicolons separate items in a series when the items have internal punctuation.

Using colons

Placed after a complete statement, a colon introduces a list or a long quotation (but not a form of the verb *to be*).

Using dashes

Dashes enclose a sentence interrupter that you want to emphasize.

Using parentheses

Parentheses enclose incidental information in a sentence.

Using quotation marks

1. Put quotation marks around the titles of short works or works contained within longer works.
2. Use quotation marks around definitions.

3. Set off words that you use in a special way with quotation marks.
4. Use quotation marks around a speaker's exact words (but not reported speech).
   a. Capitalize the first word of a complete quoted sentence.
   b. Place a comma after words that introduce the quotation, including the words that identify the speaker.
   c. End quotations with a comma, a question mark, or an exclamation point. Place all periods and commas inside the final quotation mark. Place question marks and exclamation points inside the final quotation mark if they're part of the quotation, but outside the final quotation mark if they're not part of the quotation.
   d. Use quotation marks around the *entire* quotation, not each sentence in the quotation.
   e. Each time you quote a new speaker, begin a new paragraph.

EDITING FOR MASTERY

Mastery Exercise 1

Correcting Punctuation Errors

The following passage contains fifteen punctuation errors, aside from the first error, which has been corrected as an example. Some punctuation marks are missing, and others are incorrect.

The Final Escape of Harry Houdini (1874–1926)

(1) Harry Houdini's real name was Ehrich Weiss, and he was born on March 24, 1874, in Budapest, Hungary. (2) He took his stage name from a famous French magician. (3) At the age of twenty, he married Wihelmina Rahner; who used the name Beatrice Houdini, and served as his stage assistant in his death-defying escapes from: ropes, chains, coffins, and underwater traps.

(4) Houdini's many daring escapes continually forced him to defy death. (5) He became obsessed and fascinated with the subject, therefore he often had visions of his own end. (6) But none of his fantasies were as simple accidental and tragic as the actual event.

(7) Before an afternoon performance in Montreal on October 22, 1926 Houdini was lying on a sofa in his dressing room. (8) A university student, who earlier had drawn a picture of the magician came backstage to meet Houdini and brought along two friends. (9) One was an amateur boxer named J. Gordan Whitehead. (10) The boxer asked, "Can you withstand punches to the midriff, as the press has claimed"? (11) Houdini nodded, and Whitehead immediately hit the magician violently in the stomach. (12) Houdini gasped, jumped to his feet, and explained that first it was necessary to tense his muscles—which he then did. (13) Whitehead may have punched him several more times.

(14) The following night, Houdini developed stomach cramping and fever on a train to Detroit. (15) He later began his performance but collapsed from a ruptured appendix. (16) He was given twelve hours to live. (17) Ironically, Houdini's wife was recovering from a case of food poisoning in the same Detroit hospital. (18) The magician decided there and then, that whoever died first would attempt to contact the survivor.

(19) Houdini fought on for several days, he underwent two operations (20) On Halloween night, he told his brother, "I'm tired of fighting." "I guess this thing is going to get me." (21) Then he died. (22) Houdini's body was placed in the coffin from which he always escaped in his act, in hopes that he'd escape once again. (23) Attached to Houdini's will was a letter he had written to his wife just days before. (24) In it he said. "When you read this I shall be dead. Dear Heart, do not grieve. I shall be at rest by the side of my beloved parents and wait for you." (25) His escape from death never took place, and he had to wait seventeen years for his wife.

Scorecard: Number of Errors Found and Corrected _____

Mastery Exercise 2

Correcting Punctuation Errors

The following passage contains fifteen punctuation errors, aside from the first error, which has been corrected as an example. Some punctuation marks are missing, and others are incorrect. Write your corrections above the lines.

Nostradamus (1503–1566): Prophet or Fake?

[delete comma]

(1) A lively little astrologer with a long beard had been invited to Paris in 1556 to entertain the royal court of King Henry II of France. (2) The predictions of this man, Nostradamus would soon make him famous. (3) One of them seemed ridiculous: a one-eyed man would soon be king. (4) The other one was rather vague. (5) "The young lion will overcome the older one in a field of combat in a single fight." "He will pierce his eyes in their golden cage—two wounds in one—and then he will die a cruel death."

(6) On July 1 1559, King Henry was wounded in a tournament by a lance, that punctured his left eye and then his throat. (7) The king, who was the only one-eyed ruler in French history died in terrible pain ten days later. (8) The words of Nostradamus now inspired both awe and fear. (9) The leaders of the Roman Catholic Church wanted to burn him at the stake as a magician and sorcerer. (10) Poor people thought his prediction had actually been a curse and burned him in effigy. (11) Queen Catherine, the king's widow protected and saved him.

(12) Born Michel de Notredame on December 14, 1503, this future prophet planned to become a doctor. (13) When bubonic plague swept through southern France in 1525; he traveled around to treat the victims of this terrible disease. (14) Other doctors then al-

most refused to give him a medical license out of jealousy. (15) After a second outbreak of the plague killed his first wife, and children, Nostradamus—as he now called himself, once again treated the sick and became known as a miracle-worker. (16) Consequently, he received a lifetime pension. (17) He later married a wealthy widow who had six children with him. (18) Nostradamus gave up medicine and involved himself in two forms of mysticism; magic and astrology. (19) He studied the stars and claimed to receive the secrets of the future from an eternal voice.

(20) Nostradamus wrote his prophecies in verses that mixed words from French, Italian, Greek, Spanish, Hebrew, and Latin. (21) He claimed "that his odd writing protected him from the punishment by rulers who were unhappy with his predictions of their futures." (22) But many people say that he was deliberately vague; so his writing could be interpreted in many ways. (23) As a result, almost four hundred different studies of his work have been published, each tried to unlock the secrets of prophecies that continue up to the year 3797. (24) "My writings will be better understood by those who come after my death", he wrote.

(25) According to some scholars, Nostradamus also predicted how he would die when he wrote, "Close to bench and bed will I be found dead." (26) One evening, after announcing that he would not survive the night he died, and his body was discovered the next morning near his writing desk in his bedroom.

Scorecard: Number of Errors Found and Corrected _____

27 Checking Spelling, Apostrophes, Hyphens, and Capitals

Spelling and related matters may seem to be trivial issues. But trivial issues can distract your readers from the important one: the content of your writing. You should therefore pay close attention to spelling, apostrophes, hyphens, and capitalization as you edit your work. This chapter will help you

- learn the rules
- give yourself practice in applying them

SPELLING

You can eliminate many spelling problems if you follow some simple practices:

1. *Develop a healthy mistrust for the way you spell words.* "Good" spellers are often bad ones who suspect errors and check them in the dictionary or on computer spell checkers. If you compose by hand, circle words whose spelling you aren't sure of and then look them up as you edit. The dictionary will not only show you how to spell the words, but it will show you how to pronounce them, where to separate them between syllables, and what their forms are in different tenses, as plurals, or as different parts of speech.

2. *Carefully pronounce words you aren't sure how to spell,* look them up in the dictionary, and learn the spellings that correspond to those pronunciations. But because English is a combination of several languages, each with its own spelling rules, a sound can be spelled in many ways. So keep that dictionary handy. And don't rely entirely on a computer spell checker. It can give you the "correct" spelling of a word—but not the word you want to use.

UNIT 5	Go Electronic
Chapter 27	Use the following electronic supplements for additional practice with your writing: • For chapter-by-chapter summaries and exercises, visit the Writing with Confidence Companion Website at http://www.ablongman.com/meyers.
Writing with Confidence ©2003	• For work with the writing process, visit The Longman Writer's Warehouse at http://longmanwriterswarehouse.com (password needed). • For additional practice in grammar, use The Writer's ToolKit Plus CD-ROM.

3. *Look for root words in longer, more complex words.* For example, *member* is inside *remember* and *differ* is inside *different*. This advice is especially important in words with a silent letter or a hard-to-recognize vowel sound. For example, *finite* is in *definite* and *labor* is in *laboratory*.

4. *Don't confuse words that sound or look alike (their/there/they're, its/it's, and so on).* Check your dictionary repeatedly until you can clearly distinguish one word from the other.

5. *Use memory games to remind you of tricky spellings.* For example, everybody wants to eat two deSSerts, but nobody wants to be stranded in a deSert more than once. You'll find tips throughout this chapter to help you remember tricky spellings.

6. *Keep your own spelling list of problem words* (preferably on flash cards so that you can study each one separately) and write each word in a sentence. Underline or capitalize the troublesome part of the word: proBABly, choiCe, studYing. Consult Appendix B at the back of this book for additional help with many tricky spellings.

7. *Carefully proofread your papers,* whether you write them by hand or keyboard them into a computer. You should catch a number of careless errors in the process. Use computer spell-checking programs—but don't rely on them entirely. They can't think for you, and they won't catch every mistake.

The following rules should also help improve your spelling.

The Long and Short Vowel Sounds

Carefully pronouncing words will help you spell them only if you know which letters represent the various sounds. That's especially true with the **vowels**, which can have a number of sounds and spellings.

The Long Vowel Sounds.   When you say the names of the vowels, you are pronouncing the long vowel sounds. But most often when spelling these long vowel sounds, you must *combine two vowels*, either together or separated by a single **consonant**. Here are some examples:

Sound	Spelling	Example
long *a*	*ai*	main, lain, chain
	ay	hay, say, pay
	ei	sleigh, reign
	a consonant *e*	fate, hate, crate
long *e*	*ee*	seem, meet, three
	ea	beat, dream, league
	ie	believe, achieve, brownie
	(c)*ei*	receive, deceive, conceive
	final *y*	happy, ugly, unity
	e consonant *e*	precede, Chinese, complete

Continued

If Your First Language Is Not English

Pay special attention to vowel sounds, which can be confusing. Many languages don't have a short *i* sound, and English letters *i* and *e* pronounce as *e* and *a*. For example, *bit* in English is pronounced like *beat* in many languages. And *bet* in English is pronounced like *bait* in many languages. Proofread your work carefully.

Sound	Spelling	Example
long *i*	*ie*	pie, tie, flies
	igh, ign	light, sigh, sign
	y	sky, fly, cry
	i consonant *e*	nice, cite, line
long *o*	*oa*	boat, coat, roam
	final *o*	piano, auto, potato
	old	sold, scold
	o consonant *e*	chrome, wrote, role
long *u*	*oo*	boot, shoot, food
	ui	fruit, juice
	ew	new, few, crew
	final *ue*	clue, argue, true
	u consonant *e*	cute, huge, refuse

The Short Vowel Sounds.   A single vowel is usually pronounced as a short vowel sound. Compare these words:

Short vowel sounds	Long vowel sounds
hat	hate
bat	bait
man	main
bet	beat, beet
pet	Pete
bit	bite
quit (*u* always follows *q* and is not considered a vowel in this position)	quite
hop	hope
hot	hotel
lot	load
cut	cute
subtle	suit

TIPS

For Spelling Words with *ie* or *ei*

To keep these spellings straight, remember this rhyme:

I before *e*
Except after *c*
Or when sounded like *a*
As in *neighbor* or *weigh*.

1. *i* before *e*: believe, relief
2. except after *c*: receive, conceive
3. or when sounded like *a*: eighty, sleigh

Some exceptions: caffeine, either, their, foreign, protein, leisure, weird, seize.

Although nothing can provide an instant cure for misspelled long and short vowel sounds, the list should help. And each time you hear a vowel sound you aren't sure how to spell, check your dictionary. You'll learn more about spelling long and short vowel sounds later, when the chapter discusses doubling final consonants.

EXERCISE 1 — Writing Long Vowels

Write two or three words using the vowels supplied. Don't use any of the words from the list already given.

1. long *a*

ai *claim, bait, train* _____   ay _____

ei _____   *a* consonant *e* _____

2. long *e*

ee _____   ea _____

final *y* _____

3. long *i*

ie _____   igh, ign _____

final *y* _____   *i* consonant *e* _____

4. long *o*

oa _____   final *o* _____

old _____   *o* consonant *e* _____

5. long *u*

oo _____   ui _____

ew _____   ue _____

u consonant *e* _____

EXERCISE 2 — Choosing the Correct Spelling

Circle the correctly spelled word.

1. (brief) / breif   5. chief / cheif

2. field / feild   6. reciept / receipt

3. conciet / conceit   7. decieve / deceive

4. frieght / freight   8. thier / their

Plurals of Nouns and Singulars of Verbs

Add –*s* or –*es* to make plural nouns and present-tense, third-person-singular verbs. Both nouns and verbs follow the same spelling rules for taking –*s* or –*es*.

 Add –*es* to nouns or verbs ending in *ss, ch, sh, z,* or *x.*

boss, wax, reach, wish = *bosses, waxes, reaches, wishes*

 Add –*es* to most nouns or verbs ending in –*o.*

tomato, potato, do = *tomatoes, potatoes, does*

Some exceptions: radios, pianos, stereos

▶ **Change final –*y* to –*i* and add –*es* after a consonant.**

> study, try, sky = *studies, tries, skies*

▶ **Do not change final –*y* after a vowel; merely add –*s*.**

> boy, play, buy = *boys, plays, buys*

▶ **Change noun (but not verb) endings from –*f* or –*fe* to –*ve* before adding –*s*.**

> Leaf, knife, wife = *leaves, knives, wives*
>
> *Some exceptions:* beliefs, chiefs, safes, chefs

EXERCISE 3	Forming Plurals

6. Edit
5. Revise
4. Write
3. Organize
2. Prewrite
1. Explore

Make the following nouns plural.

1. knife *knives* _____

2. half _____

3. self _____

4. hoof _____

5. shelf _____

6. chief _____

▶ **Add –*s* to most other nouns and verbs.**

> Lamp, pie, make, walk = *lamps, pies, makes, walks*
>
> *Some exceptions:* child = *children*, man = *men*

EXERCISE 4	Adding Word Endings

6. Edit
5. Revise
4. Write
3. Organize
2. Prewrite
1. Explore

Add –s or –es to these words, and change word endings when necessary.

1. ride *rides* _____

2. beach _____

3. beauty _____

4. rush _____

5. tax _____

6. flower _____

7. rose _____

8. witch _____

9. breath _____

10. key _____

Suffixes

A **suffix** is an ending attached to a **root word** to form a new word. Here are some examples:

Root word	Suffix	New word
agree	–ment	agreement
grace	–ful	graceful
sad	–ness	sadness

Note the rules for the spelling of words when suffixes are added:

▶ **Change –y to –i if the letter before –y is a consonant.**

Root word	Suffix	New word
busy	–ness	business
happy	–er	happier
pretty	–est	prettiest
angry	–ly	angrily
deny	–al	denial
beauty	–ful	beautiful

Note: Never change final *y* to *i* before the suffix *–ing:* denying, trying

▶ **Don't change a –y that comes after a vowel.**

Root word	Suffix	New word
play	–ed, –ing	played, playing
lay	–er	layer
employ	–ment	employment

EXERCISE 5	Adding Suffixes

6. Edit
5. Revise
4. Write
3. Organize
2. Prewrite
1. Explore

Combine the following root words and suffixes, making whatever changes are necessary.

1. destroy + er *destroyer* _____

2. stay + ed _____

3. apply + cation _____

4. ugly + est _____

5. pay + ment _____

6. witty + cism _____

7. fly + er _____

8. fly + ing _____

9. happy + ly _____

▶ **Drop final –e when the suffix begins with a vowel.**

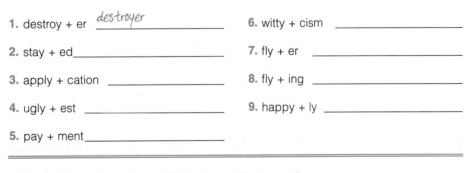

Root word	Suffix	New word
ridicule	–ous	ridiculous
argue	–ing	arguing
strangle	–ing	strangling

Some exceptions: hoeing, canoeing

▶ With most words ending in *–ce* or *–ge*, do not drop the final *–e*.

courag*e*ous	notic*e*able

▶ Keep final *–e* when the suffix begins with a consonant.

Root word	Suffix	New word
hope	*–ful*	hopeful
complete	*–ly*	completely
time	*–less*	timeless

Some exceptions: acknowledgment, argument, judgment, truly, awful

---

EXERCISE 6 — Combining Root Words and Suffixes

6. Edit
5. Revise
4. Write
3. Organize
2. Prewrite
1. Explore

Join the following root words and suffixes, making whatever changes are necessary.

1. hate + ful _hateful_____

2. awe + ful_____

3. dance + ing _____

4. sincere + ly_____

5. fame + ous _____

6. amuse + ment _____

7. dine + ing _____

8. admire + ation _____

▶ The suffix *–ly* changes adjectives to adverbs without changing the spelling of the root word (except that final *–y* may become *–i*).

This rule is especially important for root words ending in *–l* (making *–lly*) or root words ending in *–e* (making *–ely*):

Root word	New word
real	really
sure	surely
sincere	sincerely
careful	carefully

One exception: true = truly

EXERCISE 7 — Adding -ly to Root Words

6. Edit
5. Revise
4. Write
3. Organize
2. Prewrite
1. Explore

Change the following adjectives to adverbs by adding –ly.

1. ideal _ideally_____

2. bare _____

3. usual _____

4. sure _____

5. angry _____

6. necessary _____

7. real _____

8. true _____

▶ **For short vowel sounds, double the final consonant.**

As you saw earlier in the chapter, a combination of vowel-consonant-vowel (such as *–ate, –ine,* and *–ope*) usually creates a long vowel (which sounds the same as the name of the vowel):

hate	Pete	bite	hope	cute

However, a combination of vowel-consonant-consonant creates a short vowel sound, as in the following examples:

hat	hatter
pet	petted
bit	bitten
hop	hopped
cut	cutting

▶ **Doubling the consonant makes the vowel before it short.**

If the vowel sound remains long, the consonant does not double. Contrast these words:

(to cause a scar)	scar	scarring, scarred
(to frighten)	scare	scaring, scared
(to get rid of)	rid	ridding
(to ride, as in a car)	ride	riding
(to hop, like a bunny)	hop	hopping, hopped
(to wish)	hope	hoping, hoped
(to slice)	cut	cutter
(attractive)	cute	cuter

EXERCISE 8	Adding Suffixes

Add suffixes to the root words, doubling the final consonant when necessary.

6. Edit
5. Revise
4. Write
3. Organize
2. Prewrite
1. Explore

1. win + ing *winning* _____

2. tune + ing _____

3. write + ing _____

4. stop + ed _____

5. run + ing _____

6. hit + ing _____

7. heat + ing _____

8. stir + ing _____

Don't double all final consonants of words with more than one syllable.

A root word can have more than one **syllable**—a grouping of letters containing a single vowel sound. With multisyllable root words, double the final consonant only if the accent falls on the syllable immediately before the suffix:

commit′ ted	occurr′ ed
begin′ ning	submit′ ted
preferr′ ed	expell′ ed
Exception:	offer off′ erred off′ erring

When the accent falls on another syllable, do not double the consonant:

hap′ pened	lis′ tened
an′ swered	coun′ selor
pref′ erence	trav′ eled

These rules also help in determining when to double consonants in other situations:

apple	*but*	ape
beggar	*but*	begin
rummage	*but*	union

EXERCISE 9   Doubling Final Consonants

Combine the following root words and suffixes, doubling the final consonant of the root word when necessary. Be careful to note where the accent falls.

1. defer + ed *deferred* _____

2. unravel + ing _____

3. parallel + ing _____

4. compel + ed _____

5. prefer + ence _____

6. occur + ed _____

EXERCISE 10   Recognizing Correct Spelling

Circle the correct spelling.

1. runing / (running)

2. diferent / different

3. stuborn / stubborn

4. refered / referred

5. writing / writting

6. gramar / grammar

7. occured / occurred

8. comming / coming

9. biten / bitten

10. sitting / siting

Prefixes

A **prefix**—an addition to the beginning of a root word—never affects the spelling of the root. No letters are dropped or doubled:

Prefix	Root word	New word
un-	natural	unnatural
dis-	integrate	disintegrate
mis-	spell	misspell
il-	logical	illogical
in-	accurate	inaccurate
im-	moral	immoral
co-	operate	cooperate

EXERCISE 11 | Identifying Correctly Spelled Words

6. Edit
5. Revise
4. Write
3. Organize
2. Prewrite
1. Explore

Circle the correct spellings.

1. (disinterested) / dissinterested

2. unnable / unable

3. inumerable / innumerable

4. unnerve / unerve

5. disatisfied / dissatisfied

6. ilegal / illegal

7. immaterial / imaterial

8. missapply / misapply

9. misstake / mistake

10. disagree / dissagree

EXERCISE 12 | Correcting Misspellings

6. Edit
5. Revise
4. Write
3. Organize
2. Prewrite
1. Explore

Correct each of the following misspelled words. When the spelling rules won't help you, use a dictionary or look at the list of commonly misspelled words in Appendix B.

1. accross   *across* _____

2. adress _____

3. alot _____

4. arguement _____

5. athelete _____

6. basicly _____

7. begining _____

8. beleive _____

9. brillient _____

10. buisness _____

11. carefuly _____

12. childrens _____

13. choosen _____

14. comming _____

15. competion _____

16. definate _____

17. delt _____

18. diffrent _____

✓ TIPS

For Using Memory Devices

1. StationERy is papER.
2. Old AGE is a trAGEdy.
3. Bad gramMAR will MAR your writing.
4. The LLs are paraLLel in this word.
5. He is BUSY in his BUSIness.
6. The princiPAL is your PAL.
7. TOGETHER we went TO GET HER.
8. To write ALL RIGHT as one word would be ALL WRONG.
9. AFFECT is a verb that begins with A for AC-TION.
10. Strange but true, there is a LIE in beLIEf and beLIEve.
11. Don't let the IR in theIR IRk you.
12. There is an ITCH in wITCH.
13. WhICH one has the sandWICH?
14. HERE is in tHERE and wHERE.
15. There is no word in English that begins with RECCO. Recommend means Re commend.
16. FULL loses an L at the end of a word: THANKFUL, GRATE-FUL, HELPFUL, etc.

19. dinning _____
20. disapoint _____
21. discribe _____
22. dosen't _____
23. eigth _____
24. entrence _____
25. enviroment _____
26. existance _____
27. explaination _____
28. extremly _____
29. finaly _____
30. freind _____
31. goverment _____
32. grammer _____
33. heigth _____
34. hisself _____
35. hopeing _____
36. imediately _____
37. interlectual _____
38. intresting _____
39. jewlry _____
40. knowlege _____
41. localy _____
42. lonly _____
43. misspell _____
44. necesary _____

45. ocasion _____
46. occurance _____
47. perfer _____
48. possble _____
49. potatoe _____
50. preceed _____
51. priviledge _____
52. probly _____
53. recieved _____
54. rember _____
55. sacrafice _____
56. sence _____
57. seperate _____
58. shinning _____
59. sincerly _____
60. studing _____
61. suceed _____
62. suprise _____
63. temperture _____
64. themselfs _____
65. tomatoe _____
66. truely _____
67. trys _____
68. usualy _____
69. writen _____
70. writting _____

THE APOSTROPHE [']

The rules for using apostrophes are actually rather simple. The **apostrophe**—a little hook above the line where a letter (or letters) would normally be—has only three functions: to form possessives of nouns, to form contractions, and to make letters plural.

Possessives

▶ **Add 's to make a singular noun possessive.**

When something belongs to someone, that person possesses it. There are several ways to express possession or ownership:

> the house that belongs to Jerry
>
> the car my neighbor owns
>
> the room of my brother

However, a simple apostrophe *(')* + *s* added to a noun signals possession in a shorter and more direct way:

> *Jerry's* house
>
> my *neighbor's* car
>
> my *brother's* room

This form of the noun is called the **possessive**.

Although a house, a car, and a room are concrete and material, a person can also possess abstract, nonmaterial things:

> the idea of my friend = my *friend's* idea
>
> the explanation made by the teacher = the *teacher's* explanation
>
> the ambition that Rafael has = *Rafael's* ambition

Creating Memory Devices

In your collaborative group, try your talents at creating memory devices for the following words. Report your results to the whole class.

1. piece
2. attendance
3. comparative
4. existence
5. friend
6. misspell
7. disappoint
8. capitol (building)
9. different
10. marriage

EXERCISE 13 | Forming Possessives

6. Edit
5. Revise
4. Write
3. Organize
2. Prewrite
1. Explore

Rewrite each of the following using apostrophe + –s.

1. the book that belongs to Tom ___Tom's book_____

2. the coat that Judy has _____

3. the work done by Willie _____

4. the personality of Karen _____

5. the apartment that belongs to Maria_____

6. the bicycle that the boy owns _____

7. the statement made by Mr. Johnson_____

▶ **Add ' to make a plural noun ending in –s possessive.**

As you know, most plural nouns end in *–s:*

> friends   boys   classes   the Smiths
>
> teachers   students   parents   the Gonzalezes

You make these words possessive by adding ' after the –s:

> the books that belong to more than one boy = the *boys'* books
>
> the car that belongs to my neighbors = my *neighbors'* car
>
> the attitude of my parents = my *parents'* attitude

For Keeping the Possessive Forms of Pronouns Straight

Personal pronouns already have their possessive forms built in; they do not take apostrophes:

Singular	Plural
my house	*our* house
your house	*your* house
his house	
her house	*their* house
its house	

The correct placement of the apostrophe is important; it tells the reader whether the possessive noun is singular or plural:

> the *boy's* house (singular—one boy)
>
> the *boys'* house (plural—more than one boy)

All singular nouns should add *'s*, even if they end in *s*.

> *Carlos's* smile
>
> the *boss's* desk

EXERCISE 14 Making More Possessives

6. Edit
5. Revise
4. Write
3. Organize
2. Prewrite
1. Explore

Rewrite each of the following expressions, using 's or '.

1. the lounge for women _the women's lounge_

2. the idea of my boss _____

3. the house that belongs to Ms. Jones _____

4. the room that belongs to the children _____

5. the day for every mother _____

6. the schedules of the professors _____

7. the laws of Texas _____

8. the best restaurant in the city _____

▶ **Use *'s* or *'* to show possession with objects and time.**

Objects can also possess things, as in these examples:

> the front tire of the bicycle = the *bicycle's* front tire
>
> the new stoplights of the streets = the *streets'* new stoplights

Even some time expressions use *'s* or *s'*. Notice that the phrases with apostrophes sound more graceful than the ones with *of:*

> the pay of a week = a *week's* pay
>
> the work of two years = two *years'* work

EXERCISE 15	Editing for Apostrophes

6. Edit
5. Revise
4. Write
3. Organize
2. Prewrite
1. Explore

Insert the missing apostrophes in each of the following sentences.

1. I'm taking a week ^'s vacation soon.

2. The rooms air conditioner needs to be repaired.

3. A few hours work should take care of the problem.

4. This years schedule allows more time off than last years schedule.

5. The cars front fenders were dented in two separate accidents.

6. I'll be off on New Years Day.

EXERCISE 16	Spelling Words Ending in -s

6. Edit
5. Revise
4. Write
3. Organize

Circle the correct spelling in parentheses.

1. It was the (companies / (company's)) responsibility.

2. The Mets scored five (runs / run's) in the ninth.

3. He (runs / run's) a large business.

4. Four men were shot in the (movies / movie's) opening scene.

5. I ate at the (cities / city's) best restaurant.

6. She (lights / light's) the fire each night.

7. The trees have lost their (leaves / leaf's).

8. He (says / say's) that the coat doesn't fit.

✔ **TIPS**

For Correcting Errors with Apostrophes

Some people want to put apostrophes before every final –s. Remember that apostrophes signal possession, not plurals or third-person-singular verbs.

Contraction

Use an apostrophe to replace the missing letter(s) in a contraction.

A **contraction** is a joining of two words that requires omitting a letter or several letters from the second word. An apostrophe occupies the spot of the missing letters:

> do not = *don't* (' replaces *o*)
>
> cannot = *can't* (' replaces *no*)
>
> it is = *it's* (' replaces *i*)
>
> they are = *they're* (' replaces *a*)
>
> they would = *they'd* (' replaces *would*)

EXERCISE 17	Forming Contractions

6. Edit
5. Revise
4. Write
3. Organize
2. Prewrite

Make the following pairs of words into contractions, placing apostrophes properly.

1. he is *he's*   **3.** it has _____

2. we will _____   **4.** they are _____

5. we are _____   **8.** it is _____

6. has not _____   **9.** does not _____

7. you are _____   **10.** can not _____

EXERCISE 18	Editing for Apostrophes

6. Edit
5. Revise
4. Write
3. Organize
2. Prewrite
1. Explore

Add apostrophes where necessary.

1. It^'s cold today.

2. Were going to get it done.

3. Well have to see what she says.

4. What do you think hell do?

5. I dont know what youre asking me.

6. Its purpose is clear.

7. Whos there?

8. Theyre always getting into trouble.

Collaborative Activity 2

Correcting Apostrophe Errors

Write five sentences containing words that need apostrophes, but omit the apostrophes. Exchange papers by passing to the left and add the apostrophes. Exchange papers again to the left so a third student may check the work.

Plurals of Letters

Add *'s* to form the plurals of letters used as letters.

When you need to make a letter or group of letters plural, add an apostrophe before the final –s so that your readers don't mistake the –s for one of the letters:

> Watch your *p's* and *q's*.
>
> Billy already knows his *ABC's*.
>
> Maria got all *A's*.

HYPHENS [-]

Hyphens always join. They join two or more words to make them one, or they keep words joined when you must break them at the end of a line.

Hyphens to Join Words

Hyphenate two-word numbers.

In formal writing, use a hyphen to join all two-word numbers between twenty-one and ninety-nine, as well as all fractions:

thirty-five		one hundred
fifty-one	*but*	321 (Use numerals for numbers that require three or more
two-thirds		words to write out.)

EXERCISE 19 — Hyphenating Numbers

6. Edit
5. Revise
4. Write
3. Organize
2. Prewrite
1. Explore

Hyphenate the following numbers if necessary.

1. twenty⌃one

2. three hundred

3. forty six

4. one thousand

5. three fourths

6. eighty two

▶ **Hyphenate between a prefix and a capitalized noun.**

> pro-American   anti-Chinese

▶ **Hyphenate between the prefixes *self–*, *all–*, and *ex–* (meaning "former") and all nouns.**

> self-confidence   ex-husband   all-world

▶ **Hyphenate words with *–in-law*.**

> mother-in-law   brothers-in-law (Note how the plural is formed.)

▶ **Hyphenate two or more words acting as a single adjective before a noun.**

> a three-piece suit   a four-star movie
> a good-for-nothing guy   a ten-foot pole

But don't hyphenate these groups of words when they don't precede nouns:

> That guy has always been good for nothing.
> The movie received four stars from many critics.

EXERCISE 20 — Hyphenating Words

6. Edit
5. Revise
4. Write
3. Organize
2. Prewrite
1. Explore

Hyphenate the following groups of words as necessary.

1. an ex⌃officer of the group

2. two sisters in law

3. a self made woman

4. a two man job

5. a pro Russian speech

6. a hard to get out of bed morning

▶ **Check your dictionary about hyphenating compound words.**

A **compound word** is formed from two or more complete root words (like *background*). There are three different ways to write compounds:

If Your First Language Is Not English

Unlike the practices in many languages, adjectives in English don't change to show the plural. Therefore, a hyphenated word before a noun (in the adjective position) always takes a singular form:

A two-*star* movie (not *stars*)

a five-*foot* ladder (not *feet*)

1. As one word:

Root word	Root word	New word
horse	fly	horsefly
through	out	throughout
school	house	schoolhouse

Notice that these compound words do not drop any letters from their root words.

2. As hyphenated words:

Root word	Root word	New word
heavy	duty	heavy-duty
go	between	a go-between
give	(and) take	give-and-take

3. As two separate words (these are not really compound words):

monkey wrench	heat wave	grand piano

Use your dictionary when you're unsure about hyphenating or spelling a compound word.

EXERCISE 21   Writing Compound Words

6. Edit
5. Revise
4. Write
3. Organize
2. Prewrite
1. Explore

Create a compound word by adding a second root word after each of the words below.

1. day *daylight* _____

2. run _____

3. bitten _____

4. house _____

5. news _____

6. ground _____

7. chair _____

8. maker _____

9. half _____

10. under _____

Syllables

▶ **Hyphenate words at the end of lines only between syllables.**

A **syllable** is a complete sound that must include a vowel. For example, the word *understand* has three complete sounds: un der stand. When you must hyphenate a word at the end of a line, break the word only between syllables. You cannot hyphenate a one-syllable word such as *go, make,* and *seen:*

accu-rate		stra-ight (one syllable)
intel-lectual	*but not*	
com-munity		pict-ure (the syllable break is at *pic-ture*)

Here are some hints about breaking words into syllables.

1. Break syllables after complete root words:

transfer-able   spell-ing   play-er

2. Break syllables after prefixes or before suffixes:

un-interesting	sad-ly
trans-port	govern-ment

3. Break syllables between two consonants—unless the consonants form one sound, such as *–th, –sh, –sc,* or *–ch:*

cap-tain	south-ern
volun-tary *but*	
hus-band	reach-ing

Consult your dictionary if you are unsure of the syllable breaks.

4. Break already hyphenated words only at the hyphen.
   Since two hyphens in one word will confuse your reader, break a hyphenated word only at its hyphen:

Poor:	un-Amer-ican
Better:	un-American

In fact, try not to break a hyphenated word between lines.

5. Don't hyphenate a contraction.

Incorrect:	does-n't is-n't

6. Don't leave only one letter at the end or beginning of a line.

Poor:	a-live cloud-y
Better:	alive cloudy

And don't trust a computer to hyphenate for you. It doesn't know the difference, for example, between *pre-sent* (verb) and *pres-ent* (noun) or *pro-ject* (verb) and *proj-ect* (noun).

EXERCISE 22   Hyphenating Between Syllables

6. Edit
5. Revise
4. Write
3. Organize
2. Prewrite

Divide each word with a hyphen, unless the word cannot be divided.

1. unnecessary *unnec- essary*   **3.** stepped _____

2. repeat _____   **4.** waited _____

5. watered _____   8. aren't _____

6. seemed _____   9. guardhouse _____

7. ex-president _____   10. attention _____

CAPITALIZATION

Capitalize sentences, names, and titles according to the following rules.

▶ **Begin every sentence with a capitalized word.**

> **In the beginning, the book was slow reading.**
>
> **He said that he felt fine.**

▶ **Capitalize the pronoun** *I.*

> **I** *but* we he they his myself

Capitalize names of people, places, courses, organizations, languages, and words formed from them.

If Your First Language Is Not English

Nationalities and names of languages aren't capitalized in Spanish, but they are in English:

I speak Spanish.
He is French.

> Howard   Fleet Street
>
> the National Audubon Society   English
>
> New York   New Yorker
>
> Main High School (*but* high school)
>
> China
>
> Biology 111 (the name of a course) *but* biology (not a course name)

EXERCISE 23	Capitalizing Proper Nouns

6. Edit
5. Revise
4. Write
3. Organize
2. Prewrite
1. Explore

Underline the letters that should be capitalized.

1. russian

2. george herman "babe" ruth

3. the corner of prairie road and central street

4. mathematics 101

5. mathematics

6. california wine

7. i, you, him

8. american civil liberties union

9. spanish

▶ **Capitalize a person's title before his or her name.**

> Mayor Juarez   *but*   He is the mayor.
>
> Professor Williams *but*   Who is your English professor?
>
> President Bush   *but*   George W. Bush is president.
>
> Dr. Williams   *but*   She is a doctor.

Capitalize names of areas or countries.

Don't capitalize these terms when they mean only a direction:

The North won the Civil War.	She is from the West.
but	*but*
We are traveling north.	Which way is east?

 Capitalize the names of days, months, and holidays.

Don't capitalize the seasons of the year:

Tuesday		summer
March	*but*	spring
Independence Day		fall

 Capitalize all major words in titles.

Don't capitalize little words—short prepositions, conjunctions, and articles—unless they're the first or last words in the title or subtitle:

For Whom the Bell Tolls

The Mummy Returns

"Crocodile Rock"

Journal of the American Medical Association

"What to Listen For"

EXERCISE 24	Capitalizing Nouns

6. Edit
5. Revise
4. Write
3. Organize
2. Prewrite
1. Explore

Underline the letters that should be capitalized.

1. tuesday

2. winter

3. august

4. the wild west

5. a reverend

6. the reverend mr. haley

7. the wind is coming from the east.

8. webster's collegiate dictionary

IN SUMMARY	Spelling, Apostrophes, Hyphens, and Capitals

Adding final –s or –es

1. Add –*es* to words ending in *s*-like sounds or most words ending in *o*.
2. Change –*y* to –*i* after a consonant and add –*es*.
3. Change most nouns ending in –*f* or –*fe* to –*ve* before adding –*s*.

Adding a suffix

1. Change *-y* to *-i* after a consonant.
2. Keep final *-e* before a suffix beginning with a consonant.
3. Before a suffix beginning with a vowel, double the final consonant to make a short vowel sound. Don't double the final consonant to make a long vowel sound.

Using apostrophes

1. To show possession, add *-'s* to all singular nouns, but add just an apostrophe to plural nouns ending in *-s*.
2. To make a contraction, put the apostrophe in the place of the omitted letter(s).
3. To make letters plural, add *-'s*.

Using hyphens

1. Hyphenate two-word numbers from *twenty-one* to *ninety-nine* and all fractions.
2. Hyphenate a prefix and a capitalized noun.
3. Hyphenate prefixes *self-*, *all-*, or *ex-* and a noun, and all words with *-in-law*.
4. Hyphenate two or more words acting as a single adjective before a noun.
5. If you break a word at the end of a line, hyphenate only between syllables.

Capitalizing

1. Capitalize the first word of every sentence or title.
2. Capitalize the pronoun *I*.
3. Capitalize names of people, places, organizations, courses, languages, and words formed from them.
4. Capitalize a person's title when it is used before the name.
5. Capitalize areas or countries (but not directions).
6. Capitalize names of days, months, and holidays (but not seasons of the year).
7. Capitalize words in titles, except short prepositions, conjunctions, and articles.

EDITING FOR MASTERY

Mastery Exercise 1

Correcting Spelling and Other Matters

The following passage contains twenty errors in spelling, apostrophe use, hyphenation, and capitalization, excluding the first error, which has been corrected as an example. Correct each error above the line.

The Origins of the "Happy Birthday" Song

Believe

(1) ^~~Beleive~~ it or not, the tune you have heard at countless birthday party's is copyrighted, and the copyright owners often recieve royalties when its sung. (2) The melody was writen by two sisters from Kentucky, Mildred and Patty Smith Hill, and was first published under the title "Good Morning to All" in 1893. (3) The song was never meant for

birthday celebrations, but instead welcomed youngsters enterring a class room each morning. (4) It took a diffrent role as a result of a theft.

(5) Mildred Hill, who composed the melody, was a church organist, a concert pianist, and an authority on african-american spirituals. (6) She died in Chicago at the age of fifty seven. (7) Her sister Patty Smith Hill had writen the original lyric's for the song while she was principal of a kindergarten in Louisville, Kentucky, where Mildred also taught.

(8) The Hill sisters copyrighted their song on October 16, 1893. (9) However, on March 4, 1924, it apeared without thier approval in Robert H. Colemans songbook. (10) Although the song still had its original title, Coleman changed part of the lyrics to say, "Happy birthday to you."

(11) The song was then published sevral times over the next ten years, often with small changes in the lyrics. (12) By 1933, everyone knew the song as "Happy Birthday to You." (13) A year later, when the birthday tune was sung every night in a Broadway Musical, another Hill sister, Jessica, took the case to court. (14) She was fed up with the theft of the song and the total absence of royalty's to her brothers and sisters. (15) She won her lawsuit. (16) The Hill family owned the rights to the melody and had to be payed every time the song was part of a commercial production.

(17) The results of the suit were immediate. (18) The Western Union company, which had deliverred a half-million singing birthday greetings, stoped using the piece. (19) It was dropped from two plays on Broadway. (20) And in another play entitled "Happy Birthday," it's star, Helen Hayes, spoke the lyrics so the producers could avoid paying royalties.

(21) Dr. Patty Smith Hill died at the age of seventy eight, aware that she and her sister had started an amazing birthday tradition.

Scorecard: Number of Errors Found and Corrected _____

Mastery Exercise 2

Correcting Spelling and Other Matters

The following passage contains twenty errors in spelling, apostrophe use, hyphenation, and capitalization, excluding the first error, which has been corrected as an example. Correct each error above the line.

The Ghostly Rhyme (A Chinese Legend)

Collaborative Activity 3

Checking Your Answers
Compare your answers to Mastery Exercise 1 in your collaborative group and report your results to the whole class.

(1) Long ago, a wise man was sent to the jungle after he complained about dishonesty in the ^goverment. (2) He built a small hut near a stream among the cinnamon
government
trees. (3) He brought the water for his tea in a bamboo diper and ate the fish he caught, the fruit he picked, and the vegtables he grew in a small patch. (4) But usualy he spent his day reading.

(5) When a friend asked him why he lived in such a lonly spot, he was supprised. (6) "But I'm not alone," he said. (7) "My books have told me all about these hills. (8) I have the spirits of the wood's for company." (9) Later when he developed a cough, his friends tried to get him to come down to the city to see a doctor, but he refused. (10) "The smell of Pine is the best medicine," he said.

(11) One day, he picked up a book by his favorite poet, but worms had eatten away the outside edges of the pages. (12) He opened the book to read a poem and found that the last line was missing, which he could not rember. (13) He tryed to recall it by reciting the next-to last line over and over: (14) "The sun on my old garden shine's . . ." (15) He soon forgot to eat and even sleep.

(16) One day, his friend's found him dead still inside his hut, with the book in his lap. (17) Saddly, they buried him with the book, but that night the sound of the wind shaking the leafs of the cinnamon trees sounded like someone sighing. (18) The raindrops fell like someone impatiently taping a finger.

(19) Then his ghost appeared reading the poem aloud but stopped just before the last line. (20) At first people were frightened, but they realized that his ghost was harmless. (21) Eventually, though, he began to haunt the main street and shout out the words of the poem. (22) People beged the old man to go away.

(23) At last, a poet went up to the hut in the woods, sat down, and waited for the wise man to come. (24) The ghost finaly appeared and read from the book. (25) The poet recognized the poem, and when the wise man ended before the last line, the poet asked him to continue. (26) Once again, he read but stopped at the same place. (27) "The sun on my old garden shines . . ."

(28) "But I am gone," the poet finished. "No flesh confines."

(29) The ghost smiled in releif and closed his book. (30) He dissapeared, and no one ever saw or heard him again.

Scorecard: Number of Errors Found and Corrected _____

28 Writing the Right Word

Words that look alike or sound alike cause even the most experienced writers to mistake one for the other. Computer spell checkers aren't much help, either, for the words may be correctly spelled but incorrectly used. If you tend to confuse certain words, you can study them in this chapter. Whatever the case, try to focus on *one word* in a look-alike or sound-alike pairing—the one that occurs or confuses you most often. Prepare your own mental or written list of sound-alikes and look-alikes to watch out for as you revise.

This chapter will help you examine many of the most common look-alikes and sound-alikes by

■ identifying the most common confusions among these words

■ suggesting ways to keep them straight

THE MOST COMMON SOUND-ALIKES AND LOOK-ALIKES

> "The difference between the right word and the almost right word is the difference between lightning and the lightning bug."
>
> —Mark Twain

The following four categories of errors are especially troublesome and therefore deserve special attention.

Contractions

The contractions of *is* or *are* function as both the subject and verb of a sentence or clause:

Contraction	Meaning	Example
it's	it is (or it has)	*It's* a nice day.
who's	who is (or who has)	*Who's* driving tonight?

Continued

Contraction	Meaning	Example
they're	they are	*They're* talking right now.
you're	you are	*You're* doing a good job.

People often confuse contractions with these possessive words:

Possessive word	Example
its	The dog has *its leash*.
whose	*Whose briefcase* is this?
their	The students all handed in *their* assignments.
your	*Your* finger may be broken.

People also sometimes confuse *were*, a past-tense form of to be, with *we're*:

We *were* vacationing in Mexico.

We're planning to go there again next year.

One other source of confusion is the place words *there* and *where*. *There* looks like *they're* and *their*, and *where* looks like *we're* and *were*.

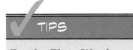

TIPS

For the Place Words

If you have trouble distinguishing between *their/there* and *we're/where*, simply remember that the place words both contain the word *here*: t*HERE* w*HERE*

EXERCISE 1 | Identifying Correct Word Choice

6. Edit
5. Revise
4. Write
3. Organize
2. Prewrite
1. Explore

Underline the correct word in the parentheses.

1. Because (we're/were/where) all so accustomed to using aluminum foil, (it's/its) probably surprising to learn that the product wasn't invented until 1947.

2. (It's/Its) inventor, Richard S. Reynolds, first worked for his uncle, R. J. Reynolds, (whose/who's) company made cigarettes and loose tobacco that (we're/were/where) wrapped in thin sheets of tin and lead.

3. Reynolds later established his own business, the U.S. Foil Co., from (we're/were/where) he continued to wrap tobacco and candy.

4. He then quickly began to use a new wrapping material called aluminum when (its/it's) price began to drop in the late 1920s.

5. Reynolds soon offered people an impressive list of products for use in (there/their/they're) homes and hobbies: aluminum siding and windows; aluminum pots, pans, and kitchen utensils; and aluminum boats.

6. But (its/it's) another product, which Reynolds created in 1947, that is most responsible for introducing Americans to the benefits of this metal: Reynolds' Wrap.

7. Today (your/you're) likely to use aluminum products in all sorts of ways.

Collaborative Activity 1

Writing Sentences
Write a sentence for each of the words highlighted in this chapter. Then exchange your sentences with another student and correct each other's work.

Too/Two/To

Here are three more frequently confused sound-alikes:
Too means *also* or *more than enough*:

TIPS

For *Too*
This sentence should help you remember the meanings of *too* with two *oo*'s: The *zoo* was *too* crowded, *too.*

We are coming, *too.* (also)

We have *too* many problems. (more than enough)

Two means the number 2.

To is used in all other cases.

EXERCISE 2	Identifying Correct Word Choice

6. Edit
5. Revise
4. Write
3. Organize
2. Prewrite
1. Explore

Underline the correct word in the parentheses.

1. Back in 1886, John S. Pemberton used an iron pot (too/<u>to</u>/two) mix a batch of a drink, later (too/<u>to</u>/two) be called Coca-Cola.

2. Pemberton had returned (too/to/two) Atlanta, Georgia, after the Civil War (too/to/two) open a drugstore.

3. A friend named the drink after its (too/to/two) main ingredients: coca, the dried leaf of a plant, and cola, from the kola nut.

4. (Too/To/Two) years later, Pemberton died, and ownership of the soft drink was sold (too/to/two) a company for $2,300.

5. Soon the public began (too/to/two) call the drink *Coke,* which the company felt was (too/to/two) informal a name.

6. In 1920, the company gave in (too/to/two) the public's practice and registered the name *Coke* as a trademark.

The *of* Error

When you speak, you probably use the following contractions:

could've = could have	would've = would have
should've = should have	might've = might have

The *–'ve* ending in each contraction sounds like the preposition *of.* So many people write "could of" when they mean *could have* and so forth:

Incorrect:	He should of done it.
Correct:	He should have ('ve) done it.
Incorrect:	I might of gone.
Correct:	I might have ('ve) gone.

Remember that *of* cannot follow the words *could, should, would, might,* and other helping verbs.

| EXERCISE 3 | Identifying Correct Word Choice |

6. Edit
5. Revise
4. Write
3. Organize
2. Prewrite
1. Explore

Underline the correct word in the parentheses.

1. Ivory Soap's famous ability to float might never (of/<u>have</u>) happened if it hadn't been for a lucky accident.

2. In 1878, an employee of Procter & Gamble should (of/have) turned off the soap-mixing machine before he went to lunch.

3. Leaving the machine on so long could (of/have) been dangerous, but the result was that the machine created a different kind of soap.

4. The employee could easily have gotten rid (of/have) the soap, but he didn't.

5. He should (of/have) told his bosses about the error, but he packaged it like any other batch instead.

6. The lengthy mixing process must have added a lot (of/have) air to the soap, and as a result, it floated.

7. People loved it, so an employee who might otherwise (of/have) been fired was a company hero.

Three Words Ending in –d

Notice the –d endings on these words that precede *to*:

| used (to) | supposed (to) |

The sounds of the letters *d* and *t* are almost identical. Many people therefore drop the final –d before *t* in *supposed to* or *used to*. That final –d is important, though, for it indicates a past-tense verb (*used*) or a past participle form (*supposed*):

We *used* to vacation in Michigan.

We are *supposed* to call later.

Another word that creates problems is the past-participle verb form *prejudiced*, which also requires a final –d:

Incorrect: He is prejudice against me.

Correct: He is *prejudiced* against me.

Prejudice can be a noun that does not end in –d:

Racial *prejudice* makes me angry.

EXERCISE 4	Identifying Correct Word Choice

Underline the correct word in the parentheses.

1. In 1917, Edwin Cox (use/<u>used</u>) to go door to door, selling a new product, aluminum cookware.

2. Many homemakers were (prejudice/prejudiced) against such newfangled inventions, so Cox had a hard time even demonstrating his product.

3. He needed a gimmick he could (use/used) to overcome this (prejudice/prejudiced) and get him into people's kitchens.

4. He knew that people hated when food stuck to pans, so he (use/used) his imagination and developed a pad that combined steel wool with soap.

5. These little pads were extremely popular. Although he gave each homemaker a free sample, most women asked for more, and Cox soon became (accustom/accustomed) to questions about where to buy the product.

6. A few months later, Cox quit the door-to-door selling he (use/used) to do so he could manufacture his little pads—called "S.O.S." for "Save Our Saucepans."

COMMONLY CONFUSED WORDS

Aside from the errors you've just seen, a number of errors show up in sound-alikes and look-alikes. We'll examine a number of the most common ones throughout the rest of the chapter.

Accept/Except

Accept means "to receive":

> He *accepted* the reward.

Except means "excluding" or "but":

> Everyone *except* him is here.

EXERCISE 5	Identifying Correct Word Choice

Underline the correct word in the parentheses.

1. George Eastman's new camera had many good selling points, (accept/<u>except</u>) that it had no trademark.

2. He felt that a trademark must be short, strong, and unusual to be (accepted/excepted) by the general public.

3. He made up a nonsense word, Kodak, which he thought would be (acceptable/exceptable).

4. Today everyone knows the word, (accept/except), perhaps, creatures on Mars.

Advice/Advise

Advice is a noun:

> We got *advice*.

Advise is a verb:

> He *advised* us to be careful.

TIPS

For *Advice/Advise*
Advice is nice, but only the wise *advise*.

EXERCISE 6 | Identifying Correct Word Choice

6. Edit
5. Revise
4. Write

Underline the correct word in the parentheses.

1. At a fair in 1904, Abe Doumar overheard an ice-cream seller complain that he had run out of ice-cream dishes. Doumar (adviced/<u>advised</u>) him to make a cone from a waffle, fill it with ice cream, and double his price.

2. It was good (advice/advise). The seller made a good profit from this new dish, the ice cream cone.

3. Two years later, Doumar followed his own (advice/advise) and set up an ice-cream stand on Coney Island and later in Norfolk, Virginia.

4. Many years after Doumar's death, his sons were still operating the same ice-cream stand. Perhaps the moral is that it is more blessed to take than to give (advice/advise).

If Your First Language Is Not English

You may have difficulty distinguishing between the first vowel sounds in *affect* and *effect*. You may also have difficulties with the *–c* (pronounced like "s") and *–s* (pronounced like "z") spellings in *advice* and *advise*.

Affect/Effect

Used as a verb, *affect* means "to influence" or "change":

> Old age *affected* his ability to walk.

Used as a noun, *effect* is the result of a cause:

> What will be the *effect* of the new law?

TIPS

For *Affect/Effect*
His *age affected* his actions. His actions had an excellent *effect*.

EXERCISE 7 | Identifying Correct Word Choice

6. Edit
5. Revise
4. Write
3. Organize
2. Prewrite
1. Explore

Underline the correct word in the parentheses.

1. From 626 to 582 B.C., when he died, the Hebrew prophet Jeremiah warned the Israelites to reform their ways or God would destroy their temple, but his warnings had little (affect/<u>effect</u>).

2. In fact, the only (affects/effects) of his predictions were to anger the king and create threats against Jeremiah's life.

3. Nothing (affected/effected) the prophet's courage, however, and while living in hiding, he dictated his prophecies to one of his followers.

4. One day, Jeremiah begged a woman to give up her sinful behavior, warning that Jerusalem would soon be attacked by people from the north. His pleas had no (affect/effect).

5. Realizing that he couldn't (affect/effect) human behavior, he said his famous words: "Can the leopard change his spots? Then may ye also do good, that are accustomed to evil."

An/And

An is the article used before a vowel sound:

> *an* egg, *an* opportunity, *an* hour

And is a joining word.

> He huffed, *and* he puffed, *and* he blew the house down.

✓ **TIPS**

For *An/And*
An apple *and* a pear.

EXERCISE 8 | Identifying Correct Word Choice

6. Edit
5. Revise
4. Write
3. Organize
2. Prewrite
1. Explore

Underline the correct word in the parentheses.

1. The can—or tin canister, as it was first called—was developed in 1810 by a British man named Peter Durand (an/<u>and</u>) was used to supply food to the Royal Navy during the Napoleonic Wars.

2. But no one had ever developed a convenient way to open the can, (an/and) British soldiers had to tear open their rations with bayonets, pocket knives, or—when all else failed—rifle fire.

3. In fact, some historians claim that the bayonet, invented in the French town of Bayonne, was not intended to be (an/and) article for piercing bodies but for piercing cans.

4. Ezra J. Warner of Waterbury, Connecticut, patented the first practical can opener in 1858. It was (an/and) odd machine with a large blade that cut hands (an/and) fingers as often as it cut cans.

5. The modern-day can opener—with a cutting wheel that rolls around the can's rim—was patented by William W. Lyman in 1870. It was revolutionary in concept (an/and) design, (an/and) it was (an/and) immediate success.

Breath/Breathe

Breath is a noun:

> She caught her *breath.*

Breathe is a verb:

> She *breathed* deeply.

TIPS

For *Breath/Breathe*
If the vowel sound is long *e*, there is silent –*e* at the end.

EXERCISE 9 | Identifying Correct Word Choice

6. Edit
5. Revise
4. Write
3. Organize
2. Prewrite
1. Explore

Underline the correct word in the parentheses.

1. *Life Savers* were originally advertised as "Crane's Peppermint Life Savers—5¢—For That Stormy (<u>Breath</u>/Breathe)."

2. *Smith Brothers Cough Drops* have been a favorite since about 1850 with people who coughed or couldn't (breath/breathe) because of a cold.

3. The first submarine was invented in 1620 by a Dutchman named Cornelius J. Drebbel, who figured out a way to get oxygen to fifteen rowers so they could (breath/breathe) under water.

4. The men could stay under for fifteen hours—a long time to exist with no (breaths/breathes) of fresh air.

Buy/By

As a verb, *buy* means "to purchase":

> Where did you *buy* that hat?

By, a preposition, has several meanings, including "near to," "at," and "by means of":

> We placed the plants *by* the window. We were finished *by* 10:00 A.M.
>
> Bill paid for his college education *by* working every summer.

TIPS

For *Buy/By*
You should *buy* it *by* credit card.

EXERCISE 10 | Identifying Correct Word Choice

6. Edit
5. Revise
4. Write
3. Organize
2. Prewrite
1. Explore

Underline the correct word in the parentheses.

1. William Collins Whitney (1841–1904), an American millionaire, would (<u>buy</u>/by) expensive things for the most trivial reasons.

2. Once, for example, in order to give an enormous ball for his friends, he decided to (buy/by) a brownstone building on Fifth Avenue in New York.

3. He then furnished it (buy/by) going on a four-year tour of Europe to (buy/by) antiques, stained-glass windows, and fireplaces.

4. (Buy/By) the end of his tour, however, he had made his most outrageous purchase, (buying/bying) an entire ballroom from a castle in France and shipping it back to New York (buy/by) boat.

5. The ball he gave for his 500 guests was an enormous hit, highlighted (buy/by) a fountain that gushed 1,200 bottles of champagne.

For *Clothes/Cloths*
Clothes sounds like *close,* which also contains an *–e.* *Cloths* has no *–e.*

Clothes/Cloths

Clothes are what people wear. *Cloths* is the plural of *cloth*—a piece of fabric.

EXERCISE 11   Identifying Correct Word Choice

Underline the correct word in the parentheses.

1. When we think of good (<u>clothes</u>/cloths), we don't usually consider underwear.
2. But three men did think about making high-quality (underclothes/undercloths).
3. Their names have not become household words associated with (clothes/cloths), but their product, B.V.D., has.
4. The initials represent the last names of the three men—Bradley, Voorhees, and Day—who turned millions of (clothes/cloths) into underpants and undershirts.

For *Conscience/Conscious*
Science is in *conscience,* and both teach you something.

Conscience/Conscious

Your *conscience* tells you that you are being bad or good. To be *conscious* means that you are awake and aware.

EXERCISE 12   Identifying Correct Word Choice

Underline the correct word in the parentheses.

1. In 1895, King C. Gillette, a traveling salesperson, (<u>consciously</u>/consciencely) decided to invent something that people would use a few times, throw away, and then pay to replace.
2. Apparently the idea of planned obsolescence did not bother Gillette's (conscious/conscience).
3. One day as he was shaving, he (unconsciously/unconsciencely) thought of the first disposable blade to be inserted into a razor. It became known as the Gillette blade.

For Distinguishing Between Noun and Adjective Endings
The *rent* is *different.* The *dance* had *elegance.*

–ence/ –ent; –ance/ –ant

–Ence and *–ance* are noun endings:

The *difference* was amazing.

The *significance* of the event was great.

–Ent and *–ant* are adjective endings:

> It has a *different* meaning.
>
> It has a *significant* meaning.

EXERCISE 13 | Identifying Correct Word Choice

6. Edit
5. Revise
4. Write
3. Organize
2. Prewrite
1. Explore

Underline the correct word in the parentheses.

1. In Cleveland in 1912, a candymaker named Clarence Crane decided to create something (difference/<u>different</u>): a mint he could sell in the summer.

2. Up to then, most mints were imported, but Crane figured he could cut the price by making them in the United States and not be (dependence/dependent) on European factories.

3. He came up with an (excellence/excellent) idea; he had a pill maker manufacture the mints.

4. But Crane was (ignorance/ignorant) of one (importance/important) problem: the machinery would work only if it punched a hole in the middle of each candy.

5. Crane had an (elegance/elegant) solution to the problem—he decided to call the mints *Life Savers*.

Fine/Find

Fine, as an adjective, means "acceptable" or "excellent." As a noun, it means "a penalty you must pay":

> You did a *fine* job on this assignment.
>
> If you get caught speeding, you must pay a *fine*.

TIPS

For *Find/Fine*
How can I *find* a *fine* job?

Find means "to discover" or "locate":

> We never *find* a place to park near school.

EXERCISE 14 | Identifying Correct Word Choice

6. Edit
5. Revise
4. Write
3. Organize
2. Prewrite
1. Explore

Underline the correct word in the parentheses.

1. You'll never (<u>find</u>/fine) a more influential book than Dale Carnegie's *How to Win Friends and Influence People.*

2. Although it was originally published in 1936, you can still (find/fine) the hardcover or paperback editions in just about any bookstore.

3. The book offers some (find/fine) advice. No one succeeds alone, so we must get along with and influence others to do what we want them to do.

4. Read the book, and you'll (find/fine) these words: "There is only one way under high heaven to get anybody to do anything. Did you ever stop to think of that? Yes, just one way. And that is by making the other person want to do it."

Know/No; Knew/New

Know means "to be familiar with" or "understand." Its past tense is *knew:*

> I *know* your brother, and I *knew* your sister in high school.

No is a negative word. And *new* is the opposite of old:

> Our old car has *no* radio, but we're buying a *new car* soon.

TIPS

For *Know/No* and
Knew/New

The knight *knew* he had *no*
nose.

EXERCISE 15 | Identifying Correct Word Choice

6. Edit
5. Revise
4. Write
3. Organize
2. Prewrite
1. Explore

Underline the correct word in the parentheses.

1. You may not (<u>know</u>/no) the origin of the phrase, "Don't look a gift horse in the mouth."
2. Contrary to popular opinion, it has (know/no) relation to the gift of the Trojan horse but comes instead from St. Jerome in around 400 A.D.
3. The man (knew/new) that a gift should be appreciated for the thought and spirit behind it, not for its value.
4. Since a (knewborn/newborn) horse is worth more than an old one, people generally examined a horse's teeth to determine its age.
5. Therefore, Jerome, who accepted (know/no) payment for his writing, advised people with this phrase: "Never inspect the teeth of a gift horse."

Led/Lead

Led (pronounced like *head*) is the past tense of *lead* (pronounced like *need*):

> General Washington *led* the army into battle.

Lead is a heavy metal:

> *Lead* pipes are no longer used in plumbing.

TIPS

For *Lead/Led*

A *head* like *lead.*
I *fed* (past) him and *led*
(past) him away.

EXERCISE 16 | Identifying Correct Word Choice

Underline the correct word in the parentheses.

1. In 1914, Carl Eric Wickman couldn't sell his Hupmobile—a seven-passenger automobile—which (lead/<u>led</u>) him to start a bus service with it.

2. The bus (lead/led) its passengers on a two-mile trip between two small towns in Minnesota.

3. After Wickman added more and larger buses, their long, sleek appearance and (lead/led)-gray color caused someone to say that they looked like "greyhounds streaking by."

4. The comment, of course, (lead/led) to the name "Greyhound Bus."

Lie/Lay

Lie means "to recline":

> I am going to *lie* down.
>
> The pen is *lying* on top of the book.

The forms of *lie* are as follows:

Present tense	Past tense	Past participle
lie, lies	lay	lain

Lay, which usually means "put," is something you do to an object:

> I am going to *lay* this book on the table.

Its forms are as follows:

Present tense	Past tense	Past participle
lay, lays	laid	laid

✓ TIPS

For *Lay/Lie*
The chicken *laid* an egg, and then she *lay* down to sleep.

EXERCISE 17 | Identifying Correct Word Choice

Underline the correct word in the parentheses.

1. The continents of the earth (lie/lay) on huge slabs of rock—or plates—that slide over the earth's core very slowly, at a rate of one to eight inches a year.

2. Sometimes this movement of the continents causes earthquakes, which result from the pressure of one plate (lying/laying) against another as they move.

3. Other times, this movement causes a gap between plates, and the hot melted rock that has (laid/lain) beneath the plates shoots out in the form of a volcano.

4. Geologists believe that the continents all (lay/laid) in one large land mass, called *Pangaea,* about 230 million years ago.

5. The continent of North America, like the other continents, is not (lying/laying) still. It drifts away from Europe at a rate of three inches a year.

Lose/Loose

Lose means "to misplace" or "not to win":

> Did you *lose* your book? Did you *lose* the game?

Loose is an adjective that means "not tight":

> My pants are *loose*.

TIPS

For *Lose/Loose*
Loose as a *goose*.

| EXERCISE 18 | Identifying Correct Word Choice |

Underline the correct word in the parentheses.

1. If you were to bet that the Baby Ruth candy bar was named after the baseball player Babe Ruth, you would (<u>lose</u>/loose).

2. Don't (lose/loose) track of the actual facts: the candy was named after the oldest daughter of President Grover Cleveland.

3. Tell somebody the true story. What do you have to (lose/loose)?

Mine/Mind

Mine is a possessive word:

> This pen is *mine*.

Mind as a noun means your "brain" or "intellect." As a verb, it means "to object":

> Einstein had a brilliant *mind*.
>
> Do you *mind* if I close this window?

TIPS

For *Mine/Mind*
A good *mind* is not hard to *find*. It's *mine!*

| EXERCISE 19 | Identifying Correct Word Choice |

Underline the correct word in the parentheses.

1. Nowadays it's common to think that you should look out for your best interests, and I'll look out for (<u>mine</u>/mind).

2. This brings to (mine/mind) the expression, "Charity begins at home."

3. Ironically, the phrase, first written in 1642 by Sir Thomas Browne, was not intended to praise selfishness. Browne was discouraged that so many people didn't seem to (mind/mine) their own poverty or ignorance and would not try to better themselves.

4. Therefore, he (reminded/remined) his readers, "How shall we expect charity toward others when we are so uncharitable to ourselves? 'Charity begins at home' is the voice of the world; yet is every man his greatest enemy, and, as it were, his own executioner?"

Passed/Past

Passed is the past tense and past participle of the verb *to pass*:

> We *passed* the house.

Past is a preposition meaning "beyond." It can also be a noun or adjective meaning "before the present":

> We went *past* (beyond) that house.
>
> That is *past* (before the present) history.

TIPS

For *Passed/Past*
The verb *pass*—without a *–t*—is *passed*.

EXERCISE 20	Identifying Correct Word Choice

6. Edit
5. Revise
4. Write
3. Organize
2. Prewrite
1. Explore

Underline the correct word in the parentheses.

1. The sewing needle appeared very early in humankind's (<u>past</u>/passed).

2. Needles of ivory, bone, and walrus tusk have been found in caves from 40,000 years in the (past/passed).

3. But almost that many years had (past/passed) before people created a better way than sewing by hand.

4. In 1830, a tailor named Barthélemy Thimmonier, of Lyon, France, invented a simple sewing machine that far sur(past/passed) the speed with which an experienced tailor could make stitches.

5. Only a short time had (past/passed) before Thimmonier was turning out military uniforms for the government.

6. However, an angry mob of tailors, who were afraid of being put out of business, stormed (past/passed) the entrance to his factory, destroyed all eighty of his machines, and nearly killed the inventor.

7. Thimmonier fled to another town, where he died in poverty, but the idea of a sewing machine was (past/passed) on to many others, including two men from Boston: Elias Howe and Isaac Singer.

Quiet/Quite/Quit

Quiet means "not noisy." Notice the ending, *–iet*. The two vowels are pronounced as separate syllables:

> It was a *quiet* night.

Quite means "very" or "a great deal of." Notice the ending, *–ite*. The ending is a silent *–e*:

> He is *quite* tall. He has *quite* a problem going through doorways.

TIPS

For *Quiet/Quite/Quit*
It was *quite* a *bite*, but he *quit* after a *bit*—and then was *quiet*.

And *quit* means "to stop" or "resign." Notice the ending, *–it:*

> Maria *quit* smoking, and Ralph *quit* his job.

EXERCISE 21	Identifying Correct Word Choice

6. Edit
5. Revise
4. Write
3. Organize
2. Prewrite
1. Explore

Underline the correct word in the parentheses.

1. The man who invented Birds Eye frozen foods was, (quiet/<u>quite</u>/quit) naturally, named Clarence Birdseye.

2. He was an explorer who, in 1916, was able to keep meat and vegetables (quiet/quite/quit) fresh by storing them in freezing water.

3. Back in the United States, he started a frozen-food company that became (quiet/quite/quit) successful.

4. In 1929, Birdseye decided to (quiet/quite/quit) the business and sold it to the Postum Company.

5. When Postum split the trademark into two words—Birds Eye—Clarence Birdseye kept (quiet/quite/quit) about the change, for his family had originally spelled its name that way.

Rise/Raise

Rise means "to get up without help":

> The sun *rises* in the east.

✔ **TIPS**

For *Rise/Raise*
He always *pays* when he gets a *raise.*

Raise as a verb means "to lift or increase something." As a noun, it means "an increase in pay":

> *Raise* your hand if you know the answer.
>
> Susan just got a *raise*, so she can afford a larger apartment.

EXERCISE 22	Identifying Correct Word Choice

6. Edit
5. Revise
4. Write
3. Organize
2. Prewrite
1. Explore

Underline the correct word in the parentheses.

1. The origin of the expression "Steal my thunder" might (rise/<u>raise</u>) a few eyebrows.

2. John Dennis, an English playwright 200 years ago, created a method of (raising/rising) a noise like a thunderclap and used it in his new play.

3. The thunder was a great success, but the play didn't (raise/rise) enough money to continue beyond a few performances.

4. A short time later, Dennis attended a performance of Shakespeare's *Macbeth,* only to discover that the director was using his method of making thunder. He (raised/rose) to his feet and proceeded to (raise/rise) a ruckus.

5. "That's my thunder, by God!" he said, with his voice (raising/rising) louder and louder. "The villains will not play my play, but they steal my thunder."

Sit/Set

Sit means "to seat yourself":

> Please *sit* down.

Set means "to put something down":

> Please *set* the glass on the table.

TIPS

For *Sit/Set*
Set the *bet* down.

EXERCISE 23 | Identifying Correct Word Choice

Underline the correct word in the parentheses.

1. The first photograph was made in 1826, when a French inventor coated a metal sheet with a special solution, exposed it to light, and (sit/set) it on a windowsill to dry.

2. He photographed an object, of course, since no person could (sit/set) still for as long as it took to make an exposure.

3. Motion pictures began in America some time between 1867 and 1871, when one man bet another that a running horse couldn't lift all four legs off the ground at once. They (sit/set) up a series of cameras along a racetrack, which photographed the horse as it galloped past—with, at various points, all four legs off the ground.

4. Edwin Land invented the Polaroid camera in 1947. He wanted to take a picture of his daughter and develop it while she was still (sitting/setting).

Then/Than

Then is a time expression meaning "afterward" or "later":

> I studied for two hours and *then* took a break.

Than is used in a comparison:

> Juan gets higher grades *than* anyone else in class.

TIPS

For *Then/Than*
Then tells you *when.*

EXERCISE 24 | Identifying Correct Word Choice

Underline the correct word in the parentheses.

1. In the music world, composers who write nine symphonies seem to be cursed. Six composers have done so and (then/than) died.

6. Edit
5. Revise
4. Write
3. Organize
2. Prewrite
1. Explore

2. Ludwig van Beethoven (1770–1827) is more famous (then/than) the other five. The composer had just completed his ninth symphony and was planning a tenth, but (then/than) he caught a cold. He died a few months later.

3. Anton Bruckner (1824–1896), an Austrian, was almost unknown until the end of his life; (then/than) he was recognized as a great composer. He died while finishing his ninth symphony.

4. (Then/Than) came Antonin Dvorák (1841–1904). His ninth symphony, *From the New World,* was performed in New York in 1893, but he died a little more (then/than) eleven years later without completing another symphony.

5. The other three composers were, first, the Russian A. K. Glazunov (1865–1936); (then/than), the Bohemian Gustav Mahler (1860–1911); and finally, the British Ralph Vaughan Williams (1872–1958).

6. Mahler suffered from heart disease and was terrified of the curse of the ninth symphony. Therefore, he completed his ninth and (then/than) immediately began work on a tenth, but the effort was more (then/than) his heart could take. He soon died.

There is/It is

There is/are and *it is* aren't look-alikes or sound-alikes, but some people confuse the two expressions. Both usually function as sentence-starters; that is, they have no meaning in themselves but merely begin a sentence. Don't use them often, but when you do, use them properly.

You may begin a statement with *there is* or *there are* to show the location or to say that something or someone exists:

> *There is* a knife in the drawer under the sink.
>
> *There are* only two solutions (in existence) to the problem.

Use *it is* when you want to express an attitude or opinion:

> *It is* too bad that he is sick.
>
> *It is* a shame that he can't come to the graduation.

And use *it is* to discuss weather, temperature, conditions, distance, and time:

It is cold today.	*It is* 78 degrees in this room.
It is dark and wet outside.	*It is* three miles from here to the bank.
It is 3:15.	

Don't confuse *it is* expressions with *there is/are:*

Incorrect:	It's a lot of chores that I have to do.
Correct:	*There are* a lot of chores that I have to do.

✔ TIPS

For *There Is/It Is*
There is a *bear* in *here.*

EXERCISE 25	Identifying Correct Word Choice

6. Edit
5. Revise
4. Write
3. Organize
2. Prewrite
1. Explore

Underline the correct word in the parentheses.

1. (It's/There's) hardly anything simpler than the brown paper bag.

2. (It's/There's) so popular that Americans use more than forty billion a year.

3. Charles Stilwell invented a machine to make paper bags in 1883, when he realized that (it was/there was) a need for the product.

4. (It was/There were) paper bags before Stilwell's invention, but (it was/there were) two problems with them: they couldn't stand up on their own, and they couldn't be easily folded or stacked.

5. (It was/There was) brilliant of Stilwell to make flat-bottomed bags that could stand up by themselves; (it was/there was) the most attractive feature to grocers and market baggers.

6. When supermarkets opened in the early 1930s, (it was/there was) a big increase in the number of items sold and packaged in stores, so (it was/there was) a big increase in the sales of paper bags.

Whether/Weather

Whether suggests a choice; it is used in the same way as *if* in indirect questions:

> I don't know *whether* he can afford a vacation.
>
> He wanted to know *whether* the test was hard.

Weather refers to the temperature and atmospheric conditions:

> The *weather* has been mild this year.

TIPS

For *Whether/Weather*
Wet weather, and neither word has *h*.

EXERCISE 26	Identifying Correct Word Choice

6. Edit
5. Revise
4. Write
3. Organize
2. Prewrite
1. Explore

Underline the correct word in the parentheses.

1. Most historians claim that General William T. Sherman said, "War is hell," but he was never sure (whether/weather) he really said it.

2. Before his death in 1891, the general looked through all his private papers to determine (whether/weather) the words were actually his.

3. There are several accounts of when the words were said. One version goes back to 1863 in the Civil War, when Sherman's troops were crossing a bridge in bad (whether/weather). The commander supposedly said to the passing soldiers, "War is hell, boys."

4. It's debatable (whether/weather) he made the statement then. Two other claims are that he used the expression at a military academy graduation in 1879 or in a speech to Union veterans in 1880.

5. In fact, no one can prove (whether/weather) Sherman ever said, "War is hell."

IN SUMMARY	To Distinguish Sound-alikes and Look-alikes from Each Other

1. Contractions with *to be*, such as *it's* and *they're*, should not be confused with similar words such as *its* or *their*.
2. *To*, *two*, and *too* are spelled differently and have different meanings.
3. The contraction for *have*, *'ve*, sounds like *of* but should not be replaced with *of*.
4. Other words discussed in this chapter can be confused, but if you follow the tips and are careful in your word choice, you can avoid picking the wrong word.

EDITING FOR MASTERY

Mastery Exercise 1

Editing for Correct Word Choice

The following passage contains eighteen errors in sound-alike and look-alike words, aside from the first error, which has been corrected for you as an example. Correct each error above the line.

The Mysterious Disappearance of Amelia Earhart (1897–1937)

(1) Perhaps ^no ~~know~~ American woman of the 1930s was as famous as the flier Amelia Earhart, who's accomplishments were well known and admired buy women and men. (2) She was born in Kansas, graduated high school in Chicago in 1915, and then took up flying. (3) In 1928, her flight across the Atlantic with two men lead to her fame as an outspoken model of "rugged feminism." (4) She married the rich publisher George Putnam in 1931. (5) But she refused to except the role of a housewife and continued to fly. (6) She set the record for a flight across the Atlantic Ocean in 1932, and her later achievements where almost as impressive.

(7) By 1937 she was use to taking risks, so she attempted a more difficult feat then any she had done in the passed: an around-the-world flight with navigator Fred Noonan. (8) There departure from Miami in June attracted great attention. (9) The world applauded when Earhart reached New Guinea and then set off for an island in the

Pacific on July 1. (10) Within a short time, however, she would loose radio contact with people on the ground. (11) No one new weather she had crashed or made and emergency landing, and the Navy could not fine any sign of the plane. (12) The newspapers were filled with theories about Earhart's fate for months. (13) While many people believed that she was a great pilot, others said she wasn't and had tried to difficult a task. (14) Perhaps she simply ran out of fuel and ended in a watery grave.

(15) To this day, it's a lot of difference theories about what happened to her. (16) Did the Japanese capture and murder her? (17) Did she land on some remote island and die a quite death? (18) The mystery of Earhart's disappearance may never be solved.

Scorecard: Number of Errors Found and Corrected _____

Collaborative Activity 2

Checking Your Answers
Compare your answers to Mastery Exercise 1 in your collaborative group, and report your results to the whole class.

Mastery Exercise 2

Editing for Correct Word Choice

The following passage contains eighteen errors in sound-alike and look-alike words, aside from the first error, which has been corrected for you as an example. Correct each error above the line.

The Beginning of the Elvis Era: 1956

(1) ^~~Its~~ *It's* an excepted fact that Elvis Presley became the first superstar of rock in 1956. (2) Without his influence, popular music might of followed a much difference course. (3) Presley, more then anyone else, defined the age of rock 'n' roll with his first hit, "Heartbreak Hotel." (4) The knew record quickly raised to the top of the record charts in February. (5) Hardly any time had past before this twenty-one-year-old singer released another song, an then another, and another. (6) He let lose a barrage of nineteen songs in twelve months, and three songs rose to number one. (7) His sexy movements on stage also lead TV shows to change there photography of live performances.

(8) Elvis Aron Presley, who use to be a truck driver for the Crown Electric Company of Memphis, Tennessee, also appeared in his first movie, *Love Me Tender,* in 1956. (9) And nothing was quiet as eagerly anticipated as his appearance on Ed Sullivan's show in September. (10) As cameras shot Presley from the waist up, the teen-aged audience went out of their mines. (11) There screaming drowned out his singing. (12) *The New York Times* called his behavior "burlesque," and *Music Journal* later labeled his performances "filthy," with their "whining, moaning, and suggestive lyrics." (13) Only Jackie Gleason, who booked Presley for a television show in 1956, wasn't prejudice against him. (14) Gleason didn't think the young singer was to wild and called him "a guitar-playing Marlon Brando."

(15) Presley didn't understand the criticism. (16) He later said of himself: "I never thought of my performing style as wicked. Wicked? I don't even smoke or drink." (17) After

two breatheless years on the pop scene, Elvis Presley sold and amazing 28 million records and appeared on bestseller charts fifty-five times. (18) He earned a fortune, became a legend, and took the title of "the King." (19) Popular music would never be the same again.

Scorecard: Number of Errors Found and Corrected _____

29 Keeping Verbs in Order

You probably already know a great deal about verbs and word order even if you can't explain every grammatical rule. For example, you wouldn't say or write the following combination of words:

Friend my to the drove some store groceries for.

Rearranged, these words make a sentence. Try unscrambling them. _____

Did you write "My friend drove to the store for some groceries"? If so, you applied many grammatical rules in order to create that sentence.

If you feel less than confident about verb forms and related matters, however, this chapter will help build your confidence by

- explaining verb tenses and phrases
- giving you practice in understanding and writing complex verb forms
- suggesting different ways to phrase questions
- clarifying sentence order when you use objects and adverbs
- explaining how to express negative statements

THE CONTINUOUS TENSES

The two most common continuous tenses, present and past, are formed in similar ways.

UNIT 5	Go Electronic
Chapter 29	Use the following electronic supplements for additional practice with your writing: • For chapter-by-chapter summaries and exercises, visit the Writing with Confidence Companion Website at http://www.ablongman.com/meyers. • For work with the writing process, visit The Longman Writer's Warehouse at http://longmanwriterswarehouse.com (password needed). • For additional practice in grammar, use The Writer's ToolKit Plus CD-ROM.
Writing with Confidence ©2003	

In the Present

> "Good order is the foundation of all good things."
>
> —Philosopher Kenneth Burke

There are two present tenses in English, but they communicate entirely different meanings.

The **simple present tense** discusses habitual actions—actions that happen all of the time, most of the time, or some of the time:

> I *go* to my English class three days a week.
>
> My instructor usually *assigns* a short composition on Friday.

It can also discuss current feelings, observations, facts, or statements involving no action:

> I *like* cauliflower, but I *hate* spinach. (feelings)
>
> I *hear* a noise, but I *don't see* anything. (observations)
>
> The earth *revolves* around the sun, and the moon *orbits* the earth. (facts)
>
> We *don't have* a car. Cars *cost* too much. (statements involving no action)

Notice that present-tense verbs have only two endings. Verbs that agree with *I, we, you,* or *they* do not end in *–s.* Verbs that agree with *he, she,* or *it* must end in *–s.* In most questions or negative statements, they take the helping verb *do* or *does,* based on the same subject–verb agreement. (See Chapter 10.)

The **present continuous (or progressive) tense** discusses actions that are happening now or planned for the future.

> *I'm going* to my English class now.
>
> *We're handing* in our compositions on Monday.

Verbs in the present continuous tense always include two parts: a present-tense form of the verb *to be* (*am, is,* or *are*) + an *–ing* word.

EXERCISE 1 | Writing Present Tenses

6. Edit
5. Revise
4. Write
3. Organize
2. Prewrite
1. Explore

Rewrite each of the following sentences, changing from the simple present to the present continuous tense, or vice versa.

Simple present tense

1. We often walk home after classes.

2. My brother-in-law sleeps fourteen hours a day.

3. _____ every week.

4. Jason often has a party on the weekend.

5. Mrs. Highnose doesn't watch television.

Present continuous tense

1. *We're walking home after classes today.*

2. _____ right now.

3. My father is washing the car now.

4. _____ this Saturday.

5. _____ now.

6. It gets cold in here once in a
while.

6. _____
today.

In the Past

Like the two present tenses, the two most important past tenses express entirely different meanings.

The **simple past tense** discusses a completed action or situation in the past, often at a stated time:

> Stanislav *passed* the test yesterday and *felt* wonderful.
>
> We *didn't see* the movie.

Most verbs in the simple past tense end in *–ed*, but some are **irregular**, meaning they show past tense in some other way (see Chapter 11). In questions or negative statements, past-tense verbs take the helping verb *did*.

The **past continuous** (or **progressive**) **tense** discusses actions in progress at a specific time or period of time in the past:

> I *was studying* at midnight.
>
> They *were working* all day yesterday.

The past continuous tense often appears in combined sentences joined by *when, while,* or *as:*

> I *was taking* a shower *when* the telephone *rang.*
>
> Tom *tried* to study *while* his sister *was watching* TV.

Verbs in the past continuous tense always include two parts: a past-tense form of the verb *to be* (*was* or *were*) + an *–ing* word.

In many languages, the *forms* of words—their beginnings, endings, or internal changes—convey a great deal of grammatical information. But in English, the *order* of words often determines how they function grammatically. Take, for example, the word *wash*. If you shift it to different positions in a sentence, it can be a noun, a verb, or an adjective—even though its form doesn't change:

As a verb: I always *wash* clothes on Saturday.

As a noun: When do you do the *wash?*

As an adjective: Saturday is my *wash* day.

The rules that govern English word order are generally consistent, so you can master them.

EXERCISE 2	Writing Past Tenses

6. Edit
5. Revise
4. Write
3. Organize
2. Prewrite
1. Explore

Rewrite each of the following sentences, changing the simple past tense to the past continuous tense, or vice versa.

Simple past tense

1. *I studied for the test this morning.*

2. _____
yesterday.

3. _____
every day last week.

4. Bill got a haircut yesterday.

5. They didn't listen to the news during dinner.

Past continuous tense

1. I was studying for the test when you called.

2. Our telephone wasn't working for several hours.

3. They were doing the wash again this morning.

4. _____
when the barbershop caught on fire.

5. _____
last night.

6. _____

when _____

this morning?

6. Who was watching the children

while you were shopping?

EXERCISE 3	Combining Sentences About the Past

6. Edit
5. Revise
4. Write
3. Organize
2. Prewrite
1. Explore

Combine each of the following pairs of sentences, using when *or* while.

1. Mario had dinner. His cat sat down in his spaghetti. *Mario was having dinner when his cat sat down in his spaghetti.*

2. I talked to my friend. Several hundred-dollar bills dropped from my pocket. _____

_____

3. Mr. Gotbucks smoked a cigar. His chauffeur drove the car._____

_____

4. They fell in love. They danced cheek to cheek. _____

_____

5. His wife washed the dishes, swept the floor, and threw out the garbage. Mr. Hogg

read the paper._____

_____

6. I took a bath. The house caught on fire. _____

_____

MORE VERB PHRASES

A verb can contain as many as four words—which together make a **verb phrase**. The last word in a verb phrase is called the **main verb**; all the other words in the phrase are called **helping verbs**. Although verb phrases may seem complicated, the rules for writing them are entirely consistent. We'll examine those rules as follows.

Two-Word Verb Phrases

There are four categories of two-word verbs: *to be* as the helping verb, *to have* as the helping verb, *to do* as the helping verb, and fixed-form helping verbs.

To Be.   The helping verb is *to be*, followed by one of the two verb forms:

1. An *–ing* **word**, which creates a continuous tense:

he is I am they are	seeing (present continuous tense)
she was you were	seeing (past continuous tense)

Collaborative Activity 1

Writing in the Present and Past

Write eight affirmative statement sentences—two in the simple present tense, two in the present continuous tense, two in the simple past tense, and two in the past continuous tense. Exchange papers by passing to the left, and

1. Correct any errors you find.
2. Change each sentence into a negative statement.
3. Change each sentence into a question.

Then exchange papers again by passing to the left for a third student to check.

2. A **past participle**, which forms the **passive voice** (see Chapter 11):

she is I am we are	} seen (present tense, passive voice)
I was they were	} seen (past tense, passive voice)

To Have.   The helping verb is *to have*, followed by one of two verb forms:

1. A **past participle**, which creates a **perfect tense** (see Chapter 11):

he has they have	} seen (present-perfect tense)
we had	seen (past-perfect tense)

2. An **infinitive**, which in the present tense expresses the same meaning as *must* (The infinitive is actually two words, since it begins with *to*.):

she has they have	} to see (must see)
I had	to study (This past-tense idea cannot be expressed with *must*.)

EXERCISE 4   Writing in the Perfect Tenses

6. Edit
5. Revise
4. Write
3. Organize
2. Prewrite
1. Explore

Complete each of the following sentences by including a verb phrase in the present-perfect or past-perfect tense.

1. I don't want to see that movie because ___I've seen it before.___

2. Bill apologized for being rude after he _____

_____

3. I can't take a coffee break now because _____

_____ already.

4. Carmen felt terrible after _____

_____

5. Wilbur couldn't drive a car after_____

_____

6. All the students were overjoyed because _____

_____

EXERCISE 5   Writing Statements with Have to

Complete each of the following sentences by including a verb phrase with have to, has to, *or* had to. *In these sentences, the verb means* must.

1. I couldn't watch television last night because___I had to study for an examination.___

2. That is a very dangerous intersection, so drivers _____

_____

3. If they want to avoid an accident. _____

_____

4. I have a paper due tomorrow, so _____

_____

5. When you visit Europe, you _____

_____

6. Mr. Kim was very sick yesterday, so _____

_____

7. If you need to pay your tuition, _____

_____

Collaborative Activity 2

Writing Two-Word Verb Forms

Write sentences with two-word verbs—two with *to be*, two with *to have*, two with *to do*, and two with the fixed-form helping verbs. In your group, exchange papers by passing to the left, and do the following:

1. Correct any errors you find.
2. Change each sentence into a negative state-ment—or each negative into an affirmative.
3. Change each sentence into a question.

Then exchange papers again by passing to the left for a third student to check.

To Do. The helping verb is *to do*—for questions, negative statements, or emphasis with any main verb except *to be.*

1. In questions:

> *Do* you *like* sports? *Does* he *like* sports? *Did* he *eat* dinner?

2. In negative statements:

> I *don't like* sports. He *doesn't like* sports. He *didn't eat* dinner.

3. For emphasis in affirmative statements:

> I *do like* sports. Oh yes, he *does like* sports. You're wrong; he *did eat* dinner.

Notice that in all three categories:

- The first verb (the helping verb) determines the tense and subject–verb agreement.
- The second verb (the main verb) never changes for tense or subject–verb agreement.

EXERCISE 6 | Writing Negatives with Do

Write an appropriate negative statement after each of the following statements.

1. I worked yesterday. *I didn't get much rest.*

2. Abraham Lincoln died in office. _____

_____

3. It often rains in Oregon during the winter. _____

4. In Europe, most children start school when they are seven. _____

_____

5. Most college students these days hold part-time or full-time jobs._____

_____

_____

6. I drove to work this morning. _____

_____

Fixed-Form Verbs.   The helping verb is a fixed-form verb, which never changes its form (although we express the past-tense meanings of *can* and *will* with the verbs *could* and *would*). The main verb is a partial infinitive (without *to*), so it cannot change for tense or agreement:

I, we, you he, she, they	can could will would shall should may might must	go, have, be

Exception: Ought is *followed by a complete infinitive:* ought to go *or* ought to be

The main function of these verb phrases is to discuss ability, possibility, obligation, choice, or necessity in the present or future:

Ability:	I	can	study now (or later).
Possibility:	I	may might could	study now (or later).
Obligation:	I	ought to would should shall	study now (or later) if I had the chance. study now (or later).
Choice:	I	may will might	study now or later.
Necessity:	I	must	study now (or later).

EXERCISE 7   *Writing Helping Verbs*

6. Edit
5. Revise
4. Write
3. Organize
2. Prewrite
1. Explore

Each of the sentences below already has a helping verb. Complete each one, using an appropriate main verb.

1. I am *composing great sentences now.* _____

2. At 8:00 P.M. yesterday, we were _____.

3. I've _____ many times.

4. Has our teacher _____ yet?

5. I had _____ before coming to school today.

6. I could _____ many years ago.

7. You should _____.

Three-Word Verb Phrases

There are two main groups of three-word verbs: those for the active voice and those for the passive voice. In the **active voice**, the subject performs the action of the verb, and in the **passive voice**, the subject is passive—it receives the action of the verb. We'll examine both main groups here.

Active-Voice Phrases.   You've already seen these combinations in two-word verbs:

1. a fixed-form helping verb + short infinitive
2. *have* + a past participle or full infinitive
3. *be* + an *–ing* word

Three-word verbs in the active-voice simply extend these combinations:

Fixed-form verb	Have	Past participle or full infinitive
might, may, could, etc.	have	done to go

Fixed-form verb	Be	*–ing* word
might, may, could, etc.	be	doing

Here is how these verb phrases function.
   Three-word verb phrases with *have* interpret past actions or circumstances:

Bill didn't feel well yesterday, so he	must have been sick. could have had a cold. might have had the flu. may have had the flu. should have stayed home.

Or they describe a change in a past action or condition beginning with the conditional word *if:*

If I had known that Bill was sick, I	would have called him.
	could have taken him to the doctor.
	might have gone to his house.

Or, with *will have* and the past participle, they form the **future-perfect tense**, which describes an action or event already completed before a later time in the future.

Ten years from now, Joe	will have graduated from college.
	will have gotten a good job.
	will have married and (will have) had children.

Three-word verb phrases with *be* express possibilities, conclusions, or plans about the present or future:

I don't know where Bill is now. He	could be working.
	might be working.
	ought to be working.
	may be gone.
Bill isn't home now, so he	must be working.
By this time next week,	Young will be flying to Korea.

Passive-Voice Phrases.   Three-word verbs in the **passive voice**—in which the subject is being acted upon—discuss a continuing action. To do so, these verb phrases also extend patterns you've already seen:

1. *be* + an *–ing* word (this forms a continuous tense)
2. *be* + a past participle (this creates the passive voice)

The passive-voice continuous tenses combine the patterns with forms of *be* as the first word and the *–ing* word, followed by the past participle:

Be	*–ing* word	Past Participle
am, is, are	being	done, served, taken, tested, etc.
was, were		

Here are some examples of sentences with three-word verbs in the passive voice:

The food *is being prepared* now.

The instructions *were being explained* when I left.

| EXERCISE 8 | Writing Three-Word Verb Phrases |

Complete each of the following sentences, using an appropriate three-word verb phrase. The first word of the phrase has been provided.

1. You can't drive on Wilson Avenue now.   *It is being repaired.* _____

2. Fidel isn't at his desk. He could_____

3. Please don't go into the kitchen. The floor is _____

_____

4. When I last saw my old car, it was _____

5. If I had known that you couldn't use your car, I would _____

_____

6. By this time next year, I will_____

Four-Word Verb Phrases

Four-word verbs are extensions of three-word verbs. The first helping verb must be fixed-form, and the second word must be *have*. Then comes *been*, the past participle of *be*:

might have been

Either an *–ing* word or past participle can complete the verb phrase:

might have been going   might have been gone

These four-word verbs express meanings similar to those of three-word verbs. Four-word verb phrases that end with *–ing* words interpret the past but express continuous actions:

Manuel wasn't home yesterday. He	could have been working. must have been working. might have been working. may have been working.
However, Manuel was sick yesterday. He	should have been resting.
If Manuel had been smart, he	would have been resting.

Four-word verbs ending in past participles are passive voice expressions that interpret the past:

The radio didn't work. It	could have been dropped on the floor. might have been broken by my son. must have been broken by someone.
The radio wasn't fixed, but	it should have been fixed.

EXERCISE 9 | Writing Four-Word Verb Phrases

Complete each of the following sentences, using an appropriate four-word verb phrase.

1. Norma was watching wrestling on TV last night when she *should have been studying.*

2. I didn't receive my final grades last week. They_____

_____

3. Claudia came home with many grocery bags, so she _____ in

the afternoon.

4. Main Street was still closed to traffic last week. It _____ three

weeks ago.

5. This song wasn't written by Mozart, but it _____

_____ by Haydn.

6. Your telephone line was busy all last night. Your teenage son _____

_____

INDIRECT QUESTIONS

As you know, some sentences ask a question:

> How can I get to the train station?

But some sentences imply that a question is asked without really asking it:

> I want to know how I can get to the train station.

This is an **indirect question**. It is actually part of a statement, so its word order and end punctuation follow the pattern for statements, not direct questions. Compare these sentences:

> *Direct question:*   Where is the office?
>
> *Indirect question:*   I wonder where the office is.

Note these differences:

- A **direct question** ends in a question mark and begins with a verb before the subject.
- An **indirect question**—since it is a statement—ends in a period and begins with the subject before the verb:

An indirect question can also be included in a statement that makes a request—or even as a dependent clause in a direct question. Here are examples:

> *Request:*   Please tell me *where the registrar's office is.*
>
> *Question:*   Can you tell me *where the registrar's office is?*

Finally, *quoted* direct questions differ from indirect questions in word order, punctuation, and verb tense. Quotations reproduce the exact words of the speaker—in the same order and tense. But indirect questions adjust word order and tense to fit within the statement that introduces them. Carefully note the tense differences in the following examples:

Direct question	Indirect question
He asked me, "Are you all right?"	He asked me if I was all right.
He asked me, "Were you working?"	He asked me if I had been working.
He asked me, "Will you come?"	He asked me if I would come.
He asked me, "Can you come?"	He asked me if I could come.
He asked me, "Did you come?"	He asked me if I had come.
He asked me, "Have you finished?"	He asked me if I had finished.

Collaborative Activity 5

Writing More Questions

Write nine sentences—three direct questions, three indirect questions, and three sentences with quoted direct questions. In your group, exchange papers by passing to the left, and rephrase the sentences. Make direct questions to indirect questions, indirect questions to direct questions, and quoted direct questions to indirect questions that aren't quoted. Exchange papers again by passing to the left so a third student checks your work.

EXERCISE 10	Writing Indirect Questions

6. Edit
5. Revise
4. Write
3. Organize
2. Prewrite
1. Explore

Rewrite each of the following direct questions as an indirect question, beginning with the words provided.

1. Do you need any help? I want to know *if you need any help.*

2. How are your parents? I would be interested to hear _____

3. Where is room 814? Can you tell me _____

4. When does the class begin? He asked me _____

5. Did you study for the final examination? I wanted to know if _____

6. When can I call the doctor? He inquired about when _____

OBJECTS AFTER VERBS

Objects, which receive the action of verbs, can be placed between or after verbs, depending on the type of verbs. We'll look at both situations here.

Objects with Phrasal Verbs

When you write a sentence using an action verb (that tells what a subject *does, did,* or *will do*), the normal word order is subject–verb–object. The object can be a noun or pronoun.

Subject	Verb	Noun object	Pronoun object
We	picked	some grapes	(them).
Bill	dropped	the plate	(it)
I	took	the dishes	(them).

Suppose, however, that you change the meaning of a verb by adding another word that looks like a preposition:

picked up	dropped off	took out

These two-word expressions are called **phrasal verbs**, and with them the placement of the object is more complicated. With many phrasal verbs, a noun-object can precede or follow the second verb word:

I *picked up* some grapes at the store. I *picked* some grapes *up* at the store.

Bill *dropped off* the book at my house. Bill *dropped* the book *off* at my house.

Try writing the sentence "I _____ the dishes" in two ways, using *took away* as the verb.

_____

_____

Did you write, "I took away the dishes," and "I took the dishes away"? Then you understand the flexibility of noun-objects.

Unlike noun-objects, however, pronoun-objects *must* come between the two words of the phrasal verb:

> I *picked* them *up.*
>
> Bill *dropped* it *off.*
>
> I *took* them *out.*

But some phrasal verbs cannot be separated by objects in this way. In general, the following rules apply.

 A two-word verb that *moves or changes the condition* of an object can take a noun-object either before or after the second verb word.

> We *put* the dishes *away.* We *put away* the dishes. (The verb *put away* moved the dishes.)
>
> I *cheered* my friend *up.* I *cheered up* my friend. (The verb *cheered up* changed the mental condition of your friend.)

 A phrasal verb that *does not* move or change the condition of an object cannot be separated. In this case, the object must come after the complete verb.

> I *ran into* an old friend yesterday.
>
> I always *count on* you for help. (The objects don't move or change in these sentences.)

Common Phrasal Verbs

The following reference lists of common phrasal verbs may be helpful.

Separable verbs:

ask out	dress up	help out
back up	drink up	hold up
blow up	drive back	keep down, on, up
break down, off, up	drop off	knock out
bring about, out, up	dry off, up	leave on, out
build up	dust off, up	let in, on, off, out, up
burn up	eat up	look over, up
buy out, up	figure out	make up
call back	fill in, out, up	mix up
call off	find out	open up
check out, over, up	fix up	pass out, up
cheer up	follow up	pay off, out
clean out, up	get back, down, out	pick out, up
cool off, up	give away, up	plug in, up
cross off, out	hand in, out	point out
cut off, up	hang up	put aside, away, down,
do over	have on	in, off, on, up

rub off
set up
shut down, off, out
slow down, up
speed up
stand up
straighten out, up
sweep out, up

take away, back, off, on,
out, over, up
talk out, over, up
tear up
tell apart
think over
try on, out
turn around, down, in,

up
use over, up
warm up
wash out, up
wear out
wipe off, up
work out
write down, off

Inseparable verbs:

agree on
allow for
amount to
ask for
back out of
become of
bump into
care about
come across
come along with
come back to, out of,
over to, through with,
up to
count on
deal in, with
do without
drop in, on, out of

into, off, on, out, over,
feel like
get ahead of
get into, off, on, out of,
over, through with
go into, on with
grow out of
hear about
hold on to
keep on with, up with
look at, for, out for
meet with
occur to
part with
plan on
put up with
read up on

run into, across, off
with, out of, over
see about
send for, away for
side with
speak about, for, of
stand by, up for
stick to
take up with
talk about, back to
think about, back on, of
try out for
turn into
wait for, on
walk out on
watch out for
work on

Collaborative Activity 6

Composing Sentences

Write at least ten sentences using different phrasal verbs from the lists just given. Then, in a collaborative group, exchange papers by passing to the left and check each other's work.

EXERCISE 11	Writing Phrasal Verbs

6. Edit
5. Revise
4. Write
3. Organize
2. Prewrite
1. Explore

Write a sentence using each of the following phrasal verbs and its object.

1. (*verb*) make up (*object*) the examination *Alicia made up the examination she had missed.*

2. (*verb*) put off (*object*) studying _____

_____

3. (*verb*) look up (*object*) it _____

_____

4. (*verb*) throw away (*object*) an old dress _____

_____

5. (*verb*) try on (*object*) them _____

_____

6. (*verb*) take out (*object*) the lettuce _____

_____

7. (*verb*) do over (*object*) it _____

_____

8. (*verb*) find out (*object*) the secret of long life _____

_____

9. (*verb*) get back (*object*) him _____

_____

10. (*verb*) give up (*object*) smoking _____

_____

Direct and Indirect Objects

Many verbs take a **direct object**, which receives the action of the verb:

Subject	Verb	Direct object
1. A repairman	fixed	the broken window.
2. The company	will open	a branch store.

But some verbs take two objects: a direct object, which receives the action of the verb, and an **indirect object**, which receives the direct object.

Subject	Verb	Indirect object	Direct object
3. The repairman	sent	us	the bill.
4. The branch store	should offer	its customers	many services.

Notice the order of the objects in sentences 3–4: *the indirect object comes before the direct object.*

There is a second way to write a direct object and an indirect object in a sentence. You may write the direct object *first* and then follow it with *to* (or sometimes *for*) plus the indirect object:

Subject	Verb	Direct object	Indirect object
5. The repairman	sent	the bill	to us.
6. The branch store	should offer	many services	to its customers.
7. Richie	mixed	drinks	for his guests.

These are the only two ways to place direct and indirect objects. They should *never* be placed in this order: *to* (or *for*)—object—direct object.

Incorrect:	I lent to Juan my pen.
Correct:	I lent Juan my pen. I lent my pen to Juan.
Incorrect:	Richie mixed for his guests a drink.
Correct:	Richie mixed a drink for his guests.
	Richie mixed his guests a drink.

EXERCISE 12	Writing Two Objects

6. Edit
5. Revise
4. Write
3. Organize
2. Prewrite
1. Explore

Rewrite the following sentences, reversing the order of the objects.

1. In 1837, the famous showman P. T. Barnum sold the public his first hoax. <u>In 1837, the famous showman P. T. Barnum sold his first hoax to the public.</u>

2. Over 10,000 New Yorkers bought tickets for themselves. _____

_____

3. Barnum showed them a 161-year-old ex-slave. _____

_____

4. After her death and autopsy, the newspapers told her real age—eighty—to the public.

_____

_____

5. Naturally, Barnum did not give refunds to anyone. _____

_____

EXERCISE 13	Writing More Objects

6. Edit
5. Revise
4. Write
3. Organize
2. Prewrite
1. Explore

Using the verbs in parentheses, write sentences containing both direct and indirect objects. Be sure to vary the object word order.

1. (give) <u>Tomas gave me a piece of paper. or Tomas gave a piece of paper to me.</u>

2. (tell) _____

3. (make) _____

4. (sell) _____

5. (send) _____

6. (bring) _____

ADVERBS

Collaborative Activity 7

Changing Sentences

Exchange the sentences you wrote in Exercise 13 by passing them to the left. Rewrite each, changing the order of the objects. Then have a third student check them.

Remember that **adverbs** tell *when, where, why,* or *how* an action occurs. Phrases and even whole clauses can be adverbs:

> (When) *After John Jacob Astor had made millions of dollars as a fur trader,* he opened the Astor Hotel (later the famous Waldorf-Astoria) in New York.

And single words (usually ending in *–ly*) or phrases can be adverbs:

Single Words	
(how much)	Eighteenth-century clock maker Levi Hutchins *intensely* disliked oversleeping.
(how)	He awoke *promptly* at 4:00 A.M. each day.
(when)	But *sometimes* he would sleep past his normal waking hour.

Continued

Phrases	
(why and when)	*As a result*, Hutchins set out to invent the first alarm clock in 1787.
(how)	He combined a clock and a bell *in a unique way*.
(when)	He wrote, "It was simplicity itself to arrange the bell to sound *at the predetermined hour*."

Single Adverbs

As the following examples show, you can place an adverb in many locations in a sentence for emphasis or variety:

Levi Hutchins *intensely* disliked . . . (between the subject and the verb)

He awoke *promptly* . . . (after the verb)

. . . *sometimes* he would sleep . . . (before the subject)

or

. . . he would *sometimes* sleep . . . (between the helping verb and the main verb)

However, an adverb rarely goes between a verb and its object or objects:

Incorrect:	Levi Hutchins disliked intensely oversleeping.
Incorrect:	He combined in a unique way a clock and a bell.

EXERCISE 14	Editing Misplaced Adverbs

6. Edit
5. Revise
4. Write
3. Organize
2. Prewrite
1. Explore

Underline the adverb, the adverb phrase, or the adverb clause in each of the following sentences. Then draw an arrow to the spot where the misplaced adverb should be located in each sentence.

1. Three men and a giraffe shared <u>cheerfully</u> a box lunch.

2. Throw Momma from the train a kiss.

3. Smoking a hand-rolled cigarette, the man turned on quickly the radio.

4. The man walked down the block his dog.

5. I sent very promptly the answer he wanted to him.

6. Johnnie kissed on a moonlit night his girlfriend.

Placing Two or More Adverbs

When a sentence contains several adverbs, you may wish to spread them around for variety or emphasis, as in this example:

when	where	why
In 1843, a man *in Troy, Ohio*, was fined $10 *for kissing a married lady*.		

Or you could put them all at the end of the sentence:

> A man was fined $10 *in Troy, Ohio, in 1843 for kissing a married lady.*

But when you stack up all the adverbs at the end of a sentence, the choices become more limited. In a sentence with no object after the verb, place the adverbs in this order: verb—how—where—when—(why). For example:

> The first U.S. bank robbery **occurred** *in New York in 1831.*
> verb — where — when
>
> President W. H. Harrison **died** *of pneumonia in Washington after only thirty days in office.*
> verb — how — where — when
>
> Private bathtubs **appeared** *in a New York hotel in 1844, perhaps for sanitary reasons.*
> verb — where — when — why

In a sentence with an object after the verb, place the adverbs in this order: how—verb—object—where—when—(why). For example:

> Robert M. Green *happily* **invented** the ice-cream soda *in Philadelphia in* 1874.
> how — verb — object — where — when
>
> Whitcomb Judson **put** the first zipper *on boots in 1893 so people would not have to tie their shoes.*
> verb — object — where — when — why

EXERCISE 15   Writing Adverbs

6. Edit
5. Revise
4. Write
3. Organize
2. Prewrite
1. Explore

Collaborative Activity 8

Changing Sentences

Exchange the sentences you wrote in Exercise 15 by passing them to the left. Rewrite any in which the adverbs can be placed differently. Then discuss and compare the first and second versions to see which are most graceful.

Write five sentences. Each must include at least two adverbs from the following list.

happily	loudly
slyly	briskly
uneasily	on several occasions
smartly	from one place to another
swiftly	to his high-rise apartment
drowsily	fourteen hours a day
in May of this year	from Nevada to California
on the sidewalk	after the term ends
since he called his parents	although he walks like a three-legged turtle
because he is always tired	at work
in more than one way	when Manuel saw the ten-dollar bill

PAST PARTICIPLES AND PRESENT PARTICIPLES

Past participles (such as *spoken, seen, tired*) and *–ing* words, or **present participles**, are formed from verbs. But they often function as adjectives. Here's how to distinguish between their meanings.

- Present participles express a feeling or action created by the noun they modify:

Collaborative Activity 9

Correcting Sentences

Write five sentences, each of which uses one of the following words as an adjective: *exciting, baked, married, boring,* and *written.* In your group, exchange papers by passing to the left and correct the sentences.

> We heard some *shocking* news. (The news created shock in the people who heard it.)
>
> The book was *interesting*. (The book created interest in me.)

Often that feeling or action is continuing, was continuing, or will be continuing:

> Don't touch that pot of *boiling* eggs.
>
> I tried to stay out of the *falling* rain.

- Past participles express a feeling or action received by the noun they modify:

> The *shocked* man couldn't believe the news. (The man received the shock.)
>
> I am *interested* in the book. (I receive the interest from the book.)

Often that feeling or action is completed, was completed, or will be completed:

> These *boiled* eggs are cold.
>
> I will pick up some *fallen* rocks by the side of the road.

EXERCISE 16 **Writing Present or Past Participles**

6. Edit
5. Revise
4. Write
3. Organize
2. Prewrite
1. Explore

Complete each of the following sentences with the appropriate past- or present-participle form of the verb in parentheses.

1. The man sounds (irritate) *irritated.* _____

2. The movie was very (interest) _____ to me.

3. I always enjoy well-(perform) _____ plays.

4. The (explode) _____ bomb is not dangerous now, but it hurt several soldiers.

5. Three (injure) _____ soldiers had to be taken to the hospital.

6. The (break) _____ branch made a loud noise.

7. The (bore) _____ audience slept through the lecture.

DOUBLE NEGATIVES

In most languages, a statement can have two, three, or even four negatives. In English, though, a negative statement can have only one negative word. The word can be *not*, which makes the verb negative:

> I did *not* do anything last night. I did*n't* have any money.

Or the negative word (usually *no, nothing, nowhere,* or *no one*) can appear elsewhere in a sentence with an affirmative verb:

> I did *nothing* last night. I had *no* money.

You *cannot* use two negatives to express a negative idea. That is an error called a **double negative**:

Incorrect:	I did*n't* do *nothing* last night.
Correct:	I *didn't* do *anything* last night. Or I *did nothing* last night.

In fact, two negatives can actually express an affirmative idea:

Correct:	It's *not uncommon* to see ducks in the pond. (It's quite common to see the ducks.)
Correct:	I *never* do *nothing*. (I always do something.)

Here is a list of the most common negative words, along with their affirmative versions:

Negatives	Affirmatives
no one	anyone
nobody	anybody
nothing	anything
nowhere	anywhere
no	any
none	any
never	ever

Two other words are negative in meaning: *hardly* and *scarcely.* They mean *almost no, almost none,* or *almost never:*

> I had *hardly any* homework this week. (almost no homework)
>
> The Wilsons *scarcely ever* go out. (almost never)

Like other negative words, they need to stand alone. They cannot be used with another negative:

Incorrect:	We didn't have hardly any money.
Correct:	We had *hardly any* money.

EXERCISE 17   Eliminating Double Negatives

Cross out one of the two negatives in each of the following sentences and write any changes above the line.

          anything

1. Nobody ever says ^~~nothing~~ unkind to Bruno.

2. Reno never has no luck at cards.

6. Edit
5. Revise
4. Write
3. Organize
2. Prewrite
1. Explore

3. When Mr. Swift explains something, it doesn't make no sense.

4. I've scarcely spent no money this week.

5. I don't like to borrow nothing from other people.

6. We didn't go nowhere on our vacation.

7. You can't hardly find an honest person these days.

8. I didn't notice no difference between those two pizzas—I ate them both.

IN SUMMARY | To Keep Verbs in Order

1. Write continuous tenses with the present- or past-tense forms of *to be* + *–ing* to express continuing actions in the present or past.

2. Form two-word verbs with these patterns:
   a. *be* + *–ing* (for continuous tenses)
   b. *be* + past participle (for passive voice)
   c. *have* + past participle (for perfect tenses)
   d. *have* + infinitive (for obligation or necessity)
   e. *do* + simple form of the verb (for negatives in present or past tense)
   f. fixed-form verbs + simple form of the verb (for ability, possibility, obligation, choice, or necessity)

3. Form three-word verbs with these patterns:
   a. fixed-form helping verb + *be* + *–ing* (for active voice) or past participle (for passive voice)
   b. fixed-form helping verb + *have* + past participle (for active voice), or fixed-form helping verb + *be* + *being* + past participle (for passive voice)

4. Form four-word verbs with these patterns:
   a. fixed-form helping verbs + *have* + *been* + *–ing* (for continuous tenses)
   b. fixed-form helping verbs + *have* + *been* + past participle (for passive voice)

5. Write direct questions using this word order: verb–subject–verb? Write indirect questions with this word order: subject–verb.

6. When a phrasal verb moves or changes the condition of the object, place a noun object after or between the parts of the verb, and place a pronoun object only after the verb. When a phrasal verb *does not* move or change the condition of the object, place both noun and pronoun objects after the verb.

7. Place direct and indirect objects in either of these patterns:
   a. verb–indirect object–direct object
   b. verb–direct object–*to* (or *for*)–indirect object

8. Place a short adverb
   a. before the subject
   b. between the subject and verb
   c. after the verb (unless the verb takes an object);

9. When there is no object after the verb, use this order: verb–how–where–when–(why).

10. When there is an object after the verb, use this order: how–verb–object–where–when–(why).

11. Use past participles as adjectives to express a completed action or an action that the modified noun did not perform; use present participles as adjectives to express a continuing action that the modified noun is performing.

12. Make a negative with *not* on the verb or with *no* before a noun or pronoun—but *don't make the negative twice.*

EDITING FOR MASTERY

Mastery Exercise 1

Editing Verb Forms and Word Order

The following passage contains fifteen errors in verb forms, placement of adverbs, placement of direct and indirect objects, use of phrasal verbs, use of past and present participles as adjectives, and use of negatives—aside from the first error, which has been corrected as an example. Make your corrections above the lines.

The Designer Jeans Fad (1970s)

(1) Blue jeans were ^~~inventing~~ *invented* by an immigrant named Levi Strauss during the great California Gold Rush in 1849. (2) Strauss planned to make for the miners canvas tents, but when he couldn't hardly sell any, he decided to manufacture pants. (3) The canvas would not wore out, and the copper rivets prevented any tears or separations at the seams. (4) However, the design of this clothing soon changed. (5) Cowboys were preferring tight pants, so they sat in water to get wet their jeans and then lay out in the sun to shrink them. (6) The copper rivet at the crotch had to be removed because it burned miners who sat too near a campfire. (7) Rivets were eliminated from the back pockets in the 1930s after schoolteachers complained that the jeans were scratching badly the wooden seats of the children's desks.

(8) These pants for working people became in the same decade a hot fashion item when an advertisement appeared in *Vogue* magazine. (9) It showed two society women who were having on tight jeans in a look called "western chic." (10) Another fad happened in the 1950s, when people rolled their jean cuffs and wore tight sweaters and dark sunglasses. (11) These fashion trends, however, weren't nothing compared to the one that erupted in the 1970s.

(12) The designer jeans fad was began when young people decorated their faded, shabby pants with patches, stitches, painted messages, and cheap jewelry. (13) Teenagers were interesting in a way to express themselves through clothing. (14) Clothing makers spotted soon a new market and introduced expensive, tight-fitting jeans decorating with jewels, sequins, and lace.

Collaborative Activity 10

Checking Your Answers

Compare your answers to Mastery Exercise 1 in your collaborative group, and report your results to the whole class.

(15) As famous designers got the jeans market into, they replaced the decorations with expensive designer labels (for the labels were what people paid for), usually stitched across the right rear pocket. (16) Jordache, Sasson, and Sergio became synonyms for fashionable jeans. (17) The pants that had once been intended for hard work would become now the clothes for serious play. (18) In fact, Calvin Klein jeans, in spite of their high price of $50 (or because of it), were selling at the rate of 250,000 pairs a week. (19) Levi Strauss himself would have being flattered.

Scorecard: Number of Errors Found and Corrected _____

Mastery Exercise 2

Editing Verb Forms and Word Order

The following passage contains fifteen errors in verb forms, placement of adverbs, placement of direct and indirect objects, use of phrasal verbs, use of past and present participles as adjectives, and use of negatives—aside from the first error, which has been corrected as an example. Make your corrections above the lines.

The Sneaker Fad (1980s to the Present Time)

(1) At one time, a single, inexpensive pair of gym shoes was ^worn ~~wearing~~ by children and adults for all sports. (2) But in the 1980s, the sneaker was came out of the gymnasium and into the world of fashion, especially among young people. (3) There weren't no more simple black canvas high-tops with rubber soles. (4) They were replacing by high-tech shoes that gave to an athlete an advantage in running and jumping.

(5) The shoes could be make of leather, suede, or nylon. (6) They might have also shock-absorbing heels, air-cushioned soles, and inflatable tops. (7) Kids were most interesting in designer sneakers like Nike's $110 Air Jordan and Reebok's $170 Pump. (8) The entire sneaker industry sold in 1989 more than 400 million shoes, up from 347 million the previous year. (9) The Converse Shoe Company claimed that 58 percent of its sales had came from children eighteen and under.

(10) Companies such as Adidas and Puma began making high-tech sneakers in the 1960s, and Nike brought out even fancier athletic shoes in the next decade. (11) Working women put on them instead of high heels for walking to the office. (12) The emphasis on fitness, jogging, and workout videos helped to increased the market for specially designed shoes.

(13) However, the real mania came when kids, particularly inner-city kids, used in the 1980s footwear as a way to make a personal statement. (14) A study of sporting goods stores showed that many inner-city youngsters were buying at least once a month expensive new sneakers. (15) Experts claimed that young drug dealers had been estab-

lished the trends for new designs in sneakers. (16) The Los Angeles Police Department accused shoe companies of making huge profits from drug money.

(17) The shoe companies wouldn't agree to none of these changes. (18) They said that sneakers cost so much because of all the high-tech features. (19) But several shoe manufacturers decided to be socially responsible (and to stop all the bad publicity). (20) They gave to the inner-city schools some of their profits to fix their gyms and out-door basketball courts.

Scorecard: Number of Errors Found and Corrected _____

30 Mastering the Little Words: Articles and Prepositions

No one notices articles and prepositions when you use them correctly. But when you don't, your writing sounds odd and even unclear. This chapter will examine some solutions to typical "little word" problems. You'll learn

- when to use *a/an, the,* or no article
- when to use which prepositions for time, place, and other special meanings

ARTICLES

The articles—*a, an,* and *the*—help your reader understand whether you are using a noun in a general or a specific way. But some people confuse *a* with *an,* and many nonnative speakers of English have difficulty distinguishing when to use *a/an, the,* or no article at all.

The articles entered English long ago simply as different pronunciations of the words *one* ("an") and *that* ("the"). So in actual usage, *a/an* replaces *one,* and *the* replaces *that.* We'll be looking more specifically at the rules for using these articles. Although the rules, unfortunately, don't explain all the uses of the articles, they explain most of the uses.

A/An

▶ Use *a* before consonant sounds, *an* before vowel sounds.

Remember that the articles entered the language as sounds, and sound still determines their use. The beginning sound—not the spelling—of a word determines whether *a* or *an* precedes it. *An* goes before *vowel sounds:*

UNIT 5	Go Electronic
Chapter 30	Use the following electronic supplements for additional practice with your writing: • For chapter-by-chapter summaries and exercises, visit the Writing with Confidence Companion Website at http://www.ablongman.com/meyers.
Writing with Confidence ©2003	• For work with the writing process, visit The Longman Writer's Warehouse at http://longmanwriterswarehouse.com (password needed). • For additional practice in grammar, use The Writer's ToolKit Plus CD-ROM.

If Your First Language Is Not English

Many languages—Russian, Polish, and Persian, for example—do not use articles or use them in different ways from the way English does. And many languages do not use prepositions in the same way English does.

| *an* elephant | *an* awful experience |
| *an* enormous task | *an* overcharge |

And for ease of pronunciation, *a* goes before *consonant sounds:*

| *a* lesson | *a* shoe |
| *a* chair | *a* doctor |

When a word beginning with a *u* sounds as if it begins with *y*, use the article *a*.

Long *u* is pronounced like the word *you*, so its sound begins with the sound *y*, a consonant sound. Therefore, *a* precedes words beginning with long *u:*

a unit	*a* unique experience	*a* useful product
	but	
an uncle	*an* unusual experience	*an* ugly mess

When an *h* at the beginning of a word is silent, use the article *an*.

The first sound of words beginning with silent *h* is a vowel. Therefore, *an* precedes these words:

an hour	*an* honor	*an* heir
	but	
a happy moment	*a* humorous story	*a* historian

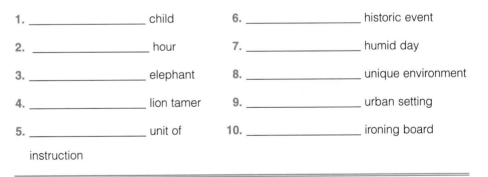

EXERCISE 1 | Writing *A* or *An*

6. Edit
5. Revise
4. Write
3. Organize
2. Prewrite
1. Explore

Place a *or* an *before each of the following words or phrases.*

1. _____ child
2. _____ hour
3. _____ elephant
4. _____ lion tamer
5. _____ unit of instruction

6. _____ historic event
7. _____ humid day
8. _____ unique environment
9. _____ urban setting
10. _____ ironing board

If Your First Language Is Not English

In many languages, you can write "I am student," but in English, you must include the *a* because you mean "I am one of many students." Here are further examples:

He is *a* lawyer.

It is *an* adjective.

She is only *a* little girl.

Singular Countable Nouns: *A/An* versus *The*

With singular countable nouns, use *a* or *an* to mean "any one."

There are two kinds of nouns in English:

1. **countable nouns** (you can put a number before them): one day, three apples, five people
2. **uncountable nouns** (you cannot put a number before them): water, music, honesty, luggage

As you know, the article *a/an* means the same thing as the number *one.* Therefore, use *a/an* only before a singular countable noun.

Here are some examples of *a/an,* meaning "any one" or "one of many":

> Take *a* pencil. (any one pencil; there are many choices)
>
> I just ate *an* apple. (one of many possible apples)
>
> *A* robin built its nest in that tree. (not a specific robin; it could be any one robin)

The

▶ **Use *the* to point out a specific one.**

Unlike *a,* which means "any one," *the* points to something specific—as does the word *that.* So *the* means a *specific one* or a *particular one.* Note that in the following examples the phrase or clause after the noun makes it specific:

> What is *the* assignment for Wednesday? (specifies and distinguishes it from other assignments, such as those for Monday and Friday)
>
> *The* new Chevrolet that Linda bought is beautiful. (specifies and distinguishes it from other cars or Chevrolets)
>
> Let's eat *the* pie your mother made. (specifies and distinguishes it from other pies, perhaps made by someone else)

EXERCISE 2	Writing The

6. Edit
  5. Revise
   4. Write
    3. Organize
     2. Prewrite
      1. Explore

Make each of the following general nouns specific by changing a/an *to* the *and adding a descriptive phrase or clause after the noun. Use several different structures throughout.*

General

1. a red book

2. a new car

3. an old woman

4. a gardening tool

5. a large table

6. an oddly shaped pear

Specific

1. the red book on the table
   or
   the red book that I bought yesterday
   or
   the red book sitting in my room

2. _____

3. _____

4. _____

5. _____

6. _____

▶ **Use *the* when you mean *the only one.***

Sometimes, there is only one of something in a room, a house, or the whole world. In such cases, the noun is specific—because there is no other choice. So the article *the* precedes the noun:

> *The roof* of this house leaks. (The house has only one roof.)
>
> What time does *the clock* say? (There is only one clock in the room.)
>
> *The* sky is cloudy today. (There is only one sky.)

Use *the* to refer to nouns you have already mentioned.

After you've mentioned a noun, you've specified which one you mean.
Therefore, use *the* if you discuss it further:

> Would you buy *a used car* from that man?
>
> Yes, but only if *the car* (now specified) had a five-year guarantee.

EXERCISE 3	Adding Articles

6. Edit
5. Revise
4. Write
3. Organize
2. Prewrite
1. Explore

Write the omitted articles a/an *or the* above the lines.

1. In 1843, ^*a* gentleman from Abbeville, South Carolina, refused ^*a* challenge to ^*a* duel.
   As ^*a* result, his neighbors were so happy that they gave him ^*a* barbecue.

2. In 1849, Elizabeth Blackwell was first woman doctor to practice in the United States.

3. In 1862, twenty-three-year-old man invested $4,000 of his life's savings in oil refinery.
   His name was John D. Rockefeller.

4. In 1864, motto "In God We Trust" appeared on coins for first time.

5. In 1870, Mississippi sent new senator to the U.S. Congress. He was Hiram R. Revels,
   first black man ever to serve in Senate.

6. In 1871, fire started in barn on West Side of Chicago. It swept through city, destroy-
   ing $200 million in property.

Plural Countable Nouns and Uncountable Nouns: Using *The* or Nothing

**Use *the* before all specific nouns; use no article before general plural-
countable or uncountable nouns.**

You cannot place *a/an* before a plural noun. So you must use *the* or no article at
all. *The* indicates a specific plural noun; no article indicates a nonspecific (or general) plural noun. Compare these examples:

> *The three birds on the windowsill* (specific) are pigeons.
> *but*
> *Birds* (in general) are interesting animals.
>
> *The people on my block* (specific) are friendly.
> *but*
> *People* (in general) are attending college in larger numbers.

Collaborative Activity 1

Adding Articles
Write ten sentences,
leaving out the articles.
Include examples of all the
rules just given. In your
group, exchange papers by
passing to the left and add
articles where they are
needed. Then exchange
papers again by passing to
the left for a third student
to check.

Don't place an article before an uncountable noun used in a general sense.
Compare these examples:

> *The water* in Lake Erie (specific) is polluted.
> *but*
> *Water* (in general) covers most of the Earth.

EXERCISE 4	Adding The

6. Edit
5. Revise
4. Write
3. Organize
2. Prewrite
1. Explore

Write the above the lines where the *is needed in the following sentences.*

1. I loved ^*the* movie I saw this weekend.

2. Beginning of movie was particularly exciting.

3. I attend church on Main Street.

4. You should read newest book on fat-free cooking.

5. You ought to try new high-protein diet mentioned in today's newspaper.

6. Dogs make good pets.

Additional Advice about *A/An* and *The*

▶ **Some names require *the*.**

Use *the* before the names of countries that end in *–s* or contain the word *Republic*:

> *the* Netherlands (but just Holland)
>
> *the* British Isles (but just Great Britain)
>
> *the* People's Republic of China (but just China)

Use *the* before the names of rivers, oceans, and seas (but not lakes):

> *the* Nile River   *the* Mediterranean Sea
> *the* Atlantic Ocean   Lake Superior
>
> *Exception: the* Great Salt Lake

Use *the* before college names that begin with the words *College or University:*

> *the* University of Illinois   *the* College of Liberal Arts and Sciences
>   *but*
> Boston College   Indiana University

EXERCISE 5	Adding Missing Articles

6. Edit
5. Revise
4. Write
3. Organize
2. Prewrite
1. Explore

Write the above the lines where it is needed.

1. *The* _____ Caspian Sea

2. _____ University of Pittsburgh

3. _____ Lake Ontario

4. _____ Germany

5. _____ Northwestern University

6. _____ Canada

7. _____ Republic of Bolivia

8. _____ Atlantic Ocean

9. _____ College of DuPage

10. _____ United Arab Republic

Some words replace articles before nouns.

When you place one of the following words before a noun, you cannot use an article. All of these words specify the noun in some way:

every	any	much
each	no	which
either	enough	what
neither	many	his, her, their, and so forth
some	more	Bill's, Mary's, and so forth

Some words go before articles.

Articles usually precede adjectives before a noun:

> the large, round bowl
>
> a dirty old T-shirt

But don't confuse the following five words with adjectives. They're actually adverbs that precede articles:

both *(the)*	half *(the* or *a)*	all *(the)*	many *(a)*	such *(a)*
Examples:	*Both the* men are here.		*Half the* pie is gone.	
	I never saw *such a* fight before.		*Many a* problem can be solved.	

PREPOSITIONS

> "You know my methods. Apply them."
>
> —Sir Arthur Conan Doyle, The Sign of Four

A **preposition** is a little word such as *in, on, off, under,* and *through.* It goes before (*pre–* means "before") a noun or pronoun to show the *position* of the noun or pronoun in space or time within a sentence. For example, phrases containing a preposition + a noun added to the sentence "I saw a fire" can locate the position of the fire and locate the time the action occurred:

> I saw a fire *in* the attic *on* Wednesday.

There are many prepositions and thousands of expressions that use them. Those uses can be confusing, but they're not impossible to learn. We'll look at some of the most common prepositions and their uses. For a list of common expressions using prepositions, see Appendix C.

To Indicate Time

1. *At* a specific or precise time:

> Class ends *at* 3:50 P.M.
>
> *At* midnight, the next day begins.

2. *By* a specific time (means no later than that time):

> Jill said she might be ready as early as 4:30 but certainly *by* 6:00.

3. *Until* a specific time (continuing up to that time):

> Last night Juanita studied *until* 11:00.

4. *In* a specific time period (usually measured in hours, minutes, days, months, or years):

> I will be leaving *in* five minutes.
>
> World War II ended *in* 1945.
>
> *in* the morning, *in* the afternoon, or *in* the evening (but *at* night)

5. *For* a duration of time:

> I have been a student *for* thirteen years.
>
> We have been best friends *for* a long time.

6. *Since* a starting date or time:

> They have been living next door to us *since* 1991.
>
> No one has eaten *since* 8:15.

7. *On* a specific day or date:

> Most people are paid *on* Friday.
>
> The doctor can see you *on* June 12.

8. *During* a continuing time period (or within the time period):

> I was ill *during* the night.
>
> We'll be away from the office *during* the next few hours.

9. Miscellaneous time expressions:

> *on* time (that is, promptly)
>
> *in* a while
>
> *at* the beginning or end (of a day, month, or year)
>
> *in the* middle (of a day, month, or year)
>
> *from* time to time (that is, occasionally)

EXERCISE 6	Writing Prepositions

6. Edit
5. Revise
4. Write
3. Organize
2. Prewrite
1. Explore

Write an appropriate preposition to indicate time in each blank space.

1. <u>On</u> August 1, 1903, a car arrived in New York, completing the first cross-country automobile trip. It had been traveling _____ July 11, when it left San Francisco.

2. _____ June 1905, the Pennsylvania Railroad opened its route between New York and Chicago. The first train made its trip _____ eighteen hours. _____ the next week the New York Central Railroad started its own eighteen-hour train service. Both trains operated _____ only two weeks, and since they had both crashed, killing nineteen people.

3. Most cars _____ the first years of the twentieth century were expensive, costing as much as $2,800. Then came Henry Ford's "universal car," the Model T. _____ several years his cars were priced at $850, but later, the Model T sold for $290.

To Indicate Place

1. *In* a country, area, state, city, or neighborhood:

in France	*in* Michigan	*in* Boston	*in* Lincoln Square

2. *On* (the surface of) a street or block:

We live *on* Wells Avenue.	They work *on* Main Street.

3. *At* a specific address:

We live *at* 1621 Wells Avenue.	We work *at* 945 Main Street.

4. *At* an intersection of two streets:

Let's meet *at* (the corner of) Main Street and Madison.

EXERCISE 7	Writing More Prepositions

6. Edit
5. Revise
4. Write
3. Organize
2. Prewrite
1. Explore

Write an appropriate preposition in each space.

The Origin of a Song

(1) In 1939, the Montgomery Ward store, located <u>on</u> State Street _____ Chicago, was looking for something unusual for its Santa Claus to give to

parents and children. (2) Robert May, who worked _____ the store _____ the advertising department, suggested an illustrated poem, printed _____ a booklet, that families would want to keep _____ their homes and reread each holiday season. (3) May recommended a shiny-nosed reindeer, a Santa's helper; and an artist friend of May's spent hours _____ a local zoo creating sketches of reindeer. (4) May thought about names for his character everywhere he went: _____ work, _____ home, even while standing _____ the corner waiting for a bus. (5) Finally, one day his four-year-old daughter said that she preferred Rudolph.

(6) That Christmas, 2.4 million copies of the "Rudolph" booklet were handed out _____ Montgomery Ward stores everywhere _____ the country. (7) In 1949, a song about Rudolph became so popular that the red-nosed celebrity became a familiar image _____ Germany, Holland, Denmark, Sweden, Norway, England, Spain, Austria, and France.

For Vehicles and Chairs

1. *In(to)* and *out of* for small vehicles (like cars) and chairs with arms:

> I got *in(to)* the cab as someone else was getting *out of* it.
> My father likes to sit *in* his big, comfortable chair.

2. *On* and *off (of)* for large vehicles (such as planes, trains, buses, and boats) and armless chairs or any long seat (such a bench or a sofa):

> We rode *on* the subway and got *off* at our stop.
> He's sitting *on* that bench over there.
> The man *on* the wooden chair is his brother.

EXERCISE 8   Writing More Prepositions

6. Edit
5. Revise
4. Write
3. Organize
2. Prewrite
1. Explore

Write the correct preposition in each space.

1. Years ago, people came to the United States *on*_____ ocean liners. Now almost everyone comes here _____ a plane.

2. We took a ride _____ our new car. We got _____ it at the park and walked around for a while.

3. Some of the people are sitting _____ the couch, and some of them are sitting _____ armchairs.

4. Where do you usually get _____ the bus? Where do you get _____ it?

5. Would you please get _____ that table and sit _____ a chair.

Other Prepositions

1. *For* a reason or *for* someone who benefits:

> Bill went to the barber *for* a haircut.
>
> I bought a present *for* my sister.

2. *About* a subject (or *on* a subject):

> We were talking *about* our plans for next week.
>
> I recently read an article *about* (or on) space travel.

3. *Between* two; *among* three or more:

> We shared the sandwich *between* the two of us.
>
> The five members of the board discussed it *among* themselves.

4. *From* a starting point; *to* a destination:

> We drove *from* Kansas *to* Alaska.

5. *Toward* (in the direction of) a place:

> I walked *toward* the beach but turned south before I arrived at the beach.

6. *Into* (entering) a place or space:

> He just went *into* that room through the back door.

7. *In* (inside of) a place or space:

> He has been running *in* the gym; he hasn't gone outside.

Collaborative Activity 2

Adding Prepositions

Write twenty sentences, leaving out the prepositions. Include examples of all the prepositions explained in this chapter. In your group, exchange papers by passing to the left and add the missing prepositions. Then exchange papers again by passing to the left for a third student to check.

8. *On* a surface:

> The book is *on* the table.
>
> The portrait is hanging *on* the wall.

9. *Off* a surface:

> I took the book *off* the table.
>
> The painting fell *off* the wall.

EXERCISE 9	Writing Still More Prepositions

Write an appropriate preposition in each of the following spaces.

The United States Enters World War II

(1) Japan made an alliance to fight _with_ Germany and Italy _____ 1940. (2) Throughout 1941, the United States moved closer and closer _____ war, but it didn't join the fighting. (3) _____ March 1941, the United States passed a law that allowed supplies to go from the United States _____ Britain.

(4) President Franklin D. Roosevelt began to make a number of speeches _____ the possibility of war. (5) _____ Sunday, December 7, 1941, General George C. Marshall received a message _____ a Japanese attack _____ the Pacific. (6) He sent messages of warning _____ the Philippines, the Panama Canal Zone, and San Francisco. (7) However, the warning didn't get _____ Pearl Harbor _____ Hawaii. (8) _____ 7:55 that same morning, Japanese planes flew _____ Pearl Harbor, filled with bombs _____ the American ships. (9) By 10:00 A.M., eighteen ships were sunk or badly damaged, and about 2500 people were killed. (10) When President Roosevelt heard _____ the attack, he immediately went on radio _____ the purpose _____ informing the American people of the Japanese attack. (11) The next day, Congress declared war _____ Japan and its allies.

EXERCISE 10	Writing In or On

6. Edit
5. Revise
4. Write
3. Organize
2. Prewrite
1. Explore

Write on or in in each space below.

1. You will find the book _on_ the desk and find the papers in the drawer.

2. I will meet you _____ the corner of Fifth and Main.

3. The new table is _____ the corner of the room.

4. I think I left my book _____ my bed.

5. Bill isn't feeling well; he is staying _____ bed today.

6. We haven't gone to a movie _____ a month.

7. Sue is usually _____ time, so she should be here _____ a few minutes.

8. Who is _____ charge of this department?

To Repeat the Meanings of Prefixes

A **prefix** is something attached to the beginning of a word. For example, the prefix *re–* means "again," so the word *review* literally means "view again." Many prefixes in English came from Latin:

Prefix	Meaning	Examples
ad–, ac–, ap–, a–	to	admit, acceptable, apply, agree
con–, com–	with	converse, communicate
ex–, e–	from	excuse, emigrate, exit
in–, im–	in	involved, implicit

Many times—but not always—a word with one of these prefixes also repeats the meaning of the prefix in a preposition following the word:

ad mitted *to* a school; *ac* ceptable *to* me; *ap* ply *to* the school; *a* gree *to* a contract

con versed *with* me; *com* municated *with* a friend

ex cused *from* class; *e* migrate *from* a country

in volved *in* a crime; *im* plicit *in* his statement

A large list of common expressions using prepositions is in Appendix C on pages 423–425. You may wish to memorize these expressions, perhaps in groups of ten at a time. Or you may use the list for a reference as you write and edit your papers.

IN SUMMARY   Mastering the Little Words

To use articles with singular nouns

1. Place *a* before consonant sounds, including long *u*.
2. Place *an* before vowel sounds and silent *h*.
3. With singular countable nouns, use *a/an* when you mean "one of many."
4. Use *the*
   a. to point out a specific or particular one.
   b. when you mean the only one.
   c. to refer to nouns you have already mentioned.

To use articles with plural and uncountable nouns

1. Place *the* before specifics.
2. Use no article before unspecifics.

To use articles with names

1. Use *the* with country names ending in *–s* or containing the word *Republic*.
2. Use *the* with river, ocean, or sea names—but not names of lakes.
3. Use *the* with the names beginning with the words *College* or *University*.

To use prepositions

Consult the guidelines found in this chapter.

EDITING FOR MASTERY

Mastery Exercise 1

Supplying Articles and Prepositions

Insert the twenty-five missing articles and prepositions in the blank spaces.

The Ford Model T (1908–1928)

The Model T Ford was a fragile-looking automobile, but it became _the_ most popular car in American history. Henry Ford sold almost 16 million Model T's (1) _____ years 1908 and 1928. (2) _____ Model T was introduced (3) _____ 1908 and cost $850. It was (4) _____ immediate best-seller, not only because of its low price, but because it was (5) _____ powerful, dependable, and simple enough to make it practical (6) _____ the average American to own and drive.

The Model T, whose nickname was the "Tin Lizzie," sold well (7) _____ the farms and (8) _____ small towns where half (9) _____ country lived. Furthermore, people could drive it (10) _____ the rough roads (11) _____ rural America (12) _____ the early 1900s. And people could depend (13) _____ the Model T. As (14) _____ popular joke expressed it, (15) _____ Model T owner wanted to be buried (16) _____ his Tin Lizzie. When friends asked why, he replied, "Oh, because (17) _____ thing pulled me out of every hole I ever got into, and it ought to pull me out of this one."

Henry Ford didn't invent the Model T; it was developed (18) _____ a team of engineers (19) _____ his Ford Motor Company plant. But he brought together brilliant people who found ways to mass-produce (20) _____ car on (21) _____ moving assembly line. He cut costs by building only one model and developing new methods (22) _____ production. He would then lower (23) _____ price of his cars, which increased sales. In 1924, Americans bought as many Tin Lizzies as all other cars combined, and next year the Model T sold for (24) _____ all-time low price of $290. Ford told Americans: "I am going to democratize the automobile, and when I'm through, everybody will be able to afford one and about everybody will have one." (25) _____ the time he died in 1947, he had fulfilled his promise.

Scorecard: Number of Errors Found and Corrected _____

Collaborative Activity 3

Checking Your Answers
Compare your answers to Mastery Exercise 1 in your collaborative group and report your results to the whole class.

Mastery Exercise 2

Supplying Articles and Prepositions

Insert the twenty-five missing articles and prepositions in the blank spaces.

Cornelius Vanderbilt (1794–1877): A Rich American

Cornelius Vanderbilt, who later became known as _the_ _____ "Commodore" because of his success in shipping, was born in New York, on May 27, 1794. As a young man, he was dedicated (1) _____ making money fast. He quit school (2) _____ the age of eleven and was working (3) _____ himself at sixteen. He bought (4) _____ small boat using money he borrowed (5) _____ his parents and took passengers (6) _____ Staten Island (7) _____ Manhattan daily. He quickly succeeded (8) _____ this business and bought three sailing boats. But he sold (9) _____ boats in 1817 to take advantage of the opportunity to learn the steamboat business.

For several years, Vanderbilt took care of (10) _____ steamboats of another man. But he started his own steamboat business (11) _____ 1829. By 1835, he was earning $60,000 a year, and by 1846 the Commodore was (12) _____ millionaire. (13) _____ main reason (14) _____ his success was that he destroyed his competitors. He cut his fares and offered better service to drive (15) _____ competition out of business. He soon owned more than a hundred boats.

When gold was discovered in California in 1849, Vanderbilt quickly increased his wealth. He established the Accessory Transit Company, which took gold hunters to California (16) _____ boat and on land. His company charged $300 for (17) _____ entire trip, by far the cheapest rate available. Soon Vanderbilt was making (18) _____ million dollars yearly, and he bragged in 1853 that he was worth $11 million.

In 1860, Vanderbilt lost interest (19) _____ boats and decided to enter the railroad business. Looking (20) _____ a bargain, he bought two railroads and then made them into one profitable company. He also purchased the New York Central Railroad (21) _____ spite of efforts to stop him, and he eventually began (22) _____ first route (23) _____ New York and Chicago.

When he died (24) _____ January 4, 1877, the eighty-two-year-old Vanderbilt was the richest man in the United States. He left a fortune to Central University in Nashville, Tennessee, which later changed its name (25) _____ Vanderbilt University. His son William Henry Vanderbilt inherited more than $90 million.

Scorecard: Number of Errors Found and Corrected _____

Use these checklists as you edit your paragraphs and essays. Read over your drafts more than once, checking for a different group of items each time. As the term progresses, you should become more efficient in this practice. Highlight the items on the lists that especially apply to you, and narrow your focus to those items in the repeated readings.

PARAGRAPHS

☐ Are my paragraphs unified and coherent? (see pp. 32-34)

☐ Have I joined sentences correctly? (see pp. 66-71)

☐ Are my sentences varied? (see pp. 195-205)

☐ Have I eliminated unnecessary repetition? (see pp. 200-201)

ARTICLES AND PREPOSITIONS

☐ Have I used the articles *a/an* and *the* correctly? (see pp. 372-377)

☐ Have I used prepositions correctly? (see pp. 377-383)

VERBS

☐ Are my verb tenses correct and consistent? (see pp. 348-351)

☐ Do my subjects and verbs agree? (see pp. 110-111)

☐ Are my verb endings and irregular verb forms correct? (see pp. 124-127; 131-140)

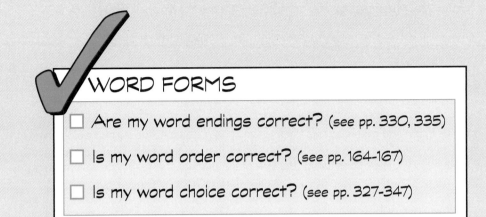

WORD FORMS

- ☐ Are my word endings correct? (see pp. 330, 335)
- ☐ Is my word order correct? (see pp. 164-167)
- ☐ Is my word choice correct? (see pp. 327-347)

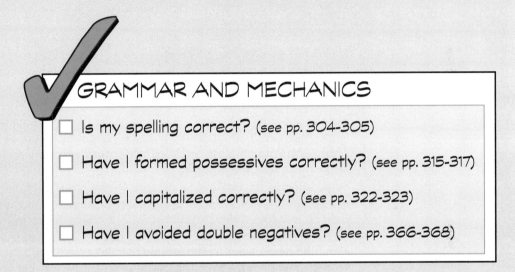

GRAMMAR AND MECHANICS

- ☐ Is my spelling correct? (see pp. 304-305)
- ☐ Have I formed possessives correctly? (see pp. 315-317)
- ☐ Have I capitalized correctly? (see pp. 322-323)
- ☐ Have I avoided double negatives? (see pp. 366-368)

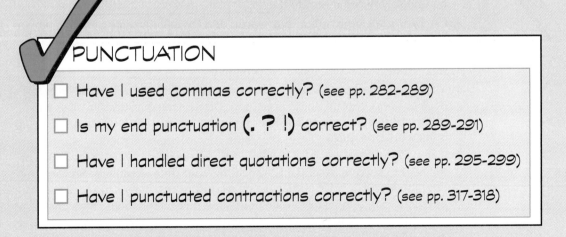

PUNCTUATION

- ☐ Have I used commas correctly? (see pp. 282-289)
- ☐ Is my end punctuation (. ? !) correct? (see pp. 289-291)
- ☐ Have I handled direct quotations correctly? (see pp. 295-299)
- ☐ Have I punctuated contractions correctly? (see pp. 317-318)

Reading Selections

Every good writer is a good reader. Reading provides you with models of writing, along with inspiration to write, ideas to write about, and information to discuss in writing. The following selections should interest you. The authors are professional writers—many of them famous—and even students like you, who had great stories to tell and worked hard to tell them well. Each selection discusses issues that you face each day—or issues that perhaps you've never considered. But one of the purposes of reading is to learn what other people have learned and wish to share with you in their writing.

Read a selection at home and consider the questions that follow it. The questions—as well as the suggestions for writing—will give you additional practice in building the skills you've been working on throughout this book.

The key to reading well is to *read with a purpose*. You should know what to look for and how to understand a reading. Here's some advice to follow as you read these selections—and any selections any time:

1. **Expect to return to a selection after you've read it.** Purposeful reading involves reviewing what you've read to be sure you understand its ideas. That's especially important as you study. You don't have to reread every word, but you have to be able to locate the important ideas.

2. **Highlight or underline main ideas.** Look for thesis statements and topic sentences and identify them, either with a highlighting pen or by underlining. Then, when you return to the selection for further review and study, you can locate main ideas quickly.

3. **Make notes in the margins of the text.** Record your reactions to a sentence or a paragraph: statements of agreement or disagreement ("great!" "yeah, right!"); reactions ("this reminds me of . . ."); objections ("but what about . . .?"); thoughts about things you could discuss in class or in writing ("how about the issue of . . .?"). Think of these notes as a dialogue you're having with the author of the text. The purpose of reading is to get you to think, not simply to swallow ideas, so record your thoughts.

4. **Reread while you're reading.** If you don't understand a sentence or idea, go back and reread the sentence or sentences that precede it. The puzzling passage may then make more sense. But if it doesn't, note the problem in the margin so you can return to it later, or perhaps discuss it with others.

5. **Circle or underline unfamiliar words,** and try to determine their meaning in context—from the sentence and the paragraph they're in. If you must look them up, do so after you finish reading. Then reread the selection. You'll go much faster—and understand much more.

6. **Make journal entries in response to readings.** If the selection raises questions or ideas, capture them in writing. Discuss the questions in class and collect ideas that you can use later if you write about the selection for homework or a quiz.

7. **Know how fast you read—and how fast you read different things.** One of the keys to success in school is budgeting your time effectively. So you ought to know how long it takes you to read twenty pages in social science or twenty pages in history. Time yourself with each textbook. How many pages have you finished in fifteen minutes or an hour? That way, you can set aside enough time to read carefully and thoroughly so you can plan your week's activities.

8. **Take frequent breaks.** Don't try to read a long, difficult selection straight through. Reading with a purpose can be hard work. Pause and rest every fifteen minutes or half hour. But don't take long breaks, or you'll find excuses not to read.

Needing and Wanting Are Different
Jimmy Carrasquillo

* * * *

We all must decide on our priorities, especially when money is involved. Many teenagers think they will be happy if they can buy a car, have all the latest CDs or video games, or eat out with their friends several nights a week. And many teenagers find themselves working too many hours at part-time jobs while their schoolwork suffers. In the following article, Jimmy Carrasquillo, a high-school senior, describes his problems with balancing work, school, and athletics. As you read it, notice how he got into trouble, how he woke up—literally—and saw what the trouble was, and what he has learned from the experience.

Jimmy Carrasquillo's essay first appeared in Newsweek *magazine.*

1   "Mom, can I have some money?" Those are the words my mother used to hear all the time. In return, I heard, "Why don't you get a job? Not to make me happy, but so you have your own money and gain a bit more responsibility." So last year I got a job with Montgomery Ward's photo studio, working about twenty-five hours a week. For $5 an hour, I was a telephone salesman, trying to persuade people to come in for a free photograph.

2   All this was during football season and I was on the team as a kicker. To do football and homework and my job at the same time became really hard. I was burning out, falling asleep at school, not able to concentrate. My first class was physics and I hated it. I'd just sit there with my hand on my cheek and my elbow on the desk, and start dozing. One day the teacher asked my partner what I was doing and she said, "Oh, he's sleeping." The teacher came to the back of the class and stared at me. The whole class looked at me for about two minutes and laughed.

3   My third-period history teacher was really concerned. She was cool. A lot of the time, I'd fall asleep in her class. She'd scream, "Wake up!" and slam her hand on my desk. I'd open my eyes for about two minutes, pay attention and go back to sleep. She asked me if I could handle school, football and work. I said, "Yeah. I'm doing OK so far." She said, "Why? Why all this?"

4   I told her it was for the things I needed, when actually it was for the things I wanted. Needing and wanting are different. Needing something is like your only shoes have holes in them. But when a new pair of sneakers came out and I liked them, I'd get them. My parents didn't feel it was right, but they said, "It's your money, you learn to deal with it." Within two years I had bought thirty pairs. My parents would laugh. "You got your job, you got your money—but where's your money now?" They didn't realize how much my job was hurting my schoolwork.

5   My priorities were screwed up. On a typical night I did about an hour of homework. A lot of times it was hard for me to make decisions: do I want to be at work or do I want to be at practice? Do I want to worry about what I'll have in the future? Sometimes I felt there was no right choice. One week in the winter I had to work extra days, so I missed a basketball game and two practices. (I'm on that team, too.) When a substitution opportunity came at the next game, the coach looked at me and said, "OK, we're running I-5," a new play they had developed during the practice I had missed. I told him I didn't know it, so he told me to sit back down. I felt really bad, because there was my chance to play and I couldn't.

6   I really did resent work. If I hadn't been so greedy, I could have been at practice. But I kept working, and the job did help me in some ways. When you have a lot of responsibilities, you have to learn to balance everything. You just grow up faster. At home, your parents always say, "I pay the bills so while you're here you're under my rules." But now with my money I say, "No, no. You didn't pay for that, I did. That's mine."

7   Slowly, I've come to deal with managing money a lot better. At first, as soon as I had money, it was gone. Now it goes straight into my bank account. This year I decided not to work at all during the football season. I have a lot more time to spend with other players after the game and feel more a part of the team. I've only fallen asleep once in class so far. I'm more confident and more involved in my classes. My marks are A's and B's, a full grade better than this time last year. I'm hoping that will help me get into a better college. I don't go shopping as much. I look at all the sneakers in school and think, "I could have those," but I don't need them. Last year I thought that being mature meant doing everything. But I'm learning that part of growing up is limiting yourself, knowing how to decide what's important, and what isn't.

Questions for Analysis

1. Paragraph 1 suggests the reasons that Jimmy Carrasquillo decided to get a job. What were they?

2. Paragraph 2 does not begin with a topic sentence. What is the topic sentence? Underline it. Find and underline the topic sentences in paragraphs 3–7.

3. What, according to Jimmy, is the difference between wanting and needing? What example does he cite to illustrate these differences?

4. This essay essentially describes the trouble Jimmy got into from trying to work so many hours. But, aside from the money he made, did the experience benefit him? If so, what were those benefits, and where does he describe them?

5. Paragraph 7 draws a number of contrasts. List them. Then write in your own words what main lessons they show that Jimmy has learned.

Writing Assignments

1. Discuss an important lesson you've learned the hard way. What happened, and what did it teach you?

2. Discuss a time when someone helped you understand and perhaps correct a mistake you were making. What happened? What was the result?

3. Write your own definition of maturity and illustrate it with two examples: one of immature behavior and another of mature behavior.

The Struggle to Be an All-American Girl
Elizabeth Wong

* * * *

Many people in the United States are bilingual, speaking one language at home or in their community and another language at school or work. And many people face conflicts between the traditions and desires of their parents and their own desires to assimilate—fit in— within the "all-American" culture. Elizabeth Wong was one of those people. Her mother insisted that Elizabeth and her brother attend a Chinese language school, and the essay that follows explores the conflicts involved. As you read it, notice the physical description that reinforces Wong's feelings toward the school. Notice the contrasts between the lessons of the Chinese school and the American school, the life in Chinatown and outside of Chinatown, and the attitudes toward speaking Chinese and speaking English.

Elizabeth Wong, who grew up in Los Angeles's Chinatown, is an award-winning Chinese playwright whose works focus on Asian American subject matter. Among her plays are China Doll, Letters to a Student Revolutionary, *and* Kimchee & Chitlins. *She is the staff writer for the television sitcom* All-American Girl.

Before reading the essay, use your dictionary to look up the following words:

1. stoic   3. repress
2. dissuade   4. maniacal

5. ideograph
6. pedestrian (adjective)

7. pidgin
8. exasperation

1 It's still there, the Chinese school on Yale Street where my brother and I used to go. Despite the new coat of paint and the high wire fence, the school I knew 10 years ago remains remarkably, stoically the same.

2 Every day at 5 P.M., instead of playing with our fourth- and fifth-grade friends or sneaking out to the empty lot to hunt ghosts and animal bones, my brother and I had to go to Chinese school. No amount of kicking, screaming, or pleading could dissuade my mother, who was solidly determined to have us learn the language of our heritage.

3 Forcibly, she walked us the seven long, hilly blocks from our home to school, depositing our defiant tearful faces before the stern principal. My only memory of him is that he swayed on his heels like a palm tree, and he always clasped his impatient twitching hands behind his back. I recognized him as a repressed maniacal child killer, and knew that if we ever saw his hands we'd be in big trouble.

4 We all sat in little chairs in an empty auditorium. The room smelled like Chinese medicine, an imported faraway mustiness. Like ancient mothballs or dirty closets. I hated that smell. I favored crisp new scents. Like the soft French perfume that my American teacher wore in public school.

5 There was a stage far to the right, flanked by an American flag and the flag of the Nationalist Republic of China, which was also red, white and blue but not as pretty.

6 Although the emphasis at the school was mainly language—speaking, reading, writing—the lessons always began with an exercise in politeness. With the entrance of the teacher, the best student would tap a bell and everyone would get up, kowtow, and chant, "Sing san ho," the phonetic for "How are you, teacher?"

7 Being ten years old, I had better things to learn than ideographs copied painstakingly in lines that ran right to left from the tip of a moc but, a real ink pen that had to be held in an awkward way if blotches were to be avoided. After all, I could do the multiplication tables, name the satellites of Mars, and write reports on *Little Women* and *Black Beauty*. Nancy Drew, my favorite book heroine, never spoke Chinese.

8 The language was a source of embarrassment. More times than not, I had tried to disassociate myself from the nagging loud voice that followed me wherever I wandered in the nearby American supermarket outside Chinatown. The voice belonged to my grandmother, a fragile woman in her seventies who could outshout the best of the street vendors. Her humor was raunchy, her Chinese rhythmless, patternless. It was quick, it was loud, it was unbeautiful. It was not like the quiet, lilting romance of French or the gentle refinement of the American South. Chinese sounded pedestrian. Public.

9 In Chinatown, the comings and goings of hundreds of Chinese on their daily tasks sounded chaotic and frenzied. I did not want to be thought of as mad, as talking gibberish. When I spoke English, people nodded at me, smiled sweetly, said encouraging words. Even the people in my culture would cluck and say that I'd do well in life. "My, doesn't she move her lips fast," they would say, meaning that I'd be able to keep up with the world outside Chinatown.

10 My brother was even more fanatical than I about speaking English. He was especially hard on my mother, criticizing her, often cruelly, for her pidgin speech—smatterings of Chinese scattered like chop suey in her conversation. "It's not 'What it is,' Mom," he'd say in exasperation. "It's 'What is it, what is it, what is it!'" Sometimes Mom might leave out an occasional "the" or "a," or perhaps a verb of being. He would stop her in mid-sentence: "Say it again, Mom. Say it right." When he tripped over his own tongue, he'd blame it on her: "See, Mom, it's all your fault. You set a bad example."

11 What infuriated my mother most was when my brother cornered her on her consonants, especially "r." My father had played a cruel joke on Mom by assigning her an American name that her tongue wouldn't allow her to say. No matter how hard she tried, "Ruth" always ended up "Luth" or "Roof."

12 After two years of writing with a moc but and reciting words with multiples of meanings, I finally was granted a cultural divorce. I was permitted to stop Chinese school.

13   I thought of myself as multicultural. I preferred tacos to egg rolls; I enjoyed Cinco de Mayo* more than Chinese New Year. At last, I was one of you; I wasn't one of them. Sadly, I still am.

*Fifth of May, which is a Mexican national holiday celebrating its independence from France in 1862.

Questions for Analysis

1. What is the thesis—the main point—of the essay? Wong develops her essay through a series of contrasts, often using very specific details. Underline each one. How do these contrasts support the thesis?
2. Wong's story combines description, narration, and comparison-contrast. What comparisons or contrasts does she make? Underline them.
3. What did Wong learn in Chinese school? Was it only the Chinese language?
4. Wong says in the eighth paragraph that Chinese "was a source of embarrassment." Why?
5. What do you think Wong means by comments in paragraph 13, especially the concluding sentence?

Writing Assignments

1. Wong probably would never go back to the Chinese language school. Describe a place that you would never go back to again and make clear to the reader why.
2. Describe a behavior of an adult (a parent, perhaps) that used to embarrass you and explain why. Or, describe some aspect of your background that used to embarrass you and explain why.
3. Visit a place from your childhood that you haven't been to in a long time. Describe it now and compare it to how you remembered it.
4. Contrast at least one way in which your behavior at home is different from your behavior outside of home. Develop the contrast through specific examples.
5. Explain why Elizabeth Wong was embarrassed by her grandmother's and mother's speech. Cite examples from Wong's essay to support your explanation.

Alligator
Bailey White

* * * *

Probably every family has an eccentric—someone whose behavior is odd but also entertaining. Young children often find this behavior fascinating. How could that person be so brave, or foolish, or weird? The following essay by Bailey White describes the rather unusual relationship between a young child's aunt and an alligator. As you read it, notice how the behavior of the aunt and alligator are described as a step-by-step process. Notice how the process moves from "taming" the alligator, to "teaching" it to bellow, and then to making the alligator appear without asking. Notice, too, how the relationship between the aunt and alligator changes.

Bailey White, who was born in 1950 in Thomasville, Georgia, is a commentator on National Public Radio and author of several books including Mama Makes Up Her Mind *and* Quite a Year for Plums. *She lives in the same house in which she grew up.*

1   I remember as a little child watching my Aunt Belle's wide rump disappear into the cattails and marsh grass at the edge of a pond as she crawled on her hands and knees to meet a giant alligator face to face. She was taming him, she said. We children would wait high up on the bank with our eyes and mouths wide open, hoping that the alligator wouldn't eat her up, but not wanting to miss it if he did.

2   Finally Aunt Belle would get as close to him as she wanted, and they would stare at each other for some minutes. Then my aunt would jump up, wave her arms in the air, and shout, "Whoo!" With a tremendous leap and flop the alligator would throw himself into the water. The little drops from that splash would reach all the way to where we were standing, and my aunt would come up the bank drenched and exultant. "I have to show him who's boss," she would tell us.

3   Later, Aunt Belle taught that alligator to bellow on command. She would drive the truck down to the edge of the pond and gun the engine. We would sit in the back, craning our necks to see him coming. He would come fast across the pond, raising two diagonal waves behind him as he came. He would haul himself into the shallow water and get situated just right. His back was broad and black. His head was as wide as a single bed. His tail would disappear into the dark pond water. He was the biggest alligator anyone had ever seen.

4   Then my aunt would turn off the engine. We would all stop breathing. The alligator would swell up. He would lift his head, arch his tail, and bellow. The sound would come from deep inside. It was not loud, but it had a carrying quality. It was like a roar, but with more authority than a lion's roar. It was a sound you hear in your bones. If we were lucky, he would bellow ten times. Then Aunt Belle would throw him a dead chicken.

5   The day came when she could just walk down to the pond and look out across the water. The alligator would come surging up to the bank, crawl out, and bellow.

6   By this time he was very old. My aunt got old, too. Her children had all grown up. She got to where she was spending a lot of time down at the pond. She'd go down there and just sit on the bank. When the alligator saw her, he'd swim over and climb out. He never bellowed anymore. They would just sit and look at each other. After a while my aunt would walk back to the house. The alligator would swim out to where the water was deep and black, and float for a minute; then he'd just disappear, without even a ripple. That's how he did.

7   But one day he didn't come when Aunt Belle went to the pond. He didn't come the next day, or the day after. All that summer, Aunt Belle walked around and around the pond looking, listening, and sniffing. "Something as big as that, you'd know if he was dead, this hot weather," she'd say. Finally, she stopped going down to the pond.

8   But sometimes, on the nights of the full moon in springtime, I can hear an alligator bellow. It comes rolling up through the night. It's not loud, but it makes me sit up in bed and hold my breath. Sometimes I hear it ten times. It's a peaceful sound.

Questions for Analysis

1. In paragraph 1, Bailey White provides details about the children's reactions to Aunt Belle's meetings with the alligator. What do the details reveal about the children's feelings and thoughts?

2. At the end of paragraph 2, the aunt is described as "exultant." Without looking up the word in the dictionary, tell what it seems to mean.

3. Paragraphs 4 and 5 describe how Aunt Belle trained the alligator to come to the edge of the pond and bellow. What detail—more than any other—suggests the reason that the alligator became trained?

Writing Assignments

1. Have you ever had a pet? Describe your relationship with it, especially how it behaved or behaves typically or in a particular situation.

2. Have you or someone you know ever housebroken a pet or taught an animal a trick? Explain how the process worked.

3. Do you have or did you have a relative or friend who behaved or behaves oddly? Describe that behavior.

4. In your own words, write an explanation of what the alligator meant to Aunt Belle.

Hellraiser
Jessica Shattuck

* * * *

Teenage life in poor communities is often filled with violence, and teenagers may not have a realistic view of the dangers or consequences involved. Gangs can be glamorous attractions, and TV and movie violence glorifies guns and death. But have you known anyone who has died or suffered greatly as a result of guns? The report that follows describes the activities of one woman to combat the use of guns in her community. As you read it, notice how it first presents the where–when–who–what information, then describes the programs that the woman has sponsored in her community. Notice, too, how the report uses quotations to illustrate and dramatize its main ideas.

Before you read the report, use your dictionary to define the following words:

1. prevalence
2. canvass (verb)
3. vigil

1   As a longtime education reformer and domestic violence counselor in Guadalupe, Arizona, Socorro Hernandez Bernasconi thought she had seen the worst problems facing young people in her town. But in 1990, she came face to face with a new threat to Guadalupe's youth—the prevalence of guns in the community.

2   A mother of seven children and one of the first people from Guadalupe to obtain a college degree, Bernasconi says, "My home was a safe haven—we had no alcohol, no guns . . . but that wasn't enough." Bernasconi says her nineteen-year-old son Sergio killed himself at a party with friends while imitating the game of Russian roulette depicted in the movie *The Deer Hunter.*

3   In recent years, Guadalupe, a town of 5,400 south of Phoenix populated mostly by Latinos and Yaqui Indians—close to half of whom are under the age of nineteen—has seen a sharp increase in the number of youth-related violent deaths. Bernasconi says three teenagers died of gunshot wounds in the first month of 1998 alone.

4   Determined to change the circumstances that she believes helped cause her son's death, Bernasconi left her job as the director of a local women's shelter to organize young people against gun violence. She founded a community group called GLAAD (Guadalupe Libre Alcohol, Armas y Drogas) and started a program urging teenagers to give up their firearms in exchange for rewards. With no institutional support or funding, she canvassed local organizations for donations of items she could trade for the guns, acquiring computers from the learning center, bicycles from the fire department, and vouchers for free guitar lessons from area musicians. The teenage members of GLAAD spread the word and, little by little, the guns began to trickle in.

5   But rather than turning the firearms over to the police department for destruction, as most gun-redemption programs do, GLAAD gives the weapons it collects to local welders who turn them into artwork and tools, ensuring they will not find their way back to the streets.

6   Inspired by the biblical verse Isaiah 2:4 ("They shall beat their swords into ploughshares"), Bernasconi had a welder make the first rifle GLAAD collected into a shovel, and had another group of guns made into candlesticks for the altar of a Guadalupe church.

7   "Socorro brings all of us together in teaching our kids not to use guns," says Ramon Guzman, one of the welders who works with GLAAD. "The shovel at the end of the rifle barrel reminds kids, 'You use guns, you're digging your own grave.'" One of Guzman's creations has been used to bury several of Guadalupe's recent victims of gun violence.

8   "We're experts at recycling," Bernasconi says. "When it comes to people who are into drugs and violence and destructive ways of life, the pieces we've made are symbols of the change they can undergo too."

9   In addition to the gun-redemption program, she has instituted a ride-along system in which local kids and community leaders accompany cops on their beats. She has also

organized vigils at the scene of violent crimes, and started a college scholarship fund, which has raised $12,000 through youth-run car washes over the last two years.

10 Most important, Bernasconi has gotten the young people themselves involved in the process of change. "Guadalupe is too small a town for how many people get killed," says fifteen-year-old Mary Alvarez, one of the teens who is involved in GLAAD. "Hopefully, getting these guns off the streets will help change that."

Questions for Analysis

1. What is the meaning of the title? Who is the "hellraiser"?
2. What led Socorro Hernandez Bernasconi to start GLAAD? How does its program differ from other programs in which people turn in their guns for rewards? What transition in paragraph 5 signals that difference?
3. Several of the pieces of art made from melted guns symbolize ideas. What are these pieces of art and what do they represent?
4. When Bernasconi says, "We're experts at recycling," in paragraph 8, what kind of recycling is she referring to? Is there more than one kind?
5. How many other kinds of programs has she started? What words identify them for the readers?

Writing Assignments

1. Have you ever witnessed an act of violence—intentional or accidental? Describe what happened.
2. Do you know someone who has been active in trying to help others? Describe what that person does, or, if you know, tell how that person became active.
3. Describe the activities of an organization in your community, at your college, or elsewhere—especially an organization that is working to improve the lives of people or animals.
4. Write a one-paragraph summary of the main ideas of this report. Include only the most important details, not the examples. Write the summary in your own words; do not copy from the report.

Two Views of the Mississippi
Mark Twain

* * * *

The context in which we view anything determines how we interpret what we see. How does what we see affect our lives at that moment? In the following essay, Mark Twain contrasts his youthful admiration for the Mississippi River with his adult concerns for navigating a boat across the river. As you read the essay, notice the order in which he first presents the details—and how he later establishes contrasts by presenting the details in precisely the same order. Notice how the word choice in the first description reinforces the beauty and poetry of the river, while the word choice in the later description reinforces the practical applications of what Twain sees.

Mark Twain (1835–1910) was the pen name of Samuel Langhorne Clemens, and, as you can guess from this essay, he worked on a riverboat when he was young. He is the author of many novels, including Tom Sawyer *and* Huckleberry Finn, *and of countless short stories and essays.*

Before reading the essay, use your dictionary to look up the following words:

1. shoal
2. compass (verb)
3. sow (verb)

1   Now when I had mastered the language of this water, and had come to know every trifling feature that bordered the great river as familiarly as I knew the letters of the alphabet, I had made a valuable acquisition. But I had lost something which could never be restored to me while I lived. All the grace, the beauty, the poetry, had gone out of the majestic river! I still keep in mind a certain wonderful sunset which I witnessed when steamboating was new to me. A broad expanse of the river was turned to blood; in the middle distance the red hue brightened into gold, through which a solitary log came floating black and conspicuous; in one place a long, slanting mark lay sparkling upon the water; in another the surface was broken by boiling, tumbling rings, that were as many tinted as an opal; where the ruddy flush was faintest, was a smooth spot that was covered with graceful circles and radiating lines, ever so delicately traced; the shore on our left was densely wooded, and the somber shadow that fell from this forest was broken in one place by a long, ruffled trail that shone like silver; and high above the forest wall a clean-stemmed dead tree waved a single leafy bough that glowed like a flame in the unobstructed splendor that was flowing from the sun. There were graceful curves, reflected images, woody heights, soft distances; and over the whole scene, far and near, the dissolving lights drifted steadily, enriching it every passing moment with new marvels of coloring.

2   I stood like one bewitched. I drank it in, in a speechless rapture. The world was new to me, and I had never seen anything like this at home. But as I have said, a day came when I began to cease from noting the glories and the charms which the moon and the sun and the twilight wrought upon the river's face; another day came when I ceased altogether to note them. Then, if that sunset scene had been repeated, I should have looked upon it without rapture, and should have commented upon it, inwardly, after this fashion: "This sun means that we are going to have wind tomorrow; that floating log means that the river is rising, small thanks to it; that slanting mark on the water refers to a bluff reef which is going to kill somebody's steamboat one of these nights, if it keeps on stretching out like that; those tumbling 'boils' show a dissolving bar and a changing channel there; the lines and circles in the slick water over yonder are a warning that that troublesome place is shoaling up dangerously; that silver streak in the shadow of the forest is the 'break' from a new snag, and he has located himself in the very best place he could have found to fish for steamboats; that tall dead tree, with a single living branch, is not going to last long, and then how is a body ever going to get through this blind place at night without the friendly old landmark?"

3   No, the romance and beauty were all gone from the river. All the value any feature of it had for me now was the amount of usefulness it could furnish toward compassing the safe piloting of a steamboat. Since those days, I have pitied doctors from my heart. What does the lovely flush in a beauty's cheek mean to a doctor but a "break" that ripples above some deadly disease? Are not all her visible charms sown thick with what are to him the signs and symbols of hidden decay? Does he ever see her beauty at all, or doesn't he simply view her professionally, and comment upon her unwholesome condition all to himself? And doesn't he sometimes wonder whether he has gained most or lost most by learning his trade?

Questions for Analysis

1. What is the thesis of the essay? Where in the first paragraph does Twain state the thesis? Where (in the third paragraph) does he state it more explicitly?

2. What sentence in the second paragraph establishes the transition from a poetic view of the Mississippi to a matter-of-fact, practical view?

3. Compare the language of the two views of the Mississippi. Make a grid on a sheet of paper by drawing a line down the middle. On one side, list the details of the first description, and on the other side list the parallel details of the second. What do you notice about the language Twain uses for each?

4. At the end of his essay, Twain says he pities doctors. Why? How does the point relate to his two views of the Mississippi?

Writing Assignments

1. Describe a place that you view differently as an adult from the way you viewed it as a child. Contrast the two views and explain why they have changed.

2. Describe a place that you view differently from the way someone else views it. Explain why your views differ.

3. Discuss whether Twain lost or gained something important as he saw the Mississippi in a different light as an adult.

Divining the Strange Eating Habits of Kids
Ellen Goodman

* * * *

Everyone who has teenage children or has ever been a teenager should enjoy and understand this essay. As you read it, notice how Ellen Goodman first establishes a "problem" that she then tries to solve. Notice how she then explains her mistaken interpretation of the cause of the problem. Finally, notice her categories or classifications of real causes for the problem.

Ellen Goodman, who was born in 1941, is a Pulitzer Prize winning columnist and the author of many books, including Value Judgments *and (with co-author Patricia O'Brien)* I Know Just What You Mean: The Power of Friendship in Women's Lives. *She has received many awards for her work in furthering the causes of civil rights and the rights of women.*

Before reading the essay, use your dictionary to look up the following words:

1. refrain
2. dire
3. divine (verb)

4. anthropology
5. intrinsic
6. nomadic

1   As a parent who works with words for a living, I have prided myself over many years for a certain skill in breaking the codes of childspeak. I began by interpreting baby talk, moved to more sophisticated challenges like "chill out" and I graduated with "wicked good."

2   One phrase, however, always stumped me. I was unable to crack the meaning of the common cry echoing through most middle-class American households: "There's Nothing to Eat in This House!"

3   This exclamation becomes a constant refrain during the summer months when children who have been released from the schoolhouse door grow attached to the refrigerator door. It is during the summer when the average taxpayer realizes the true cost-effectiveness of school: It keeps kids out of the kitchen for roughly seven hours a day. A feat no parent is able to match.

4   At first, like so many others, I assumed that "NETH!" [as in "Nothing to Eat in This House"] was a straightforward description of reality; if there was NETH, it was because the children had eaten it all. After all, an empty larder is something you come to expect when you live through the locust phase of adolescence.

5   I have one friend with three teenage sons who swears that she doesn't even have to unload her groceries anymore. Her children feed directly from the bags, rather like ponies. I have other friends who buy ingredients for supper only on the way home so that supper doesn't turn into lunch.

6   Over the years, I have considered color-coding food with red, yellow and green stickers. Green for eat. Yellow for eat only if you are starving. Red for "touch this and you die."

7   However, I discovered that these same locusts can stand in front of a relatively full refrigerator while bleating the same pathetic choruses of "NETH! NETH!" By carefully observing my research subjects, I discovered that the demand of "NETH!" may indeed have little to do with the supply.

8   What then does the average underage eater mean when he or she bleats "NETH! NETH!" You will be glad to know that I have finally broken the code for the "nothing" in NETH and offer herewith, free of charge, my translation.

9   NETH includes:

10   1. Any food that must be cooked, especially in a pan or by convectional heat. This covers boiling, frying or baking. Toasting is acceptable under dire conditions.

11   2. Any food that is in a frozen state with the single exception of ice cream. A frozen pizza may be considered "something to eat" only if there is a microwave oven on hand.

12   3. Any food that must be assembled before eaten. This means tuna that is still in a can. It may also mean a banana that has to be peeled, but only in extreme cases. Peanut butter and jelly are exempt from this rule as long as they are on the same shelf beside the bread.

13   4. Leftovers. Particularly if they must be reheated [See 1.]

14   5. Plain yogurt or anything else that might have been left as a nutrition trap.

15   6. Food that must be put on a plate, or cut with a knife and fork, as opposed to ripped with teeth while watching videos.

16   7. Anything that is not stored precisely at eye level. This includes:

17   8. Any item on a high cupboard shelf, unless it is a box of cookies and:

18   9. Any edible in the back of the refrigerator, especially on the middle shelf.

19   While divining the nine meanings of "NETH!" I should also tell you that I developed an anthropological theory about the eating patterns of young Americans. For the most part, I am convinced, Americans below the age of 20 have arrested their development at the food-gathering stage.

20   They are intrinsically nomadic. Traveling in packs, they engage in nothing more sophisticated than hand-to-mouth dining. They are, in effect, strip eaters who devour the ripest food from one home, and move on to another.

21   Someday, I am sure they will learn about the use of fire, not to mention forks. Someday, they will be cured of the shelf-blindness, the inability to imagine anything hidden behind a large milk carton. But for now, they can only graze. All the rest is NETHing.

Questions for Analysis

1. Who is Ellen Goodman's audience, and what is her purpose in writing to them? Where does she state her point, and what is it?

2. Goodman writes a classification with nine categories. She does not state her criterion for classification. What is it?

3. After listing the nine meanings of NETH, Goodman makes several other observations. Are they irrelevant to her point? Why or why not?

4. How would you describe Goodman's attitude toward teenagers? What evidence from the essay supports your viewpoint?

5. Goodman writes several sentence fragments. Underline them. Why do you think she chooses to do so?

Writing Assignments

1. Write a paragraph or an essay in which you categorize the items that do not get put away or thrown out in a typical teenager's room.

2. Why do you think that, in Goodman's words, "Americans below the age of 20 have arrested their development at the food-gathering stage"? What from Goodman's categories supports your argument?

3. Why do teenagers tend to "travel in packs"? Cite examples from your own experience or the experience of people you know to support your explanation.

The Natchez Indians
Adapted from The People's Almanac #3

* * * *

We tend to think that the customs of our culture and community are "natural." Men, women, and children have certain roles, and so do the leaders of the community. Think about who takes or took the main responsibility for raising the children in your family. Think about the class structure in your society or culture. Who are your leaders? Whom do you look up to? What determines membership in the higher or lower classes? The following essay describes a culture that has disappeared, but that, while it existed, was unique. As you read it, notice its descriptions and classifications of the four levels within the society. Notice its discussion of the importance of women. And notice its discussion of how and why the society disappeared.

1   The Natchez were a Native American tribe that lived on the bank of the Mississippi River near what is now Natchez, Mississippi. They may have come to that area from Mexico. Although they were farmers, they also hunted, made pottery, and wove clothes. They created a society in which everyone knew his and—more important—*her* role. Unfortunately, their way of life, and the people themselves, died out in a period of less than 200 years.

2   The society of the Natchez was based on their religion. The high priest ruled the Natchez, who worshiped him as the "Great Sun," a descendant of the sun god. There were four classes in the Natchez society. The highest class was the Suns, who were rulers and priests and relatives of the Great Sun. The second highest class were the Nobles, and the third highest were the Honored Men. The lowest class, known as Stinkards, served the upper classes. But people rose from one class to another because all people of the upper classes had to marry below them.

3   Although the high priest was the main ruler, the true powers behind Natchez society were women. When a Great Sun died, for example, his mother or sister chose the next Great Sun from among his brothers or sons. Female Suns also led privileged lives. Their husbands were commoners and had to wait on them and obey their commands. If the husband was unfaithful to a Sun woman, she could have him beheaded. But she was allowed as many lovers as she desired.

4   In 1700, about 4,000 Natchez people lived peacefully in farming communities and grew squash, corn, pumpkins, and beans. But they soon engaged in bloody battles with the French who had settled on their land. In 1729, the French commander of a fort on Natchez territory ordered them to give him their main village for his personal plantation. The Natchez were outraged. They killed 200 Frenchmen, captured 400 women and children, and burned the fort. The French fought back and slaughtered the Natchez.

5   This was the beginning of the end of the tribe. About 400 surrendered and were sold into slavery in the Caribbean Islands. The rest of the survivors—no more than 450—joined other Native American tribes for protection. The slaves soon died, and the rest of the Natchez lost their tribal identity and language. During the 1800s, the United States government forced them to settle in a territory that is now part of Oklahoma. By 1900, there were only 20 Natchez left, and in a short time they disappeared. A unique culture and people were erased forever.

Questions for analysis

1. Why is an entire essay necessary to define the Natchez? What is the purpose of each paragraph in the composition?

2. Which sentence in paragraph 1 provides a formal definition of the Natchez? What is the function of the body sentences of the paragraph? What is the function of the last sentence of the paragraph?

3. The last two sentences of the opening paragraph introduce key ideas discussed later in the essay. Underline those ideas. Which paragraphs specifically discuss each of the ideas? Identify the idea with a one- or two-word label.

4. Find and underline topic sentences in paragraphs 2, 3, and 5. Does the topic sentence always begin the paragraph?

5. In your own words, write a short summary of the powers of women described in paragraph 3.

Writing Assignments

1. Write a description of the differing roles of the people in your own family or immediate community. Who is primarily responsible for each important task—making money, caring for children, preparing meals, and so on? Who shares these responsibilities? Give examples.

2. Describe a typical gathering of your family or community in which different generations perform different roles. It might be an important holiday, a reunion, a traditional dinner, or a monthly or yearly event. What things happen, and who does each one?

3. Have there been any important changes in the roles people perform in your family or community? Describe one change, showing what used to happen before the change and what happened or happens afterward.

The Writing on the Wall
Adapted from The People's Almanac

* * * *

There are many things around us that we see every day but don't think about very much. One of the traits of a good writer is to consider and analyze these things and to discuss them in ways that make us think about them. The following essay on graffiti is an example. As you read it, notice that it begins with a definition and then continues with a three-part classification. Notice the examples of each part of the classification. And notice the purpose of the essay—to entertain.

Before you read the essay, use your dictionary to define the following words:

1. archaeologist
2. motive
3. vandalism

1   The term *graffiti*—a plural noun, by the way—comes from an Italian word that means scribbling or scratching, and archaeologists use it to refer to the writings and drawings on the walls of caves or ancient buildings. Most people, however, are familiar with modern graffiti, such as the writings and pictures found on the walls of washrooms, buildings, subway cars, and billboards. Those with a mind toward classifying these scribbles have divided them into three types, based on the motives of the graffiti-maker: identity graffiti, message or opinion graffiti, and art graffiti. A fourth type, dialogue graffiti, overlaps the other three.

2   Identity graffiti represent an attempt by someone (let's assume he is male) to immortalize his existence by writing his name and the date, announcing his current romance ("John loves Mary"), or simply stating, "I was here." This urge to leave a personal imprint seems as to be old as the human race. Signatures of ancient Greek soldiers are still scratched on the sphinx and on the Great Pyramid at Giza in Egypt.

3   The writer of messages or opinions likes to tell the world exactly what is on his or her mind. Most message graffiti make political statements, although some also deal with philosophy, religion, the arts, and sex. Here are a few examples:
   "We are the people our parents warned us about."
   "Carry me back to old virginity."
   "May your life be like a roll of toilet paper—long and useful."

4   The drawers of art graffiti display their greatest achievements in big cities, where inner-city kids decorate walls with spray-painted creations. Instead of leaving a simple message, these unpaid exterior decorators write their own names (or the names of their gangs) in swirls, curlicues, and flourishes of all colors. Some graffiti artists cover a building wall with complex designs or murals. Although most of these graffiti are only vandalism, some spray-painters have been paid to do murals for office buildings. An art gallery in New York even held a graffiti exhibit.

5   Sometimes graffiti-makers start talking back to each other, and a graffiti dialogue is born. These dialogues can develop into long-winded conversations, with several scribblers getting into the act. A subway poster for a job retraining program showed a complicated electrical unit with a question written underneath: "When this circuit learns your job, what are you going to do?" Then came the graffiti responses: "Go on relief," "Pull the plug," and "Become a circuit breaker." Another poster asked, "Did you make New York dirty today?" and received the obvious comeback: "New York makes me dirty every day."

6   No matter what their purpose, graffiti are ways for ordinary people to communicate. Graffiti have several advantages: they are free, uncensored, and available to everyone. Graffiti have been both hated and enjoyed throughout history and will no doubt survive, in spite of occasional cleanup and paint jobs. A scribbler in a New York washroom summed it up: "Everything has its place, even the stupid writings in this cold john."

Questions for Analysis

1. What are the four categories of graffiti discussed in the essay? What criterion is used for classifying them? Why does the fourth type overlap the other categories?

2. What phrases at the beginning of paragraphs 2 through 5 introduce the category to be explained and illustrated? Are any of the categories defined? Which ones?

3. What examples for each category does the essay cite? Do any paragraphs include more than one example?

4. In your own words, write a summary of the reasons that people make graffiti. Do not copy from the essay.

Writing Assignments

1. Choose another way that people often communicate: by letters, memos, e-mails, telephone, messages left on the refrigerator, or messages left on telephone answering machines. Divide the subject into categories (for example, the types of messages left on the refrigerator) and illustrate each category with one or more examples.

2. Pretend you are a visitor from another planet and must explain to its inhabitants some behavior you observe here. Examples might be the strange rituals of taking tests, traveling from one place to another, decorating people's bodies with clothing and other devices, or eating and drinking amazing things. Divide the behavior into categories and describe each one.

3. Do you or the people you know speak differently to different groups—to people your age of the same sex or opposite sex, to parents, to grandparents, to young bosses, to teachers? Choose several ways in which the speaking is different, and illustrate each one.

Teen Gangbangers: An Ignored Issue
Mike Royko

* * * *

The problems of crime among poor children in the inner city are complex, and this newspaper column shows just how complex the problems are. It was written in 1992, so its claims about the lack of violence in prep schools are ironically out of date. Nevertheless, you'll probably find the story and its argument compelling.

The author of the essay, Mike Royko, was a Pulitzer Prize winning columnist for the Chicago Tribune *and the author of many books. He writes in typical newspaper style, with very short paragraphs that will fit into the narrow columns of a newspaper. He also writes in sentence fragments, which are characteristic of his conversational style.*

As you read the essay, notice how Royko begins and ends it with a reference to the presidential debates. Notice how he first provides background information about a young gangbanger named Jawon and then quotes the principal of an elementary school, who describes the problems Jawon creates. Also notice how Royko summarizes the main points near the end of the essay. There are probably no words in the essay that you need to look up.

1   If the presidential candidates of both parties want to enliven their debates, they might talk about what they'll do with Jawon.

2   Jawon, 14, lives on the West Side of Chicago. No permanent address. He and his fellow gang members pick out an abandoned building and call it home.

3   The cops assume that his source of income is crime. Theft, extortion, maybe drug errands for older gang members. He can barely read or write and doesn't attend school, but he has street smarts.

4   Lately, he has been showing up around the Herbert Elementary School, 2131 W. Monroe St. But not to learn. Just the opposite. He teaches young kids how to join the gang, what hand signals and gang colors to wear to avoid being shot.

5   Kids are valuable to gangs. Because of their age, they can shoot someone or run drugs or pull a stickup and get a lighter rap.

6   Jawon has already learned to handle a gun. He's currently awaiting a hearing for wounding another boy in the face during a gang dispute.

7   And he can drive a car. Not only drive it but bust in, hot wire the ignition, tear out the radio, and go joy riding.

8   The police got him for that, too, after he and his pals stole a car belonging to a teacher at the Herbert school. They wouldn't have been caught if they hadn't smashed into another car, injuring a couple of people.

9   All that, and he's still seven years short of being able to legally buy beer. But there's more.

10   Recently, a boy's sports jacket was stolen at the school. Jackets are a serious matter. Kids are gunned down for not surrendering them.

11   When the parents complained to the principal, the suspects were gathered in the school office. One was Jawon's cousin, who brought Jawon for moral support.

12   The principal describes the meeting:

13   "I had nine boys in there and the mother of the kid whose jacket was stolen, and I was questioning them. Then I left the room to call in another boy.

14   "Before I came back, the mother told me that Jawon was intimidating the kids right in front of her.

15   "His cousin had taken the jacket. We later found out that he had stolen it for Jawon. So Jawon told them: 'You better say that we didn't do it or I'm going to get a Uzi and blow you away.'"

16   If a 14-year-old in a prep school says he is going to blow you away with an automatic weapon, you might chuckle. But on the West Side and other city neighborhoods like it, there are probably 100 automatic weapons for every tennis racket.

17   "So I went back in and told Jawon he had to leave," the principal says. "He wouldn't. I told him I was ordering him out. He got out of his seat and started swearing at the kids and threatening them.

18   "I got up and he starts throwing punches at me. I finally got him off me and out of the office, but as he left, he was swearing and he said he'd be back to blow me away."

19   There was a time when the principal might have called Jawon's parents in to discuss the boy's behavior. But nobody knows where Jawon's parents are. Maybe Jawon doesn't.

20   So the principal called the police and filed aggravated battery charges.

21   That made three criminal charges against Jawon: the earlier shooting of the other kid, which was still pending; the theft of the teacher's car; and the assault on the principal.

22   When they went to court, the judge continued the case and ordered Jawon to stay away from the school and not to bother the principal or anyone else. The probation officer (Jawon's on probation for the car theft) was told to report any bad behavior.

23 Jawon nodded and went back to the street, where he will roam until sometime in March when another hearing will be held. Unless he kills someone before then.

24 That thought has crossed the principal's mind, who was more than a bit upset when Jawon was set free.

25 "I have to say to you I'm a little angry. No, a lot angry. There's nothing to prevent him from getting a gun and blowing me away. The judge told Jawon that he doesn't want him near the school. What are they going to do if he doesn't obey?

26 "What's this telling the kid? That he can do anything he wants. It will continue until he murders someone. He's already shown that he has access to guns and that he's willing to use one.

27 "One of my jobs is protecting students from gang activity. I can't even protect myself. How am I supposed to protect the kids?

28 "If he comes around and I call the police, what am I going to charge him with—trespassing? Hell, he shot a kid in the face and he's on the streets. Are they going to put him away for trespassing?"

29 Questions, questions. And who has the answers? We have a kid of 14, no parents, living a gang life. No skills or prospects other than crime. And there are thousands like him.

30 Is there anything in the president's crime package about that? Not that I've noticed.

31 A principal fears death. And he's not the only one. What do the candidates propose to do about that sort of educational environment?

32 An adolescent says he'll get an Uzi. He just might. The gangs now consider a six-shooter an antique. What will the candidates do to keep military hardware out of the hands of the Jawons?

33 You can rap the judge. But we have a national surplus of young criminals and a shortage of cells. Shall we build more prisons? Sure, and what will you say when the tax bill comes?

34 Yes, you could devote a speech to Jawon. Or even a State of the Union speech. The silence would be deafening.

Questions for Analysis

1. Mike Royko tells Jawon's (and the principal's) story to make a point: that children like Jawon pose serious and complex problems. What problems does Royko directly mention? What others does he imply?

2. If Royko had discussed the problems without telling Jawon's story, would he have made his point as strongly? Why or why not?

3. Royko makes comparisons throughout his essay. Underline them. How does each one develop the point of the essay?

4. Royko also challenges a number of assumptions that people make about gang-bangers—the assumptions of people who don't deal with gangs and those of people who do. Why? How does Royko fit these challenges into his argument?

5. Royko often writes sentence fragments in his columns, and this column has a lot of them. Are they effective? Why or why not?

Writing Assignments

1. Write a proposal to try to solve one of the issues that Royko mentions in his essay. Begin by summarizing what Royko says about the issue. Then describe your proposal, and explain how it might solve (or begin to solve) the problem.

2. Write about a student who was disruptive in one of your classes. Explain what happened and suggest why you think the student was disruptive.

3. Has a teacher, a counselor, or another person (perhaps a minister) ever helped you in a difficult situation? Describe the situation and how the person helped you.

The Legacy of Generation Ñ
Christy Haubegger

* * * *

Like all minority groups, Latinos tend to be stereotyped in a number of ways. In the following essay, Christy Haubegger has a bit of fun with the negative stereotypes, and she also presents some surprising facts about Latinos. As you read, notice that Haubegger's main method of development is cause-effect. Also notice the topic sentences in each body paragraph, which also serve as transitions. Finally, notice how Haubegger uses statistics to support her main ideas.

Christy Haubegger was born in Houston, Texas, in 1968 and received a law degree from Stanford University. She is the founder, president, and publisher of Latina *magazine, the first magazine for Hispanic women.*

Before beginning to read, use your dictionary to look up the following words:

1. manifest destiny
2. assimilate
3. condiment
4. demographic
5. senescence

1   About 20 years ago, some mainstream observers declared the 1980s the "decade of the Hispanic." The Latino Population was nearing 15 million! (It's since doubled.) However, our decade was postponed—a managerial oversight, no doubt—and eventually rescheduled for the '90s. What happens to a decade deferred? It earns compounded interest and becomes the next hundred years. The United States of the 21st century will be undeniably ours. Again.

2   It's Manifest *Destino*. After all, Latinos are true Americans, some of the original residents of the Américas. Spanish was the first European language spoken on this continent. Which is why we live in places like Los Angeles, Colorado and Florida rather than The Angels, Colored and Flowered. Now my generation is about to put a Latin stamp on the rest of the culture—and that will ultimately be the Ñ legacy.

3   We are not only numerous, we are also growing at a rate seven times that of the general population. Conservative political ads notwithstanding, this growth is driven by natural increase (births over deaths) rather than immigration. At 30, I may be the oldest childless *Latina* in the United States. More important, however, while our preceding generation felt pressure to assimilate, America has now generously agreed to meet us in the middle. Just as we become more American, America is simultaneously becoming more Latino.

4   This quiet *revolución* can perhaps be traced back to the bloodless coup of 1992, when salsa outsold ketchup for the first time. Having toppled the leadership in the condiment category, we set our sights even higher. Fairly soon, there was a congresswoman named Sanchez representing Orange County, a taco-shilling Chihuahua became a national icon and now everyone is *loca* for Ricky Martin.

5   We are just getting started. Our geographic concentration and reputation for family values are making us every politician's dream constituency. How long can New Hampshire, with just four Electoral College votes—and probably an equal number of Hispanic residents—continue to get so much attention from presidential candidates? Advertisers will also soon be begging for our attention. With a median age of 26 (eight years younger than the general market), Latinos hardly exist outside their coveted 18–34 demographic. Remember, we may only be 11 percent of the country, but we buy 16 percent of the lipliner.

6   The media will change as well, especially television, where we now appear to be rapidly approaching extinction. Of the 26 new comedies and dramas appearing this fall on the four major networks, not one has a Latino in a leading role. The Screen Actors Guild released employment statistics for 1998 showing that the percentage of roles going to Hispanic actors actually declined from the previous year. But, pretty soon, the cast of "Friends" will need to find some *amigos*. Seeing as they live in New York City, and there's almost 2 million of us in the metropolitan area, this shouldn't prove too difficult.

7   Face it: this is going to be a bilingual country. Back in 1849, the California Constitution was written in both Spanish and English, and we're headed that way again. If our children speak two languages instead of just one, how can that not be a benefit to us all? The re-Latinization of this country will pay off in other ways as well. I, for one, look forward to that pivotal moment in our history when all American men finally know how to dance. Latin music will no longer be found in record stores under FOREIGN and romance will bloom again. Our children will ask us what it was like to dance without a partner.

8   "American food" will mean low-fat enchiladas and hamburgers served with rice and beans. As a result, the American standard of beauty will necessarily expand to include a female size 12, and anorexia will be found only in medical-history books. Finally, just in time for the baby boomers' senescence, living with extended family will become hip again. *Simpsons* fans of the next decade will see Grandpa moving back home. We'll all go back to church together.

9   At the dawn of a new millennium, America knows Latinos as entertainers and athletes. But, someday very soon, all American children can dream of growing up to be writers like Sandra Cisneros, astronauts like Ellen Ochoa, or judges like José Cabranes of the Second Circuit Court of Appeals. To put a Latin spin on a famous Anglo phrase: It is truly *mañana* in America. For those of you who don't know it (yet), that word doesn't just mean tomorrow; *mañana* also means morning.

Questions for Analysis

1. What is Haubegger's thesis? Where does she state it?
2. According to Haubegger, what are some of the causes of the "decade of the Hispanic"? What will be some of the effects? Which topic sentences serve to introduce these causes and effects?
3. Who will benefit from these effects?
4. In paragraph 2, Haubegger writes an intentional fragment. Underline it. Why do you think she writes the fragment?
5. Haubegger mixes humorous or trivial statistics and details about Latinos with more significant information. Why? Underline the most significant information.
6. Haubegger also suggests that some common terms will need to be redefined. Which ones? How?

Writing Assignments

1. Describe how the influence of a group (for example, teenagers, immigrants, or African Americans) has changed some aspect of American culture (food, music, dance, dress, speech, and so on) in the past decade or two.
2. Who has influenced you the most in any one of the following ways: your choice of dress, in your religious faith, your decision to study in college, your choice of a profession, or your favorite leisure activities? How has the person influenced you?
3. Explain the most important benefits to American society that Haubegger thinks Latino culture is creating.

My Fifteen Minutes of Fame
Mark Schlitt

* * * *

Sometimes an (almost) innocent moment can turn into a long nightmare. That's what happened to Mark Schlitt, a former student at Truman College. He survived the experience and went on to a successful college career. As you read his story, notice how Mark gets ever deeper into trouble. And notice how the trouble unfolds in specific details: characters, places, and objects have names.

1   When I was eleven, my brother and I became famous in one day. It all started because we felt persecuted by our mother's mad obsession with wholesome food. Even my little sisters stared blankly at her lima beans. We wanted ice cream and my father hadn't uttered the code word—ice—for what seemed like years. We sat in the summer heat and swallowed our vegetables with disgust. Something had to be done, so after dinner we began plotting.

2   The next day my brother kept mom busy while I slid into her bedroom. After finding her purse, I gently pulled a bill from her wallet, put the purse back, and retreated into the hallway. I took a deep breath, stuffed the bill in my pocket, and tried to walk casually past mom without looking at her face.

3   As I went out the front door I gave my brother the sign. He ran out to the curb where I was waiting and panted, "Whaddya get?"

4   Glancing at the kitchen window nervously I said, "She didn't have any change; all I got was a buck." I held out a crumpled bill.

5   "That ain't a buck, that's ten bucks!" my brother said in amazement. Then he looked at me and said, "You're gonna get in trouble for this." I looked at the kitchen window again for signs of my mother. My brother stood on the curb waiting until he asked, "Well, whad're we gonna do now?" I felt like strangling him. My hand fidgeted with the bill in my pocket as I imagined the business end of my mother's ruler on my butt. "Are ya gonna get ice?" my brother said, interrupting my reverie. Then the taste of ice cream mixed with Bosco came to mind. Every time my mother caught me in a lie she washed my mouth out with Lava soap. I imagined looking innocent and saying, "I found the money, Ma; I didn't take it." The Lava soured the Bosco in my brain.

6   But my mom's face never appeared in the window and the sun kept telling me how good and cold ice cream would be.

7   We took off for town, arguing all the way. We decided to change the bill at the Ben Franklin, but we had to buy something to look legitimate. A Duncan see-through yo-yo caught my brother's eye. We argued, agreed on co-ownership, sealed it with spit-on-the-palm, and left. Eight dollars and some change remained. We were rich.

8   The saleslady in the Ben Franklin stared at us like goldfish in her five-and-ten fish bowl as we stood on the sidewalk tearing the plastic wrapper off the yo-yo. I pointed to a sign on Jansma's Bakery window across the street: "Chocolate Eclairs—Four for a Dollar." We weren't allowed these cream-filled dreams at home—my mother was too mean—so we had to make up for lost time. After buying four eclairs we stood on the boulevard imitating pus-filled sores at each other.

9   But ice cream was still on my mind, so like two millionaires we strolled down to Rexall's. My mother's words, "Thou shalt not . . ." were lost in the noise of the swarm of kids inside the drugstore. My brother and I debated over the cooler filled with ice cream. We couldn't agree on what kind to buy. A small crowd gathered. We decided on a whole carton of Fudgsicles. Suddenly everyone liked us.

10   Even Gustuli, the kid that used to beat me up every day, was my pal. The power of money made my head swell and I couldn't see myself sitting down to lima beans ever again. We were now philanthropists, revered and respected for our wealth. In the alley behind the drugstore we stood like Mafia bosses, fudgsicles jutting from our mouths.

11   Someone had fireworks for sale, but the deal had to be made in a secret place. We decided to meet in Hank's barn. My brother and I got there before anyone else, so we sat in the sun-lit straw and waited. Hank never seemed to be around and it looked like he never used the barn. As big to me as a cathedral and filled with dark corners and a nice musty smell, Hank's barn was one of my favorite places.

12   We were forbidden to play in the barn because it was dangerous and Hank didn't like trespassers. I sucked on a Fudgsicle and thought about the time Hank had caught my brother and me in his pear tree. He looked old and angry while pointing his gun at us. I thought he would shoot, but he let us down and told us to get.

13   Finally, the kid with the firecrackers showed up, accompanied by a bunch of other guys. I bought some Chasers and Black Cats while my brother and the other kids ran

around the barn hollering. Someone with a deck of cards suggested a poker game. We played cards in the tiny loft room, filled with streaming sun and straw dust, while the little kids played their games on the barn floor. My brother kept taunting me to walk the beam. Bored with cards, I finally agreed, but dared my brother to walk it with me. We went out, one at a time, tippy-toeing over the narrow joist above the barn floor to stand in the middle, where we had to raise one leg and then get back to the wall without falling off.

14　　Walking the beam was exciting, but the fireworks in my pocket promised new thrills. My brother and I talked about throwing some in a huge barrel, but someone suggested putting one in a rat-hole. Toward the back of the barn, in one of the stalls, we found a huge rat-hole. We rigged a string of firecrackers together, lit the wick, jammed them into the hole, and backed away as the fireworks fizzled. Smoke trailed from the rat's front door. I looked for water in the barn, but the only buckets around were filled with dust. We tried to smother the fire by stuffing the hole shut. Our friends vanished. A disoriented rat appeared from nowhere and ran for the door where Hank stood holding a shovel.

15　　I can't recall much of what happened after that, except the look of sadness on my mom's face when the police officer opened the back door to let us out of the squad car.

Questions for Analysis

1. In the first sentence of the story, what does the word *famous* mean? What kinds of "fame" have the brothers experienced by the end of the story?

2. The opening paragraph establishes a story's setting, telling *where, when, what,* and *who*. Examine the first paragraph of the story. How does each introduce the four w's of its setting?

3. Soon after the story began, you probably guessed that Mark was going to get deeper and deeper into trouble. What, therefore, creates the suspense and tension in the story?

4. The ending of the story is puzzling—and intriguing. Does the barn burn down? Has Mark been arrested? Why do you think Mark decided not to reveal these details?

5. Mark uses a lot of slang when he quotes the dialogue of the speakers. What effect does the slang create?

6. Examine each quotation carefully for its use of capitalization, punctuation, quotation marks, and paragraphing. Make a list of the "rules" for handling quotations. You may wish to compare your list with those of your classmates.

Writing Assignments

1. Mark Schlitt didn't plan on getting into deep trouble, but each event seemed to cause another. Summarize these events.

2. Tell the story about a time when you accepted a dare that led to trouble. Don't try to write as long a story as Mark Schlitt's (which actually was eight handwritten pages long).

3. Use dialogue as the primary way to tell the story of a funny moment from your childhood.

Liked for Myself
Maya Angelou

* * * *

The desire to be accepted is a strong influence on all of us, especially if the person who accepts us is someone whom we admire. In the story that follows, an excerpt from I Know Why the Caged Bird Sings, Maya Angelou takes us back to her childhood (when her name was Marguerite Johnson), the year after her parents had divorced and she was sent to live with her grandmother in Arkansas. There she meets and is befriended by an older woman, named Mrs. Flowers. Description plays a large role in this story. As you read this story, notice the details that reveal the personality of Mrs. Flowers—the descriptions of her physical appearance, her actions, and her words. Notice the lessons that she teaches young Marguerite as well.

Maya Angelou, who was born in 1928, is a famous African-American poet, essay writer, actress, producer, director, and civil rights activist, who read a poem at the inauguration of President Bill Clinton. She is the author of ten best-selling books.

Before reading the story, use your dictionary to look up the following words:

    1. taut   3. infuse
    2. benign   4. mead

1   For nearly a year, I sopped around the house, the store, the school and the church, like an old biscuit, dirty and inedible. Then I met, or rather got to know, the lady who threw me my first life line.

2   Mrs. Bertha Flowers was the aristocrat of Black Stamps. She had the grace of control to appear warm in the coldest weather, and on the Arkansas summer days it seemed she had a private breeze which swirled around, cooling her. She was thin without the taut look of wiry people, and her printed voile dresses and flowered hats were as right for her as denim overalls for a farmer. She was our side's answer to the richest white woman in town.

3   Her skin was a rich black that would have peeled like a plum if snagged, but then no one would have thought of getting close enough to Mrs. Flowers to ruffle her dress, let alone snag her skin. She didn't encourage familiarity. She wore gloves too.

4   I don't think I ever saw Mrs. Flowers laugh, but she smiled often. A slow widening of her thin black lips to show even, small white teeth, then the slow effortless closing. When she chose to smile on me, I always wanted to thank her. The action was so graceful and inclusively benign.

5   She was one of the few gentlewomen I have ever known, and has remained throughout my life the measure of what a human being can be. . . .

6   One summer afternoon, sweet-milk fresh in my memory, she stopped at the store to buy provisions. Another Negro woman of her health and age would have been expected to carry the paper sacks home in one hand, but Momma said, "Sister Flowers, I'll send Bailey up to your house with these things."

7   She smiled that slow dragging smile, "Thank you, Mrs. Henderson. I'd prefer Marguerite, though." My name was beautiful when she said it. "I've been meaning to talk to her, anyway." They gave each other age-group looks. . . .

8   There was a little path beside the rocky road, and Mrs. Flowers walked in front swinging her arms and picking her way over the stones.

9   She said, without turning her head, to me, "I hear you're doing very good school work, Marguerite, but that it's all written. The teachers report that they have trouble getting you to talk in class." We passed the triangular farm on our left and the path widened to allow us to walk together. I hung back in the separate unasked and unanswerable questions.

10   "Come and walk along with me, Marguerite." I couldn't have refused even if I wanted to. She pronounced my name so nicely. Or more correctly, she spoke each word with such clarity that I was certain a foreigner who didn't understand English could have understood her.

11   "Now no one is going to make you talk—possibly no one can. But bear in mind, language is man's way of communicating with his fellow man and it is language alone which separates him from the lower animals." That was a totally new idea to me, and I would need time to think about it.

12   "Your grandmother says you read a lot. Every chance you get. That's good, but not good enough. Words mean more than what's set down on paper. It takes the human voice to infuse them with the shades of deeper meaning."

13   I memorized the part about the human voice infusing words. It seemed so valid and poetic.

14   She said she was going to give me some books and that I not only must read them, I must read them aloud. She suggested that I try to make a sentence sound in as many different ways as possible.

15   "I'll accept no excuse if you return a book to me that has been badly handled." My imagination boggled at the punishment I would deserve if in fact I did abuse a book of Mrs. Flowers. Death would be too kind and brief.

16   The odors in the house surprised me. Somehow I had never connected Mrs. Flowers with food or eating or any other common experience of common people. There must have been an outhouse, too, but my mind never recorded it.

17   The sweet scent of vanilla had met us as she opened the door.

18   "I made tea cookies this morning. You see, I had planned to invite you for cookies and lemonade so we could have this little chat. The lemonade is in the icebox."

19   It followed that Mrs. Flowers would have ice on an ordinary day, when most families in our town bought ice late on Saturdays only a few times during the summer to be used in the wooden ice-cream freezers.

20   She took the bags from me and disappeared through the kitchen door. I looked around the room that I had never in my wildest fantasies imagined I would see. Browned photographs leered or threatened from the walls and the white, freshly done curtains pushed against themselves and against the wind. I wanted to gobble up the entire room and take it to Bailey, who would help me analyze and enjoy it.

21   "Have a seat, Marguerite. Over there by the table." She carried a platter covered with a tea towel. Although she warned that she hadn't tried her hand at baking sweets for some time, I was certain that like everything else about her the cookies would be perfect.

22   They were flat round wafers, slightly browned on the edges and butter-yellow in the center. With the cold lemonade they were sufficient for childhood's lifelong diet. Remembering my manners, I took nice little lady-like bites off the edges. She said she had made them expressly for me and that she had a few in the kitchen that I could take home to my brother. So I jammed one whole cake in my mouth and the rough crumbs scratched the insides of my jaws, and if I hadn't had to swallow, it would have been a dream come true.

23   As I ate she began the first of what we later called "my lessons in living." She said that I must always be intolerant of ignorance but understanding of illiteracy. That some people, unable to go to school, were more educated and even more intelligent than college professors. She encouraged me to listen carefully to what country people called mother wit. That in those homely sayings was couched the collective wisdom of generations.

24   When I finished the cookies she brushed off the table and brought a thick, small book from the bookcase. I had read *A Tale of Two Cities* and found it up to my standards as a romantic novel. She opened the first page and I heard poetry for the first time in my life.

25   "It was the best of times and the worst of times . . ." Her voice slid in and curved down through and over the words. She was nearly singing. I wanted to look at the pages. Were they the same that I had read? Or were there notes, music, lined on the pages, as in a hymn book? Her sounds began cascading gently. I knew from listening to a thousand preachers that she was nearing the end of her reading, and I hadn't really heard, heard to understand, a single word.

26   "How do you like that?"

27   It occurred to me that she expected a response. The sweet vanilla flavor was still on my tongue and her reading was a wonder in my ears. I had to speak.

28   I said, "Yes, ma'am." It was the least I could do, but it was the most also.

29   "There's one more thing. Take this book of poems and memorize one for me. Next time you pay me a visit, I want you to recite."

30   I have tried often to search behind the sophistication of years for the enchantment I so easily found in those gifts. The essence escapes but its aura remains. To be allowed, no, invited, into the private lives of strangers, and to share their joys and fears, was a chance to exchange the Southern bitter wormwood for a cup of mead with Beowulf or a hot cup of tea and milk with Oliver Twist. When I said aloud, "It is a far, far better thing that I do, than I have ever done . . ." Tears of love filled my eyes at my selfishness.

31   On that first day, I ran down the hill and into the road (few cars ever came along it) and had the good sense to stop running before I reached the store.

32   I was liked, and what a difference it made. I was respected not as Mrs. Henderson's grandchild or Bailey's sister but for just being Marguerite Johnson.

33   Childhood's logic never asks to be proved (all conclusions are absolute). I didn't question why Mrs. Flowers had singled me out for attention, nor did it occur to me that Momma might have asked her to give me a little talking to. All I cared about was that she had made tea cookies for me and read to *me* from her favorite book. It was enough to prove that she liked me.

Questions for Analysis

1. What is the thesis of this story? Where is it stated?

2. Although Angelou tells a story, she actually examines a series of contrasts. List them.

3. Mrs. Flowers talks to Marguerite about the importance of language. What does she say is most important?

4. What do you think Angelou means in the first sentence of paragraph 33?

Writing Assignments

1. Has an adult—or even a person a few years older than you—served as a role model for you? How did the person influence your life? Write about this person. Cite specific examples of what the person did and, if possible, how these actions affected you.

2. Describe an experience that awakened your interest in or love for some activity—reading, playing a sport like basketball or soccer, working with computers, singing or playing a musical instrument, or any other pastime you enjoy.

3. What values do you think Maya Angelou considered most important as an adult? Describe these values, supporting your interpretations with evidence from what she learned from Mrs. Flowers.

Living with "The Look"
Robert Hughes

* * * *

Many of us cannot hide our surprise and curiosity when we see someone who acts in an unusual way. Think about a homeless person muttering to herself, a musician performing on the street, or a small child talking in very adult-like sentences. In the following essay, Robert Hughes discusses his feelings as the parent of a child who often is looked at with surprise and curiosity. As you read it, notice how it describes the child's attractive appearance, the child's unusual behavior, and people's reactions to the child. Notice, too, how Hughes attempts to analyze and classify the reasons for their reactions.

Robert Hughes, who was born in 1949, is the author of many articles and is currently working on a book about his autistic son.

Before you read the essay, use a dictionary to define the following words:

1. autism
2. bourgeoisie
3. anthropologist
4. gravitate

5. magnanimous
6. conjecture
7. speculate

1   I am walking down a busy Chicago street with Walker, my autistic eleven-year-old son, and people are staring at him. He's a boy blessed with terrific good looks—tall and straight, with big, dark eyes, glossy hair and a movie star's smile—but this isn't what's turning heads.

2   Walker isn't actually walking down the street; he's running and somehow skipping at the same time. And he isn't talking to me; he's loudly singing "Jingle Bell Rock," though this is the middle of July. And he isn't, like me, trying unsuccessfully to look everywhere but into people's eyes; he's looking and smiling directly at everyone he passes with his fingers in his ears, his elbows flared out on either side. And, further baffling the bourgeoisie, he occasionally stops, shouts, spits twice and pulls up his shirt.

3   Although I'm secretly proud of every bit of this sidewalk routine of his, I'm all too aware of the faces of the people we pass. Some smile, even laugh appreciatively, at his obvious joy. Some nod to me sadly and knowingly: "Ah, I know how hard your life must be," they seem to say. Some flinch in exaggerated horror as though from some ghastly space alien from Warner Brothers. Others are cool, spot him far off and pretend not to see him when they pass. Still others are so used to such surpassing weirdness in the city that our little show comes nowhere near their threshold of surprise.

4   One reaction, however, is more puzzling to me than all the others. I have come to think of it as "The Look." The passerby's face becomes still and thoughtful. The eyes become narrow, like those of the cunning psychiatrist in an old movie when he asks a patient what the inkblots look like. A hand goes up to the lips and, shifting into field anthropologist mode, the eyewitness stops and stares and nods silently as though making a mental note to write this one down in the journal. It's a locked-on-target look. A piano falling onto the pavement nearby wouldn't jar the stunning logical processes at work.

5   Having been upset by The Look about a thousand times, and being something of an amateur field anthropologist myself, I have often asked this question: "Why do these people act this way?" The best answers that I have been able to come up with are these:

   (a) They are heartless and rude and should be tortured in some hideous way for upsetting a really nice father.

   (b) They are ignorant and think that humans come in solidly "normal" and "abnormal" forms and have no doubt about what kind they themselves are.

   (c) They saw the movie *Rain Man* and are now experts on autism.

   (d) They are fearful and are trying to achieve distance from a scary sight by trying to regard it as a rare scientific phenomenon.

   (e) They are curious, as the father would be, too, in their situation, at seeing a normal-looking boy acting strangely.

   (f) They aren't even aware that they have an expression on their faces and actually feel sympathetic toward the boy.

   (g) They really are psychiatrists, and their work is a big help to humanity.

6   Which answer I choose is largely dependent on my mood. If I'm feeling defensive and hypersensitive (most of the time), I gravitate toward letters a, b and c. If I'm feeling wise and magnanimous (not very often), I go for letters d, e and f. And if I'm feeling light-hearted (once or twice a year), I amuse myself with some variation of g.

7   But I know that I can conjecture forever and never really be sure what The Look means.

8   One thing I am sure of is the look on Walker's face. Unable to talk normally, he deploys a heavy arsenal of expression and movement to communicate. The beaming smile, the direct gaze, the skip-running and shout-singing, even the vigorous spitting—all of it—tells me Walker is working his audience hard. "Here I am! Look at me! I'm having fun! Aren't you impressed?" The message goes out, and some people, remarkably, seem to pick it up. Most, understandably, do not.

9   But what about my face, my look? Inside the house I do a fair job of attempting to see the world as Walker sees it and understanding him as far as possible on his own terms. Thus, a game of catch is, for us, not a Ward and the Beaver experience in the backyard. Performed Walker style, catch is an "extreme sport," with rules that are reinvented by him daily. Currently the game must be played in the house while Walker jumps wildly on his exercise trampoline, and there must be loud music playing, and he must catch the ball and throw it back while airborne. At unpredictable moments, Walker must leap off the trampoline and dash in and out of the room. The one unvarying rule is this: Dad must never stop paying attention. The result is that I long ceased aching for the "normal" game of catch and learned to love the in-house version we share.

10   At home, I stretch my notions of the "appropriate" to accommodate Walker's ideas on: a bedroom (the dining room, lights on); breakfast, lunch and dinner (cooked spaghetti, no sauce); and entertainment (every morning, the video of *The Wind in the Willows*).

11   When I step outside the house, however, a different, less noble point of view grips me, and I start to speculate needlessly on how outsiders see my son. Lost in a fog of anger or avoidance or criticism, I must present an uninviting picture for him and the world to look at. Why shouldn't passersby stare at the friendly son when the father's face is cloudy with conflict and questioning?

12   So I'm working on my look. I'm shooting for, at minimum, a near-frequent smile. I want to face the sidewalk parade as Walker does, with joy and hope and, most important of all, with a saving sense of fun.

Questions for Analysis

1. Robert Hughes writes this essay in the present tense. How does that affect your reaction to the events? Would your reaction be as strong if he had written in past tense?

2. What contrasts does Robert Hughes draw between himself and his son Walker in paragraph 3? In his description of his own behavior, what is Hughes suggesting about how he feels? How does that feeling contrast to the feeling he describes in paragraph 3?

3. In paragraph 4, what are the characteristics of "The Look"? What does Hughes mean when he says, "It's a locked-on-target look"?

4. Examine Hughes's classifications of the reasons that people give his son "The Look." (He labels them "a" through "g.") Which ones do you think are most likely to be the real reasons? Why? Does Hughes provide any evidence to support your opinion?

5. Based on paragraphs 8, 9, and 10, write, in your own words, a definition and description of autism as it applies to Walker.

6. Is this an angry essay? Is it a humorous one? Does it show other attitudes? What evidence supports your reactions?

Writing Assignments

1. Describe a time when you saw someone acting in ways you found unusual and try to explain why you think the person acted that way. If possible, provide more than one explanation, as Hughes does.

2. Describe a time when you witnessed—or were responsible for—cruelty to someone who was unusual. What happened, and why do you think the cruelty occurred?

3. Like Walker, do you have your own special "games" or routines? Describe one or more of them.

Melting Pot
Anna Quindlen

* * * *

As the title of this essay reminds us, America is supposed to be a great melting pot, in which people from many backgrounds blend together. But the blending is not easy. When new groups move in, the neighborhoods change, and not always in ways that the old groups like. Think about changes you've seen in the neighborhoods where you grew up or moved into. Think about the prejudices you've faced and perhaps felt. In the essay that follows, Anna Quindlen discusses the changes in her neighborhood in New York. As you read it, notice how it begins with a discussion of the melting pot, and then how it discusses both the hatred and friendliness between groups. Notice how the essay begins in the present tense and then switches to the past tense. Notice, also, how Quindlen is able to illustrate her main ideas with her own experiences, now and as a child.

Anna Quindlen, who was born in 1953, is a Pulitzer Prize winning columnist who cur-rently writes for Newsweek *magazine. She is the author of many best-selling books. Her nonfiction books include* Thinking Out Loud, *and* A Short Guide to a Happy Life. *And her books of fiction include* One True Thing *and* Black and Blue.

Before you begin to read, use a dictionary to define the following words:

1. tabloid
2. macro
3. goiter
4. glazier
5. doleful
6. apropos
7. embattled
8. gourmand
9. plantain
10. bodega
11. interloper

1   My children are upstairs in the house next door, having dinner with the Ecuadorian family that lives on the top floor. The father speaks some English, the mother less than that. The two daughters are fluent in both their native and their adopted languages, but the youngest child, a son, a close friend of my two boys, speaks almost no Spanish. His par-ents thought it would be better that way. This doesn't surprise me; it was the way my mother was raised, American among Italians. I always suspected, hearing my grandfa-ther talk about the "No Irish Need Apply" signs outside factories, hearing my mother talk about the neighborhood kids, who called her greaseball, that the American fable of the melting pot was a myth. Here in our neighborhood it exists, but like so many other things, it exists only person-to-person.

2   The letters in the local weekly tabloid suggest that everybody hates everybody else here, and on a macro level they do. The old-timers are angry because they think the new moneyed professionals are taking over their town. The professionals are tired of being blamed for the neighborhood's rising rents, particularly since they are the ones paying them. The old immigrants are suspicious of the new ones. The new ones think the old ones are bigots. Nevertheless, on a micro level most of us get along. We are friendly with the Ecuadorian family, with the Yugoslavs across the street, and with the Italians next door, mainly by virtue of our children's sidewalk friendships. It took a while. Eight years ago we were the new people on the block, filling dumpsters with old plaster and lath, drinking beer on the stoop with our demolition masks banging around our necks like goi-ters. We thought we could feel people staring at us from behind the sheer curtains on their windows. We were right.

3   My first apartment in New York was in a gritty warehouse district, the kind of place that makes your parents wince. A lot of old Italians lived around me, which suited me just fine because I was the granddaughter of old Italians. Their own children and grandchildren had moved to Long Island and New Jersey. All they had was me. All I had was them.

4   I remember sitting on a corner with a group of half a dozen elderly men, men who had known one another since they were boys sitting together on this same corner, watching a glazier install a great spread of tiny glass panes to make one wall of a restaurant in the ground floor of an old building across the street. The men laid bets on how long the panes, and the restaurant, would last. Two years later two of the men were dead, one had moved in with his married daughter in the suburbs, and the three remaining sat and watched dolefully as people waited each night for a table in the restaurant. "Twenty-two dollars for a piece of veal!" one of them would say, apropos of nothing. But when I ate in the restaurant they never blamed me. "You're not one of them," one of the men ex-plained. "You're one of me." It's an argument familiar to members of almost any embat-tled race or class: I like you, therefore you aren't like the rest of your kind, whom I hate.

5   Change comes hard in America, but it comes constantly. The butcher whose old shop is now an antiques store sits day after day outside the pizzeria here like a lost child. The old people across the street cluster together and discuss what kind of money they might be offered if the person who bought their building wants to turn it into condominiums.

The greengrocer stocks yellow peppers and fresh rosemary for the gourmands, plum tomatoes and broad-leaf parsley for the older Italians, mangoes for the Indians. He doesn't carry plantains, he says, because you can buy them in the bodega.

6   Sometimes the baby slips out with the bath water. I wanted to throw confetti the day that a family of rough types who propped their speakers on their station wagon and played heavy metal music at 3:00 A.M. moved out. I stood and smiled as the seedy bar at the corner was transformed into a slick Mexican restaurant. But I liked some of the people who moved out at the same time the rough types did. And I'm not sure I have that much in common with the singles who have made the restaurant their second home.

7   Yet somehow now we seem to have reached a nice mix. About a third of the people in the neighborhood think of squid as calamari, about a third think of it as sushi, and about a third think of it as bait. Lots of the single people who have moved in during the last year or two are easygoing and good-tempered about all the kids. The old Italians have become philosophical about the new Hispanics, although they still think more of them should know English. The firebrand community organizer with the storefront on the block, the one who is always talking about people like us as though we stole our houses out of the open purse of a ninety-year-old blind widow, is pleasant to my boys.

8   Drawn in broad strokes, we live in a pressure cooker: oil and water, us and them. But if you come around at exactly the right time, you'll find members of all these groups gathered around complaining about the condition of the streets on which everyone can agree. We melt together, then draw apart. I am the granddaughter of immigrants, a young professional—either an interloper or a longtime resident depending on your concept of time. I am one of them, and one of us.

Questions for Analysis

1. Anna Quindlen is the child of parents of two different nationalities. Based on the information in paragraph 1, what are those nationalities?
2. The term "moneyed professionals" appears in paragraph 2. From context, what do you think it means? Likewise, the terms "macro level" and "micro level" also appear. What, from context, do they mean?
3. Based on the information in paragraphs 3 and 4, what seems to be the main reason that Quindlen got along with her neighbors?
4. What is the topic sentence of paragraph 5? What point does the sentence about the greengrocer illustrate?
5. Paragraph 6 begins with an old expression about a baby and bath water. The paragraph then describes two groups who moved out of the neighborhood. Write, in your own words, a statement of what the baby-and-bath-water expression means in this context.
6. Paragraph 7 contains a sentence about how people in her neighborhood think of squid. But the point of the sentence really isn't about squid—it's about the people. Write, in your own words, a statement about what Quindlen is saying in that sentence.
7. Paragraph 8 draws a conclusion about the melting pot. What is it? Write a summary of the point in your own words.

Writing Assignments

1. Have you ever encountered prejudice against your nationality, religion, or race? What happened? How did you react?
2. Have you ever moved from one community or country to another? Discuss one or more adjustments that you had to make.
3. Describe a change that you've seen in your neighborhood or community. What has resulted from that change? If the change was supposed to benefit the people there, has everyone benefited? Give examples.

Why I Dread Black History Month
Wayne M. Joseph

* * * *

All of us should know—and be proud of—our heritage. What do you know about the history of your own people and its heroes? And what do you know about your family's history and its personal heroes? In the following essay, which first appeared in Newsweek *magazine, Wayne M. Joseph discusses what he thinks is wrong with focusing on black history for just one month of the year. As you read it, notice his discussions of "tokenism," black history as part of American history, and the role of the family in creating an awareness of heritage.*

Before you read the essay, use a dictionary to define each of the following words:

1. hail (verb)
2. thrive
3. momentous
4. flagrant
5. insidious
6. eschew
7. perseverance
8. indigenous
9. paragon
10. laud
11. fleeting
12. icon
13. instill
14. validate

1   Every year when the month of February approaches, I'm overcome with a feeling of dread. February is hailed as Black History Month, a national observance that is celebrated neither at the school in which I am the principal nor in my own home. This may come as a surprise to even the casual observer, since I am black. In my humble estimation Black History Month is a thriving monument to tokenism, which, ironically, has been wholeheartedly embraced and endorsed by the black community.

2   For at least twenty-eight days we are bombarded by the media with reminders of great black Americans. Teachers across America dust off last year's lesson plans and speak of African kings and queens. Dr. Martin Luther King's "I Have A Dream" speech is played repeatedly and there are festivities where people wear traditional African garb and may even speak a few words of Swahili.

3   So, you might ask, what is wrong with this?

4   Black contribution to American history is so rich and varied that attempting to confine the discussion and investigation to four weeks a year tends to trivialize the momentous impact that blacks have had on American society.

5   There is also a tendency to somehow feel that "black" history is separate from "American" history. "Black" history is American history—they are not mutually exclusive. The struggles of black people in America strike at the core of our country's past and its development. One cannot, for instance, hope to thoroughly study the factors leading to the Civil War or Reconstruction without investigating the issue of slavery and the emancipation of those slaves. American music and dance has little significance without the recognition of black influences. Spirituals, jazz and the blues are a vital and important part of American culture. To speak of the experience of black people in America (as some are inclined to do during the month of February) as independent of the American social, political and economic forces at work in our country is a misreading of history at best and a flagrant attempt to rewrite it at worst.

6   Of course very few people will be courageous enough during February to say that it's irrelevant whether or not Cleopatra and Jesus were black, since their experiences have not the slightest kinship with those of black Americans.

7   It is not very difficult to understand why the distant (usually African) past is used as a way to give blacks a sense of cultural identity. In the final analysis, however, it's a hollow attempt to fill a vacuum that was created by the institution of slavery. It is widely acknowledged that one of the more insidious aspects of American slavery was that Africans of different cultures and languages were stripped of their cultural base and were forced to learn the enslaver's tongue to survive. Unlike the German, Italian and Jewish immigrants who came to this country with their own languages, religions and customs, Africans of

different backgrounds were compelled to eschew their own roots in order to survive on American soil.

8   Instead of African kings and queens who never set foot in America, it is the black people who survived the infamous "middle passage" and endured slavery who should be heralded as "kings" and "queens" for their courage and perseverance. After slavery, there were scores of blacks who endured beatings, lynchings and daily degradations indigenous to the system of discrimination in both the North and the South; yet these paragons of endurance are seldom lauded. It's as if the words "slavery" and "segregation" are to be mentioned only fleetingly during February. We should look to our own grandfathers and grandmothers to find examples of real heroism. Unfortunately, the significance of these black men and women as well as the traditional black icons—Dr. King, Malcolm X, Jackie Robinson, et al.—are lost in a month in which people are studied in isolation instead of within the historical context that produced them.

9   Black parents must try to instill in children a sense of their own history. This should include a sense of family—the accomplishments of parents, grandparents and ancestors has more relevance than some historical figure whose only connection to the child is skin color. We in the schools are often expected to fill the gaps that parents have neglected in their child's development; but for every child a knowledge of identity and self-worth must come from home to be meaningful and long-lasting. For the black child, a month-long emphasis on black culture will never fill that void.

10   There will be those, I'm sure, who will say that I should feel pleased that black people are recognized one month out of the year, knowing the difficulty black Americans have historically encountered validating their accomplishments. But being black does not entitle one to more or less recognition based solely on heritage. In a multicultural society, there is a need to celebrate our cultural differences as well as our commonalities as human beings. No one group has a monopoly on this need.

11   One month out of every year, Americans are "given permission" to commemorate the achievements of black people. This rather condescending view fails to acknowledge that a people and a country's past should be nurtured and revered; instead, at this time, the past of black Americans is handled in an expedient and cavalier fashion denigrating the very people it seeks to honor.

12   February is here again, and I'll be approached by a black student or parent inquiring as to what the school is doing to celebrate Black History Month. My answer, as always, will be that my teachers and I celebrate the contributions of *all* Americans *every* month of the school year.

Questions for Analysis

1. In paragraph 1, who, according to Wayne M. Joseph, is creating and supporting a sense of tokenism? What evidence in paragraph 2 does he provide for this argument?

2. Why is paragraph 3 only one sentence? What reaction does that create in you as a reader?

3. In paragraph 4, Joseph argues against separating "black" history from "American" history. Why does he put these words in quotation marks? Locate and underline the examples that support his argument. Then summarize, in your own words, what his main argument is.

4. In paragraph 7, what does he say is the main difference between the experience of Africans and other groups coming to this country?

5. In paragraph 8, Joseph contrasts two different sets of kings and queens. In your own words, write an explanation of this contrast.

6. The following difficult sentence appears in paragraph 11: "This rather condescending view fails to acknowledge that a people and a country's past should be nurtured and revered; instead, at this time, the past of black Americans is handled in an expedient and cavalier fashion denigrating the very people it seeks to honor."

Rewrite the sentence in simpler language—and use more than one sentence if necessary.

1. According to Joseph, who should be teaching children the history of African Americans? What should be taught in that history?

Writing Assignments

1. Did someone in your family—present or past—overcome some obstacle in a way that benefited him or her? Did anyone experience something terrible? Tell the story.

2. Do you have a particular hero? Tell who the person is and why he or she is a hero.

3. Have you had an experience in which you and someone from a different background or culture worked or played together well—or badly? Describe it.

Living Like Weasels
Annie Dillard

* * * *

Can animals think? Can animals feel what we feel? Many of us have thought about these questions. In the following passage, Annie Dillard describes a moment when she came face to face with a weasel. Her reaction is a mixture of many feelings and ideas. Look for them as you read, and consider how you would have reacted in her situation.

Annie Dillard, who was born in 1945, is the Pulitzer Prize winning author of nine books, including Teaching a Stone to Talk *and* An American Childhood. *She is currently an adjunct professor of English at Wesleyan University.*

Before you read the description, use a dictionary to define each of the following words.

1. stalk (verb)	6. grate (noun)
2. carcass	7. dismantle
3. thrust	8. enchantment
4. inexplicable	9. retrieve
5. fierce	10. careen

1   A weasel is wild. Who knows what he thinks? He sleeps in his underground den, his tail draped over his nose. Sometimes he lives in his den for two days without leaving. Outside, he stalks rabbits, mice, muskrats, and birds, killing more bodies than he can eat warm, and often dragging the carcasses home. Obedient to instinct, he bites his prey at the neck, either splitting the jugular vein at the throat or crunching the brain at the base of the skull, and he does not let go. One naturalist refused to kill a weasel who was socketed into his hand deeply as a rattlesnake. The man could in no way pry the tiny weasel off, and he had to walk half a mile to water, the weasel dangling from his palm, and soak him off like a stubborn label.

2   I have been thinking about weasels because I saw one last week. I startled a weasel who startled me, and we exchanged a long glance.

3   Near my house in Virginia is a pond—Hollins Pond. It covers two acres of bottomland near Tinker Creek with six inches of water and six thousand lily pads. There is a 55 mph highway at one end of the pond, and a nesting pair of wood ducks at the other. Under every bush is a muskrat hole or a beer can. The far end is an alternating series of fields and woods, fields and woods, threaded everywhere with motorcycle tracks in whose bare clay wild turtles lay eggs.

4   One evening last week at sunset, I walked to the pond and sat on a downed log near the shore. I was watching the lily pads at my feet tremble and part over the thrusting path of a carp. A yellow warbler appeared to my right and flew behind me. It caught my eye; I swiveled around—and the next instant, inexplicably, I was looking down at a weasel, who was looking up at me.

5   Weasel! I had never seen one wild before. He was ten inches long, thin as a curve, a muscled ribbon, brown as fruitwood, soft-furred, alert. His face was fierce, small and pointed as a lizard's; he would have made a good arrowhead. There was just a dot of chin, maybe two brown hairs' worth, and then the pure white fur began that spread down his underside. He had two black eyes I did not see, any more than you see a window.

6   The weasel was stunned into stillness as he was emerging from beneath an enormous shaggy wild-rose bush four feet away. I was stunned into stillness, twisted backward on the tree trunk. Our eyes locked, and someone threw away the key.

7   Our look was as if two lovers, or deadly enemies, met unexpectedly on an overgrown path when each had been thinking of something else: a clearing blow to the gut. It was also a bright blow to the brain, or a sudden beating of brains, with all the charge and intimate grate of rubbed balloons. It emptied our lungs. It felled the forest, moved the fields, and drained the pond; the world dismantled and tumbled into that black hole of eyes. If you and I looked at each other that way, our skulls would split and drop to our shoulders. But we don't. We keep our skulls.

8   He disappeared. This was only last week, and already I don't remember what shattered the enchantment. I think I blinked, I think I retrieved my brain from the weasel's brain, and tried to memorize what I was seeing, and the weasel felt the yank of separation, the careening splashdown into real life and the urgent current of instinct. He vanished under the wild rose. I waited motionless, my mind suddenly full of data and my spirit with pleadings, but he didn't return.

9   I tell you I've been in that weasel's brain for sixty seconds, and he was in mine. Brains are private places, muttering through unique and secret tapes—but the weasel and I both plugged into another tape simultaneously, for a sweet and shocking time. Can I help it if it was a blank?

10   What goes on in his brain the rest of the time? What does a weasel think about? He won't say. His journal is tracks in clay, a spray of feathers, mouse blood and bone: uncollected, unconnected, loose-leaf, and blown.

Questions for Analysis

1. What does the first paragraph tell us about the way a weasel hunts? The end of the paragraph describes the experience of a naturalist whose hand was "socketed" by a weasel. What does that mean? Why do you think the naturalist refused to kill the weasel?

2. In paragraph 5, Dillard describes the weasel, saying it "would have made a good arrowhead." What does she mean? What details in the paragraph develop that idea?

3. In paragraph 7, Dillard says that she and the weasel were like two lovers—or two enemies. How is that possible? She also describes many changes in the world around them. Are these changes real? Why does Dillard describe them? She also says, "If you and I looked at each other that way, our skulls would split and drop to our shoulders." What do you think she means?

4. Explain in your own words the meaning of this sentence from paragraph 8: "I waited motionless, my mind suddenly full of data and my spirit with pleadings, but he didn't return."

5. Dillard's description is filled with surprising comparisons. Find at least three and explain in your own words what they mean.

6. Dillard has many reactions to the weasel. List as many as you can find. Then write a paragraph in which you explain these reactions.

7. Dillard waits for the weasel to return, but it doesn't. Why does she wait? What do you think she wants to find out from the weasel?

Writing Assignments

1. Write about a relationship you've had with a pet. Have you ever felt that the pet was almost human? Why?

2. Write about one experience with an animal that was particularly memorable. Explain what happened and make clear why it was memorable.

3. If you could be one animal for a day, what animal would it be, and why?

A

Common Irregular Verbs

Present tense	Past tense	Past participle	Present tense	Past tense	Past participle
be (am, are, is)	was, were	been	fit	fit	fit
beat	beat	beaten	flee	fled	fled
become	became	become	fly	flew	flown
begin	began	begun	forget	forgot	forgotten
bend	bent	bent	forgive	forgave	forgiven
bet	bet	bet	freeze	froze	frozen
bind	bound	bound	get	got	gotten
bite	bit	bitten	give	gave	given
bleed	bled	bled	go	went	gone
blow	blew	blown	grind	ground	ground
break	broke	broken	grow	grew	grown
breed	bred	bred	hang	hung, hanged	hung, hanged
bring	brought	brought	have	had	had
build	built	built	hear	heard	heard
burst	burst	burst	hide	hid	hidden
buy	bought	bought	hit	hit	hit
cast	cast	cast	hold	held	held
catch	caught	caught	hurt	hurt	hurt
choose	chose	chosen	keep	kept	kept
come	came	come	know	knew	known
cost	cost	cost	lay	laid	laid
creep	crept	crept	lead	led	led
cut	cut	cut	leave	left	left
deal	dealt	dealt	lend	lent	lent
dig	dug	dug	let	let	let
do	did	done	lie	lay	lain
draw	drew	drawn	light	lit (or lighted)	lit (or lighted)
dream	dreamt (dreamed)	dreamt (dreamed)	lose	lost	lost
			make	made	made
drink	drank	drunk	mean	meant	meant
drive	drove	driven	meet	met	met
eat	ate	eaten	pay	paid	paid
fall	fell	fallen	put	put	put
feed	fed	fed	quit	quit	quit
feel	felt	felt	read	read	read
fight	fought	fought	ride	rode	ridden
find	found	found	ring	rang	rung

Present tense	Past tense	Past participle	Present tense	Past tense	Past participle
rise	rose	risen	stand	stood	stood
run	ran	run	steal	stole	stolen
say	said	said	stick	stuck	stuck
see	saw	seen	sting	stung	stung
sell	sold	sold	stink	stank	stunk
send	sent	sent	strike	struck	struck
set	set	set	strive	strove	striven
shake	shook	shaken	swear	swore	sworn
shed	shed	shed	sweep	swept	swept
shine	shone, shined	shone, shined	swim	swam	swum
shoot	shot	shot	swing	swung	swung
show	showed	shown	take	took	taken
shrink	shrank	shrunk	teach	taught	taught
shut	shut	shut	tear	tore	torn
sing	sang	sung	tell	told	told
sink	sank	sunk	think	thought	thought
sit	sat	sat	throw	threw	thrown
slay	slew	slain	thrust	thrust	thrust
sleep	slept	slept	understand	understood	understood
slide	slid	slid	wake	woke	woken
slit	slit	slit	wear	wore	worn
speak	spoke	spoken	weave	wove	woven
spend	spent	spent	win	won	won
spin	spun	spun	wind	wound	wound
split	split	split	withdraw	withdrew	withdrawn
spread	spread	spread	write	wrote	written

B

Commonly Misspelled Words

Add your own words to the list as you look up their correct spelling.

absenCe	convenIEnce	inTELLectual	priviLEGE
aCCept	counSelor	inTERest/inTEResting	proBABly
aCComplish	criticiSM/critiCIZE	inTERfere	proNUNciation
aCCoMModate	deFINITEly	inteRRupt	PSYchology
aCCurate	desPErate	iRRELevant	PURsue
achIEvement	dESCribe	jUDGment	quIET/quITE
acquaintANCE	develOP	jEWELry	realIZE
aCRoss	diffERent/diffERence	knowLEDGE	reCEIve
adverTISEment	diSAPPoint	laBORATory	recoMMend
adVICE/adVISE	DISease	leiSURE	RHyTHM
A LOT	doESN'T	liCenSe	ridicULOUS
AnSWer	duRing	lONELiness	scenERy
aPPropriate	eiGHTH	lOOse/lOse	SCHEDule
arGUment	embaRRass	mainTENance	SECRETary
artiCLE	enTRANCE	maTHEmatics	SePArate
aTHLete	enveLOPE	miLLeNNium	sIEge
attenDANCE	enviRONment	misCHIEF	simILAR
availABLE	especIALLY	miSSpell	sinCE
bEAUtiful	exaGGerate	nIEce	sinCEREly
begiNNing	EXcept	ninETY	spEEch
behaVIOR	existENCE	ninTH	straiGHT
breaTH/breathE	exPERIENCE	oCCasion	strenGTH
BUSiness	exPERIment	oCCuRRENCE	SURpriSE
calENDAR	exPLANAtion	opINion	temPERature
cEIling	exTREMEly	oPPortunity	THROUGH
certAINly	familIAR	oRIGinal	thoROUGH
chIEf	faSCinate	opTImist	ThurSday
choiCe	FeBRUary	partiCULAR	toMoRRow
chOOse/chOse	forEIGN	PAStime	unNECESsary
coMMerCIAL	genIUS	PERform	UNusually
coMMiTTee	goVERNment	PERhaps	WedNESday
compETItion	gramMAR	phoNY	**Your own words:**
conCentrate	guarANtee	phySICAL	_____
congRATulate	hEIGHT	poSSess	_____
conSCIENCE	iMMediate	preFER	_____
conSCIOUS	imporTANT	prejUDicED	_____
conSENSus	indepenDENCE	PREscription	_____
consEquently	inTEGration	preVALENT	_____

C

Common Expressions Using Prepositions

accuse someone *of* something

acquaintance *with* someone or something

affection *for* someone

afraid *of* something

agree *with* someone about something

alarmed *at* something

a lot *of* something

amazed *at* something

amused *at* or *by* someone or something

angry *at* someone

angry *with* something

approve *of* someone or something

argue *about* something

argue *with* someone *for* (or *about*) something

arrive *at* a place *in* a city or country

ashamed *of* something

ask someone *for* something

ask something *of* someone

associate *with* someone *in* some activity

assure someone *of* something

at the top *of*

aware *of* someone or something

bargain *with* someone *for* something

because *of* something or someone

believe *in* something

blame someone *for* something

by means *of*

call *on* someone socially

call *to* someone *from* a distance

call *up* someone *on* the telephone

capable *of* something

certain *of* something

challenge someone *to* something

characteristic *of* something

cheat someone *out of* something

close *to* something or someone

comment *on* someone or something

communicate something *to* someone

comparable *to* something

complain *to* someone *about* something

composed *of* something

conceive *of* something

concerned *about* someone or something

confess *to* someone

confidence *in* someone or something

confident *of* something

congratulate someone *on* something

conscious *of* something

consideration *for* someone

contempt *for* someone or something

contribute *to* something

control *over* someone or something

convict someone *of* something

copy *from* someone

correspond *with* someone

count *on* someone *for* something

cure *for* something

cure someone *of* something

deal *with* someone or something

decide *on* something

dedicate something *to* someone

defend someone *from* something or *against* something

delighted *with* someone or something

delight *in* someone or something

demand something *of* someone

depend *on* someone *for* something

deprive someone *of* something

designed *for* something

desire *for* something

die *of* or *from* a disease

different *from* someone or something

disagree *with* someone *about* something

disappointed *in* something

disappointed *with* someone

disgusted *with* someone or something

displeased *with* someone or something

distrust *of* someone or something

do something *about* something

doubt *about* someone or something

dream *of* or *about* something

due *to* someone or something

duty *to* someone

engaged *to* someone

escape *from* something

excel *in* something

exception *to* something

excuse *for* something

excuse someone *from* something

explain something *to* someone

failure *of* someone *in* something

faithful *to* someone or something

fall *in* love *with* someone

fascinated *with* someone or something

fearful *of* something

fond *of* someone

for the purpose *of*

for the sake *of*

full *of* something

grateful *to* someone *for* something

guard *against* something

guess *at* something

hear *about* something

hear *of* something

hint *at* something

horrified *at* something

in case *of*

in common *with*

independent *of* someone or something

in favor *of*

influence *over* someone

inform someone *of* something

in place *of*

inquire *into* something

in search *of*

in spite *of*

in the course *of*

intent *on* something

interfere *with* someone or something

introduce someone *to* someone

invite someone *to* something

irrelevant *to* something

knock *at* or *on* a door

laugh *at* something or someone

lecture *on* or *about* something

listen *to* someone or something

look *at* someone or something

look *for* something or someone

look up something *in* a reference book

made *of* something

make something *for* someone

mistaken *for* someone

need *for* something

obligation *to* someone

on account *of*

opportunity *for* someone or something

opposition *to* someone or something

pay someone *for* something

pay something *to* someone

pity *for* someone

point *at* someone or something

popularity *with* someone

prefer something *to* something

prejudiced *against* someone or something

protect someone *from* something

provide something *for* someone

punish someone *for* something

qualification *for* a job

quarrel *with* someone *over* something

quote something *from* someone

reason *for* something

reason *with* someone *about* something

recover *from* an illness

related *to* someone

rely *on* someone or something

remind someone *of* something

reply *to* someone *about* something

require something *of* someone

research *in* something

responsible *to* someone *for* something

result *from* a cause

result *in* a consequence

result *of* a cause

rob someone *of* something

satisfactory *to* someone

search *for* something

send *for* something

shocked *at* something

shocking *to* someone

similar *to* someone or something

smile *at* someone

stare *at* someone

start *with* something

supply someone *with* something

sure *of* something

sympathy *with* or *for* someone or something

take advantage *of* someone or something

take care *of* someone or something

talk *over* something *with* someone

talk *to* someone *about* something
tell someone *of* or *about* something
thankful *for* something
think *of* or *about* or *over* something
threaten someone *with* something
tired *of* something

trust *in* something or someone
trust someone *with* something
wait *for* someone or something
weary *of* something
work *for* or *on behalf of* someone or something
worry *about* something

Answers to Chapter Exercises

(Odd Numbered Items Only) and to Mastery Exercise 1 in All Chapters

Chapter 2

Exercise 1

3. to inform or entertain

5. to persuade

Exercise 2

Possible answers.

3. a. challenging academic program, excellent choice of courses, fine teachers and counselors

 b. fine teachers, excellent tutors and counselors, excellent developmental courses, friendly and nonthreatening atmosphere

 c. fine teachers, excellent counselors for foreign students, many clubs for foreign students, excellent tutors in English

Exercise 3

1. to entertain—and persuade students to do well in school

3. that students fail because they don't try and they can succeed if they do try

Chapter 3

Exercise 1

Possible answers.

3. a trend in music; a trend in dress; surfing the Internet

5. how the writer became interested in a hobby; typical experiences with the hobby

Exercise 2

Paragraph C Sentence 1

Paragraph E Sentence 1

Paragraph G Sentence 6

Exercise 3

Sample answers

3. People who bury their pets in cemeteries have too much time and money on their hands.

5. Sports are boring.

Exercise 4

Sample topic sentences.

Paragraph C Cats probably emerged as pets much later than dogs.

Paragraph E Cats later suffered much worse fates outside of Egypt.

Exercise 8

Paragraph 3 The origins of nursery rhymes
Delete sentence c.

Paragraph 5 came for a number of reasons
Delete sentence d.

Exercise 9

1. Sentence 17—the final sentence

3. (1) the cookie (2) chocolate (3) chocolate chip cookie (4) xocoatl (6) chocolate powder (7) solid chocolate (8) hard chocolate, chocolate chip (9) the cookie (10) first chocolate chip cookie (11) the inn's owner (12) chocolate pieces . . . butter cookies . . . the Toll House Inn cookie (13) For chocolate bits . . . Chocolate Bar (14) Nestlé . . . bar (15) free chocolate (16) The cookie . . . chocolate chips (17) Aztec Indians . . . chocolate

5. The Aztecs, the Spanish, a candy maker in Holland, a British company, (possibly) Ruth Wakefield, the Nestlé Company

Chapter 4

Exercise 1

1. three points: extraordinary attractiveness, incredible physical talent, and exemplary character. The opening sentences are introductory and serve to attract the reader's interest.

3. (2) handsome, magnificent body on his 6½ foot frame, shaves his hair, broad shoulders and rippling muscles (3) dodges defense and makes spectacular shots, scores a lot of points . . . top scorer, "Air Jordan" moves . . agility and leaping ability, jumps in air and can stay there for a long time, smart . . . and tries to keep his teammates disciplined (4) team captain shows cool and controlled leadership and gentility, never fights, and calms down teammates, puts on his suit and politely answers questions, donates money to charity, sponsors community services

Chapter 5

Exercise 2

3. The Republican party

5. Two

7. He

9. The future president

Exercise 4

3. would be [to die]

5. would die [being]

7. held [dying]

9. would have been [to outlive, coming, according]

Exercise 5

3. Mary (fragment)

5. attended (fragment)

7. <u>husband</u> appeared

9. <u>Mumler</u> produced

Exercise 6

Possible answers.

3. put

5. was

7. wanted

9. won

11. abolished

Exercise 7

Possible answers.

3. *He* lifted . . .

5. no error

7. no error

Exercise 8

3. front, he went . . .

5. downstairs when the sobbing grew louder, although . . .

7. no change

Exercise 9

3. soldiers who were acting as guards told him . . . president who had . . .

5. . . . story, which the president . . .

Exercise 10

3. sentence

5. fragment (add a clause)

Mastery Exercise 1

Possible changes

South (3) *now* that . . .

(4) he *was* telling . . . (5) *by* preparing . . .

(7) post, (8) either

(9) rang out, (10) *Lincoln* slumped . . .

(11) stage, (12) *in* the process . . .

(14) horse (15) *which* was . . .

(16) theater (17) *where* he died'. . . next morning,

(18) throwing . . .

(19) or another, (20) *Abraham* Lincoln . . .

(21) discovered: (22) *John* Wilkes Booth . . .

(24) to be hanged, (25) *including* Mary Surratt . . .

Chapter 6

Exercise 1

1. and

3. for

5. but

7. nor

Exercise 2

3. . . . the cash box, *but* he did not harm . . .

5. . . . an angry poem, *but* it also contained . . .

7. . . . not amused, *so (and)* it offered . . .

9. . . . handkerchief, *or* he might . . .

11. . . . passenger, *nor* have I ever treated . . .

Exercise 6

3. . . . possible; *therefore,* he . . .

5. . . . brave; *otherwise,* they would never . . .

7. . . . water; *nevertheless,* they were . . .

Exercise 8

Sample combinations.

3. Critics claimed that couples "embrace at the pelvis," and they said that couples "whirl about in a posture of copulation."

5. The waltz was rapidly becoming popular with lower-class people all over Europe, and it was first danced at a royal ball in England in 1816.

Mastery Exercise 1

(2) . . . police, *but (; however,)* they were more concerned . . .

(3) . . . strange; *they (, for)* they had lived . .

(4) . . . anyone; *(, and)* in fact, they . . .

(5) . . . 1940, *and (;)* he never saw . . .

(6) no change

(7) . . . the house, *and (for) (;)* Langley fetched . . .

(8) . . . windows; *(, for)* he was . . .

(9) no change

(10) . . . the house, *and (;) they* cleared away . . .

(11) no change

(12) . . . been, *and (;)* Langley's body lay . . .

(13) . . . Homer, *and* he was crushed . . .

(14) . . . of dollars, *and (;)* the Collyers' . . .

(15) . . . Homer, *but* . . .

Chapter 7

Exercise 1

3. I. C. . . . Owens felt tense . . . D. C. *because* a German . . .

5. D. C. *Although* Hitler claimed . . ., I. C. the meaning . . .

7. D. C. *When* the trade . . ., I. C. Jesse Owens . . .

Exercise 2

Possible answers.

3. . . . to participate *because* he had sprained . . .

5. *When (Because, After)* he got off to a perfect start, . . .

7. *When* Owens won the 220-yard dash . . .

9. *As (When)* Owens completed four events in forty-five minutes . . .

Exercise 4

Possible answers.

3. *Although planning* to become a tailor at Carlisle, Thorpe attracted . . .

5. *While continuing* to compete . . .

Exercise 5

Possible answers.

3. *When (After)* the world later learned . . . the world was astonished.

5. *Although* Thorpe played for only a few dollars, he was technically . . .

Mastery Exercise 1

Possible answers.

(3) . . . was thrilled when . . . (omit comma)

(4) The Bulgarians drew loud cheers (5) *when* they marched . . . (join)

(6) were jeered *because* they didn't (omit semicolon)

(8) *Although* his fellow African-American teammate . . . (omit *but*—or retain *but* and omit Although) . . .

(9) . . . for the broad jump, (10) Owens fouled . . . (add comma and join)

(11) . . . tired (12) *because* he had just run . . . (join)

(13) *When* Owens felt a hand on his shoulder, (14) *he* turned . . . (join)

(17) . . . his second jump (18) *although* Luz Long tied it . . . (join and omit comma)

(20) *After* landing on his final jump, (21) *Owens* was congratulated . . . (join)

(22) *While* collecting four gold medals in all, (23) Owens didn't receive . . . (join)

Chapter 8

Exercise 1

3. . . . her *husband, who* refused . .

5. Henry II of *England, who* demanded . . .

Exercise 2

3. who seemed to sneeze just before dying from illness.

5. , who had basically similar ideas,

7. that killed many people in Italy

Exercise 5

Possible answers.

3. The first New Year's festival began in the city of Babylon, [which is] the capital of ancient Babylonia, [which is] now part of Iraq.

5. The Babylonians also performed a play to honor the goddess of fertility, and they had an enormous parade that included music, dancing, and performers who wore costumes.

7. Roman rulers and government officials made the months and years longer because they wanted to lengthen the time when their terms of office lasted.

9. Roman emperors continued to change the calendar for the next century, and in 46 B.C. Julius Caesar adjusted the calendar so the year dragged on for 445 days.

11. The holiday came back during the Middle Ages, when the British celebrated it on March 25, the French on Easter Sunday, and the Italians on Christmas day.

Exercise 6

Possible answers.

3. A few months later, de Mistral thought of a better way to fasten fabrics when he was on a hunting trip with his dog.

5. De Mistral noticed tiny hooks on their ends while examining the burrs under a microscope.

Mastery Exercise 1

(3) It seemed *logical that* (omit comma) . . .

(4) . . . in *1957, when* the first (replace semicolon with comma) . . .

(5) . . . in a human, which was only (change *that* to *which*, preceded by a comma) . . .

(6) The person *who* developed (change *which* to *who*) . . .

(7) . . . the Jarvik-7, *in* 1979.

(9) Barney *Clark,* a retired dentist . . .

(10) . . . *later* (11) *with* an artificial heart . . .

(12) . . . *Clark,* (13) *who* lived . . .

(14) . . . strokes resulting from blood clots (remove semicolon).

(17) *recommended that* . . . (remove comma)

Chapter 9

Exercise 1

Possible answers.

3. The governor was *furious; he* put Pep on trial and sentenced the dog to life imprisonment.

5. The story has a happy *ending; Pep's* fellow inmates loved him, and he could switch cellmates at will.

Exercise 2

Possible answers.

CS 3. Every evening *when* he returned on a train, Hachi was always there to greet him.

CS 5. Hachi, *who* lived for ten more years, went to the train station every evening and patiently waited for his master.

CS 7. *Because* Hachi always met the evening trains, he became a familiar sight to Japanese travelers.

9. correct

Exercise 3

Possible answers.

3. They kept repeating in *Swahili, a language* he did not know well, that Dian was dead until he finally understood them.

5. *Four days later,* the fifty-four-year-old woman was buried in the station's animal cemetery in a spot next to the graves of some mountain gorillas that she loved so dearly.

7. McGuire was accused of a crime and fled the *country; however,* there were other, more obvious suspects.

Mastery Exercise 1

Possible answers.

(2) . . . gorillas; *consequently,* they . . .

(3) . . . world *although* there were only 250 . . .

(5) . . . distance, *but* later on she . . .

(6) . . . body language, *and* she also nibbled . . .

(7) . . . understandable; *she* had been . . .

(8) . . . goldfish, *and* when it died . . .

(9) *After* she saw gorillas . . .

(10) She left Africa *but then* returned . . .

(13) . . . authorities *who* wanted (remove comma) . . .

(14) . . . attractions, *and* she threatened . . .

Chapter 10

Exercise 1

3. areas

5. females

7. lions; zebras

Exercise 2

1. hunt

3. lives, joins

5. kills

Exercise 3

1. women

3. lice

5. teeth

Exercise 4

3. own

5. rains

7. write

Exercise 5

3. make

5. seems

Exercise 6

3. is ('s)

5. are ('re)

7. are ('re)

Exercise 7

3. *There are also* small . . .

5. *They're* kept . . .

7. . . . *leopards are*

Exercise 8

3. don't

5. don't

7. doesn't

Exercise 9

3. has

5. don't have (haven't)

7. doesn't have (haven't)

Exercise 10

1. Are

3. Do

5. Does

Exercise 11

3. are

5. are

Exercise 14

3. <u>of this social club</u> *don't*

5. <u>of pizzas, french fries, garlic bread, onion rings, and nachos</u> usually *disappears*

Mastery Exercise 1

(1) . . . cats *have* always . . .

(2) . . . some *cats* . . . others *work* . . .

(3) . . . job . . . these days *is* . . .

(4) . . . but it *doesn't* . . .

(5) . . . some tests of intelligence *show* . . .

(7) . . . everyone *knows* . . .

(8) There *are* . . . all the breeds *have* . . .

(9) *They're* the only animals . . . that *walk* . . .

(11) . . . it *has* . . .

(13) *It's* the only animal . . .

(14) . . . *are* the female cat and the male cat?

(17) . . . he *doesn't* stick . . .

Chapter 11

Exercise 1

3. Pr

5. P

Exercise 2

(3) showered, rushed

(5) started

(7) developed, crumbled

(9) extended

(11) called, changed

(13) baked, received

(15) piled

(17) visited, watched, considered

(19) criticized, adopted

Exercise 4

3. were

5. was

7. was

9. were, was

Exercise 5

3. Bill wants to know if he can borrow your car.

5. Jeannette thinks that she will graduate in two years.

Exercise 6

3. They *have remained* . . .

5. . . . *has served* . . .

Exercise 7

3. protected

5. have searched, have discovered

7. have guarded

Exercise 8

3. haven't been

5. hasn't been

Exercise 9

1. been, was

3. (had) worked, sent

Exercise 10

3. laid

5. paid

7. heard

Exercise 11

3. bought

5. felt

7. lost, taught, meant

Exercise 12

3. became, led

5. fought, found

7. wound, was, had

9. came

11. wound, had

Exercise 13

3. rang

5. sank, handed

Exercise 14

3. put

5. quit

7. cut, spread, shut

Exercise 15

3. drew, fell

5. broke, swore, overate

7. had done, wrote, had grown

Mastery Exercise 1

(2) . . . Ponce de Leon *discovered* Florida . . .

(5) The king of Spain *had* removed . . .

(6) . . . he *could* find.

(7) . . . didn't *mention* . . .

(9) . . . had *sought* . . .

(10) . . . had *gone* looking for the fountain.

(14) That attraction *drew* . . .

(15) . . . Louella McConnell *told* . . .

(16) She *saw* . . .

(17) . . . from a box *buried* near the tree.

(21) . . . a millionaire *named* Henry Flagler . . .

(22) . . . where McConnell *charged* admission . . .

(24) . . . he *gave* up his plans . . .

(25) . . . who *made* . . .

(26) . . . was *discovered* . . .

Chapter 12

Exercise 1

3. . . . and *he* . . .

5. *He and I* . . .

7. . . . *they* are . . .

Exercise 2

Possible sentences.

3. Sam works harder than we (do).

5. The counselor talks to you more often than (she does) to me.

Exercise 3

Possible changes.

3. . . . until *the company* could fix the problem

5. . . . which outsold *them* all.

7. no change

Exercise 4

Possible changes.

3. . . . *people* don't repair calculators; . . .

5. . . . *the industry* think of next?

Exercise 5

Possible changes.

3. He̶ *The attendant* then strolled . . .

5. he̶ *the person* must not assume . . .

Exercise 6

Possible changes.

3. . . . gazed at *his or her* image . . .

5. *If people* dropped . . . *they* would soon die, or that the gods were sparing *them* . . .

7. . . . that *people's* health changed . . . that *they* could determine *their* condition from it.

Exercise 8

3. yourselves

5. himself (or herself)

7. I

Exercise 10

Possible answers.

3. However, we do know the identity of the man *who first called a bagel a "bagel."*

5. In 1653, the first coffeehouse in Vienna was opened by a Polish man *who introduced a new bread called the* beugel.

Mastery Exercise 1

Possible revisions.

(2) . . . where *Edison and his coworkers* invented . . .

(4) . . . because *Edison* was . . .

(6) . . . *the person* made *Edison's* hearing worse.

(7) . . . educating *himself* . . .

(8) . . . *these* experiments . . . *the company* fired him.

(12) . . . his assistants and *he* perfected.

(13) . . . *was* earning him national fame.

(14) . . . for *himself or herself.*

(17) . . . for *him* (or *himself*) . . .

Chapter 13

Exercise 1

3. peacefully

5. badly

Exercise 2

3. This man <u><in simple clothes</u>

5. Settlers <u><on the frontier,</u> began calling him Johnny Appleseed <u><in a spirit of humor or ridicule</u>

7. buried <u><in Johnny Appleseed Park,</u> <u><near Fort Wayne, Indiana</u>

Exercise 3

3. Jefferson <u><wearing plain working clothes</u> . . .

5. formed . . . <u><offering their services</u> . . .

Exercise 4

3. myth, <u><invented by writer George Lippard</u> . . .

5. was coined <u><to refer</u> . . .

Exercise 5

3. Dr. Richard Schuckburgh <u><who wrote the first version of "Yankee Doodle"</u>

5. song <u><that made fun of the colonials' appearance</u>

Exercise 6

Possible answers.

3. Sam Wilson served as the drummer boy *at the age of eight* . . .

5. . . . been settled with the *Treaty of Paris* in 1783 . . .

7. Another war, *which was also fought against Britain,* . . .

9. One day, *when asked by government inspectors what the "U.S." stood for,* a meat packer . . .

Exercise 7

Possible revisions.

3. *At the age of thirty-five,* Adams . . .

5. Ironically, John Adams died *at 6:00 in the evening* . . .

Exercise 8

Possible revisions.

3. Unhappy with both teaching and the clergy, *Adams turned to his true love, the law.*

5. His reputation and political future could have been damaged *when he defended* the British soldiers who shot some Massachusetts citizens in the Boston Massacre.

Exercise 9

Possible combinations.

3. Because this brilliant and very patriotic young man was sure that a national language would unify the country, he began his research in 1803.

5. Webster then began to work on a much longer dictionary, which he finished two decades later.

7. When Webster died in 1843, George and Charles Merriam bought the rights to Webster's dictionary.

Mastery Exercise 1

Possible revisions.

2. . . . a man without a beard *in a solid black hat and topcoat.*

3. no change

4. The first pictures of him *in a red hat* . . .

5. The flowing beard, *which appeared during Abraham Lincoln's presidency,* was inspired . . .

6. Uncle Sam was such a popular figure *in the late nineteenth century* . . .

7. no change

8. Pictures of a tall, thin man, *who resembled the original Uncle Sam,* Sam Wilson, . . .

9. However, the most famous portrayal of Uncle Sam, *the one most frequently reprinted and most widely recognized,* . . .

10. no change

11. The poster *showing Uncle Sam dressed in his full flag costume* sold four million copies . . .

12. *Contrary to the popular belief,* Flagg's Uncle Sam . . .

Chapter 14

Exercise 1

1. flatter

3. shinier, more expensive

5. more useful

Exercise 3

3. the most unusual

5. the silliest

Exercise 4

Possible answers.

3. the least talented.

5. less than her siblings.

Exercise 6

3. more commonly

5. more likely

Exercise 7

3. well, better

5. bad, the worst

5. badly, the worst

Mastery Exercise 1

(2) . . . disappeared so *quickly.*

(3) . . . *harder* to believe.

(9) . . . *more complete* . . .

(11) . . . lived *happily* . . .

(12) . . . hurt their crops *badly* . . .

(13) . . . the *most* important part of the colonists' diet.

(14) . . . the same *as* chicken but was a little *tougher.*

(18) . . . device that worked *well* . . .

(19) . . . called very *loudly* . .

Chapter 15

Exercise 1

3. we

5. her

Exercise 2

Possible answers.

3. *They* will really . . .

5. *Students* who want . . . *They'll* laugh . . .

Exercise 4

3. was

5. thought, was

7. knew, could

Exercise 6

(3) . . . but she *would* eventually become . . .

(7) . . . so she *could* explore Tibet without him for fourteen years.

(11) . . . until he *died* . . .

(15) after she *had* emerged from the cave in 1916.

Exercise 7

1. avoid the accident

3. a good student

5. overtired

7. ran back

Exercise 10

Possible answers.

3. . . . and also *their customs.*

5. . . . and *called* on Alexandra . . .

7. . . . remained in their disguises and *were* undetected.

9. . . . made her return to Tibet and *live* there . . .

Mastery Exercise 1

(2) . . . *people* could hear . . .

(3) . . . *was* awakening from . . .

(4) . . . and *blotted* out the sun.

(5) . . . and then *fell* back into the volcano.

(6) . . . and *rained* stones all over the mountainside.

(7) . . . and *escaped* in their boats.

(8) *They* lived to tell . . .

(9) . . . or *in the public baths.*

(11) . . . and *set* others on fire.

(12) . . . and *suffocated* the rest.

(14) . . . *would* be preserved in the ash . . .

(15) . . . *people* could visit the city . . .

Chapter 16

Exercise 1

Possible answers.

3. repeat

5. examine,

7. murder, kill

9. remove

Exercise 2

Possible answers.

3. constructed, erected, assembled, threw together

5. lifted, swiped, stole, looted, boosted

Exercise 3

Possible answers.

3. The university library contains every book you can imagine.

5. The dog's fleas are bigger than grapes.

Exercise 5

Possible answers.

3. generous, extraordinary, unselfish, benevolent

5. gigantic, enormous, awesome, huge, towering

Exercise 6

3. Seven men were sleeping on the floor at the end of the party.

5. A train will be arriving from Philadelphia in a few minutes.

Exercise 8

Possible revisions.

3. Bus fare is pretty (somewhat, slightly) high in this city.

5. By reading the directions on an examination first, I know exactly what is expected of me.

Exercise 9

Possible revisions.

3. I like art because it allows me to be creative.

5. Anita seems to have a lot of self-confidence.

Exercise 10

Possible combinations.

3. When his host showed him an easy target, a baby bear (or cub), Roosevelt refused to shoot it.

5. Morris Michtom, the owner of a toy store in Brooklyn, New York, was so inspired by the cartoon that he and his wife made a soft brown bear.

7. The bear and many more sold quickly, developing a fad that became very popular.

9. The president sent a handwritten note to Michtom granting him permission.

Exercise 11

3. Getting rid of every cliché is difficult.

5. Honest politicians are rare.

Mastery Exercise 1

Possible revisions, which reflect goals that students probably will only approximate.

2. Germans surrounded the Americans and attacked them.

3. Furthermore, the American division also was getting "friendly fire" from their own army.

4. The division commander Major Charles W. Whittlesey knew that his many of his men had been killed or hurt, and they had almost run out of rations and medical supplies.

5. To stop more "friendly fire" from coming at the division, Whittlesey decided to write a note to his superiors at division headquarters in Rampont.

6. He asked them to stop bombing the division.

7. The only one way to get the message to head-quarters twenty-five miles away was to send it by carrier pigeon.

8. Whittlesey sent up five pigeons with the message, but German marksmen killed each one of them immediately.

9. He put the message inside a capsule attached to the leg of the only pigeon left, Cher Ami, which means "dear friend" in French.

10. After a short flight, Cher Ami landed on the branch of a nearby tree and decided to groom feathers.

11. Major Whittlesey knew that this situation was so bad, he had to make the bird fly.

Chapter 26

Exercise 1

3. Catherine of Aragon, Anne Boleyn, Jane Seymour, Anne of Cleves, Catherine Howard, *and* Catherine Parr.

Exercise 2

(5) . . . (later Tuskegee), *and* his mother . . .

(11) . . . and sympathized with him, *for* they were convinced . . .

Exercise 3

Possible changes.

3. *When his friends and neighbors talked,* he no longer heard . . .

5. . . . an alphabet as a syllabary, *eighty-six characters representing all the sounds of spoken Cherokee.*

7. The task took Sequoyah twelve years *in all.*

Exercise 4

Odd numbered items only.

(5) Within a few months, *a group* of almost entirely . . .

(7) *In 1828,* Sequoyah and other Cherokees arrived . . .

(9) Charles Bird King, *a famous painter,* asked him to sit . . .

(11) Although most Cherokees refused to leave Tennessee and Alabama, *Sequoyah's* . . .

Exercise 5

3. no commas

5. an awkward, tall basketball player

Exercise 6

3. After December 5, 2005, Kathy will be an attorney.

5. July 4, 1776, in Philadelphia, Pennsylvania.

Exercise 7

Odd numbered items only.

(3) *Consequently,* a large battalion . . .

(7) . . . over the *land,* over the members of the local government, *and* over many other matters.

(9) At the meeting of the entire *tribe,* all the groups agreed to live in peace.

(11) *However,* Sequoyah still could not rest.

(13) Where were these lost Cherokees, *who did not know of his alphabet or the new Nation?*

Exercise 8

3. NBC

5. The Environmental Protection Agency is called the EPA.

Exercise 9

3. other.

5. forest?

Exercise 10

3. population.

5. today.

Exercise 11

3. . . . into the ground; however, their council house . . .

5. . . . religious ceremonies; each contained . . .

Exercise 12

1. Nathaniel Hawthorne, *The Scarlet Letter;* Mark Twain, *Huckleberry Finn;* Herman Melville, *Moby-Dick;* William Faulkner, *The Sound and the Fury;* F. Scott Fitzgerald, *The Great Gatsby;* and Ernest Hemingway, *For Whom the Bell Tolls.*

3. Bear Wallow, Kentucky; Pewee, Kentucky; Bulls' Gap, Tennessee; Difficult, Tennessee; Hot House, North Carolina; Improve, Mississippi; Scratch Ankle, Alabama; and Dime Box, Texas.

Exercise 13

3. fashions: a neon tee shirt, jeans torn at the knees, orange and green spiked hair, and seventeen pierces in her left ear.

5. take one from column A, two from column B, and your choice of two from column C or D.

Exercise 14

3. (the first planet beyond normal eyesight to be observed)

5. —in fact there is no wind, no sound, no life.

Exercise 15

3. Cold Mountain

5. The Producers is a very popular Broadway production.

Exercise 17

3. Martha told me, "I have been working late."

5. Mr. Joseph asked where the registrar's office was (is).

Exercise 18

3. "Well, . . . night," *m*urmured . . . author. "When will this end?"

5. servants, "Why . . . immortal?"

7. "Please," *m*umbled Theodore Roosevelt, "*p*ut . . . lights."

Mastery Exercise 1

(3) . . . *Rahner, who* used . . . *from* [delete colon] . . .

(5) . . . subject; *therefore,* he

(6) . . . *simple, accidental,* and tragic . . .

(7) . . . *1926,* Houdini was lying on a sofa in his dressing room.

(8) . . . who earlier had drawn a picture of the *magician,* came backstage . . .

(10) . . . *as the press had claimed?"* [question mark inside end quotation mark]

(18) . . . *then that* whoever died [remove comma]

(19) . . . for several *days; he* underwent two operations . . .

(20) . . . his brother, "I'm tired of *fighting. I* guess this thing is going to get me." [combine quotations]

(24) . . . *said,* "when . . .

Chapter 27

Exercise 2

3. conceit

5. chief

7. deceive

Exercise 3

3. selves

5. shelves

Exercise 4

3. beauties

5. taxes

7. roses

9. breathes

Exercise 5

3. application

5. payment

7. flier

9. happily

Exercise 6

3. dancing

5. famous

7. dining

Exercise 7

3. usually

5. angrily

7. really

Exercise 8

3. writing

5. running

7. heating

Exercise 9

3. paralleling

5. preference

Exercise 10

3. stubborn

5. writing

7. occurred

9. bitten

Exercise 11

1. disinterested

3. innumerable

5. dissatisfied

7. immaterial

9. mistake

Exercise 12

3. a lot

5. athlete

7. beginning

9. brilliant

11. carefully

13. chosen

15. competition

17. dealt

19. dining

21. describe

23. eighth

25. environment

27. explanation

29. finally

31. government

33. height

35. hoping

37. intellectual

39. jewelry

41. locally

43. misspell

45. occasion

47. prefer

49. potato

51. privilege

53. received

55. sacrifice

57. separate

59. sincerely

61. succeed

63. temperature

65. tomato

67. tries

69. written

Exercise 13

3. *Willie's* work

5. *Maria's* apartment

7. Mr. *Johnson's* statement

Exercise 14

3. Ms. *Jones's* house

5. *Mother's* Day

7. *Texas's* law

Exercise 15

3. A few *hours'* work

5. The *car's* front fenders

Exercise 16

1. company's

3. runs

5. city's

7. leaves

Exercise 17

3. it's

5. we're

7. you're

9. doesn't

Exercise 18

3. *We'll* . . .

5. *don't . . . you're* . . .

7. *Who's* . . .

Exercise 19

3. forty-six

5. three-fourths

Exercise 20

3. a self-made woman

5. a pro-Russian speech

Exercise 21

Possible compound words.

3. fleabitten

5. newspaper

7. chairman

9. halftime

Exercise 22

3. stepped

5. wa-tered

7. ex-president

9. guard-house

Exercise 23

3. *Prairie Road* and *Central Street*

5. no capitalization

7. *I* . . .

9. *Spanish*

Exercise 24

3. *August*

5. no capitalization

7. *The*

Mastery Exercise 1

Only corrected words appear.

(2) parties . . . receive . . . it's

(3) entering . . . classroom . . .

(4) different

(5) African-American

(6) fifty-seven

(7) written . . . lyrics

(9) appeared . . . their . . . Coleman's

(11) several

(13) musical

(14) royalties

(16) . . . paid

(18) delivered . . . stopped

(20) its

(21) seventy-eight

Chapter 28

Exercise 1

3. where

5. their

7. you're

Exercise 2

3. two

5. to, too

Exercise 3

3. have

5. have

7. have

Exercise 4

3. use, prejudice

5. accustomed

Exercise 5

2. accepted

3. acceptable

Exercise 6

3. advice

Exercise 7

3. affected

5. affect

Exercise 8

3. an

5. and, and, an

Exercise 9

3. breathe

4. breaths

Exercise 10

3. by, buy

5. by

Exercise 11

3. clothes

Exercise 12

2. conscience

3. unconsciously

Exercise 13

3. excellent

5. elegant

Exercise 14

3. fine

Exercise 15

3. knew

5. no

Exercise 16

3. lead

Exercise 17

3. lain

5. lying

Exercise 18

3. lose

Exercise 19

3. mind

Exercise 20

3. passed

5. passed

7. passed

Exercise 21

3. quite

5. quiet

Exercise 22

3. raise

5. rising

Exercise 23

3. set

Exercise 24

3. then

5. then

Exercise 25

3. there was

5. It was, it was

Exercise 26

3. weather

5. whether

Mastery Exercise 1

(1) whose, by

(3) led

(5) accept

(6) were

(7) used, than, past

(8) Their

(10) lose

(11) knew, whether, an, find

(13) too

(15) there's, different

(17) quiet

Chapter 29

Exercise 1

3. My father washes the car every week.

5. Mrs. Highnose isn't watching television now.

Exercise 2

3. They did the wash every day last week.

5. They weren't listening to the news last night.

Exercise 3

Possible answers.

3. While Mr. Gotbucks was smoking his cigar, his chauffeur was driving the car.

5. While his wife was washing the dishes, sweeping the floor, and throwing out the garbage, Mr. Hogg read the paper.

   (His wife was washing the dishes, sweeping the floor, and throwing out the garbage when Mr. Hogg read the paper.)

Exercise 5

Possible answers.

3. I have to finish it tonight.

5. he had to stay home.

Exercise 6

Possible answers.

3. The sun doesn't shine very much.

5. They don't have much time to relax.

Exercise 7

Possible answers.

3. eaten at that restaurant

5. eaten breakfast

7. take a vacation

Exercise 8

Possible answers.

3. is being mopped

5. have lent you mine

Exercise 9

Possible answers.

3. must have been shopping

5. could have been written

Exercise 10

3. where room 814 is.

5. you had studied for the final examination.

Exercise 12

3. a 161-year-old ex-slave to them.

5. did not give anyone refunds.

Exercise 14

3. the man [quickly] turned on the radio [quickly].

5. I gave him the answer to the question. [the answer to the question to him].

Exercise 16

3. performed

5. injured

7. bored

Exercise 17

Possible answers.

3. it doesn't make *any* sense.

5. I don't like to borrow *anything* . . .

7. You *can* hardly find . . .

Mastery Exercise 1

(2) . . . make *canvas tents for the miners,* but when he *could hardly* sell any . . .

(3) . . . . would not *wear* out . . .

(5) Cowboys *preferred* tight pants . . . to get *their jeans wet* . . .

(7) . . . the jeans were *badly scratching* . . .

(8) . . . became a hot fashion item *in the same decade* . . .

(9) . . . who *had* on tight jeans in a look called "western chic."

(11) . . . weren't *anything* . . .

(12) . . . was *begun* when young people . . .

(13) Teen-agers were *interested* . . .

(14) Clothing makers *soon spotted* . . . jeans *decorated* . . .

(15) . . . got *into* the jeans market . . .

(17) . . . would *now become* . . .

Chapter 30

Exercise 1

1. a

3. an

5. a

7. a

9. an

Exercise 3

3. *a* twenty-three-year-old, *an* oil refinery

5. *a* new senator, *the* first, *the* Senate

Exercise 4

3. *the (a)* church on Main Street.

5. *the* new high-protein diet in today's newspaper.

Exercise 5

3. _____

5. _____

7. the

9. the

Exercise 6

1. *since* July 11

3. *in* the first. *For* several

Exercise 7

(1) in

(3) at

(7) in

Exercise 8

1. on

3. on, in (on)

5. off (off of), in (on)

Exercise 9

(1) in

(3) In, to

(5) On, about, in

(7) to, in

(11) against (on)

Exercise 10

3. in

5. in

7. on, in

Mastery Exercise 1

(1) in the

(2) The (3) in

(4) an (5) [none needed] (6) for

(7) on (8) in (9) the

(10) on (11) in (12) in

(13) on

(14) a (15) a (16) in

(17) the

(18) by (19) at

(20) the (21) a

(22) of

(23) the

(24) the (an)

(25) at

Glossary

Action verb: a verb that states what a subject does, did, or will do.

Active voice: a sentence structure in which the subject performs the action of the verb.

Adjective: a word or group of words that describe a noun or pronoun.

Adverb: a word or group of words that describe a verb (or a word formed from a verb, such as *–ing word* or an *infinitive*), telling *when, where, why, how,* or *how often* the action happens or happened. Adverbs can also describe adjectives or other adverbs (especially adverbs such as *very, really, too,* and *somewhat*).

Adverb clause: a clause beginning with a subordinating conjunction such as *if, because, when,* or *before* that functions as an adverb.

Antecedent: the word or words that come before a pronoun and which the pronoun refers to.

Apostrophe: a punctuation mark ['] that shows possession before or after *–s* on nouns, replaces omitted letters in contractions, or forms the plurals of letters before adding *–s*.

Appositive: a noun that adds identifying information about a noun that precedes it.

Articles: the words *a, an,* and *the,* which determine whether a noun is specific or not specific.

B

Body: the central part of a paragraph or essay that develops and explains the topic sentence of the paragraph or the thesis statement of the essay.

Brainstorming: a part of prewriting in which you list thoughts as they come to you.

C

Case: the grammatical role of a pronoun as subject, object, possessive, and so on.

Causal analysis: an organization that examines the causes of an event or the results of an event. It is also called *cause–effect organization.*

Cause–effect organization: see *Causal analysis.*

Chronological order: an organization of events according to how they occur in a time sequence. This organization is found most often in narratives, process analysis, and cause–effect papers.

Classification: an organization that divides the subject matter into categories determined by one criterion, or standard.

Clause: a group of words containing both a subject and a verb. Every sentence must contain at least one clause, although many sentences contain more than one.

Cliché: a tired and overused expression.

Climax order: an organizational arrangement going from the least important to the most important information and often ending dramatically.

Clustering: a part of prewriting in which you explore and organize your thoughts in a chart. Begin by writing and circling the topic in the middle of the page, then draw lines (or branches) to circles in which you write related ideas. You can also draw branches and attach circles to each of the related ideas until you fill up the whole page.

Coherence: a quality in which the relationship between ideas is clear throughout a paragraph or essay.

Collective noun: a noun such as *class, orchestra,* or *team* that represents a group of people or things. Most—but not all—collective nouns are grammatically singular.

Colon: a punctuation mark [:] that functions like an equal sign. It is most often used to show that the last words of a grammatically complete statement are equal to what follows—usually a list or long quotation.

Comma: a punctuation mark [,] used for separating ideas or, with two commas, enclosing ideas.

Comma-spliced sentence: a sentence containing two independent clauses incorrectly joined by a comma. This is a serious, but common, grammatical error.

Common noun: a noun that represents but does not name something and is therefore not capitalized.

Comparative form: the form of an adjective or adverb ending in *–er* or preceded by *more,* showing that the two things being compared are not equal.

Comparison–contrast: an organization that shows similarities and differences between two or more subjects. The organization can be whole-to-whole or part-to-part.

Complex sentence: a sentence containing an independent clause and a dependent clause that begins with a word such as *after, because, if, who, that,* or *which.*

Compound predicate: a predicate containing two or more verbs.

Compound sentence: a sentence containing two independent clauses, each of which could be a sentence by itself.

Compound subject: a subject consisting of two or more nouns and/or pronouns joined by *and.*

Compound word: a word formed by joining two complete words—sometimes with a hyphen and sometimes without.

Conclusion: the last sentence of a paragraph or last paragraph of an essay, which ties together the preceding ideas and gracefully ends the work.

Conjunction: a joining word or phrase (see *coordinating conjunctions* and *subordinating conjunctions*).

Conjunctive adverb: a word that often follows a semicolon to explain how or in what way the two clauses joined by the semicolon are logically related. A conjunctive adverb is also called a *transitional word.*

Consonant: a sound represented by any of the letters of the alphabet that do not represent the vowel sounds.

Contraction: a joining of two words that requires the omission of a letter or several letters from the second word.

An apostrophe occupies the spot of the missing letter(s).

Coordinating conjunction: a word that joins grammatically equal structures. There are only seven coordinating conjunctions: *for, and, nor, but, or, yet, so.*

Coordination: the joining of two or more grammatically equal structures, usually with a coordinating conjunction or a semicolon.

Countable nouns: nouns that can be either singular or plural.

Criterion: the method used in classifying things—such as by size, frequency, or age.

D

Dangling modifier: a modifier that does not modify any word or phrase in a sentence.

Dash: a punctuation mark [—] used to separate and enclose items that dramatically interrupt a sentence. Internal items require two dashes, while end items require one.

Definition: an organization that explains the meaning of a term, often by providing examples and contrasting it with similar terms.

Demonstrative adjectives: the pronouns *this, that, these,* and *those,* which go before nouns—as in "this man" or "these cars."

Demonstrative pronouns: the pronouns *this, that, these,* and *those* that are used without nouns (see *demonstrative adjectives*).

Dependent clause: a clause that cannot stand alone as a sentence but must be joined to an independent clause to complete its meaning. Most dependent clauses begin with words such as *because, although, if, that, which,* or *who.*

Detail: a smaller part of something larger. Details usually support generalizations.

Direct object: the word or words (usually nouns or pronouns) following and receiving the action of an action verb, following a word formed from a verb (such as an infinitive, a past participle, or an *–ing* word), or following a preposition.

Direct question: a question that forms a complete sentence ending in a ques-

tion mark and places the verb (or first helping verb) before the subject.

Direct quotation: the exact words of a speaker or writer, placed in quotation marks.

Double negative: a type of grammatical error in which two negative words express one negative idea. Only one negative word should be used.

E

Editing: one of the last steps in the writing process in which you check over your second or third draft for misspelled words, words left out or repeated, grammatical errors, missing word endings, incomplete sentences, and incorrect punctuation.

Effect: the result of some action or event (see *causal analysis*).

Essay: an organized discussion of a topic in a series of paragraphs—usually at least five paragraphs and often many more. Ideally, the introductory paragraph attracts the readers' attention, states the thesis of the essay, and outlines its structure. The body paragraphs present each main supporting point of the thesis. The concluding paragraph summarizes the ideas and brings the paper to a graceful end.

Example: a specific illustration of a concept.

Exclamation point: an end punctuation mark [!] that shows strong emotion.

Exclamatory sentence: a statement or strong emotion ending in an exclamation point [!].

Exemplification: the use of examples to clarify or illustrate an idea.

Expository writing (exposition): informative writing, the primary purpose of which is to explain something.

F

Fact: a statement that can be proven to be true.

Figure: a number or percentage.

Four Ws: *who, what, where, when*—usually included in a description of a scene or a narrative.

Fragment: an incomplete sentence because (1) it is missing either a subject, a verb, or both; (2) the verb is incomplete; or (3) it is only a depen-

dent clause and must be attached to an independent clause.

Freewriting: exploring your ideas in paragraph form without concern for grammar, spelling, or organization.

Future-perfect tense: a tense referring to an action or event completed before a later time in the future. This tense always contains three words: *will + have +* past participle.

H

Helping verb: the parts of the verb before the main verb, conveying the most important information about verb tense or mood.

Hyphen: a punctuation mark [-] used for joining words and for separating words between syllables at the end of a line.

I

Indefinite pronoun: a pronoun such as *everyone, nowhere,* or *something* that does not refer to a specific person, place, or thing.

Independent clause: a clause that can stand alone as a sentence.

Indirect object: a noun or pronoun following a verb that receives a direct object.

Indirect question: a question contained within a larger statement that uses the word order of a statement. An indirect question does not end with a question mark.

Infinitive: a word formed from a verb but that does not have a tense and that functions as an adjective, adverb, or noun.

–ing word: a word formed from a verb that functions either as a noun, an adjective, or an adverb. An *–ing* word can also be part of a verb if some form of *to be* precedes it, such as *is going, was going,* or *will be going* (see *present participle*).

Introduction: the beginning of a paragraph or essay, which attracts the readers' interest and usually includes the point of the paragraph in a topic sentence or, for an essay, in a thesis statement.

Irregular nouns: nouns that do not form plurals by adding *–s.*

Irregular verbs: (1) verbs that do not simply add *–s* for present-tense subject–verb agreement but make larger changes, or (2) verbs that do not form the past tense or past participle by adding –*ed*. These verbs change internally or do not change form at all.

L

Linking verb: a verb that does not express action but merely links the subject to the word or words that describe the subject. The most common linking verbs are *to be (is, am, was, were,* etc.) and the verbs representing the five senses: *look, feel, smell, sound,* and *taste.*

M

Main verb: the last word in a verb phrase, conveying the most important information about the action the verb expresses.

Metaphor: a way to make writing livelier by discussing your actual topic (such as *thinking*) in terms of another (*brewing up* or *cooking up ideas*).

Modifier: a word or group of words that function as an adjective or an adverb.

N

Narration: a story, usually told in a chronological order, or a sequence of consecutive events that build to a climax, which ends the story. A narration often includes dialogue.

Nonrestrictive relative clause: a clause that provides information not essential to the meaning of the noun it relates to, so the clause is enclosed by two commas.

Noun: a word that functions as a subject or an object and can be replaced by a pronoun. A noun usually represents a person, place, idea, or thing.

Noun clause: a clause that functions as a noun, usually beginning with *what, that, where, why,* or *when.*

Number: the singular or plural forms of nouns or pronouns.

O

Object: a word or words (usually nouns or pronouns) following action verbs; words formed with verbs (–*ing* words, past participles, and infinitives), prepositions, or other objects (see *direct object* and *indirect object*).

Object pronoun: a pronoun form (*me, us, you, him, her, it,* or *them*) that follows verbs, prepositions, or words formed from verbs.

P

Paragraph: a group of sentences that discuss a topic. A paragraph can contain ten or more sentences—or as few as one sentence—especially when used for dialogue in a story. In most circumstances, paragraphs are smaller divisions of an essay.

Parallel construction (parallelism): the repetition of the same grammatical structure for coherence or emphasis.

Paraphrase: restating ideas in your own words and sentence structure—as opposed to quoting the idea.

Parentheses: punctuation marks [( )] that enclose incidental information in a sentence. They always come in pairs.

Part-to-part organization: a way of making comparisons and contrasts between subjects by examining one part of each subject, then examining the second part of each, and so on.

Passive voice: a clause in which the subject does not act, but is acted upon. The passive voice is formed from *be* and the past participle of the verb in any tense, such as *has been done, is done, was done,* or *will be done.*

Past continuous (or progressive) tense: a tense showing an action in progress in the past, formed from the helping verbs *was* or *where* and an –*ing* word.

Past participle: a verb form that ends in –*ed* for regular verbs, although there are more than 100 irregular forms. The past participle functions as a main verb in perfect tenses (such as the present-perfect *has known,* or the past-perfect *had known*), and in the passive voice (such as *is known* or *was known*). The past participle is also used as an adjective (a *well-known* man).

Past-perfect tense: a tense used to describe past action or an event occurring prior to a later time in the past. The past-perfect tense is formed from *had* and the verb's past participle.

Past tense: a tense used to discuss completed actions in the past. All regular past-tense verbs end in –*ed*. There are more than 100 irregular verbs (see *simple past tense*).

Period: a punctuation mark [.] that ends a complete statement or is included in an abbreviation.

Person: a way of classifying personal pronouns: first person, *I* and *we;* second person, *you;* third person: *he, she, it* and *they.*

Phrasal verb: a two-word (and sometimes three-word) expression such as *get up,* which combines a verb with a second word to change the meaning of the verb.

Phrase: a group of two or more words. Unlike a clause, it does not contain a complete subject and verb.

Plural: more than one. Most plural nouns end in –*s,* but two or more nouns or pronouns can be joined to make a plural by *and.* Present-tense plural verbs do not end in –*s.*

Possessive: a word that shows ownership or possession.

Possessive adjective: a possessive word—actually a pronoun, such as *my, our, your, his, her, its,* and/or *their,* that shows possession before a noun (see *possessive pronoun*).

Possessive noun: a possessive word formed by adding –*'s* to singular nouns or –*'* to plural nouns ending in –*s.*

Possessive pronoun: a possessive word, such as *mine, ours, yours, his, hers, its,* and *theirs,* which replaces a possessive noun or possessive adjective and the noun.

Predicate: the words that make a statement or ask a question about the subject. A predicate begins with a verb.

Prefix: an addition to the beginning of a root word.

Preposition: a small word such as *in, of, on, at,* or *around* that precedes a noun or pronoun object (for example: *on the roof, by the road, under the rug, in a year*). The preposition and its object, called a *prepositional phrase,* modify a noun or a verb.

Present continuous (or progressive) tense: a tense that discusses actions that are happening now or are planned for the future. All verbs in this tense include the helping verb *is, am,* or *are* and an –*ing* word.

Present participle: an –*ing* word that functions as an adjective or adverb.

Present-perfect tense: a tense used to describe an action or condition in the past that continues up to the present. The tense is formed with *has/have* and the past participle.

Present tense: see *Simple present tense*.

Prewriting: the step in the writing process in which you think about your topic, purpose, and audience, and then explore your ideas through brainstorming, clustering, or freewriting.

Process analysis: an organizational structure that explains how to do something or how something works.

Proofreading: the last step in the writing process in which you examine the final copy for small errors and omissions.

Pronoun: a word that replaces a noun as a subject, object, or possessive word. Some pronouns have additional functions (see *relative pronouns, demonstrative pronouns,* and *reflexive pronouns*).

Proper noun: a noun that names someone or something and is therefore capitalized.

Q

Question mark: a punctuation mark [?] that ends direct questions.

Quotation marks: punctuation marks [""] that enclose direct quotations, titles of short works, definitions, and words used in special ways.

R

Reflexive pronoun: a pronoun that both performs and receives the action of the verb (such as "I wouldn't do that to myself.") The pronoun's singular forms end in *-self,* and its plural forms end in *-selves*.

Regular verb: a verb that ends in *-ed* in the past participle, or that forms its third-person singular form by adding *-s* or *-es*.

Relative clause: a clause that functions like an adjective, relating its information back to the noun that, in most cases, immediately precedes it.

Relative pronoun: the word that begins a relative clause, which relates its information back to a noun preceding the clause. The most common relative pronouns are *who, which, that,* and *whom*.

Report: a summary of decisions taken at a meeting, the details of some inci-

dent, the results of an experiment, or a set of observations.

Reported speech: a retelling in your own words of what the speaker or writer says or said. Reported speech never uses quotation marks.

Restrictive relative clause: a clause that provides essential information about the noun it relates to, so the clause is not enclosed in commas.

Root word: a word to which a suffix or prefix is added.

Run-on sentence: a sentence containing two independent clauses with nothing that joins them together. This is a very serious grammatical error.

S

Semicolon: a mark of punctuation [;] that most commonly joins two independent clauses or, less commonly, separates items in a series that contains internal commas.

Sentence: a complete statement or question containing a subject (usually a noun or subject pronoun) and a verb, which begins the statement or question about the subject.

Sequential order: an organization in which ideas are presented in consecutive steps or a sequence.

Simile: a comparison using *like* or *as,* such as "He ran *like a deer*."

Simple past tense: a tense that shows a completed action or idea in the past. Regular verbs in the simple past tense end in *-ed,* but more than 100 past-tense verbs are irregular.

Simple present tense: a tense used to discuss habitual actions, or states facts, or conditions that are true of the present. All third-person-singular present-tense verbs end in *-es*.

Singular: only one. Singular nouns usually do not end in *-s,* but the present-tense verbs that agree with them do end in *-s*.

Spatial order: an organization that presents details in space according to some arrangement such as top to bottom, left to right, or front to back. This organization occurs most often in description.

Subject: the topic (who or what) a clause makes a statement or asks a question about. Most often the subject is a noun or subject pronoun. In state-

ments, the subject usually precedes the verb; in questions, the verb precedes the subject.

Subject pronoun: a word that replaces a noun as the subject of a verb. The list of subject pronouns includes *I, we, you, he, she, it,* and *they*.

Subject–verb agreement: matching of singular subjects with singular verbs or plural subjects with plural verbs. With the exception of *to be* (*was/were*) in the past tense, only present-tense verbs change form to agree with their subjects.

Subordination: joining two clauses by making one clause dependent on the other clause.

Subordinating conjunction: a word that joins two clauses by making one clause lower in importance and dependent on the second clause. The second clause is independent and completes the meaning of the dependent clause.

Suffix: an ending added to a root word.

Superlative forms: the adjective or adverb form ending in *-est* or preceded by *most,* used to show that one of three or more things compared is greater than the others.

Syllable: a grouping of one or more letters that contain a single vowel sound.

Synonym: a word with the same or nearly the same meaning as another word.

T

Tense: the form of the verb that shows when an action or idea occurs or occurred—in the *present, past, future,* and so on. In two-, three-, or four-word verbs, the first word always indicates the tense (*doesn't want*—simple present; *didn't want*—simple past; *is going*—present continuous; *was going*—past continuous; and so on).

Thesis statement: this sentence, included in the introductory paragraph of an essay, states the central point of the essay and often outlines the organization of the essay.

Topic sentence: a sentence that states the main idea, or point, of a paragraph, which the body of the paragraph develops. Most topic sentences come at the beginning of a paragraph.

Transitional word: a word that explains how or in what way two ideas are logically related (see *Conjunctive adverb*).

U

Uncountable nouns: nouns that represent an idea or subject that cannot be counted such as *air, water,* or *furniture.*

Unity: a trait of an effective paragraph, in which each sentence develops the main idea, or topic, which is often expressed in the topic sentence.

V

Verb: a word or phrase that usually follows the subject and expresses the action the subject performs. A few verbs also link descriptive words back to the subject. Verbs generally have a tense (present, past, future, etc.) and can contain as many as four words.

Verb Phrase: a verb made up of two, three, or four words.

V

Vowel: a sound represented by the letters *a, e, i, o, u* (or a combination of these letters) that involves the passage of air through the vocal cords.

W

Whole-to-whole organization: a way of making comparisons and contrasts between subjects by examining everything about one subject and then everything about the other.

Credits

LITERARY

CHAPTER 2   **p. 10** Bill Cosby. From *Fatherhood* by Bill Cosby. Copyright © 1986 by William H. Cosby, Jr. Used by permission of Doubleday, a division of Random House, Inc.

CHAPTER 3   **p. 24** "What's the Name of That Street?," originally titled "Sesame Street." Adapted from *The Best of Uncle John's Bathroom Reader* by The Bathroom Readers' Institute. Copyright © 1995 by Bathroom Readers' Press. Reprinted with permission.

CHAPTER 5   **p. 51** Abridged excerpt from "Young Tad Lincoln Saved the Life of Jack, the White House Turkey!" (http://members.aol.com/RVSNorton1/Lincoln65.html) by Roger Norton. Reprinted by permission of the author. **p. 56** Abridged excerpts from "Mary Todd Lincoln's Ultimate Agony" (http://members.aol.com/RVSNorton/Lincoln62.html) and "Mary Todd Lincoln and Clairvoyance" (http://members.aol.com/RVSNorton/Lincoln44. html) by Roger Norton. Reprinted by permission of the author.

CHAPTER 6   **p. 71** Abridged excerpt from "Kon-Tiki" from *The Twentieth Century* by David Wallechinsky, copyright © 1995 by David Wallechinsky. Reprinted by permission of Ed Victor Ltd. **p. 74** From *The People's Almanac #3* by David Wallechinsky and Irving Wallace. Adapted by permission of the author. **p. 75** From *The People's Almanac #2* by David Wallechinsky and Irving Wallace. Adapted by permission of the author.

CHAPTER 7   **p. 77** From *The People's Almanac Presents The Twentieth Century* by David Wallechinsky. © David Wallechinsky 1995. Reprinted with kind permission from the author. **p. 83** From *The People's Almanac* by David Wallechinsky and Irving Wallace. © David Wallechinsky 1995. Adapted by permission of the author. **p. 87** From *The People's Almanac* by David Wallechinsky and Irving Wallace. © David Wallechinsky 1995. Adapted by permission of the author.

CHAPTER 8   **p. 95** From *The People's Almanac Presents The Twentieth Century* by David Wallechinsky. © David Wallechinsky 1995. Reprinted with kind permission from the author. **p. 96** From *The People's Almanac Presents The Twentieth Century* by David Wallechinsky. © David Wallechinsky 1995. Reprinted with kind permission from the author. **p. 96** From *The People's Almanac Presents The Twentieth Century* by David Wallechinsky. © David Wallechinsky 1995. Reprinted with kind permission from the author.

CHAPTER 9   **p. 90** From *The People's Almanac Presents The Twentieth Century* by David Wallechinsky. © David Wallechinsky 1995. Reprinted with kind permission from the author. **p. 101** From *The People's Almanac Presents The Twentieth Century* by David Wallechinsky. © David Wallechinsky 1995. Reprinted with kind permission from the author. **p. 104** From *The People's Almanac Presents The Twentieth Century* by David Wallechinsky. © David Wallechinsky 1995. Reprinted with kind permission from the author.

CHAPTER 10   **p. 123** Abridged excerpt from "Mind Games: Animals' Fiendish Tricks" (http://www.nua-tech.com/paddy/ethology.shtml) by Paddy Carroll. Reprinted by permission of the author.

CHAPTER 11   **p. 145** From *The People's Almanac Presents The Twentieth Century* by David Wallechinsky. © David Wallechinsky 1995. Reprinted with kind permission from the author.

CHAPTER 12   **p. 151**   Adapted from " A Food is Born: Bubble Gum" in *The Best of Uncle John's Bathroom Reader* by The Bathroom Readers' Institute. Copyright © 1995 by Bathroom Readers' Press. Reprinted with permission. **p. 152** From *The People's Almanac Presents The Twentieth Century* by David Wallechinsky. © David Wallechinsky 1995. Reprinted with kind permission from the author.

CHAPTER 13   **p. 163** From *The People's Almanac* by David Wallechinsky and Irving Wallace. Adapted by permission of the author. **p. 164** From *The People's Almanac* by David Wallechinsky and Irving Wallace. Adapted by permission of the author.

CHAPTER 16   **p. 207** Abridged excerpt from "The Pigeon Hero of World War I" from *The Twentieth Century* by David Wallechinsky, copyright © 1995 by David Wallechinsky. Reprinted by permission of Ed Victor Ltd.

CHAPTER 17   **p. 215** (FAIR USE) From *The Hundred Secret Senses* by Amy Tan, G.P. Putnam's Sons. **p. 216** Reprinted with the permission of Scribner, a Division of Simon & Schuster, Inc., from *Angela's Ashes: A Memoir* by Frank McCourt. Copyright © 1996 by Frank McCourt.

CHAPTER 19   **p. 233** From "Daddy" in *The Color of Water* by James McBride. Copyright © 1996 by James McBride. Used by permission of G.P. Putnam's Sons, a Division of Penguin Putnam Inc.

CHAPTER 21   **p. 246** From *Little House on the Prairie* by Laura Ingalls Wilder. Text copyright 1935 by Laura Ingalls Wilder, copyright © renewed 1963 by Roger L. McBride. Used by permission of HarperCollins Publishers. Please note: "Little House"® is a registered trademark of HarperCollins Publishers, Inc.

CHAPTER 25   **p. 273** From "The Bicycle" in *The Color of Water* by James McBride. Copyright © 1996 by James McBride. Used by permission of G.P. Putnam's Sons, a Division of Penguin Putnam Inc. **p. 274** (FAIR USE) From *The Heart of a Woman* by Maya Angelou, Random House, Inc.

CHAPTER 26   **p. 286** Abridged excerpt from "Cherokee History: Part One" (http://www.tolatsga.org/Cherokee1.html). **p. 301** James H. Harris. (FAIR USE) From (http://www.uelectric.com/houdini/harris.html)

READING SELECTIONS   **p. 389** "Needing and Wanting Are Different" by Jimmy Carrasquillo, *Newsweek*, November 16, 1992. Reprinted by permission of the author. **p. 390** "The Struggle to Be an All-American Girl" by Elizabeth Wong, a Los Angeles-based playwright teaching at the University of California, Santa Barbara. Permission to reprint granted by the author. **p. 392** "Alligator" from *Mama Makes Up Her Mind and Other Dangers of Southern Living* by Bailey White. Copyright © 1993 by Bailey White. Reprinted by permission of Perseus Books Publishers, a member of Perseus Books, L.L.C. **p. 394** "Hellraiser" by Jessica Shattuck, *Mother Jones Magazine* (July/August 1998), copyright © 1998 Foundation for National Progress. Reprinted by permission. **p. 395** Mark Twain. (PUBLIC DOMAIN) *Life on the Mississippi*, Mark Twain. **p. 397** "Divining the Strange Eating Habits of Kids" by Ellen Goodman, Chicago *Tribune*, August 15, 1986, copyright © 1986 The Boston Globe Newspaper Co./Washington Post Writers Group. Reprinted with permission. **p. 401** "Teen Gangbangers: An Ignored Issue" by Mike Royko, Chicago *Tribune*, January 31, 1992, copyright © Tribune Media Services, Inc. All Rights Reserved. Reprinted with permission. **p. 404** "The Legacy of Generation Ñ" by Christy Haubegger from *Newsweek*, July 12, 1999, copyright © 1999 Newsweek, Inc. All Rights Reserved. Reprinted with permission. **p. 407** Abridged excerpt from *I Know Why The Caged Bird Sings* by Maya Angelou, copyright © 1969 and renewed 1997 by Maya Angelou. Used by permission of Random House, Inc. **p. 410** "Living with 'The Look'" by Robert Hughes from *Newsweek*, September 1, 1997, copyright © 1997 Newsweek, Inc. All rights reserved. Reprinted by permission. **p. 412** "Melting Pot" from *Living Out Loud* by Anna Quindlen. Copyright © 1987 by Anna Quindlen. Reprinted by permission of Random House, Inc. **p. 415** "Why I Dread Black History Month" by Wayne M. Joseph from *Newsweek*, February 14, 1994, copyright © 1994 Newsweek, Inc. All rights reserved. Reprinted by permission. **p. 417** "Living Like Weasels" (abridged) from *Teaching a Stone to Talk: Expeditions and Encounters* by Annie Dillard. Copyright © 1982 by Annie Dillard. Reprinted by permission of HarperCollins Publishers, Inc.

PHOTO CREDITS

p. 52, Library of Congress; **p. 79**, © Corbis; **p. 83**, © Corbis; **p. 86**, © Corbis; **p. 103**, Peter G. Veit/Copyright, National Geographic Society; **p. 132**, Photographs courtesy of the George S. Bolster Collection of the Historical Society of Saratoga Springs.; **p. 134**, Photographs courtesy of the George S. Bolster Collection of the Historical Society of Saratoga Springs.; **p. 220**, ©The British Museum; **p. 223**, Museo Del Prado; **p. 224**, Library of Congress; **p. 225**, (top left) Dan Morrill; **p. 225**, (top right) David Jennings/The Image Works; **p. 225**, (bottom) © David R. Frazier Photolibrary; **p. 229**, (top right and left)Library of Congress; **p. 229**, (bottom) The J. Paul Getty Museum, Los Angeles, Walker Evans (photographer), (American 1903-1975), Subway Portrait, 1941, gelatin silver, Image 12.4 x 16.1 cm (Image: 5½ x 6¾ in.). (#84.XM.956.743); **p. 230**, The J. Paul Getty Museum, Los Angeles, Walker Evans (photographer), (American 1903-1975), Subway Portrait, 1938-1941, gelatin silver, Image 12 x 12 cm (Image: 4¾ x 4 ¾ in.). (#84.XM.956.758); **p. 249**, RUBE GOLDBERG (TM) and © of Rube Goldberg Inc. Distributed by United Media

Index